ROBBER BARON

ROBBER BARON

LORD BLACK OF CROSSHARBOUR

GEORGE TOMBS

ECW Press

Published by ECW PRESS
2120 Queen Street East, Suite 200, Toronto, Ontario, Canada M4E 1E2

LIBRARY AND ARCHIVES CANADA CATALOGUING IN PUBLICATION

Tombs, George
Robber Baron: Lord Black of Crossharbour / George Tombs.

ISBN 978-1-55022-806-9

1. Black, Conrad. 2. Publishers and publishing—Canada—Biography.
I. Title.

PN4913.B56T64 2007   070.5092   C2007-904134-5

Front cover photo: Reuters / John Gress
Back cover photo: The Canadian Press / Dave Chidley
Cover and text design: Tania Craan
Typesetting: Gail Nina
Printed by Thomson-Shore

DISTRIBUTION
CANADA: Jaguar Book Group, 100 Armstrong Avenue, Georgetown, ON, L7G 5S4
UNITED STATES: Independent Publishers Group, 814 North Franklin Street,
Chicago, Illinois 60610

PRINTED AND BOUND IN THE UNITED STATES

ECW PRESS
ecwpress.com

TABLE OF CONTENTS

The Canadian Press/The Globe and Mail/Fred Lum

CHAPTER ONE

ENTERING THE LABYRINTH

IT WAS A DARK, WINTRY DAY in December 2006, with sleek, black leafless trees silhouetted against low clouds and wet snow fading on the ground. Three months before the start of Conrad Black's trial in Chicago on fourteen counts of criminal fraud, breaches of fiduciary duty, mail and wire fraud and racketeering, I had flown from Montreal to Toronto for the day. Black — Baron Black of Crossharbour — had given me a two-hour appointment at his Georgian mansion, in the exclusive Bridle Path area, to discuss a new edition of my book about him.

I took a cab from the airport. The closer we got to Black's house, the more excited my Sikh driver became. "Oh my goodness!" he said as the ranch bungalows on small lots gave way to the gloomy neo-Gothic and garish Mediterranean suburban palaces of Toronto's arrivistes. "So many rich people live around here. Look at these houses! There must be so many gardeners working here in the spring. Tell me, sir, what do you do for a living? You are a university professor — that is a very well-paid job. So, this is the house we are going to? Oh my goodness, we have to get out at the gate and announce through the radio intercom who we are. Is your friend *also* a university professor?"

Sprawling 26 Park Lane Circle is a Can.$20-million brick mansion, with a stately portico entrance and Palladian windows, standing back from the road on an eleven-acre estate. Black sometimes jokingly referred to it as his "cottage." It was his parents' home, the place where he grew up. In the 1980s, after Black inherited the place, he hired New York-based celebrity architect Thierry Despont — whose clients included Microsoft billionaire Bill Gates — and completely rebuilt the mansion, gutting whole sections and adding an indoor pool and library. Black pays more than Can.$70,000 in annual property taxes.

As we entered the gate, the driveway curved rightward down past the entrance of the house, then looped back again, in front of the main door. Even in the first week of December, ripe green apples still clung to the branches of two huge trees. We came round an enormous weeping willow, then swept in front of the entrance.

Werner, the sixty-five-year-old German butler dressed all in white, stood at the door. With his stern, obsequious manner, he ushered me to the cloak room, off to the right as we entered, where he took my leather jacket and hung it up. He then led me back through the two-storey entry hall with barrel-vaulted ceiling, where portraits of the Prince Regent (the future George IV) and Napoleon were displayed. To my left was the stairway, where Conrad Black's father, George, had fallen over the banister upstairs in 1976 and come crashing down onto the main floor. That was the day father told son, "Life is hell, most people are bastards, and everything is bullshit."[1]

"Everything in the house has been changed," one of Conrad Black's cousins told me, "except the entrance and the stair where Uncle George fell to his death." Even Black once wrote he wasn't sure whether his father's death was voluntary. It was a touchy subject for him. For decades, George Black's depression and his sudden death had hung like a cloud over his son. Conrad had preserved the entrance and stairwell intact — it seemed a grim memorial to his father.

By the time I got there, 26 Park Lane Circle had become a gilded cage for Black. In the lead-up to his criminal trial, he had to post a $21-million bond* — the highest in the history of American criminal justice. U.S. District Judge Amy J. St. Eve set as a condition of bail that he couldn't go anywhere but Chicago,

*All monetary amounts are in U.S. dollars unless otherwise noted.

his hometown of Toronto or his $35.5-million winter ocean-front retreat in Palm Beach without first getting court approval.

Along the stairwell, I could see an enormous print of Rome from the early nineteenth century, showing St. Peter's to the left, which Black had collected as a souvenir from a landlady during his early years in London. It must have been about ten to twelve feet long. I remembered seeing it at Black's £13.1-million mansion in Cottesmore Gardens, London, when we met there in 2002 — he was forced to sell that property three years later, when his business empire had begun to disintegrate. To my right was the main living room, with a series of French doors overlooking the park. This park slopes downward onto expansive terraces, gardens and into a forest, and must be uneven terrain for garden parties, although it is a paradise for racoons.

Werner led me past a stairwell to the basement, the walls covered with handwritten correspondence in gold frames between President Franklin Roosevelt and his cousin and probable mistress Daisy Suckley. I remembered some of the letters from my 2003 visits to Black's executive suite at Hollinger International on Fifth Avenue in New York, just before he was turfed out of his job there. There were also some framed letters signed by Abraham Lincoln.

I had entered the inner sanctum of Black's private mythology. He has the habit of fusing his personality with his political heroes, papering his walls with rich symbols of power, as if some of their magnificence would rub off on him. He has a dreamy, expansive, blistering nature — blowing a fortune on fantastic decor all around him, drawing analogies between himself and colossal, larger-than-life figures (as a way, I thought, of drowning his own deep-seated insecurity).

Werner showed me to the sitting room, with some green-and-cream-striped Empire chairs I recognized from the Cottesmore Gardens mansion. A lot of things had moved around in the last couple years. There were a few million dollars' worth of Canadian paintings on the walls, cluttered like postage stamps. One was by Jean Paul Lemieux, another was a nondescript painting by Robert Pilot showing a church in Quebec, and there was a Maurice Cullen. A painting by A. Y. Jackson showed a village chapel in Quebec's Charlevoix county in winter, with some logs floating in a river in the foreground. On a low coffee table were a few books about platinum jewels and a recent book by Barbara Amiel's former husband, George Jonas. Here I waited.

I first met Conrad Black and Barbara Amiel in June 1993 when I worked at the Southam-owned daily the Montreal *Gazette*. A high-school classmate of mine, Montreal financier André Desmarais, had invited me to a private gala on the summit of Mount Royal, overlooking the St. Lawrence River, Old Montreal and the nineteenth-century mansions of the Square Mile. On that golden evening, the summit had been cordoned off for a dinner André had organized on behalf of the Americas Society — David Rockefeller's network of corporate leaders and statesmen committed to establishing political, economic and cultural links among the Americas.

Several hundred people mingled, many of them balding Latin American tycoons accompanied by glittering buxom trophy women in high heels who defied gravity in more ways than one. "These trophy wives always travel in pairs of limousines," the conference organizer told me with a knowing smirk. "One so they can stretch out their long legs and one for all their Holt Renfrew shopping bags." This was a world of high rollers. I was just a spectator.

Here was André's father, the billionaire Paul Desmarais, once Conrad Black's rival in a 1970s grab for Toronto-based conglomerate Argus Corp.

Miguel Alemán Valesco, a Mexican senator and son of a former Mexican president, was also in attendance. Here was another billionaire, David Rockefeller, then chairman of the Chase Manhattan Bank; Guilherme Frering, Brazilian co-owner of CAEMI, the world's fourth-largest iron ore producer; the controversial Argentine banker Jose Rohm; and Norman Webster, my editor-in-chief (he had previously been editor-in-chief at the *Globe and Mail*, where he had hired, then fired Conrad Black as a columnist in the 1980s). Here, too, was Conrado Pappalardo, the right-hand man of Paraguay's fascist dictator,

General Alfredo Stroessner; Ken Taylor, Canada's ambassador to Iran who had helped rescue Americans during the 1979 storming of the U.S. embassy in Tehran; and Brazilian-born Peter White, Black's old friend and first partner in the newspaper business.

Liveried waiters passed to and fro, bearing champagne on silver trays. This was the world of Conrad and Barbara. Their reputations — cultivated by their flamboyant lifestyles and deliberately provocative, caustic writings — had preceded them. Riveted to each other, they devoted a few half-interested minutes to each conversation before spotting another contact and moving on.

I introduced myself to Black as an editorial writer at the *Gazette*, since he had just purchased a minority shareholding in the Southam Group, which owned the Montreal newspaper. He was six feet, two inches tall, bulky and exuded power. He looked like a fighter who could tear people to pieces. He was blustery, pompous, wooden in speech, always looking to fit people into an intellectual framework but ever ready to dismantle that framework, a man who could go just as well into fast forward as into rewind, his eyes opening wide with delight and closing menacingly — an aggressive man who nonetheless wanted to be liked. As we spoke, Amiel tugged on Black's sleeve. Her sleek brown hair, tight-fitting black dress and high heels gave her a dramatic look. As she glanced left and right, lining up the next networking opportunity for Conrad, her eyes burned with a dull flame in which I read a peculiar combination of rage, boredom and fragility.

I had followed Black's career closely over the years. I had no sympathy for his stark neo-conservative views, I was puzzled by his withering doctrinaire Catholicism and I had often heard that he milked his media properties. I suggested that if he took over Southam, he could make the *Gazette* the flagship of the chain and build a network of national and international correspondents to take on the *Globe and Mail*. Black's response was to dump on the *Globe*. He took pleasure in debunking the paper's claim that it was the "national newspaper of record." But the idea of centring anything important in Montreal struck Black as an anachronism. He had other plans. After a few minutes, he and Amiel went off to speak to the Rockefellers, from whom he had rented a summer estate in Maine.

I could not have known in 1993 that within ten years Black and his long-time partner David Radler (a McGill University graduate, just like Black) would make the *Gazette* part of his newspaper empire, the world's third-largest, with six hundred titles in Canada, Britain, the United States, Israel and Australia. That Black would renounce his Canadian citizenship to become a baron and sit in the British House of Lords. And that I would become his biographer, interviewing him as well as some two hundred other people, from close family members to childhood buddies, business associates to competitors and critics — as I chronicled the dazzling rise and fall of a proud, destructive genius. Given the meltdown of Black's career and finances, starting in 2003–04, I would be the last person before his trial to conduct extensive biographical interviews with him as well as those closest around him.

As a boy, Conrad Black had regularly played chess with his father in the Park Lane Circle mansion. He had extended these skills and strategies from the chessboard to the world. He struck me as someone who treated people like rooks, bishops and knights, queens and kings on a chessboard, moving them around at will. Each person served or defeated his interests. Character, ambitions and morality provided him with useful insights, which he could articulate with stunning detachment, then use to strategize, manipulate and position things to his best advantage.

I had to be sure I didn't end up being Black's pawn. Here was a man who could snap his fingers and immediately get half of the front page of any newspaper in Canada. Quotable quotes rolled off his tongue, ready to be snatched up in an endless stream of newspaper articles. He loved to craft other people's ideas. He loved being the centre of attention. But as a result, he often appealed to the gallery, saying things for provocative effect that didn't reflect his true impulses.

It was challenging to make sense of a dark man, full of contradictions, rage and energy, who did not seem to understand himself. Black's speeches and writings were rich in allegory and allusions to historic grandeur and military prowess. In his autobiography, *A Life in Progress*, he compared himself to a number of historical personalities from Henry VIII to Pope Alexander VI, Napoleon, the fictional media tycoon Citizen Kane, General Douglas MacArthur and German General Heinz Guderian (at least implicitly) for his Second World War blitzkrieg strategy. Further research finds Black himself — and others — comparing him to at least five Shakespearean characters: the mournful, power-obsessed King Lear; the boisterous, back-slapping, next-round-is-on-me Prince Hal; the master of dissimulation Bolingbroke, who succeeded Richard II to the throne; the Roman politician Cassius, who suggested that Brutus murder Julius Caesar; and the ever-devious "pound-of-flesh" Shylock.

Most of these characters evoked pathos, suffering, looming defeat and the unavoidable fall from grace. I wondered whether all these analogies weren't simply a form of "grandiosity by association" — exuberant, boastful camouflage designed to protect the vulnerable, uneasy person he really was, deep inside. Unless he was just lining things up so that other people would grovel in front of his colossal ego as he laughed down at them. Whenever Black talked about himself, I had the impression I was hearing the final summing up, as if the moon were beginning to inch across the sun in a total eclipse.

At the apogee of his power in 2002, Black used his majority voting control of Hollinger International Inc. — a company with more than $2 billion in assets — to control the London *Daily Telegraph*, *The Spectator*, the *Chicago Sun-Times* and the *Jerusalem Post*. He was also part-owner of the upstart and modestly successful *New York Sun*. And until 2000 and 2001 (when he shed almost all of his Canadian assets), Black controlled 57 per cent of all daily newspaper titles in Canada. He claimed to have started with no more than a $500 investment when he and partner Peter White bought two rural newspapers in Quebec's Eastern Townships in the mid-1960s and then enlisted a third Montrealer, David Radler, as partner to buy a small daily, the Sherbrooke *Record*. But that was a calculated understatement. Black had inherited substantial wealth from his parents and grandparents.

On the editorial level, Black was widely admired for his ability to revive flagging newspapers, such as Britain's *Daily Telegraph,* and start up new ones, such as Canada's *National Post.*

On the financial level, his sprawling newspaper empire dazzled but left many wondering whether it was an enormous house of cards — incredibly complicated and highly leveraged. Yet he was the world's best-paid newspaper publisher. In 2002, according to *Crain's Chicago Business,* he received $7.1 million in salary and benefits — $1 million more than the publishers of the *New York Times,* the *Washington Post* and the *Chicago Tribune* combined. In addition, he received management fees of $6.6 million via the private holding company Ravelston Corp. In 2002, the London *Evening Standard's* "top 50 residents of Kensington & Chelsea" pegged Black's personal fortune at £194 million (Can.$405 million). The current Lord Beaverbrook told me "rich lists" such as the *Evening Standard's* only estimated assets, without counting liabilities. According to Beaverbrook, no matter how much money Black earned, he always seemed to spend more than he had — on parties, celebrity interior decorator David Mlinaric, artwork and jewels. His various residences alone were worth close to $100 million, which would be a drain on anybody's finances. Black saw his role as a builder of working capital — negotiating takeovers, starting up new properties and developing strategies to improve the editorial quality of Hollinger's media holdings. For this, he was richly rewarded with dollars and prestige. And he protected his gains by controlling votes within his companies and developing value for what he calls "continuing [long-term] shareholders." In his mind, there was a clear distinction between those shareholders and independent public shareholders.

Former business associate and member of the Hollinger board Hal Jackman compares Black to Napoleon, who achieved "outrageous success, and felt he could do it indefinitely, but the whole world eventually turned against him. Conrad did the same, pushing the envelope and doing one outrageous thing after the other, but now the public mood is very much against him. He's pushing the envelope. That's a death wish. You know that sooner or later, they'll get you. He doesn't think like rational people think. All these payments and houses have turned people against him."[2]

Everything started to unravel for Black in mid-October 2001, just two weeks before he made his triumphant entry into the House of Lords as "Baron Black of Crossharbour," in recognition of his ownership of the *Daily Telegraph*. When he entered the House of Lords, Black seemed like a new sun king, reaching the height of social achievement — here was a Montreal-born, former Canadian businessman gaining an aristocratic title and a seat in the upper chamber of the British Parliament. But I wondered whether the sunny Black wasn't being dogged by a mischievous double — a darker, self-defeating version of himself, who was undoing all that he had just achieved.

In October 2001, Tweedy, Browne Company, with about 18 per cent of Hollinger International's class A common stock, wrote to the chairman of the company's audit committee, former governor of Illinois James R. Thompson, complaining that between 1995 and 2000 Hollinger had paid $150.3 million to Ravelston, the Canadian-based holding company controlled by Black, "under an undisclosed management agreement that calls for 'strategic advice, planning and financial services,' but establishes no performance goals." The Tweedy, Browne letter said an additional $3.7 million went directly to Black. "And what have we, shareholders of Hollinger, received in return for that $154 million? The stock of our company has sagged about 30 per cent from its Initial Public Offering price. . . ."

Chris Browne, the mild-mannered managing partner at Tweedy, Browne, was concerned about the level of Hollinger International's payments to Black and several of his associates.

Browne is a white-haired, thin-lipped scion of the financial establishment of Manhattan. (He looks like a new species of wildlife: the *killer beluga*.) He is also a master of the highly political art of leveraging media coverage in order to support his billion-dollar portfolios. Tweedy, Browne's corporate offices on Park Avenue (in the same building as Henry Kissinger's office) boast a series of outsized nineteenth-century engravings of Wall Street and genteel eighteenth-century maps of the New World.

"In the late summer and early fall of 2001," Browne said, "we started noticing that management service payments to Ravelston had increased substantially. We wrote a letter to the board in October 2001, asking what criteria they used to determine whether these were reasonable payments, which were lump sum. There was no disclosure as to Conrad Black's share or David Radler's share, or how they arrived at it.... Not one director responded to our letter. Conrad did. We had a meeting with Conrad, but I wouldn't say we got a very satisfactory explanation. He said the fees would be coming down, going forward."[3]

Browne told me he had the impression that Black and his associates paid themselves management and other fees based on what they needed rather than on the objective value of services they provided.

It was not a good idea for the newly minted baron to provoke Browne, an architecture and history buff who lives alone with his border terrier, Orville. In thirty years of business, Browne has sworn twice in the office and raised his voice twice. It was not exactly a David and Goliath struggle: Black may have been a media giant, but Browne was no naive underdog — he is one of the best connected, most respected investors in New York. The contrast in temperament and manner between the two became a key part of the story. In late 2001, Browne launched an intense campaign that led to revelations of questionable business practices at Hollinger. Black could have avoided scrutiny and embarrassment had he opted to take Hollinger private, dealt proactively with Tweedy, Browne, updated business practices to reflect changes in corporate governance practices or paid closer attention to the evolving morality of the investment community that produced the Sarbanes-Oxley Act of 2002 — requiring CEOs to sign a certificate that no longer allowed them to claim ignorance if the numbers in their company financial statements didn't add up. Instead, Black dug in — accusing Tweedy, Browne of being "corporate governance terrorists."[4]

Black seemed shocked that anyone would have the temerity to question the way he ran his company. That he felt he was above the mundane concerns of society and, in particular, his shareholders is clearly stated in an e-mail to another corporate officer on August 5, 2002: "There has not been an occasion for many months when I got on our plane without wondering whether it was really affordable. But I'm not prepared to re-enact the French Revolutionary renunciation of the rights of nobility. We have to find a balance between an unfair taxation on the company and a reasonable treatment of the founders-builders-managers. We are proprietors, after all, beleaguered though we may be."

Were Black's problems a case of *hubris*—an excess of pride? Did he feel he had an inalienable right as a continuing share-holder to receive special consideration, whereas independent shareholders such as Tweedy, Browne were only along for the ride? Or was his eye off the ball as he immersed himself for two years, from 2001 to 2003, in the drafting of his encyclopedic 1,280-page biography of Franklin Roosevelt — a project he had dreamt of for decades? Whatever the explanation, Black's sense of omnipotence and self-sufficiency did nothing to deflect two forbidding challenges: investigations by the United States Securites and Exchange Commission (SEC) and the Federal Bureau of Investigation (FBI); and shareholder lawsuits alleging that hundreds of millions of dollars in payments were improper and that some of them were illegal in that they had neither been properly authorized by the board of directors nor accurately reported to the SEC.

Black was a business proprietor in the nineteenth-century mould, a self-centred man of grandeur and ambition, a man of cunning, taste and discernment, an iron-willed, ruthless entre-preneur, like a robber baron in the early decades of American industrial capitalism. And he was a press tycoon on a grand scale, someone like William Randolph Hearst, who could send printing presses a-clattering with bold, sensationalist news reports and compelling visions and ideas for the future of the North Atlantic democracies — the United States, Canada and Britain. Black used his newspapers to build up political causes he believed in — mostly neo-conservative ones — and he used them just as readily to clobber opponents into the ground. He was quite prepared to do the clobbering himself, signing pieces that demolished his own employees. He adored manipulation, devising pathways, then following them to smoke out his enemies and snatch final victory. He saw his business in naval terms — an ongoing war at sea, with cruel storms, raging battles long into the night, well-aimed salvoes and then, when he was lucky, sending his enemies to the ocean bottom.

In many ways, the decor in Hollinger International's New York offices was an extension of Black's personality — a way of illustrating his love and admiration for the great American republic and its navy. He desperately wanted that love and admiration to be returned.

From the boardroom window, there was a clear view of an early-twentieth-century skyscraper with a decrepit wooden water tower, the garish black Trump Tower and, further uptown, the concave W. R. Grace Building and eccentric Legion of Honor building. On one wall of the boardroom was a watercolour depicting the first transit by a sitting president — Franklin Delano Roosevelt — through the Panama Canal, July 11, 1934, aboard the cruiser USS *Houston*, nudging her way through the Miraflores locks, Stars and Stripes rippling in the wind, an honour guard assembled on the dockside. The watercolour had been painted long after the fact from a black-and-white photograph in the U.S. Navy archives.

Along the walls, in gold frames, were some of the controversial FDR documents that Hollinger International had acquired for $10 million — a typewritten presidential speech, as well as handwritten letters on USS *Houston* stationery from the president to Daisy Suckley. Critics have charged that the company had no business purchasing the material to help Black with his private research on FDR.

A long oak table with black speakerphones arrayed on it like threatening UFOs were visible through the open doorway of the boardroom, and one could visualize the imperial Black chairing a meeting of his distinguished board members. The decor was a way of conditioning them. Just inside the doorway of the boardroom was a framed, signed black-and-white portrait of the notorious 1930s gangster Al Capone. Black's executive assistant,

Jan Akerhielm, made a point of showing the portrait to me. Next door, in Black's office, was an oil portrait of Lord North, the incompetent British prime minister under George III who "lost" the thirteen colonies during the War of Independence. The office also boasted autographs, in gold frames, of Benjamin Franklin and the robber baron–cum–philanthropist Andrew Carnegie. Along the corridor outside was a Civil War requisition order for mules, signed by General William T. Sherman.

Black preferred elder statesmen on his boards — Conservatives in Britain and Republicans in the United States. Whether they had business experience was irrelevant. Lord Carrington, the former UK foreign secretary, defence secretary, secretary-general of NATO and member of the Hollinger and *Telegraph* boards, said he himself knew little about finance.[5]

It wasn't much different at Hollinger International, where independent board members former U.S. secretary of state Henry Kissinger and former U.S. assistant secretary of defense Richard Perle occasionally attended meetings in the New York boardroom. I met Kissinger in his Park Avenue office in September 2003, when things were already getting very hot for Black. Two Secret Service agents in navy blue suits were on duty, ready to defend Kissinger. And part of my meeting with the ever-pugnacious bulldog Kissinger involved some conditioning. While I waited in an anteroom decorated with Chinese bronzes, he left his door open so I could hear him barking into the phone: "Conrad, some Canadian journalist is here to see me. What should I do with him? Ja. Ja. Do you know him? Ja. Ja." The ground rules of the interview were that I could record everything, sitting in his office surrounded by autographed portraits of Pope Paul VI, King Hussein of Jordan and Richard Nixon. But the minute I veered off topic, he would shout at me to "turn that thing off!" He must have been interviewed tens of thousands of times. He ended up telling me that in his role as director of Hollinger International, he brought "some understanding of the international situation, and they have papers in different parts of the world. I can bring some judgment on the content of the papers that cover the subject that I know something about. It's good for the company that there are others on the board that have a more acute understanding of financial matters than I do. So that [finance] is not why I'm on the board." He said he also read the Web version of the *Daily Telegraph* every day.[6] Kissinger was so devious he made me feel extremely uncomfortable. Once the interview was over, I checked my pocket to make sure my wallet wasn't missing. I then quizzed the two Secret Service agents about how to get an airport bus back to LaGuardia, but they had never taken a bus. They knew only how to hire a limousine.

Montreal billionaire and investment counsel Stephen Jarislowsky, who has served on a number of Black's boards including the Southam board, said Conrad was a jolly rogue going through life, fooling most of the people he met and doing it with gusto. Black's naming Kissinger to the board, despite a lack of financial experience, was quite typical. "Most of the people on his boards knew nothing about finance. They were window-dressing. The Great Man likes to surround himself with Great Men. On the Argus and Southam boards in the 1990s were a judge, a general and a cardinal."[7] Jarislowsky is known for his astute financial judgment, skillful resounding statements about corporate governance and occasional on-the-record candour about his own business dealings.

Hal Jackman, who amassed a half-billion-dollar fortune running an insurance company and a Northern Ontario railway, criticizes Black for "paying a lot of money to ex-politicians to be sycophantic and be directors — it just isn't worth it."

Black gathered members of his board of directors and international advisory council together for periodic meetings, wined and dined them, exulting in the insider conversation about world politics. Many of his board and council members were thrilled to be part of such an exclusive circle of movers and shakers, although Margaret Thatcher was often jet-lagged when she turned up and promptly nodded off at the table. Even so, she collected the same rich fees as everyone else — in the range of $25,000 per day, just for sitting there. It seemed as if Black were paying for friendship with the high and mighty.

So when big institutional shareholders such as Tweedy, Browne confronted Black openly in correspondence and shareholder meetings, when they claimed Hollinger International was *their* company and he was supposed to be acting on their behalf, there was more at stake than Black's professional future. They risked shattering his proud self-image, the whole persona he had constructed for himself of a plugged-in networker above the fray, the intimate friend of presidents and prime ministers, someone who knew the nature of power and how to leverage newspapers to dominate the game. This may explain how Black could study the laws that bound him as chairman and CEO of Hollinger International, analyze them and pontificate on them in a detached way, as if he were addressing a purely intellectual problem.

Just weeks before a May 22, 2003, shareholders meeting where one investor openly accused Black of being a "thief," Black told me that the Sarbanes-Oxley Act was "an insane law" with "all sorts of absurd conditions that are in part locking the barn door after the horses have fled and in part penalizations of the habitually law-abiding."[8] He said the act is in response "to a sense of revulsion" over serious wrongdoings "involving large sums of money and large companies. I would have thought that not much needed to be done beyond the enforcement of existing criminal statutes — namely those people who did bad things should be prosecuted and, if guilty, convicted and not lightly sentenced. But when you get politics and public opinion involved, you do get a bit of pandering going — I think that is what we have seen."

Black said that "it is astonishing that the incidence of objectively bad things — felonious conduct or even invidious conduct — is as infrequent as it is," given the amount of money that changes hands in the corporate sector of countries such as the United States, Canada and the United Kingdom. "Here in the United States, you have GDP of essentially twelve trillion dollars. The private sector is almost two-thirds of that — almost eight trillion dollars. The incidence of apparent serious misbehaviour is really quite slight, and quite rare."

Black asserted that the danger emanating from the tremendous economic boom of the 1990s is that in its latter stages it was "vulgar" and some of it "economically false" and, quoting

U.S. Federal Reserve board chairman Alan Greenspan, "an irrational enthusiasm." When the bubble burst, Black recalled, there were "a lot of recriminations" and revelations of "promotional instinct trespassing into the area of fraud." But comparing this era with the 1920s "or with the era of the railway barons and robber barons," he said, "I think all in all the record is quite good."

He assailed "self-righteous . . . elements of the liberal media in the United States, and in foreign countries, trying to represent the American capitalist economy as corrupt and vulgar and exploitative, and the executive class as composed essentially of venal and morally contemptible people. I think that's highly exaggerated, and I think the response to it has been somewhat exaggerated."

In May 2002, Black was already considering the one strategy that would have solved most or all of the problems he eventually faced — buying out minority shareholders. But he discarded the idea. "I don't have the goal of privatizing Hollinger International," he said. "What I do have is the desire to take advantage, on behalf of the continuing shareholders, of the under-valuation of our stock. As long as we have the means, without over-stretching ourselves, and our own share price is the best bargain amongst all the menu of investment available to us, it is a good thing to do. I don't have the objective as such to take the public out completely. I would be happy to dispense with them completely if we could do it to our commercial advantage, but not if it means putting too much freight on the wagon and overpaying for it."

Chris Browne considers this to have been wishful thinking: "I don't think privatization was a realistic alternative on his part. The company was already too much in debt for him to have taken out the other shareholders."

In late 2003, Tweedy, Browne launched a lawsuit in Delaware Chancery Court for "recoupment of over $73 million (U.S.) in payments to Ravelston and its affiliates (including Lord Black) under Non-Competition Agreements arising from asset sales by Hollinger International."

The non-compete fees — part of the Can.$3.2-billion sale of the Southam newspaper group to CanWest Global Communications Corp. in 2000 — had been disclosed at the time, but the record was unclear about how the fees were negotiated in the first place.

One key aspect of the lawsuit was a media campaign run by Tweedy, Browne analyst Laura Jereski, an aggressive former *Wall Street Journal* reporter. (She had written a 1993 article that led to the largest libel judgment in U.S. history — $222.7 million. The award was later overturned.) Tweedy, Browne's complaint was intended to "recover the reasonable attorney's fees of counsel who assisted a stockholder's investigation of possible wrongdoing at Hollinger International and prepared formal demands to its Board of Directors."

According to Tweedy, Browne, abundant media coverage — expertly organized by Jereski — demonstrated that its investigation was of *benefit* to Hollinger International. The media coverage thus offered evidence that Tweedy, Browne deserved to receive reimbursement of the costs of its own investigation.

The propriety of non-compete fees would be one of the important issues to be evaluated in the lawsuits and securities investigations facing Lord Black.

But another vital issue surfaced on March 31, 2003, when Hollinger International made its annual 10-K filing for 2002. In the 10-K, or annual report, Hollinger International gave a mixed message about Black and his closest Canadian associates. On the one hand, the report noted "our success is largely dependent on the abilities and experience of Lord Black, our Chief Executive Officer, F. David Radler, our Chief Operating Officer, and Daniel W. Colson, The Telegraph's Chief Executive Officer, and our senior management team. The loss of the services of Lord Black, F. David Radler and Daniel W. Colson or one or more of these senior executives could adversely affect our ability to effectively manage our overall operations or successfully execute current or future business strategies." But, on the other hand, the 10-K explained to Hollinger International shareholders that "Lord Black is our controlling shareholder and there may be a conflict between his interests and your interests. . . . Entities affiliated with Lord Black and other officers and directors of the Company engage in significant transactions with the Company, which transactions may not necessarily be consummated on an arm's length basis. . . . Certain subsidiaries of the Company also have separate service agreements directly with certain Ravelston executives, as well as Black-Amiel Management Inc. and Moffat Management Inc., both affiliates of Ravelston. All of the Service Agreements were negotiated in the context of a parent-subsidiary relationship and, therefore, were not the result of arm's length negotiations between independent parties. The terms of the Service Agreements may therefore not be as favorable to the company and its subsidiaries as the terms that might be reached through negotiations with non-affiliated third parties." In other words, Hollinger International acknowledged the prestige and authority of its controlling shareholder, Lord Black, while simultaneously warning in its annual report, duly filed with the SEC, that "*Black and several close associates could be in serious conflicts of interest, using their controlling shareholder position to derive undue benefits from the company.*" Hollinger International's 10-K filing in 2002 — its annual report — makes gripping reading. It presents in broad brushstrokes the complex relationship that Black and his main Canadian partners had with the U.S.-based company.

Fortune magazine reported that at the annual shareholders meeting of Hollinger International at the Metropolitan Club in New York, on May 22, 2003, "Black and his wife, Barbara Amiel — a right-wing columnist whose looks have been compared to Gina Lollobrigida's and whose opinions would curl Rush Limbaugh's toes — waved to friends. They exchanged air kisses with Donald Trump and his girlfriend, model Melania Knauss. Black scanned the room and his lip curled. He knew what was coming — shareholders rising, one after another, to chastise him. Finally he erupted. Yes, he admitted, there was room for improvement in Hollinger's stock price. But Black was squeezing more and more cash out of his newspapers. Why, he asked, hadn't anybody commended him for *that*. 'You have a right to say whatever it is that is on your mind, all of you,' he informed his investors. 'You don't know what you are talking about, but you are still welcome as shareholders.'"9

Under increasing pressure, on June 17, 2003, Black created a special committee to conduct an independent review and investigation of allegations raised by Tweedy, Browne. The committee, advised by former SEC chairman Richard Breeden, began sifting through several years' worth of Hollinger International corporate documents, in search of irregularities.

A week before the committee was formally set up, Tweedy, Browne sent another letter to Hollinger International's board of directors, revealing that some Hollinger International assets had been sold in 2000 to Bradford Publishing, a company owned and controlled by some Hollinger board members and senior management. Tweedy, Browne thought this was self-dealing and demanded more information. Tweedy, Browne had uncovered something important. As a result of its prodding, Hollinger International later accused Black and Radler of self-dealing, alleging for example that Black and Radler set up Horizon Publications Inc. in 1998 in order to acquire newspaper assets from Hollinger International. Each held 24 per cent of Horizon's shares and had beneficial control (through people they had rewarded with shares and allegedly still influenced) of at least 73 per cent of the company's shares. This beneficial control was not made clear to the SEC, Hollinger International alleged, nor were board and audit committee members properly informed about the nature of Horizon's transactions.

In 2000, Bradford Publishing Co. was set up "as an additional vehicle for them [Black and Radler] to own other community newspapers they purchased from the Company [Hollinger International] at a price substantially below market value."

In early November 2003, despite the looming crisis at Hollinger International, Black departed on a two-week tour to promote his 600,000-word magnum opus on FDR. Covering the launch party for the book at a New York restaurant, *Washington Post* columnist Tina Brown said, "Even with hosts as luminous as philanthropist Jayne Wrightsman and fashion designer Oscar de la Renta, acceptances shrank to a small band of loyalists like Henry Kissinger and Ronald Perelman. Unfortunately for Black, a packed, convivial book party for former treasury secretary Robert Rubin was coincidentally raging in the next room. 'I am just doing a fly-by,' one society hostess said as she scurried through to the Rubin fiesta beyond."[10]

Once again, the sunny Black was dogged by the darker, self-defeating Black. It was one step forward and one step back. He had wanted to wear the proud mantle of greatness. But he was headed for humiliation. As the Hollinger scandal continued to unfold, Black was front-page news in New York, London and Toronto. And when he was forced to step down as CEO of Hollinger International, media criticism and coverage intensified. "Lord Black's appetite for empire-building outstripped his ability to pay," said the *Wall Street Journal*. "Improper payments led to mogul's demise," was the *Globe and Mail* headline. And the influential Lex column in London's *Financial Times* said, "The lid has been lifted on Hollinger's dark secrets. In a victory for shareholder activism, Lord Black has been forced to step down as chief executive. . . . He may be forced to dismantle his entire empire."[11]

Journalists, particularly in Canada, began writing in-depth articles and columns about the scandal after years of avoiding serious investigation of the litigious Black's financial empire and personal life. "The gloating of the press is misplaced," wrote *Globe and Mail* financial columnist Eric Reguly. "This is not our finest hour. Everything Tweedy, Browne came up with is in the public domain. They are not sleuths. The press simply haven't done their job."

But Black wasn't intimidated. At a book signing in a Toronto bookstore, he told a gathering of journalists: "All you fellows that are writing today that I'm finished may not have it right. I'm still chairman of the parent company. I'm still the controlling shareholder. I'm co-director of the strategic process and I'm chairman of the *Telegraph*. And I made fifty million bucks yesterday. That's a flameout I could get used to."[12]

Black was confident he could count on support from board members, whom he had handpicked and handsomely paid, to see him through the current crisis. But during the week of his book launch, Hollinger International's special committee reported the company had paid more than $32 million to Black,

David Radler, two other company officers and their Toronto-based parent company, Hollinger Inc. The committee said the payments had been neither explicitly authorized by the board of directors nor accurately reported to the SEC and that $7.2 million had gone to Black directly.

The investigation continued, and during a stormy board meeting, Black was confronted about the payments. He agreed, under pressure, to resign as chief executive officer effective November 21, although continuing as non-executive chairman and controlling shareholder. Radler resigned as well, effective immediately. Black (with the board's backing) decided to retain the New York investment bank Lazard LLC to review and evaluate Hollinger's strategic alternatives, including the sale of all or some of the company's assets. According to an insider at the meeting, Black aggressively defended his actions. But on November 19, he resigned as CEO two days earlier than planned. That meant he would not have to sign off on the company's latest quarterly financial statements. Hollinger announced that Black, Radler and the others would be returning unauthorized payments to the company by mid-2004. The SEC then issued subpoenas and requested more information from Black, Hollinger International, its auditors (KPMG) and others.

On November 21, 2003, Black was asked to resign as CEO of Toronto-based parent company Hollinger Inc., and when he refused, four independent directors — the entire audit committee of Hollinger Inc. — resigned. By early December 2003, *Forbes* magazine had named Black to its "rogues' gallery" and included the disclosure of unauthorized payments at Hollinger International among the year's worst financial scandals.

Drawing on his verbal skills, legal knowledge, powerful memory and intimidating presence, Conrad Black had achieved, over the years, an impressive string of results in the courts. With the help of keen intuition and expensive lawyers, he was adept at gaining advantage through litigation. He could also recognize when it was time to walk away or to settle when facing the possibility of serious legal difficulties. But all that began to change in December 2003, when the SEC issued a subpoena to him to testify about alleged inaccurate financial reporting at U.S.-based subsidiary Hollinger International and a number of questionable non-compete payments to himself, close associates and his private investment company, Ravelston. Black invoked the Fifth Amendment — the constitutional right not to testify for fear of incriminating himself. Many critics questioned how a responsible and reputable CEO of a large publicly traded corporation could refuse to cooperate with the SEC. "In the U.S. at least, invoking the Fifth Amendment right to refuse testimony generally leads to the termination or forced resignation of public company executives," wrote *Forbes* columnist Dan Ackman.

Black was vilified on the world's financial pages as critics questioned the elaborate corporate structure through which Ravelston Corporation, a holding company formed in 1969, controlled 78 per cent of Hollinger Inc., which in turn held 30 per cent of Hollinger International's common shares and all of its voting shares . . . leaving Black with 72 per cent of the voting rights. Some suggested he had "squandered" the multi-billion-dollar windfall he had made selling the Southam Group of newspapers to CanWest Global. Others wondered why Black and his closest associates had received tens of millions of dollars' worth of tax-free non-compete fees as part of the sale. Black insisted the payments had been authorized by the board and fully disclosed in securities filings.

But Tweedy, Browne complained to the SEC that Black and his associates had "usurped" Hollinger International's right to the non-compete fees, since the company, and not its officers, was the party selling the newspapers. There was also sharp criticism of $202.7 million in management fees paid from 1995 to 2002 to Black and his associates, while Hollinger International had posted cumulative losses since 1999 of $171 million. Minority shareholders were angry that the flow of management fees out of the company reduced earnings and kept the stock price down.

When Hollinger International made its amended 8-K filing (an ad hoc report required by the SEC when some event at a publicly traded company needs to be explained to shareholders) in May 2004, it alleged that "the scale of income diverted by the

Black Group into their own pockets during the period 1997-2003 was largely if not wholly without precedent as a proportion of the operating income of a widely-held public corporation. From 1997-2003 (estimated for 2003), Hollinger reported net income (the money left in the Company and available to other equity shareholders) of $155.4 million, after paying Black [his wife, Barbara Amiel, several associates and their respective investment companies] fees or compensation of one type or another aggregating approximately $390.7 million. Thus . . . Black and Radler used their control powers to cause the Company to pay themselves and their top associates almost 72 per cent of the Company's total net income. . . . By contrast, during the same period the top five officers of the New York Times Company and the Washington Post Company, both of which also have two-tier voting structures, received approximately 4.4 per cent of total net income in the case of the *Times*, and 1.8 per cent in the case of the *Post*." While Hollinger International alleged that these payments were part of a pattern of criminal activity, any allegations would have to be proven in a court of law.

On January 18, 2004, Hollinger International fired Black as chairman, suing him, along with Radler, Ravelston and Hollinger Inc. for more than $200 million. Black's loss of control over his press empire in February 2004 was swift and brutal. In mid-February, Black launched an $850-million suit against several Hollinger International board members and advisers, alleging they had made false and malicious representations about him, making him a social leper and a loathsome laughingstock. Two weeks later, a Delaware judge blocked his attempts to sell Hollinger International to Sir David and Sir Frederick Barclay, twin Scottish business tycoons who owned several newspapers. Instead, Hollinger International ignored Black's objections in the summer of 2004, selling off the *Daily Telegraph* to the Barclay brothers for £665 million, or $1.21 billion. By August 2004, the special committee report accused Black and Radler of running a "corporate kleptocracy," alleging they had colluded to steal $400 million from the company, to "satisfy their ravenous appetite for cash." Advised by Richard Breeden, the committee continued its investigation, at a cost to Hollinger International of $57 million between 2004 and 2006. On November 15, the SEC filed civil charges against Black, Radler and Hollinger Inc. On August 18, 2005, federal prosecutor Patrick Fitzgerald filed criminal fraud charges against Radler, the private holding company Ravelston Corp. and Hollinger lawyer Mark Kipnis.

As long as Radler remained silent, Black could be confident of muddling his way through. After all, Black had taken the Fifth Amendment. But when Radler began testifying before Hollinger International's special committee and the SEC, he kept changing his story, tripping over his many nervous and contradictory accounts. He got himself cornered. Radler accepted in August 2005 to turn state's evidence, pleading guilty to one charge of fraud that would see him get twenty-nine months in prison.

On November 17, 2005, federal prosecutors in Chicago announced that Black, former Hollinger executive Jack Boultbee and former Hollinger lawyers Kipnis and Peter Atkinson faced a raft of additional criminal charges. Prosecutors alleged that the four had planned and executed a number of fraudulent schemes, looting Hollinger International by diverting $51.8 million in tax-free non-compete payments from Hollinger International's sale of Canadian newspapers to CanWest Global, in 2000, as well as $32 million in other transactions. In addition, prosecutors alleged Black had breached his fiduciary duty by charging lavish entertainment such as his wife's birthday party and a Tahitian holiday to the company. According to FBI agent Robert Grant, "the frauds were blatant and pervasive. They extended from the backrooms to the boardroom, and from Park Avenue to the South Pacific." Black also faced nine mail and wire fraud charges, obstruction of justice charges and a possible order, if convicted, to restitute $92 million.

The irony is that Black would have been worth far more today if various rich payments, fees and special dividends hadn't been squeezed out of his companies since the 1980s.

Andrew Knight, the former editor-in-chief of the *Economist* who helped Black take over control of the *Telegraph* in 1985 (Knight was CEO of the paper until 1989), said, "In my last year at the helm, I'm told we made as much profit as the *Telegraph* made in total over its previous hundred years. I was introduced that winter to a room of U.S. investment bankers as 'the man who made Conrad Black a billionaire.' "[13]

The *Chicago Sun-Times*, sitting on a substantial parcel of prime downtown real estate, was also a valuable franchise. Black and Donald Trump had been planning to build the world's tallest skyscraper on the site. That project was put on hold following the destruction of the World Trade Center towers in the terrorist attacks of September 11, 2001. In June 2004, Trump bought Hollinger International's share in the site for $73 million, scaling the project down from an initial 150 stories to 92. The following month, the *Sun-Times* was valued at more than $1 billion, although a bidding war was expected to push the value even higher.

And the hotly contested management fees at Hollinger International had never been tied to Black's performance, reducing his motivation to get the stock price moving upward. *Globe and Mail* columnist Eric Reguly said if Hollinger International shares had followed the Dow average since they were first issued in 1994, Black's 27.9 million class A shares would be worth $865 million instead of slightly under $350 million. "The difference is $515 million, or 2½ times more than the amount . . . collected through the management contract over seven years."[14]

By December 2006, Black was rumoured to be down to his last $8 million in ready cash. His legal fees from 2004 to December 2006 were said to have passed the $30-million mark.[15] Two of his former companies, Hollinger International and Hollinger Inc., were fronting 75 per cent of his legal fees fighting off the criminal suit in Chicago and 50 per cent of his legal fees in various civil suits. But if found guilty, and once the appeal process was exhausted, Black would have to reimburse this money. The rest of his fortune was said to be mortgaged or otherwise committed, although some assets may have been tucked away abroad. Was he now technically broke?

Black came through the library of his Toronto mansion to greet me. He looked crumpled, older than I remembered him, with deep circles under his eyes. His clothes were informal, crinkled and did not match. He showed me around absent-mindedly, bringing me through the library, whose walls were covered with hardcover and multi-volume biographies, organized by theme — Lawrence of Arabia, Henry Kissinger, Winston Churchill, Margaret Thatcher, Richard Nixon and so on. To my surprise, I saw no books in French on the shelves. It seemed like an Anglo businessman's collection of "great books" more than the library of a historian who had written acclaimed, controversial biographies of Quebec premier Maurice Duplessis and Franklin Roosevelt.

Black brought me through to his study and showed me stunning custom-built models of passenger liners. He was surprised I could identify so many of them and tell their stories. "Is this the *Rex*?" I asked. "No, not wrecks, real ships." "No, I mean the Italian liner from the 1930s. Yes, it is the *Rex*. And this must be the *Conte di Savoia*. And that ship with the four funnels — that's the *M-M-M-M*. . ." I sometimes stutter when under pressure.

"Yes, that's it, George — the *Mauretania*!"

Werner offered to take our picture in front of a model of the *Titanic*, but I said that would be bad luck.

On Black's desk sat a computer and a pile of papers and correspondence. He said he didn't mind if I looked around while he typed an e-mail — he is a two-finger typist. In the centre of the room was a table of the same height as his desk with four-foot models of the battleships *Warspite* and *Iowa* (BB61) and the five- or six-foot *Normandie* coming out at a T-angle from that. Along with the models of the *Rex* and the *Conte di Savoia* on one wall was the *Empress of Britain*. On the other side of the study were models of the *France*, the *Ile de France* and the *United States*. These were the most beautiful models of liners I had ever seen. He said he had a basement full of models of all the capital ships of the Second World War, which would have to mean battleships and aircraft carriers of Japan, Italy, Germany, Britain,

France and the United States. Did he like going to sea? "Not really," he said, "I just like the ships."

Then we came back to the sofas in his library, under the dome, and began our discussion. First, the overall situation. My original biography of him had come out in 2004, but my publisher had quickly gone bankrupt. The time was now ripe for a completely revamped edition — with new publishers. As we spoke, I felt he was desperate for attention and positive feedback, hoping a new edition of my book would come out before the Chicago trial and somehow help his defence. He offered me his "full co-operation" — exclusive interviews on the short-term — if I agreed to devote an entire chapter of my new book to rebutting Tom Bower's recent biography, *Conrad and Lady Black*. "It would have to be a complete debunking of Bower. Almost every word in his book is false."[16] This was an obvious attempt on Black's part to co-opt me — to make me his instrument — since he was already lining up an $11-million libel suit against Bower. I said my role was not to defend or to blame him, but to write an objective account. I asked him personal questions, not in the interview style but more as a biographer, to find out how he was dealing with things on a human level.

Once I started work on my biography in 2002, I had to work hard to maintain a cool and formal relationship. In all our meetings since then, I was deliberately low-key. My questions were always circular. I occasionally played on his vanity, moved in a little closer, tested his defences, reminded him I was not his mouthpiece, occasionally threw in a new line of questioning, pried loose a spontaneous answer, then reiterated my independence, backed off and waited for a new opening. And now that he was facing criminal charges, I wanted to make clear that in everything I said in media coverage of the trial, I would maintain the principle that he was innocent until proven guilty. My role was not to judge him but rather to write a fair book with integrity.

"It must have been very difficult for you to go through this period," I said.

"It has been just dreadful," he replied. "I have learned how tough people are in the United States, how corrupt the justice system is, how vile and mean-spirited the media are."

"You have been judged guilty until proven innocent."

"It has been worse than that. I have been under extreme pressure, harassed practically on a daily basis by the Ontario Securities Commission and the Canada Revenue Agency, but I have finally dealt with them. The seizure of proceeds of the sale of my New York apartment was grotesque."

"It seems to have been a set-up — the way the FBI turned up just as the buyer was handing over that cheque for $9.5 million. The FBI are still holding on to the money."

"The money was basically stolen from me."

"How has your wife, Barbara, been through it all?"

"She and I both had medical exams last week and we are in great shape. If you saw her, you would see she hasn't aged or changed a bit. She doesn't want to come out in public. In fact, she knows you are here, George, but she prefers to stay upstairs, without coming down, until you have gone. It has been just terrible for her."

"How have your children taken it all?"

"I was talking to Brian Mulroney just last week about this, and he said, 'Conrad, our children don't relate to us based on what they see in the newspaper.' That's true. My children are very supportive."

Vintage Black. I had only just arrived, and even when I was asking about his children, he was already dropping names — showing that he was still on friendly terms with the former prime minister.

"You and Barbara have been identified as celebrities, so the standards of celebrity journalism apply to you. Anything you do, like stepping outside and crossing the street, is immediately a pseudo-event, and swarms of journalists descend on you."

"It is just incredible."

"But you are paying for your celebrity status. A lot of the media are only too happy to bring you down. Journalists tend to be frustrated anyway, and seeing how much money you made, and all the allegations that have been made, they are only too happy to take a swing at you."

"The situation has changed a lot, especially in Canada, in the last few months. The tone of coverage has changed. Canadian journalists are beginning to realize that I have not surrendered, not been cowed, not been destroyed. I have survived, I am still fighting, and the media respect that."

"One of your main characteristics is loyalty. You are loyal to your friends. You are loyal to your family. I mean, you still live in your parents' house."

"I have made a lot of changes to the house since their time."

"You must feel badly about David Radler. He is testifying against you — after all the many years when you were close partners, building up Hollinger."

"I didn't know him that well. I didn't see him socially."

"Now Radler has cut a deal with the Justice Department to do a bit of jail time, pay a fine, in exchange for incriminating you. What if he was the operator and you were the ideas man, all along — what if he knew he was doing things that were illegal?"

"He never told me he was committing any felony. Whenever I asked him about the legality of Hollinger transactions, he always assured me everything was perfectly legal. The case against me essentially depends on what he is saying. His cross-examination will last three weeks. He is a nervous, twitchy person. There is no case against me."

"The amounts of money paid to you were huge. If they were approved by your board members, why aren't they being held responsible, at least in part?"

"The justice system in the United States is fundamentally corrupt. The media have been working hand in hand with the SEC and the Justice Department. There is no case against me, and this will become clear when the trial begins in March 2007. Every payment I received was properly approved."

"You must feel badly about the people who did well by you but have now let you drop."

"Like whom?"

"Like Rupert Murdoch. Like Henry Kissinger — he has sued you, after all."

"In England, I am very surprised how many people have

broken off contact with me. As for Murdoch, I came out pub-licly supporting him when he was having problems and nearly went bankrupt. There was no need for him to use his papers to attack me like he has done, in *The Times* and the *New York Post*. Henry Kissinger is a different story. Have you been in touch with him since your book came out? No? Henry had no choice. He was basically cowed into suing me. He is only acting the way Richard Nixon told me he acted: 'Kissinger took enough distance from someone under fire that he could not be confused with the target by the assailants, nor with the assailants by the target, and awaited the outcome before determining whose side he was on.'"

"But you are far more loyal to other people than they have been to you."

"You are talking about betrayals. Sure. A lot of other people in Canada have remained loyal. But I did a lot for some people, I helped them make a lot of money. And they turned on me."

"Do you have any close friends?"

"I have a few close friends. None of us have a lot of close friends. My friends have remained loyal to me."

"Have you been sad through this period?"

"Of course I have been sad. It has been very, very difficult. Running a company as CEO and buying and selling assets is nothing compared to surviving through a period like this. I am actually proud of what I have managed to do. I have reorgan-ized and stabilized my finances."

While he spoke, I wondered whether he had discreetly sold off assets, making sure people did not know he was the seller.

"I almost feel I am a magician," Black continued, "consid-ering everything I have done. It is better not to talk of magic, but I am very proud of what I have done."

Then I asked the real question I had come for.

"What are you going to do, Conrad, if you *don't* win this case?"

"I can't . . ." His voice broke, and it took him a moment to regain his composure. "I can't conceive of losing. I can't think about that. We will win the case."

"But if *you* win, the prosecution will surely appeal. And if *they* win, I am sure you will appeal. This won't be over anytime soon."

Only once did he make me laugh — when he showed me the finished manuscript of his biography of Richard Nixon. Writing the book must have been therapeutic, I said. He explained it had helped him channel energy into something positive — it had been a good discipline. He asked me to outline what I was planning to do with my book.

By now, I was planning on bringing out a completely new edition. I asked if he would give me interviews. He replied that he would, in the short-term, if I gave him a reasonable guarantee that my updated book would come out *before* the start of his trial. But the trial was starting in a little more than three months. That meant I would have to complete a new edition in a few weeks! I was leaving in a week for southern Argentina to do a documentary on Patagonia for the Canadian Broadcasting Corporation and would not be back until mid-January. There was no way I could produce a completely updated manuscript by January 31.

"But you could write a hundred pages in a week, George," he said, almost pleading with me. He wanted me to take up his cause, and bring out a book that he could somehow use to bolster his criminal defence in Chicago, just three months away.

I said I would get back to him.

Applying pressure, he added that if I wanted to bring out my book later, he would be too busy to give me interviews in January or February — he would be totally absorbed by the upcoming trial. However, if I waited till after the trial, he would give me his full co-operation.

'That only works if you are acquitted,' I couldn't help thinking. 'When the judge hands down the verdict, she could ask the marshal to take you into custody right then and there. . . .'

As a result of his plea bargain, Radler would be a star witness for the prosecution at the criminal fraud trial of *USA v. Conrad Black et al.* in Chicago, providing detailed, damning testimony against his former partner. In acknowledgement of his guilt, Radler and his private investment companies agreed to reimburse a total of $71 million, part to Hollinger International, now

renamed the Chicago Sun-Times Group, and part to settle a
civil suit filed by the SEC.[17] A serious corporate fraud had been
committed. But was Black involved in this fraud and, if so, to
what extent? That was the question.

If the jury believed Radler's testimony and found Black
guilty in Chicago, he could face a long jail term in a medium-
security federal penitentiary in the United States, alongside
convicted killers, terrorists and drug traffickers. But if Black was
acquitted, Radler might get a more severe sentence, and Black's
acquittal would greatly strengthen the hand of his lawyers, who
had slapped his adversaries with more than $1 billion worth of
lawsuits.

It was all or nothing. His life had become a crapshoot.

The Canadian Press/AP/Jeff Roberson

CHAPTER TWO

CHICAGO LAW

CONRAD BLACK'S CRIMINAL TRIAL in Chicago started on the cold morning of March 14, 2007. Black had wanted Chicago to be the site of his ultimate American triumph — the place where his control of the *Chicago Sun-Times* would give him a political and business platform and his partnership with real estate developer Donald Trump — the comeback king and reality-show TV star — would result in a glamorous ninety-two-storey hotel and conference centre on the Chicago River. But Black had lost control of the *Sun-Times*, and Trump was going ahead on the super-luxury tower without him, offering residential condos at prices from $580,000 to $9 million.

In fact, Chicago had become the scene of Black's excruciating trial by fire — along with co-defendants Peter Atkinson, Jack Boultbee and Mark Kipnis. Silver Loop "L" trains clattered along elevated rail lines high above Van Buren Street. On a faded brick wall nearby, a neon sign flashed "Jesus Saves." Homeless people shuffled in the shadows of the pre-dawn twilight, blowing warmth into their hands and clinging to plastic bags containing their worldly possessions.

TV trucks from the Canadian networks CBC and CTV, and smaller TV vans from the American networks ABC, CBS and NBC had taken up position on South Plymouth Court the previous evening, their roofs bristling with satellite dishes and aerials. As dawn broke, TV journalists were already beaming live reports about the "white-collar trial of the century" to viewers hungry for news. But what was the story? Was it tragedy, tragi-comedy or thriller — or had it become, by now, a non-event, with Black's conviction simply a foregone conclusion? Journalists for newspapers, radio and TV huddled outside the Everett McKinley Dirksen Federal Courthouse, a black twenty-seven-storey glass-and-steel skyscraper designed by Mies van der Rohe in the mid-1960s, at the corner of Jackson Avenue and South Dearborn Street. In the early-morning hours, a BBC Radio reporter thrust a microphone in front of passers-by, most of whom had never heard of Black. Only one man said, "I hope he gets a very stiff sentence."

Several hundred journalists had applied for press accreditation. This meant waiting in line to show our press credentials to blue-uniformed federal marshals sporting Glock pistols and having our pictures taken. On the walls of the marshals' office were grim posters giving details of the FBI's ten most wanted fugitives. We knew seats in courtroom 1241 were limited. Some of us would end up in two media overflow rooms. Shivering in the brisk wind off the lake, we expected Conrad Black and Barbara Amiel to cross the intersection around 9:00 a.m. from the century-old Monadnock Building, where Black's American attorney, Ed Genson, had his offices.

There was something lurid and fascinating about Black's appearance in criminal court. He had pleaded not guilty to fourteen counts of wire and mail fraud, tax fraud, obstruction of justice and racketeering the previous December. If found guilty, he faced the possibility of a lifetime in prison and the forfeiture of some $92 million in assets. Even if he was acquitted, he and several associates would still face a $542-million civil lawsuit by Hollinger International, now renamed the Sun-Times Media Group, a $700-million lawsuit filed by Hollinger Inc. of Toronto, as well as class action lawsuits filed on behalf of shareholders. It was our job to report the facts and to uphold the principle that he was innocent until proven guilty.

Black had been silenced. Having lost his position in the

newspaper industry, he no longer had control of the narrative of his life. He was being interpreted by the world media. With the exception of Mark Steyn, a Black loyalist and neo-conservative still praising his former boss in *Maclean's* magazine, Peter Worthington of the *Toronto Sun* and Steve Skurka, a Toronto criminal lawyer blogging from Chicago, media interpretations were either harsh or cautious.

I worked from the assumption that Black had a 50 per cent chance of an acquittal, which meant a 50 per cent chance of being found guilty. But federal prosecutors actually have a conviction rate in criminal cases of 95 per cent, which gave Black only one chance in twenty of getting acquitted. When the American public cried for blood, the prosecutors could often provide it.

In Canada, Black was a celebrity with a dwindling constituency of people who believed in him. In Britain, as a member of the House of Lords, he was a lawmaker. But in the United States, he was alleged to be a lawbreaker on a grand scale. District Judge Amy St. Eve wouldn't let him travel to London without prior written approval. In Chicago, Black was not particularly well known, although his $21-million bond and former ownership of the *Chicago Sun-Times* raised a few eyebrows.

He had chosen as his American defence attorney Ed Genson, a famous sixty-five-year-old criminal lawyer with curly reddish-grey hair and thick glasses who habitually sported a five-day beard. Genson had contracted polio as a child and required the use of a wheelchair. He was a brilliant strategist with high-profile clients, although he had not won a case in years. He had recently represented lobbyist Larry Warner, who was convicted with former Illinois governor George Ryan on racketeering and fraud charges. He had also represented Ryan's assistant, Scott Fawell, who was convicted on corruption charges.

For his Canadian defence attorney, Black had chosen fifty-nine-year-old Eddie Greenspan, a stooped, stout man with thick grey hair and black eyebrows whose chubby head sits on his shoulders like that of a great snapping turtle sticking out of its shell. He puffed rather than spoke. Greenspan is one of Toronto's most aggressive criminal lawyers, and this was the first time he had been allowed to plead in the United States. He fantasized about winning a high-profile legal case in the city of Clarence Darrow. He would have to convince twelve jurors Black deserved to be acquitted.

The evening before the trial began, the very indiscreet public relations manager of the Palmer House Hotel told me Black would be staying at the Ritz-Carlton uptown. I was the only journalist to know this, so I took a cab up there with a driver who nearly ran over several pedestrians, then argued he wanted twenty-five cents more tip from me. I went up to the lobby on the twelfth floor of the hotel, asked permission to take some photographs of a lovely fountain in the lobby with some green metallic herons in it, then asked to leave a message at the reception for a guest.

"What name, sir?"

"Black."

"First name?"

"Conrad."

The manager came out of his office and said there was nobody by that name registered at the hotel so I couldn't leave the message. As I came out the doorway into the street, a glistening black limo pulled up, followed by a stretch security van. Barbara got out. She had huge sunglasses on, wore black as usual, and her face looked lumpier and much older than when I had last seen her. Next came Black's daughter from his first marriage, Alana, slender, beautiful, with long brown hair arranged in bangs over a face that had strong features. Then out came Black himself, wearing a grey suit, his silver hair neatly combed. I lingered off to the side, waiting to see whether I caught his eye. I didn't want to invade his privacy. He looked anxious and wan.

"What are you doing here?" he asked in his usual bemused way.

"Oh, I'm just looking for someone to have a drink with. I wanted you to know I am not like all the others." I wanted him to remember I was covering the trial in Chicago, and hoped to land an interview eventually.

"I know you are not like the others, George."

I chatted awhile with Alana, indicated to Black I wouldn't tell anyone where they were staying — they had a right to privacy — then hailed a cab and left.

As things turned out, Genson and Greenspan served as decoys, crossing the street from the Monadnock Building, hemmed in closely by a forest of TV cameras and boom microphones. The Blacks made their way into the Dirksen building through an underground entrance.

Proceedings started at 9:30 a.m. Judge St. Eve, a petite forty-one-year-old woman with auburn hair parted in the middle and wearing pearl earrings, entered the courtroom and took her place, spreading out her black robes. She wore a Stars and Stripes pin on her lapel. She was all of five feet tall and looked even smaller, sitting in front of the huge silver and rust-brown bald eagle on the seal of the United States District Court for the Northern District of Illinois. The courtroom itself was about 100 feet by 75 feet, with the clerks seated at a table in front of the judge. At one table sat the thirty-seven-year-old lead federal prosecutor, Eric Sussman, who had won convictions against the Gangster Disciples, a largely African-American Chicago-based street gang, as well as a former police detective running a jewellery theft ring. Sussman was wiry, with brown hair, a thin, inexpressive face and pursed lips. He wore a dark suit, white shirt and striped tie and could have passed for a Mormon on a mission. He was joined at the table by assistant prosecutor Jeff Cramer, who had experience prosecuting white-collar fraud cases in New York. At another table were Genson, Greenspan and Black himself. At a third table were Black's co-defendants and their attorneys. At the end of the room were seats reserved for sketch artists (no photographs were allowed in the court room), the general public and the media. Barbara and Alana took their seats on the first bench, reserved for family members of the defendants.

For the next two days, Judge St. Eve interviewed prospective jurors to establish their attitudes on tax treatment, law enforcement and other matters and to find out whether they had any fundamental bias or impediment that should disqualify them for jury duty. "If any of you are not comfortable with my questions," she said reassuringly, "just let me know."

Criminal cases involve majesty, terror, theatre and ritual — partly because the verdict depends on a small cross-section of the people, chosen at random. The prospective jurors at Black's trial were everyman and everywoman. They represented society at large, and their personal stories of struggle and survival were a cross-section of Middle America. Black listened in silence. These were the kind of people he had made a point of ignoring all his life — and now they held his destiny in their hands.

Jurors would be paid only forty dollars a day for jury duty, plus forty-eight cents a mile, for the duration of a three-month trial. A few had employers willing to support their jury duty. But some expressed concern that jury duty would result in them losing their jobs, even if their employers had no legal right to fire them on that basis. Or they could lose private health-care coverage, which was their only way to get health benefits. An overweight woman complained that she could not sit still for long periods of time without getting something to eat. An apprentice mechanic had several friends who had been arrested in drunken brawls — he was worried that serving on the jury would delay his certification as a mechanic and put a hole in the finances of his young family.

The wages they earned and the money Black was accused of looting were in two different universes. "If you heard evidence that some of the defendants made tens of millions of dollars," St. Eve said, "would you think that they had done something wrong?" "Yes," answered an Asian-American college student who barely got by juggling part-time tutoring jobs. "I don't think anyone in the United States, unless you are Donald Trump, should make money like that."

"Have you ever been charged or arrested?" St. Eve asked the candidates repeatedly. "Have any of your friends been charged or arrested?"

A surprising number of the prospective jurors had first-hand experience of crime: they were plaintiffs in class action shareholder lawsuits, had witnessed armed robbery, been defrauded by con artists, lost money in time-shares, been victimized by identify theft, been burglarized or had lost family members to violent crime. Another prospective juror had been shot at for no reason, reporting it to the police, who had simply ignored his complaint. This was a mosaic of hardship, but also of basic decency. I could imagine running into the prospective jurors at the local corner store.

"Do you have any potential bias due to your personal or professional experiences?" St. Eve asked. "Can you be objective about the evidence admitted in court? Do you understand that the government must prove its case against the defendants — that the mere fact of being charged with a criminal offence does not imply that the defendants are guilty? Everyone is innocent until proven guilty. The defendants do not need to testify if they choose not to, and the fact that they do not testify cannot be held against them."

St. Eve repeatedly questioned prospective jurors about whether they were familiar with the case, and warned them not to do independent research on the Internet or watch TV reports about Black and his co-defendants. "Can you put aside what you read in the newspaper? Because that is not evidence. Our ultimate goal is to end up with a fair and impartial jury to hear this case. It will be your obligation, if you are chosen for jury duty, to absolutely obey the instructions you are given. Does that pose a problem for you?"

She had to remind them this case was based on evidence admitted in court, and nothing else. "The law does not oblige a defendant to prove his innocence," she said. "The defendants stand innocent here today. The government has to prove beyond a reasonable doubt that they committed a crime. As the trial starts, all witnesses are equal. I will be giving you instructions in due course on the factors that can help you determine if they are telling the truth or not."

One candidate had a criminal justice degree and figured the defendants in this case "probably stole the money." Another shuddered to think how much money was involved. Another declared she did not believe in the presumption of innocence.

"Are you sure you are going to be able to understand the

issues?" the judge asked one candidate for the jury. The case involved complex financial, accounting and legal principles and very contradictory accounts of what happened when some $60 million was paid out to Black and several associates.

"I will, if it's like what I see on TV."

"Nothing that happens in this courtroom," snapped Judge St. Eve, "is like what you see on TV!"

This comment drew a broad grin from Eric Sussman. He well knew that Americans love TV. Some people's view of the criminal justice system is shaped by *Boston Legal* and *America's Funniest Police Videos*. People like sharply defined characters, simple plots, flashes of colour and outrage and surprise endings on the hour. According to the non-profit organization TV-Free America, in Washington, D.C., Americans watch an average of twenty-eight hours of TV per week. TV conditions their thinking, feeling, hopes and fears. TV is leading even serious newspapers to publish gossipy tabloid fare — all about how celebrities look, not what they do. And the boob tube was now creating tabloid justice. Sussman, Cramer and two other prosecutors in this case struck a heroic TV star pose for Reuters early in March. The caption of this stunning picture, taken against a dramatic black backdrop, could have been: "A new blockbuster series coming this fall — *Chicago Law*."

I had written about all sorts of topics — disappearances, refugees, hostages, terrorists, Aboriginal societies, desert nomads, slaves, spiritual leaders, Nobel-winning scientists and inventors. But I found the Chicago trial a tough assignment. We journalists were thrust into a labyrinth of intrigue, a swirling vortex. And here we alternated between moments of dread, anger, boredom and even vertigo, trying to follow the story as new evidence was read into the record each day.

Coming to Chicago, I had expected there to be two groups with clearly drawn interests in the courtroom, functioning like a legal seesaw. This is the norm in the adversary system of justice. Instead, I could now count at least six interest groups. First was the prosecution, who aimed to get a conviction by any means. Second, the defence, who were ready to argue that Black and the other defendants were the victims of a vast government conspiracy based on lies, deception and manipulation. For them, Black was unjustly accused — the "wrong man." Radler had pleaded guilty to fraud and he alone deserved to go to prison. Third was the judge herself, a former federal prosecutor, who was there to rule on points of evidence and of law, although judges sometimes act to consolidate the power of the government that employs them. Fourth were the jurors. Were they really qualified to judge questions of law? Were they also capable of judging questions of fact? Their role was to form an objective view of the facts of the case. But they were also there to limit the power of the judge. Given their limited knowledge of the business world, should they sit on a jury in a corporate fraud case? Should others have been chosen?

A fifth interest group were the media, who hang people in effigy every day of the week, before cases even get to trial, who prejudice cases and don't seem to know the difference between a ripping narrative and evidence admitted in court. Many journalists around me seemed less interested in reporting what actually happened that day than in predicting what would happen the next day, weaving a compelling tale held together by threads of human interest, hearsay, drama and colour.

Then there was a sixth interest group, not represented in court and not even physically present. These were corporate governance experts, led by Richard Breeden, the former SEC chairman who had been appointed by Black to the special committee at Hollinger International and had brought about his downfall. Many of Breeden's allegations of corporate malfeasance on a grand scale were serious. But the amount of money Black was alleged to have diverted from Hollinger International had melted like butter in the sun — from an alleged $1.25 billion in early 2004 including treble damages to $60 million here in Chicago. Breeden's two-year investigation had cost the company $57 million, of which Black guessed Breeden had personally received $25 million. To justify the high cost of his work, he had had to construct as damaging a case as possible. He had launched a billion-dollar corporate governance hedge fund.

In fact, by the time the trial started, $500 million had been spent on corporate investigations at Hollinger International and Hollinger Inc. and on the settlement of directors' and lawyers' insurance claims and other expenses. It's as if this money had been raked into a huge pile and burned. An additional billion dollars of shareholder value had disappeared — probably forever.

Corporate governance advocates were right to denounce the manipulative, duplicitous behaviour and self-interest of corporate executives they wanted to drive out of the company. But what if some corporate governance also involved manipulative techniques — such as commandeering the media through selective leaks of damaging information, cowing board members into submission and lobbying for absurd compensation for investigating and documenting executive improprieties?

Finally, Judge St. Eve chose twelve jury members and six alternates. Who were these people we were not allowed to identify until after the trial? I got to know some of them by name. Tina Kadisak was young, white, quite overweight, with dyed blonde hair, and often blew bubbles of chewing gum while listening with a vacant expression in her eyes. Monica Prince was a black woman in her early fifties with hair going grey at the temples. She worked for a Canadian-based employer and said she could be fair. Sandra Grubar was manager at a Chicago packaging company (a month later, she asked to be dismissed from the jury to take care of her eighty-nine-year-old father). Barbara Carroll was a black woman in her fifties with glasses and a nice smile. She regularly dozed in court. Jonathan Keag would serve as jury foreman.

Once the jurors were chosen, the *Chicago Tribune* filed an emergency motion for access to the names of jurors. The newspaper said the conclusion of the jury selection process was shrouded in secrecy and argued for the right to publish jurors' names, citing the First Amendment's guarantee of freedom of the press. Conrad Black's defence team did not want jurors' names released, and St. Eve quickly responded in writing the following week. "A number of cases, for example, address the press' request to release juror names after the return of the verdict — cases that silently reflect a practice of not releasing names and information during the pendency of a trial," she wrote. It was important to protect the secrecy of the jury's work to encourage free and open debate within the jury room. "The only external output of the jury's function is the end product — the verdict," St. Eve said. In effect, she was upholding the Sixth Amendment guarantee of the right to a fair trial.

Over the weekend, the SEC announced David Radler had agreed to pay a $28.7-million fine as part of his settlement with the SEC.[18] "Radler and others misappropriated millions of dollars from Hollinger International and made numerous misstatements to shareholders as part of their scheme," said Linda Chatman Thompson, director of the commission's enforcement division. "The tough sanctions in this settlement, including one of the largest civil penalties in recent years against an individual wrongdoer, reflect our resolve to act forcefully against corporate officers who perpetrate fraud against those whom they are supposed to serve, the shareholders of the company."

The fine underlined the gravity of the charges facing Black and his former associates. But the timing of the announcement — just days before the opening arguments in the criminal case — led to a flurry of defence motions, since the news could prejudice the interests of the defendants. Judge St. Eve adjourned the case for one day.

I thought back to my first meeting with Conrad Black, in April 2002, to discuss my biography project. At the time, arranging a meeting with Black involved months of trans-Atlantic messages. He was more often in London, in his corporate apartment in New York or in his Palm Beach mansion than in Toronto. I finally got my summons to his London residence.

Cottesmore Gardens can be hard to find. The discreet, enclosed neighbourhood for the ultra-rich — where mansions typically go for more than £10 million is hidden away near London's Brompton Oratory in the fashionable West End borough of Kensington and Chelsea. In England, it often rains suddenly. I was caught without an umbrella and found myself walking around in a very damp suit. A sleek, dark green Bentley passed in the street as I rang the doorbell, clutching an e-mail confirmation of my appointment like a wilted flower.

"Conrad Black — I mean, Lord Black — will receive you," said the fit young butler (who looked more like a secret agent than the trembling Jeeves-the-butler figure I had expected). The momentary lapse was forgivable; Black's baronial title was just six months old. Inside the mansion, I caught a glimpse of a mournful Gainsborough (a portrait of what appeared to be an eighteenth-century aristocratic youth suffering from tuberculosis); a reduced Ivor Roberts-Jones bronze of Sir Winston Churchill; an opulent sunken dining room; and a round marble table with a stylish arrangement of books by Margaret Thatcher, Henry Kissinger and other political heroes.

After a few minutes, a uniformed maid escorted me to the upstairs drawing room, running the full length of the house (actually two houses joined together) and furnished with Empire chairs and sofas. Then came the long wait, punctuated by the passage of Barbara Amiel in a low-cut black dress and leopard-skin Manolo Blahniks. She offered a Scotch, and I accepted a double. From her autobiography and many columns, I had imagined her to be an ice queen writing with a stiletto — her journalism occasionally reduced to rants on subjects she hadn't really mastered. In person, she projected the image of a woman of power. Too brainy to be anybody's trophy, she had lived a very public life — a celebrity and a fiery political columnist. Black was her fourth husband. At that time, they were one of London's leading "power couples."

Sixty-something, she looked more like a thirty-year-old cross between a young Jackie Kennedy and a Hollywood femme fatale, complete with pert, upturned nose. Although some magazine deemed her Canada's most beautiful woman in the 1980s, I found there was a disagreeable harshness in her eyes. Behind the public face was a long-suffering woman. Barbara Amiel has struggled with illness for quite some time. According to journalist Anthony Holden, "The only cloud on [Conrad and Barbara's] horizon is that she has developed a rare auto-immune disease called dermatomyositis. 'It's related to lupus,' said Black, 'but less severe. It is the reverse of AIDS. Instead of being without an immune system, you have an immune system so belligerent that it attacks healthy cells.' The need for treatment takes her 'out of commission for three to four days every two to three months.'"[19]

At one end of the room where I sat was a baby grand piano. Nearby was yet another historical reference to power — a looming portrait of Napoleon in oils. "Glory is fleeting, but obscurity is forever," Napoleon once said.

Conrad Black inevitably kept his visitors waiting. This proved to be the beginning of a relationship of sorts. I would be subjected to many long waits in luxurious decors, and Black would alternate between courtesy and veiled threats, casually mentioning biographers and journalists he had either just sued for libel or was about to.

Being talked about and being seen in the right places were important to the Blacks. The furnishings, artwork and books in Cottesmore Gardens served as carefully selected illustrations of Black's political ideas and values. It was a site of celebrity theatre where little happened by chance and everything made a statement. In the early 1980s, Black induced the pop artist Andy Warhol to do his portrait — not once but four times. It seemed he was awarding himself an excess of trophies. But it was also, surely, a good investment.

This was the sumptuous residence where the Blacks held their famous summer garden parties, one of the main events in the London glam set's social calendar. In June 2000, for example, they filled their six reception rooms with the likes of Prince Andrew, Prince Michael of Kent, the exiled King Constantine II of Greece (an Olympic gold medallist), beautiful young movie stars and an assortment of billionaires, aristocrats, Conservative historians and newspaper editors. Given Black's Christian Zionism, it seemed strange that a crusty old Nazi tank commander from the Second Panzer division also turned up.

Sitting in Black's drawing room armed with a long list of questions about governance, executive compensation and how he had sometimes boasted of having re-engineered companies (at the cost of tens of thousands of jobs), I wondered, with all the Hollinger turmoil, how he was finding the time to write an exhaustive biography of Franklin D. Roosevelt.

The question was whether Black would grant on-the-record interviews — and actually say something revealing. The answer was crucial, since my research would coincide with a darkening period in Black's corporate life. As hindsight has shown, this initial meeting took place at the apogee of his financial power, just before things began to turn, so establishing my independence was important.

He appeared at last, apologizing for the delay. Even though I had met him before, his reputation was larger than life, and I was again surprised to find a man who was neither abnormally tall nor overly pugnacious.

Black was tough, so I had to be tough back — like an iron hand in a velvet glove. I had heard and read that he was a fanatical devotee of Napoleon. But when I offered that Napoleon was a megalomaniac who launched wars that led to the death of hundreds of thousands of people — all for his own glory — and that he had usurped the revolution and in a way confiscated it, Black's response was: "Yes, I agree with that. I think he was a great general, but not a particularly admirable man."

He was guarded but courteous. Black asked why I wanted to write a book about him and in what way it would be different from his own autobiographical work. This was a very strange comment. How could my view of him ever coincide with the view he took of himself? I sat back a moment, to take the measure of the man.

"You were very ambitious, publishing your memoirs at the age of forty-nine," I replied, "but you have compressed a great deal of information into a short space — besides which, there are so many names of people that one sometimes gets lost." I told him that after finishing the book, I still did not understand who he really was, how he came to be so successful, what influence he wielded through his newspapers and what his relationship with Canada was.

"You seem unnecessarily aggressive and contrarian when stating your views," I said, "and this means that readers focus on your aggressive tone rather than on the substance of your ideas, which are interesting in their own right."

He clearly liked that comment. "What should we do about the book to ensure its accuracy?" he asked.

I figured I had about one minute to nail down control of my book. I was a novice at this while Black was a noted biographer and probably knew every pitfall of the writing profession. I told him there were several possibilities "ranging from puff pieces like Joe Haines's adulatory biography of Robert Maxwell — to a negative, destructive biography." Black said he had known Haines and thought he had destroyed his own credibility by writing such a glowing account of Maxwell, whom Black himself found colourful and entertaining but also a devious scoundrel.

I felt quite mischievous mentioning Maxwell on that first meeting — I knew that Black had periodically been compared to Maxwell in the British press. Both were outsiders who had snatched up London daily newspapers and had larger-than-life personalities. Maxwell turned out to have been a complete crook. Black had done many controversial things, but had always bashed his way back to safety.

"I don't think it would be worthwhile to have you authorize or vet my book," I told Black. "On the contrary, it is better that my book be independent and critical and written from the perspective of a historian rather than a journalist."

Black agreed, and said he would just have to trust me not to misquote him. He asked me to name four people as references, and to send him a copy of my doctoral thesis in history, so he could judge the kind of person I was. Our next meeting would be at the New York offices of Hollinger International.

During my researches, Black was not the only person to pressure me in an effort to bend my will to his advantage. Andrew Knight, the British newspaper executive who had helped Black buy the *Daily Telegraph* in 1985, gave me an interesting interview but then, fearing legal action, pressured me to tone down some of his comments.

One Saturday morning in early 2004, I got an unexpected phone call at my home in Montreal. "Hello, this is Ken Thomson." I scratched my head, trying to remember who that might be. "Ken Thomson. You interviewed me for your book about

Conrad Black."

I pulled myself together. This was Kenneth Roy Thomson — the second Lord Thomson of Fleet, the publicity-shy owner of a worldwide publishing empire that had started with the *Scotsman* and *The Times*, with a personal fortune of some $21 billion. "Yes, Mr. Thomson. What can I do for you?"

"Things are going very badly for Conrad. It is all very unfortunate, and I am not comfortable about being quoted in your book. I would like you to remove the interview. Now that so many lawsuits are being filed against Conrad, readers of your book might assume I am making fun of him."

I thought of one specific quote from the interview, done in June 2003 — which now seemed prescient. Thomson told me Black was "remarkable for the depth and breadth of his intellect, matched by a monumental ambition to play a major political and historical role on the world scene. His ownership of the *Daily Telegraph* and the *Sunday Telegraph* provides him with a premium media platform, making him a well-known business and political figure in Britain and Europe.

"His ownership of the *Chicago Sun-Times* gives him an American base on which to build, while his strategic holding in the Middle East, the *Jerusalem Post*, provides him with a small but important window on that part of the world. If he were a passive owner, Conrad Black's position would not be overly remarkable. It is his ambition, little disguised by himself, to become a prominent figure on the world stage, which elevates him to international focus. Whether he is destined to leave his mark as a chapter or as a footnote in the history of newspapers and their proprietors is not, for the moment, the point."

I asked Thomson to explain a little more why he was so uncomfortable with this statement. As he spoke, I began fidgeting at my desk with a pocket calculator, imagining the worth of the hour he was spending with me on the phone. 'Hmm. $21 billion, at 5 per cent annual interest, divided by 365 days, divided by 24 hours, comes to about $120,000!'

"But, Mr. Thomson, you read the transcript of the interview and signed it as an accurate statement and mailed it back to me! It's like a contract. How about if I make clear in the text of my book that the interview took place in June 2003? That way people will know that your comments were made before all of Conrad Black's troubles started."

He paused. "That will take care of things perfectly. Come and see me next time you are in Toronto."

It took me a while to follow up on the invitation. When I visited Ken Thomson in September 2004, he took me on a tour of his art collection on the ninth floor of the Bay, at Queen and Bay, next to his offices in downtown Toronto. Just as I came up a special escalator under a sweeping atrium, a lovely-looking young woman with short blonde hair and spike heels, piqued by curiosity, left a benefit event she was attending to visit the Thomson Gallery.

We wandered around the hundreds of valuable paintings and sketches, without speaking, stopping in front of Arctic glaciers by Lawren Harris, foothills buffalo by Paul Kane, Quebec farming scenes of old by Cornelius Krieghoff and Group of Seven paintings of trees bending under the weight of fresh snow.

Thomson introduced himself. He was tall, though stooped now that he was in his early eighties, with laughing eyes, a wry, down-to-earth smile and a familiar manner. He peered at the chic young woman visiting his gallery, complimenting her on her wonderful posture. "My wife, Marilyn, keeps telling me to stand up straight," he said, looking down at the woman's breasts. "You have *such* good posture."

Turning to me, Thomson said, "Things will end very badly for Conrad. He has taken far too much money out of his company. He got greedy, and he will pay for it. I am at the point in my life when I realize people only need three things — three square meals a deal, their family around them and their good name. I am not a religious person, but I believe we get what we ultimately deserve. This is a very negative subject, and, George, you should be using your writing talents to do something more useful in life!"

On my next visit, we walked around Thomson's office together, which featured young female assistants wearing blue jeans and, stranger yet, dogs wandering around the corridors. In our correspondence and conversations, he showed a maniacal desire to protect his privacy and good name. He had known Black for decades. They had moved in some of the same circles. They were Canada's two last newspaper barons. But in some ways, Ken Thomson was the exact opposite of Black — someone who built durable value, which he passed on to his son, and who fled any form of publicity. He died of a heart attack in his Toronto office on June 12, 2006.

On the morning of March 20, 2007, there was a nervous hush in courtroom 1241 in Chicago as the opening arguments were presented. Assistant attorney Jeff Cramer spoke for the prosecution. He presented the case in broad brush strokes, with villains and victims clearly identified. Black was villain number one. The strategy was to keep things simple and present the jury with compelling graphic images.

"You're sitting in a room with four men who stole $60 million," Cramer said. "Four men that betrayed the trust of thousands of public shareholders. Four men who decided amongst themselves that their six- and seven-figure salaries were simply not enough.

"Bank robbers wear masks and use a gun. Burglars wear dark clothing and use a crowbar. But these four — three lawyers and an accountant — dressed in ties and wore suits. These four, you see, were officers of Hollinger International. It's a newspaper company based here in Chicago.

"In 1998, the shareholders trusted these four to sell hundreds of community newspapers — small community newspapers — in Canada and the United States.

"What the shareholders didn't know was that these four secretly took some of the money from all of those sales of the newspapers for themselves — money that should have gone to the shareholders.

"And these four covered up their crime by falsifying documents to make it look to any outside observer that each transaction was a normal business deal. It wasn't. It was a theft. It was fraud. It was a crime . . .

"They decided to focus on those big newspapers. Conrad Black didn't want to focus on the small community newspapers;

newspapers like Jamestown, North Dakota, a population of about ten thousand people. That's not the target market that Conrad Black wanted. He wanted to influence world events; not just write about them, but influence world events.

"But what that resulted in is that, as they were selling these hundreds and hundreds of newspapers that were located in Canada and the United States, these four were literally working themselves out of a job because their salaries were based on four hundred or so newspapers, plus the larger newspapers, as I mentioned.

"What they decided to do was they thought they deserved some of that money — the money that belonged to shareholders. Remember, this is a public company. In the mid-1990s, they went public. The shareholders owned this company.

"These four decided that they would take the proceeds from each of those sales and put it in their pocket. And they concocted a scheme. And the scheme was to use a vehicle called a non-competition agreement to facilitate this: a non-competition agreement.

"What a non-competition agreement is, you have a buyer and seller of an asset. It could be anything, a company. And if you're going to buy a company, the last thing you want is the person who sold it to you to come back and compete with you. So, if you buy a business, you don't want them to open up right next door to you the day after you buy it. So, you enter into what's called a non-competition agreement. . . .

"Ladies and gentlemen, these are some of the most sophisticated businessmen you will ever see. They are the most sophisticated businessmen you will ever lay eyes upon. They knew this wasn't their money. It was the shareholders' money.

"Keep remembering this was the shareholders' money when they sold this business to the public. It's the woman who put Hollinger International stock into her retirement account. That's who owns this company. It's the guy who bought Hollinger International stock and put it into the college fund. That's who owns this company. It's not their company [i.e., not the defendants' company].

"And you will see, ladies and gentlemen, that they just take a little piece. They just take the tiniest pieces. But these are hundreds of millions of dollars in deals. One of these deals was several billion dollars.

"I will tell you what. If you take a little piece from deals that are worth hundreds of millions of dollars and billions of dollars, you can get to $60 million pretty darn quick. And that's what they did.

"What's wrong with it? Why can't you take $60 million from a public company that you work for? Ladies and gentlemen, besides the obvious that it's stealing, these defendants also had a duty. They had an obligation to the shareholders. You'll hear it called a 'fiduciary duty.' What a fiduciary duty is, is directors and officers have a duty to Hollinger International and its shareholders. Generally, they must consider the company's and shareholders' best interests. They must not harm the company or its shareholders. So, they have this duty to the shareholders.

"And it's a thread. It's a thread that's going to go through this trial — a fiduciary duty. And you will see them, ladies and gentlemen, breach that duty time after time after time. The shareholders have a right to expect that the officers — these defendants — don't lie to them. They have a right to expect that they are honest with them. At the very least, they can expect not to be lied to — at the very least."

Then Ed Genson wheeled around and opened for the defence, his voice ringing with mingled passion and rage. "Conrad Black is not guilty of each and every — each and every — charge in this indictment. He is innocent. And when the evidence comes in, you will see that he is innocent of any wrongdoing. Hollinger was not a company in trouble. It was built by Conrad Black. It was a company that made money for its shareholders. It was a company that had been attacked and preyed on by people who had built nothing; and who convinced others caught up in something called corporate governance to help them. It was built from nothing to be one of the world's great newspaper companies. Nothing criminal was done by Conrad Black or anybody else in this courtroom. There were no books altered. There were no false assets. Hollinger put out some of the best newspapers in the world.

"There is no issue about changing the financial records. The company was audited by the best accounting company in the world. There was no accounting magic at Hollinger.

"You have to understand — and there were questions by some of the jurors in their questionnaires — this wasn't an Enron. This wasn't a WorldCom. This wasn't a failing business. This wasn't a failing business of worthless properties. Hollinger assembled, manufactured and sold a real product. There was no accounting fraud, no bankruptcy, no unemployed employees.

"This is a healthy and successful company worth billions of dollars and producing some of the world's best newspapers. It is a healthy and successful company until the company is taken away from Conrad Black.

"This is not a story about a theft *by* Conrad Black — this is a story about a theft *from* him!

"The government tells you about public shareholders, and we share their concern; but, Hollinger's largest single-equity shareholder was Conrad Black, who was truly one of the owners; just as much of an owner as any of the public shareholders; the largest single owner of Hollinger.

"He was not stealing from himself. The company was stolen from him. Men came in and tried to find and pretended to find criminal liability when there was none there. And those men are using the United States attorney as their tool in order to justify their takeover of the company.

"Conrad Black was paid, as normal in the industry, for the value he created; for running the company; and, then, selling the assets wisely. And we will show that he sold the assets wisely.

"The government argues that certain non-compete payments that were properly given to Conrad Black and others by the buyers of some of the Hollinger papers should not have gone to Conrad Black. That's what they say.

"In fact, it was the payment to Conrad Black in the one transaction that he was directly involved which allowed this immense profit to occur for Hollinger.

"You are going to hear from government witnesses, brilliant and accomplished men, who claim they were tricked into acts they did, in fact, do willingly, and with full knowledge of the facts.

"You're going to hear about government deals, reduced charges, the government recommendations of leniency for Conrad's partner of over thirty years, David Radler.

"Radler will come into this courtroom and lie about Conrad Black to help himself. He will lie about events that Conrad did not know about and make up things that Conrad did.

"You'll hear how almost every major accusation that the government maintains or makes revolves around a transaction, a transaction performed by David Radler, which magically became a Black-orchestrated deal after Radler cuts his deal.

"You'll hear the government's use of word games while trying to establish criminal liability where no criminal acts occurred.

"You will hear about facts that weren't mentioned in the opening statement and which I plan to mention a few of, which show that Conrad Black did not violate the law —

"When I talk to you about Conrad Black, I'll tell you that it's a difficult job because it's impossible to take a man's life and talk about it in fifteen or twenty minutes. We're much too complex for that.

"And as you shall see, this is particularly true in Conrad's case. Mr. Cramer, the lead prosecutor, touched on it. He talked about the fact that Conrad Black had become — maybe not in the United States, but in the United Kingdom and Europe and Canada — a very, very prominent man; a political figure; a man . . . who has written books, a man who has written editorials, a man who goes on television and speaks out for what he believes in.

"And as Mr. Cramer wants to characterize it as ego, it is a man who has carried a message, and the same message for years, both in Canada and in every place where he actually participated with his papers.

"He's a master of language. For my purposes in this case, he goes a little too much for rhetorical flourishes. And I wish we didn't have to hear his musings. But those things that he said are nothing more than attempts by the prosecution to dissuade you from the facts of the case. They don't deal with what he did and what he didn't do. They deal with an attitude that's being made fun of and criticized.

"And I accept his attitude; but, the point is that's not what we're here for. What we're here for is to find whether, in fact, Conrad violated the law. And the end result of this is that he didn't."

It was hard to figure out Black's position. Was he a white collar "looter," as often portrayed by much of the press? This made him seem like Thomas Crowne, the upper-class scoundrel of the silver screen. Or was he instead the pilot of an airliner being hijacked by the special committee named by Hollinger International (a company that, under normal circumstances, he would still have controlled), and then by the U.S. Justice Department? The difficulty lay in the fact that the criminal charges, some of which were speculative, covered as many bases as possible. The prosecution was determined to get a guilty verdict by whatever means.

In coming weeks, proceedings in courtroom 1241 were low-key. There were skirmishes and sudden conferences between the attorneys and the judge at the sidebar, while evidence was presented and contradicted. Journalists often got frustrated that the issues did not seem clear-cut and ended up interviewing one another. This case would take a long time even to begin to make sense.

CHAPTER THREE

DREAMS OF GRANDEUR

THE ROYAL VICTORIA HOSPITAL is a sprawling, gloomy grey-stone building in the Scottish baronial style, nestled on the slopes of Mount Royal in the centre of Montreal. Pheasants and raccoons are sometimes spotted in the parking lot, while amorous students stroll farther uphill into the dense forest preserve landscaped in the nineteenth century by the celebrated architect Frederick Olmsted, famous for his design of New York's Central Park. The hospital was founded in 1893 by Canada's two most powerful business tycoons, the Scottish cousins Donald Smith, Lord Strathcona and Mount Royal, and George Stephen, Lord Mount Stephen.

It was here that Conrad Black was born on August 25, 1944, to George Montegu Black, Jr., a rising business executive, and Betty Riley Black, a member of one of Canada's leading Establishment families. George Black served as assistant deputy minister of National Defence for Air, earning a dollar a year in salary, then ran a company with a largely female labour force in Montreal manufacturing aircraft propellers. George Black's father had served as president of several Western Canadian breweries, while Betty Riley Black, originally from Winnipeg, was the granddaughter of Thomas Riley, a founder of the Great-West Life Assurance Company, who also had a minor interest in

London's *Daily Telegraph*. Each generation of Rileys since then boasted several corporate chairmen, presidents and directors. Betty's father had for many years represented Viscount Rothermere's fifty-one business interests in Western Canada.[20]

Although Conrad only lived a year of his childhood in Montreal before the family moved to Toronto, he returned for an eight-year period in early adulthood, living the most creative years of his life in Quebec.

The co-founder of the Royal Victoria, Strathcona was a decisive, transitional figure in Canada. British aristocrats had long been figureheads of political power in Canada. They symbolized the Crown, the British class structure, the hereditary nature of aristocratic rank, and they came to Canada for a few years at a time, serving as governors and military commanders. They brought with them an English Protestant value system emphasizing the social hierarchy that they dominated under the discreet cover of unspoken moral superiority — grace under pressure, self-reliance, pragmatism and a disdain for overt sexuality and expressions of emotion. The fusion of Protestant values and a vertical pecking order could result in an unquestioning, self-righteous attitude and a good deal of snobbery — as if the grasping, aggressive leaders of society had God-given rights, and were answerable virtually to nobody.

By the late nineteenth century, the structure of British and Canadian society had changed. Immigrant industrialists such as Strathcona, who arrived in North America in 1838, now enjoyed the power that British colonizers and military commanders had once had. Industrialists were empire-builders. They had the economic means to influence government, finance regiments for imperial conquest and, if necessary, pay hard cash to political parties to obtain British aristocratic titles.

The new, mostly Scottish, bourgeoisie of Montreal made their fortunes in forestry, mining, railways and the financial sector, often exploiting the resources and population of Canada's rural hinterland and vast untapped wilderness. These industrialists looked for legitimacy and approval from British role models. A noble title and a personal coat of arms were the ultimate endorsement for these hard-working colonial industrialists. It helped many of them justify the tough, take-no-prisoner measures they engaged in to acquire personal fortunes in industry and commerce.

Strathcona had spent long years in Labrador with the Hudson's Bay Company before helping to set up the Canadian Pacific Railway and driving the last spike in 1885. With his cousin Mount Stephen and three associates, he manipulated the shares of the railway company, making the equivalent of $800 million of today's money in a decade. And that was just one of their investments.

"Of course insider trading was not forbidden or even frowned on in those days," journalist and author Peter C. Newman told me. "In fact, you can make a case that these men invented it, at least in Canada."

Strathcona was the quintessential robber baron. Many Canadian business tycoons of the twentieth century aspired to be just like him.

By the 1940s, Montreal was still Canada's financial and industrial capital. But the city's Scottish business families, living in a virtual garrison, surrounded by French Canadians of a far lower social and economic status, were beginning to lose their grip on the country's major corporations. Toronto and Winnipeg were dragging wealth westward, and the once creative Scottish elite of Montreal was losing its creative edge. Nevertheless, the new business families of Ontario and Winnipeg shared some of the social values and aspirations of Montreal's Scottish bourgeoisie. They fawned over British aristocrats and built neo-Georgian mansions that rivalled Britain's landed estates. They hired European butlers and collected Rolls-Royces and bred English thoroughbreds for racing.

In 1944, George Black attracted the attention of Edward Plunket (E. P.) Taylor, Canada's leading business tycoon, and the very personification of the anglophile Canadian. With his perennial top hat, he looked something like Rich Uncle Pennybags, the mascot of the Monopoly board game. Taylor lived at Windfelds, a twenty-five-acre estate in the Bridle Path area of Toronto. From here he would run a sprawling business empire, breed Northern Dancer, the greatest sire of the twentieth century, and regularly count members of the British royal family as house guests.

In 1945, Taylor was putting together the blue-chip holding company Argus Corp., along with minority partners Colonel W. Eric Phillips and Wallace McCutcheon. He named George Black president of Canadian Breweries Ltd., an Argus affiliate that would become one of the world's leading brewers. George Black's starting salary was $15,000 a year.

When George Black moved his wife and two sons to Toronto, they seemed to fit well into the genteel world of the business elite there. They soon moved to the Bridle Path to be closer to the Taylors.

George Black was a man of intelligence and considerable force of personality. He had a direct, frank manner, and never minced words. Remembering his experience introducing non-refundable bottles at a large American brewing subsidiary, he said, "God, there was beer and blood and broken glass all over thousands of stores. . . . So naturally, it was a first-rate disaster. It was an imperial fuck-up, like the charge of the Light Brigade." He felt his main brewing competitor, Labatt, was a Machiavellian opponent, so he was comfortable adopting Machiavellian tactics himself. He got used to his role of cutting costs through massive lay-offs: "I've fired so many people in my life that it's sort of an art. I can do it without bitterness." He found beer unions a pain to deal with: "If you can't turn around and snarl at these people occasionally, they'll kick you to pieces."[21]

In a *Saturday Night* magazine profile, George Black was described as "a tall (six feet four) man with slightly greying hair, neatly dressed (preferring dark suits and conservative ties), he conducts the affairs of the enterprise from a large modern office in an impressive building in downtown Toronto. On his neat, limed-oak desk is a model propeller. Sometimes, weighing a decision, he balances the model between his fingers. All facts and facets of each problem are weighed and sifted before reaching a decision. There is no guesswork, no snap decision." The profile also described George Black's unstructured routine: "His working schedule has no fixed limits. Policy may be discussed over a nightcap with Mr. Taylor. Mornings may find him at his home at Todmorden, Ontario, examining sales reports and financial statements. At a Saturday luncheon with business associates, the talk may range from progress on the newest plant in Massachusetts to a civic centre for Toronto, from the success of a hospital campaign for funds to Canada's immigration policy."[22]

George Black was idiosyncratic. He had something quivering and restless deep in his nature, a man who wanted to be hard, but couldn't be. Conrad's first cousin (once removed) David Culver remembers George Black as "a mathematical genius, a night hawk who loved to gamble all night long, playing blackjack."[23] And Conrad described him in 1993 as complicated and sophisticated, aloof and temperamental, and "slender, cultured, humorous, enigmatic, and in his later years, melancholy."[24] He displayed considerable skill at wordplay and developed endearingly eccentric habits, such as heating the outdoor swimming pool to 85°F (29°C) until early December, despite occasional blizzards.

The Blacks were wealthy. Conrad's father managed a half-million-dollar ($2.85 million in 2007 dollars) trust fund for him until 1969, when he reached the age of twenty-five. And in 1976, Conrad inherited another $7 million (more than $25.5 million in 2007 dollars).

But the combination of rough edges and idiosyncrasy may explain why George Black never really found his way into the Canadian Establishment. He didn't really belong. For one thing, he wouldn't kiss anyone's ass. He was a proud, passionate man who loved some people but hated most, particularly those he considered pretentious. He didn't exude the understated superiority, the grace, and pragmatism and clubby charm that Establishment figures expected. As the Argus business empire grew through the 1950s, clans naturally developed. George Black sided with Bud McDougald, a millionaire investor jockeying to seize control from E. P. Taylor. Black was denied a key promotion in the Argus empire, which amounted to being fired. Even though he was just forty-eight years old, he had grown tired of the game. He felt he had made enough money and withdrew from business altogether in 1958, spending the last eighteen years of his life managing his portfolio, drinking heavily and staying up late at night reading and brooding.

Black identified closely with his father and resolved to right any wrongs he had suffered. That may explain the way he turfed George Black's former business partners out of Argus once he gained control in the late 1970s.

Remembering his mother warmly, Conrad said Betty Riley Black was "a natural, convivial and altogether virtuous person" — a champion figure skater who lived up to the Riley family traditions of athletic prowess and performance.

As a boy, Conrad was closer in looks and temperament to his father, while his older brother, Montegu, had the athletic skills and charm of their mother: the *Daily Telegraph* would write that Monte "won colours for cricket, football and hockey and developed a lifelong interest in boats after being given a DIY punt for his eleventh birthday on August 6, 1951, which was launched in E. P. Taylor's swimming pool."[25]

According to Jeremy Riley, Conrad's double first cousin (Jeremy's mother was the sister of Conrad's father, and Jeremy's father was the brother of Conrad's mother), "Montegu was an exceedingly athletic person, very personable and easy to get along with. Conrad took a long time to develop. He had lots of sharp edges as a kid."[26]

Riley said Conrad felt lost and insecure in the larger, self-contained, Riley tribe — attractive, athletic and always competing with one another. The bookish Conrad was the solitary outsider, outperformed by his boisterous, self-confident cousins who displayed seemingly effortless skill at every sport. Riley's pretty French-Canadian wife, Jean, the granddaughter of Prime Minister Louis St. Laurent, developed a certain affinity for Conrad since she also felt isolated and even subversive in the larger Riley tribe. "There is a tremendous Riley tradition of success in business and service and athletics; a very competitive family," she said. "They're all good-looking, they're all smart and good athletes. And most of them have been highly successful in their endeavours, focusing on business or engineering. It's a large family. He and his brother had first cousins. Finding himself in this quite tribal environment, being not at all athletic himself, he had had a sense of not fitting a very well-established mould. Those insecurities are what his whole life has been about correcting and addressing."[27]

Compensating for the inadequacy he felt around his cousins, Conrad concentrated on intellectual pursuits that brought him closer to his father who taught him about finance, geometry and many other subjects. But this may have isolated Conrad further from the rest of the family. Father and son often tested their memories by challenging each other to cite literary quotations or obscure facts, such as the tonnage of British battleships and passenger liners.

Jeremy Riley's older brother Ron remembers, while in university, visiting George Black in 1952: "I had been to all the fraternity parties in Toronto. Uncle George sat up waiting for me, and offered me a drink. He could produce more drinks on a little drink table than any man alive. He wanted to know how to explain to an eight-year-old boy the Pythagorean theorem. Conrad shared a lot of interests with his father. They often sat up late at night, talking about the world. Conrad learned a lot of his verbal skills from his father."[28]

Conrad, like his father, was highly temperamental, and this distressed his parents. David Culver remembers "in the early 1950s his father and mother talking to my mother in our Montreal home, saying 'we have this strange child — we don't know what to do with him.' "

George Black had long been a monarchist and loved to recount how, at the age of eight back in 1919, he had shaken the hand of the Prince of Wales. In October 1951, the young family stood in front of Sunnybrook Hospital in Toronto admiring the procession of Princess Elizabeth, who was on a royal tour of Canada. When the Queen's father, King George VI, died, George Montegu signed up for a luxurious coronation cruise package, which would include first-class passage on the world's largest and most glamorous passenger liner, the *Queen Elizabeth*, and special reserved seats at the coronation itself. The cruise and British holiday, from March to June 1953, would prove to be one of Conrad Black's formative experiences. No wonder he filled his study at 26 Park Lane Circle with custom-built models of passenger liners.

As the 83,600-ton giant with her twin funnels belching smoke was led by tugboats into the Hudson River on New York's West Side in a blaze of dangling coloured streamers, the eight-year-old Conrad realized how much he wanted to be part of this new international league. The *Queen Elizabeth* had escaped U-boat attack during the war, when she served as a troopship. She took on the Cunard Line's red, white and black livery after the war. A publicity poster from 1953 shows the *Queen Elizabeth* at night, her lights ablaze, steaming in a sea of stars under the Milky Way. She was a symbol of British power, resilience and, above all, romance. Everything onboard was done with impeccable style and polish. The ship had first-class staterooms, some of them fitted with grand pianos; dining rooms with newly printed menus every day; cinemas; theatres; shops; hairdressing salons; swimming pools; shuffleboard courts and a library.

A scene in *Gentlemen Prefer Blondes*, a 1953 comedy starring Marilyn Monroe and Jane Russell as two buxom lounge singers on a trans-Atlantic passenger liner, may give some idea of how Conrad Black behaved on board the *Queen Elizabeth*. Marilyn Monroe plays a gold-digger angling to sit at the dinner table next to "Henry Spofford III." But the rich father's son, played by George "Foghorn" Winslow, turns out to be a seven-year-old boy in a black suit and tie — just about the same age as Conrad was. Henry Spofford III is stern and bombastic. He makes droll quips to amuse the adults at the table. Conrad must have been like that.

As the Black boys raced through every part of the ship, they were thrilled by the vertical organization of command, the bustle of life in this floating city, the relentless throb of the engines driving the giant across the restless blue ocean. Liveried waiters served their parents tea on the Promenade Deck. The boys kept busy collecting copies of first-class passenger lists, the ship's daily newspaper and abstract logs, postcards and fact brochures.

Arriving in Britain was even more exciting. The young

family stayed at Claridge's, the famous London hotel, and when the time came to attend the coronation, they sat with 105,000 other people in improvised stands along the five-mile route, while three-quarters of a million more stood cheering. The Blacks watched Her Majesty pass by in her two-hundred-year-old state coach, a gilded carriage drawn by eight white horses, in a two-mile-long procession that included 15,800 men of the army, air force and navy, 15,000 policemen and 10,000 other servicemen. Sir Winston Churchill had his own carriage. Thirty-eight officers of the Royal Canadian Mounted Police, on black chargers, escorted Prime Minister Louis St. Laurent. Attendance was limited in Westminster Abbey to 8,000 due to a lack of space. Even Britain's titled nobility had to apply for lottery tickets to see whether they could get in.

Conrad Black was dazzled by the pageantry, the uniforms, the measured grace and dignity of the procession — by the way Britain had risen from the ashes and near-defeat of war to reclaim her destiny as a victorious nation at the head of a world-wide empire of dominions and colonies. The experience showed him first-hand what Canada's business class aspired to: aristocratic rank in a country that stood at the top of the global scale, and with that a grandiose, ritualized and almost mythical place in history. All eyes were focused on the Queen.

Even more extraordinary was the return voyage, which began with the Queen's coronation naval review at Spithead, near Portsmouth. Here gathered a fleet of battleships, aircraft carriers, cruisers, destroyers and yachts, as far as the eye could see, firing their salutes to honour the young Queen. The *Queen Elizabeth* and other passenger liners chartered for the occasion steamed through the fleet on their own track, tooting their whistles as they went. There was a fly-past of more than three hundred aircraft, and when night fell, the Queen fired the first of 2,500 rockets from the deck of the battleship HMS *Vanguard*, launching a brilliant fireworks display that lit up the entire fleet and the beaches. Like many English Canadians of the time, George and Betty Black saw the coronation and naval review as a confirmation of their own commitment to Canada's constitutional monarch, a reaffirmation of the historical continuity that the royal family provided. As members of the Canadian business class, they also identified with the values of a vertically ordered society.

But their son saw something greater still. He had never witnessed such a demonstration of might. It fired his imagination and helped trigger his youthful quest for grandeur and power — on his own terms. Thirty-eight years later, when he became a baron and entered the House of Lords in Westminster, flanked by a former British prime minister and a former defence secretary, he could have been fulfilling a secret promise he had made to himself at the age of eight, back in 1953.

Just a few months earlier, in November 1952, an eleven-year-old girl took passage with her mother and stepfather on another ship, heading westward across the Atlantic, from England to Canada. Nothing suggested that Barbara Amiel was destined to become the wife of a multi-millionaire and a baroness through marriage. Quite the contrary, she suffered from her family's crushing poverty and her own Jewish émigré insecurity and gawkish manner.

The motivation for Amiel's later aggressive ideology and extravagance is deeply rooted in her early years. In *Confessions*, she recounts her impoverished childhood in Watford, England. Among her mother's family were Zionists and comfortable bourgeois Communists, safely ensconced in the London suburbs. Her father had risen to the rank of colonel in General Montgomery's Eighth Army during the North African campaign of the Second World War. "It was the East End that had shaped many of my family's — and later my own — attitudes," wrote Amiel. "In this cramped Jewish quarter of London, the Russian and Polish newcomers worked, argued, and scrambled for a piece of England, bringing with them the socialist ideals and ideas of the *Bund*, the religious-political organization formed in the old country as a beginning of resistance to the authoritarian regimes under which they lived."[29]

This was a world away from the parts of London the Blacks visited in 1953.

At first, Barbara did not question socialism — that would

come later — but the pattern in Amiel's intellectual life of a complete ideological worldview, purporting to answer any question that might arise, was already there. Her adult neo-conservatism filled the ideological space left vacant by her abandonment of her youthful socialism. After her parents divorced, Amiel moved with her mother and stepfather to Hamilton, Ontario, in early 1953.

Hamilton was a manufacturing centre of steel mills, electronics plants, car assembly factories, belching smokestacks and railway lines down to the shores of Lake Ontario, where bulk carriers brought in iron ore pellets and concentrate from the Lake Superior region and steamed off with steel plates and bars. Her stepfather got a job at the open-heart furnaces of Stelco's lakeside steel plant, braving the 130°F (54°C) heat as the burning gas and hot air played on the fresh steel, returning home grimy and exhausted. The job made him sweat so much that he had to take salt tablets. The family's financial situation remained grim.

She remembers the fridge was always empty. "We were down to one large meal a day, heavy on potatoes and no seconds. From seven o'clock in the evening, when the meal was over, my sister and I would fantasize about the endless meals we would have when we were rich." But alongside her anxiety about the next meal was the anxiety of being left alone, of being irrelevant to others: "Since early childhood, fear of empty rooms had been something of a problem for me. In adolescence, when I was very often alone, I stayed out of a house or a building even in the sunny afternoon until there was someone else there. Otherwise I could find myself sitting in the middle of a room, stranded, sitting in my own urine, sitting for hours, too frightened to cry and too frightened to move."[30]

But Barbara had a redeeming quality that would help her overcome obstacles: drive. On February 12, 1955, the *Hamilton Spectator* announced on its Junior Press Club page that fourteen-year-old Barbara Amiel had won first prize in an essay contest (there were nine runners-up). She would be theatre manager for a day. An accompanying photograph showed Century Theatre projectionist William Thornberry next to a slim Barbara, dressed in a white sweater and plaid skirt. Her large nose made her look like the actor Karl Malden. Her chin was also very prominent, and conveyed a sense of determination. In later self-mockery, she said the second photograph in the paper showed her "sitting grinning maniacally in the theatre manager's office." The movie showing that day was *Black Widow*, billed as "an electrifying drama about a predatory female," with Ginger Rogers as a bitchy Broadway star and George Raft as a gravel-voiced detective.

Barbara parlayed her prize — twenty-six passes to Saturday-morning kiddie shows — into thirteen tickets to adult movies, which made her more popular among her peers. That was the year of *Rebel Without a Cause* with James Dean and the Alfred Hitchcock film *To Catch a Thief* with Cary Grant and Grace Kelly. There was something in both these films to appeal to the young Barbara. Movies provided her with fantasy material. Grace Kelly was an ice queen who ended up marrying a real prince, but Ava Gardner seemed more like the woman Barbara wanted to become — she had dark brown hair, the face of an angel and the voluptuous body of a goddess; she was glamorous, provocative and her barefoot sexuality was enticingly naive; she was good at playing the femme fatale, a sensuous woman leading her lover into impossible, doomed situations.

Amiel earned extra money working in a drugstore, a woman's clothing shop and a canning factory. Hanging out with "bad" girls, she quickly learned the facts of life and came to realize her sassy intelligence and self-conscious Jewishness made her different from other young people. She was devastated in 1956 when she learned her father had committed suicide in England — and she dwelled on this family tragedy in later years.

Barbara moved to Grantham in the north end of St. Catharines, a shipbuilding city along the Welland Canal, between Lake Ontario and Lake Erie, to get away from her mother and stepfather. At the age of seventeen, she shared a boarding house with "a woman, a daughter and a female boarder." In this rough household, she began to realize that the three of them were prostitutes, working in a bar and bringing sailors and shipyard workers home for "entertainment." She bought wax earplugs to block out the sound of frantic sex in the adjoining rooms so she could concentrate on her studies at St. Catharines Collegiate.

In 1958, Amiel was editor of the *Vox*, the school yearbook. Her editorial paid tribute to the principal. But then she admonished the school for introducing a ten-month school year: ". . . already a huge percentage of students are finding summer employment in hotel resorts, close to them — a seemingly minor problem. But let us not make the mistake of looking at it through the self-righteous glasses of the financially secure. Summer employment may mean college — the solving of family difficulties — the much needed dose of responsibility, and often with it, that invaluable lesson in life."

That comment was understandable, since she had been working part-time in ladies' dress shops since the age of fourteen, and she knew a thing or two about the underside of life. She graduated the following year from high school. Her graduation portrait suggests a face somehow changed: at eighteen, her nose no longer seemed so prominent. Someone had written a chatty, teasing description of her personality and future prospects. "Barbara Amiel: Dramatic and mixed up is Barb in a nut shell and Barb is some nut. Member of Theta Kappa Sorority, Senate and Forum, Barb edited last year's scandal sheet (the Vox) and carried on the good work (?) in the Collegiate Corner. Advocating good clean fellowship (particularly on weekends!) Barb plans honour sociology at U. of T. (that Bainy city) specializing in mass relationships!"

Conrad Black was a turbulent youth, but his turbulence was different from Barbara's. And they lived in worlds apart.

There was no easy readjustment to life back in Toronto, after the coronation cruise on the *Queen Elizabeth*. George and Betty Black were concerned that their precocious and articulate son was such a poor student at Upper Canada College (UCC), one of the country's most exclusive schools.

William Dendy wrote nostalgically of the Romanesque Revival architecture of the college, "built on a foundation of roughly finished Credit Valley sandstone, with upper walls of red

brick ornamented with terra cotta panels and string courses. . . .
The central tower, rising 165 feet above the ground, like a
church steeple above the surrounding trees, became a symbol of
the college — an ever present reminder to students, and to the
city below the hill, of the importance of the college and the
influence of the alumni that had been shaped by it."[31]

But Black could not agree. He had been a student at UCC
since 1951, and hated the place. After eating cereal alone for
breakfast, and reading through the *Globe and Mail*, the young
Conrad would get into a chauffeur-driven car, for the daily
three-and-a-half-mile ride to school. Looking through the
window, he found the journey from the Bridle Path into
Toronto depressing. The city was less appealing than Montreal
or New York City, where the family often vacationed. "Those
were lovely cities, and still are. Toronto now is a rather nice city,
but it wasn't then," he said. "None of the telephone or electric
wires were underground, so you had these horrible telephone
poles everywhere with masses of thick wires strung between
them; there was no aesthetic to it at all."

"My sense of Conrad at the time," said John Fraser, his classmate at UCC, "was that he was a prisoner, a fully developed adult
in a child's body. He was a responsible person — his brother was
older but much less mature."[32]

Fraser remembers Conrad comparing UCC to a prison camp.
One day he saw teachers watching a fistfight in the schoolyard
from their windows.

"Look at them," Black said to Fraser. "Don't you want to
throw up?"

Fraser, watching the two boys fighting below, looked quizzi-
cally at his friend.

"No, I don't want to throw up," said Fraser. He found the
fight exhilarating.

"Not those idiots," said Black, with perfect contempt. "Look
at the windows. Our Gauleiters are enjoying the show. What
puppets we are."

Fraser said Black was right. "Most of the prep masters were
watching the fight with evident satisfaction. 'Blowing off steam,'
I suspect they were thinking. Conrad ascribed darker motiva-

tions to their 'voyeurism.'"

"This place is a concentration camp," said Black, "but most of the inmates are oblivious to the fact."[33]

"That's the way Conrad talked then," said Fraser. "That's the way he talked when he was ten. Big words and strong statements."

Black was filled with a noticeable rage. His long-time friend Peter White said he "kicked holes in walls when he got upset as a child, threw knives around, things like that."[34]

He felt "profound revulsion" during his years at UCC because of the rampant violence, abuse and humiliation he experienced. Absolute power was invested in the master, who would single out boys and cane them for arbitrary and often invented reasons. The class was drawn into a perverse and sadistic relationship with the teacher who asked the boys to vote on whether a caning should be administered. The swish of birch, alder, swagger stick, whip, riding crop or fishing rod punctuated the school day, as teachers applied brute force to break the will of their students.

In his autobiography, Black denounced the school's "penal system — the several sadists and few aggressively fondling homosexuals on the faculty, and the more numerous swaggering boobies who had obviously failed in the real world." At first, he said he was "slightly perverse, intermittently irreverent, and generally unlucky," but he evolved "from a skeptic, to a rebel, to an insurrectionist — an anarchist."

Conrad was caned repeatedly, in one instance by a teacher "who applied himself so strenuously to his task that both his hearing-aids sprang from his elephantine ears and he glowered, flush-faced, after me, like an incredibly aged and demented fugitive from outer space."[35]

Compounding Black's unease was his cloistered home life in the suburbs. Recalling his early years in the Bridle Path, which "was in those days out in the country," Black said, "there was virtually nobody my own age right around, so it wasn't a very conventional neighbourhood. And it was before there was this huge plethora of television channels or a need of any television sets. So I read a lot, compared to my peers, I guess."

One childhood companion was an older boy, Norman Elder, who lived next door and sometimes came over to thumb through *Who's Who* with Black. The two fantasized about fame and fortune. Elder also went to UCC, had a flair for sports and saw himself as a future explorer. In a 1982 interview, Elder remembered his boyhood friendship with Conrad: "I'd call George Black and say, 'I'll be over in about ten minutes.' I'd arrive in fifteen and be told, 'You are now five minutes and thirty seconds late.'"[36]

As the tragic events of his later life and death indicate, Elder had a perverse streak in his personality. In 1997, he pleaded guilty to indecent assault on ten teenaged boys over a twenty-year period. His million-dollar Victorian house on Toronto's Bedford Road was full of odd items collected during his world travels, such as a sixteen-foot python and an assortment of lizards, piranhas, a boa constrictor, an enormous pig that slept under his bed and a giant tortoise he liked to ride down the street. He also took in homeless people. When I called Elder's number in early 2004, I spoke to a young man who identified himself as "John," and who said Elder had hanged himself the previous October. "He just got fed up, he was ready to meet his maker, he was a good man. It was hard for Norman and Conrad to keep in touch, Norman being in jail and all. They were out of touch the last fifteen years. . . . Norman and I drove by Conrad's place once, on the Bridle Path. Huge fence, six and a half feet high, a foot thick, with these huge stone pillars every thirty feet or so. The fence must have cost as much to build as the house did. That's Conrad for you. He's a good man, nothing like what they say in the press."

According to John Fraser, "Norman Elder is dead, that's for sure. And there were seven police cars outside the house from hell — it was a *bad* place and known to be a *bad* place for years. I don't know if he hanged himself, but he died under strange circumstances. You don't have seven squad cars for nothing."

From the age of ten, Black stayed up late into the night reading biographies of history's political and military giants, such as de Gaulle, Roosevelt, Sir Winston Churchill and Napoleon. He was enthralled by their personalities, hopes and sorrows, by their victories, defeats and comebacks. He regularly discussed the drama of power with his father, who encouraged the boy's passion for history and often challenged his memory of facts. George Black also stimulated his son's penchant for strategy by playing chess with him. They often discussed Machiavellian strategy, and Conrad formed an opinion of Roosevelt as "extremely secretive, devious, inscrutable and conniving, always working toward the implementation of a plan that no one could divine." He went beyond the external masks of leadership to study the colourful rogues on the inside.

He was treated as a young adult at home. But at school, he was a delinquent child fit to be whipped. The contrast was too much for him. Many boys developed survival strategies — becoming teacher's pets; managing never to get caught or keeping their backs to the wall. But Black confronted authority head-on. Fraser noticed he liked to push to the limit, creating uproar, then seeking some advantage from the confusion that followed. He was affirming his personality, and getting caught and punished was his way of voicing his contempt for the system.

Conrad was inventive in his mischief, once picking the chief disciplinarian's lock and shuffling the records so that boys awaiting punishment would be exonerated and an unfriendly classmate would be punished. Most infamously, he entered the school's central office from which he copied students' academic records and stole final exam questions that he quietly sold — for $1,400 ($10,200 in 2007 dollars) — to boys listed as underperformers. He was caught and expelled on June 9, 1959. George Black intervened with the headmaster, arguing unsuccessfully that his fourteen-year-old son was simply showing a youthful flair for capitalism.

"Conrad went from hero to pariah in three days," said Fraser. "It is not true [as some people later claimed] that he was burned in effigy in front of his house. But some students must have gone and shouted something. He must have been traumatized by the expulsion — he had been the hero of the hour for a few days. I didn't know there were exams for sale — I have a seven in physics to prove it."

Black remained friends with Fraser and named him editor of *Saturday Night* magazine in the late 1980s.

Fraser said that at UCC "Conrad wanted them to know he was there, and he was protesting. . . . The scenario of pushing things to the limit and daring people is still there."

In fact, Black was a rebel, but he wanted to be an *Establishment* rebel. He already had a quirky and passionate longing, based on intensive reading, for values and social institutions in decline and just about to disappear. He had a burning, mythical attachment to heroes of the past, which made him seem strangely out of time and place. His public outbursts were quite spontaneous, but the outrage he provoked always seemed to buoy him upwards to a higher level.

More recently, an obvious parallel with the UCC episode was Black's contempt for Hollinger International's public shareholders that led to his resignation from the company and the media ridicule that followed. His theft of exam questions was wrong, but to him it was directly proportional to the violence and abuse he experienced at the school. They messed with him and had to pay. But he also paid — through his expulsion, public humiliation and the disappointment he brought to his parents. After the UCC experience, Black's father sent him to Trinity College School, where he was given the nickname of "China Black." But on March 22, 1960, the school authorities asked that he be withdrawn after he threw a radiator cap full of ink at a teacher. He managed to stay on, as an "extra-mural student," and completed grade twelve at Thornton Hall, a "cram school."

"I remember clearly one day in September 1960," said Brian Stewart, a Thornton classmate, "this skinny kid smoking a cigarette, and someone said 'that guy got into trouble at Upper Canada over stolen papers.' I had heard Conrad knew about French history, which interested me. Right off the bat, we found we had a lot in common: the Second World War, the war in Algeria, American politics. I had never met someone with such a breadth of interests. We became fast friends."[37]

Stewart — later one of Canada's most distinguished journalists — was a good intellectual match for Black. "Even as a sixteen- or seventeen-year-old, Conrad's world was global. This was very rare in Toronto in the 1950s. He always felt imprisoned in his age and in Toronto, and in a world that was too small for him. . . . Conrad was a liberal, a firm believer in FDR. Roosevelt came up in our conversations frequently at the time, even in the 1950s. He knew chapter and verse about Roosevelt. He believed Roosevelt had saved America during the Depression."

It was Black's admiration for Roosevelt that so angered his father. ". . . I'll smash the records," he would threaten. "Do you hear me, damn it?"

In 1960, Conrad preferred Kennedy to Nixon. "He saw Kennedy as a welcome change after Eisenhower's uninspiring leadership, without flash and drive, with his dithering," said Stewart. "There was no dream in America. Conrad saw Kennedy as giving America the challenge it always needs. And during the Cold War, and particularly during the 1962 Cuban Missile Crisis, Kennedy showed real leadership. A lot of young people were much more caught up in reading the news than they are today. Conrad was left of centre in the Democratic Party."

Black was naturally interested in girls. But dating was an awkward affair: he had spent years in private boys' schools and didn't know much about women. According to Brian Stewart, Black developed a strong crush on Caroline Dale Harris — a glamorous Toronto beauty "who broke many hearts" and would later marry a French tennis pro. Stewart said that after pursuing her without much success, Black went out with another pretty woman — Lynn Sifton "from the famous, horsey and very wealthy Sifton family." The Siftons were a bedrock Establishment family, descended from Sir Clifford Sifton, who had launched the family newspaper empire in 1899. Lynn Sifton later went out with Hal Jackman, who loomed large in Black's business dealings in the 1970s and 1980s (the friendship between Jackman and Black cooled in the 1990s). In his late teens, Black enjoyed occasional trips away to Montreal, the United States or Europe, where he was released from his Toronto reputation and background as well as the prudery of life in the "Queen City" of the early 1960s.

In 1959, Barbara Amiel entered the University of Toronto to

take an honours degree in philosophy and English. Journalist Larry Zolf, a fellow student, remembers her as "left wing in those days, a Trotskyite, bright as a whip. She was beautiful — with an aquiline nose. She had a nose job. . . . She was funny, loyal to her friends."[38]

While at the University of Toronto, Amiel married Gary Smith, whose father, before the Communists came to power in Cuba, had built the Riviera Hotel and Casino in partnership with the notorious gangster Meyer Lansky. Meyer Lansky had personally clubbed rivals with iron bars, and built up a criminal organization based on bootlegging, gambling, tax evasion and violence. He had hung out with Bugsy Siegel, Lucky Luciano and other murderers. He spent his final years attempting to escape from what he had wrought — to a new life in Israel or Paraguay. According to biographer Robert Lacey, "Meyer Lansky knew he had something to hide. He had broken the law. He had consorted with killers, and he had ridden on the fear that their violence generated — knowingly, willingly, and to his own personal profit."[39] Smith and Amiel's marriage lasted nine months.

For some reason, Amiel later boasted about the family connections of her first husband — it made her seem more notorious. "I have never been to Cuba," Amiel wrote in 1997, in one of her weirdest *Daily Telegraph* columns. "The Canadian family of my first husband built a casino in Havana in pre-Castro days. It was big and expensive and the sort of place one might go on a flashy honeymoon. I saw newspaper photos showing my extremely beautiful blonde mother-in-law, wearing fur coats and jewels, waving like Eva Peron. I could almost smell the perfume. By the time I got married, the Havana Riviera had been expropriated by Castro to house some ministry or other. I am ashamed to say in those days I never thought much about the ethics of political theft, especially when it was the theft of casinos financed in part by the gangster Meyer Lansky. In my early twenties, my notion of property rights and their relationship to liberty was shaky." Amiel devoted the remainder of her *Daily Telegraph* column to Castro's Communist excesses.[40]

During her years at the University of Toronto, Amiel became addicted to codeine when she discovered it provided instant relief from debilitating muscle fatigue. Soon the drug became an escape, and she was devouring up to twenty pills at a time. "It was best not to wear nail polish or lipstick so that the distinctive blue tinge of phenacetin poisoning would be quickly seen," she later wrote. After codeine came an addiction to the anti-depressant Elavil, and when she found it humiliating that she was unable to stop, Amiel sought help at Toronto's Addiction Research Foundation. Treatment was successful, although in later years her extravagant spending seemed like a new form of dependence. *Le Monde* described Amiel's shopping extravagance as "la boulimie dépensière" — a morbid hunger for spending.

Amiel first got a first-hand view of Communism in 1962, when she attended the World Youth Festival, a Soviet-sponsored propaganda effort aimed at young people. "I have no excuse but I have some shame," she later wrote of her three weeks of travel through East Germany, Poland and the USSR. The grey, dreary, heavily polluted East had no appeal for her. She was disturbed by the lack of public spontaneity and freedom of the locals she tried to talk to and by the young Western Communists accompanying her who clung blindly to their ideology despite what they saw. Amiel will never forget the young East German girls crowding around her in the locker room of a Dresden school desperate to buy lipstick, face powder or anything she was willing to sell; the tap on the shoulder and a whispered "Verboten . . . not done . . . not here" when she began dancing the twist on a school dance floor as students nervously edged away from her; or the "inevitable we-clap-you-clap line-up (the socialist form of applause) on the platform at the end of public performances of any kind."[41]

Amiel is a romantic intellectual, with a messianic strain rooted in her parents' Judaism. She compared herself, at least implicitly, to George Orwell, Malcolm Muggeridge, Arthur Koestler and Albert Camus, who had seen Communism face-to-face before condemning it. In addition, she writes, "I am a wandering Jew. I always have my toothbrush handy. My allegiance is not to any piece of earth or particular set of rock outcroppings. My allegiance is to ideas, and most especially to the extraordinary idea of individual liberty. That idea is still here in the North American landscape, a landscape I have come to love. I do not wish to leave. But my suitcase is always packed. I do not feel bound to any country or any popular will more than to my own conscience. I would leave here as easily as I would have left Germany when its people elected Hitler to power."[42] Through this overt romanticism, Amiel presented herself as a woman of conscience ready to accept the bitter cup of exile.

During the 1960s, she worked as a researcher at the Canadian Broadcasting Corporation. Patrick Watson, then one of Canada's most distinguished TV journalists (and later the chairman of the CBC), remembers, "Barbara was skinny. She came in on a bicycle where we produced *This Hour Has Seven Days*, at the corner of Maitland and Jarvis in Toronto. She was very attractive, very lean, spectacularly flat-chested."[43]

In 1964, Barbara was working as a script assistant at CBC, and had an abortion when close to five months pregnant. The doctor "wore a black rubber apron and the pain was excruciating," she wrote. "Later, in hospital after haemorrhaging, I was told I escaped never being able to have children because of the masses of antibiotics the doctor took care to prescribe." She felt even then that abortion was morally wrong, and later described it as "murder."[44] The experience added to her fragility.

In the late 1950s and early 1960s, following on the heels of Marilyn Monroe and Ava Gardner, pouting sex kittens of the cinema such as Brigitte Bardot and Honor Blackman were in vogue as the image of femininity. But those perfect profiles, surging bustlines and romps in tight-fitting leather suits put a lot of pressure on millions of more "normal" women to be perfect. Besides, sex goddesses of the screen could spontaneously make love without ever running the risk of getting pregnant. They were objects of fantasy. In later years, Barbara made her mark in society as a sexy bombshell with a pert nose, wearing a low-cut Chanel dress. She had constructed this self-confident persona for the world to enjoy, but on the inside there seems to remain a shrill, insecure woman, prone to unrestrained rage and self-mockery, as a way of jockeying for attention.

In September 1962, Black enrolled at Carleton University in Ottawa, where he spent a good deal of time carousing — a young Prince Hal. He also found time to play cards with senators and Members of Parliament, picking up a lot of inside political gossip. Canada had a Progressive Conservative prime minister, the eloquent, somewhat paranoid westerner John Diefenbaker.

"Mr. Diefenbaker was an interesting man, personally," said Black, "and if you read many of his speeches as prime minister, they were very interesting and well done. Those who mock him as an absurd figure, I think, are unjust. But I don't think there is a legacy for him as a prime minister."

Black said Diefenbaker made an important contribution to human rights by "the tearing down of such remaining barriers as there were to . . . I think he used to call them 'hyphenated Canadians'. . . who were neither of British nor of French ancestry. Beyond that, he was a personality — a colourful figure in Parliament . . . for forty years. He wasn't really a serious head of government, and of course, his huge majority of 1958 disintegrated in one term, and he wasn't an effective prime minister."

Although Black was interested in politics, he did not apply himself to his studies in the fall of 1962. According to history professor Naomi Griffiths, "I taught first-year courses at Carleton, and when the students were failing at Christmas, I would write them letters. I wrote that sort of letter to Conrad, suggesting he had to face a choice: withdrawing and getting his money back or coming and seeing me so we could work things out. The course was 'apes to atoms, and atoms to apes' — on the entire breadth of Western civilization. He pulled through: he was eighteen, thin as a rail, and desperately unhappy . . . because he had left Upper Canada College under a cloud. He had come to Ottawa, determined to establish what he was about, and he had spent three months trying to get to know people."[45]

While Black was at Carleton, the Nobel Prize winner and former president of the U.N. General Assembly, Lester Pearson, returned to take over the federal Liberal Party, defeating Diefenbaker in 1963. Pearson maintained Canada's status as an honest broker during the Cold War — a mediator between the United States and the Soviet Union. Perhaps because of his humility and self-deprecating manner, Pearson has sometimes been written off as an idealist when, in fact, he was arguably the most outstanding representative of the Canadian internationalist tradition. He was also a strong supporter of multilateralism and an occasional critic of the United States. In 1970, Pearson told me the United Nations "has done some very important things in the field of security, because it has, I think, on one or two occasions, prevented small wars from developing into large wars. And who knows? By being there and by intervening, it may have saved the world from world war."[46]

Black felt constrained in Canada and was impatient to explore the wider world. On one of their trips together to Europe, Brian Stewart noticed Black's "fascination for newspapers — the feel, the touch, the masthead, the amount of advertising." And above the newspapers, controlling the levers of power, was a larger-than-life newspaper owner. Travelling in Spain in the early 1960s, Black devoured a biography of William Randolph Hearst. Stewart learned of Black's fascination with Hearst, the model for Orson Welles's masterful *Citizen Kane*. "He'd go on about Hearst and quote him endlessly," Stewart said. Hearst had turned his back on his father's mining interests to take over an indifferent San Francisco newspaper and spin it into a nationwide chain — the most powerful of its day. Hearst redefined newspapers in the early twentieth century and used them in a methodical, Machiavellian way to fuel his greed, ambition and rage. He was a malignant narcissist, both press tycoon and robber baron, who destroyed people who dared get in his way. He was an American aristocrat, with a Californian ranch as big as Rhode Island. But the press empire he built crumbled away during his lifetime.

Strange to say, Black has sometimes gone on the record comparing himself directly to the character of Citizen Kane and therefore indirectly to Hearst. Was he looking for a grandiose fiction to latch on to, a mythical figure he could use to define and fasten his own volatile personality? He wanted to construct a persona of his own.

Black and Stewart's interest in politics was rewarded in 1964 following a chance meeting at a Chinese restaurant in Ottawa between Black and Peter White, a bright, bilingual Quebecker who was working for Liberal cabinet minister Maurice Sauvé. White was from Montreal and had a vast network of connections in Quebec. Many of his English-speaking contemporaries looked disdainfully on French Quebec as a provincial backwater.

White spoke flawless French. His owlish and scholarly appearance (due mainly to thick-framed glasses) was deceptive: he was first and foremost a political animal. White and Black struck up a friendship, and the young ministerial assistant procured invitations for Black and Stewart to join an inter-parliamentary group as guests at the Democratic Party convention in Atlantic City. Hard-talking Texan Lyndon Johnson had been serving as U.S. president since the assassination of John F. Kennedy in November 1963, and he would be accepting the party nomination to run against the Republican candidate, Barry Goldwater.

"We were kind of American news junkies, at a time when Bobby Kennedy was there and the first race riots broke out in Philadelphia," said Stewart. "Martin Luther King won the Nobel Peace Prize later that year. We were fascinated by the 'great society' — by LBJ's vision. Conrad was a passionate follower of the Democratic Party — welfare reform, money for the cities, head starts in school. You had a very hopeful period from Kennedy to the early years of Johnson, before Vietnam."

The 1964 election campaign was the culmination of a change in American politics, as portentous as FDR's use of fireside chats and radio through his campaigns — politics had become theatre and was being played out on television. It was a journalists' campaign. "Politicians have always gone where the crowds have gathered," writes David Halberstam, "and by 1963 the crowds were gathering every night in their own living rooms. In some ways the change was not so obvious, either to the pols or to the public, because the 1964 election obscured it; it was a campaign without subtlety, without closeness. Johnson was so clearly going to swallow Goldwater. But what was clear to print reporters working in 1964 was that the whole schedule had changed, the campaigns were different now — no longer run to catch the main editions of the big East Coast newspapers, but run to catch the evening news shows with, above all, film. To be telegenic."[47]

Black loved the Stars and Stripes, the banners, the crowds, the campaign badges, the grandeur of it all, the feeling that this was something that really mattered — a great political party in the greatest nation on Earth choosing its destiny.

Johnson gave one of the worst speeches of his campaign, but it didn't really matter. "I report tonight as president of the United States," he said, "and as commander in chief of the armed forces on the strength of your country and tell you it is greater than any adversary. I assure you that it is greater than all the combined might of all the nations, in all the wars, in all the history of this planet. And I report our superiority is growing."

There was no mention of Vietnam, and LBJ brought down the house. Robert Kennedy received a standing ovation that lasted a full twenty-two minutes. After the tragedy of his brother's assassination in Dallas, less than a year earlier, it seemed to many a new beginning. But Black and Stewart experienced the ugliness of racial despair when, on the same trip, they drove to Philadelphia to see the race riot. "Several blocks were torched," Black later wrote. "Others had been trashed; hundreds were injured, and large groups of surly and belligerent black toughs milled and roamed about. A brick apparently launched from an upper floor narrowly missed our windshield. A clairvoyant was not required to foretell that black urban violence could become an American growth industry."[48]

The contradiction was apparent to Black. On one side was a great, powerful figure poised to transform society and, on the other, the uncontrollable masses that held that greatness in contempt and rejected the exalted dreams of a leader they considered illegitimate. It was a contradiction that he was to recognize again in the passionate nationalism of Quebec in the late 1960s — a pivotal contradiction that would eventually move him from the left toward something he would call "integral conservatism."

In the spring of 1965, Peter White and Conrad Black shared an apartment for three months in Ottawa. "Conrad was a nocturnal person," White recalls, "and I had a day job, so I had to go to bed, and I'd get up and be in the office by nine o'clock, but Conrad had no such constraints. He would go out drinking with his buddies at Carleton and come back at three or four in the morning, and stay up until five or six in the morning and then go to bed and sleep most of the day. His father, George, was carrying on a similar regime back on Park Lane Circle. George was retired at this point, and would stay up all night long, drinking Scotch or whatever, watching television until all the stations went off the air, hoping, if he was lucky, to find a Groucho Marx movie to watch before the last station closed down for the night, and then he would telephone Conrad. I won't say he was in his cups, but he had had a certain amount to drink, and he wanted to have a long conversation with his young son, then nineteen. Conrad knew this would happen every night. He had the option of going to bed and being wakened by his father at three or four in the morning or waiting up until the call came through. And I would always eavesdrop in a semi-comatose state, at Conrad's end of those calls. The two of them had a very close relationship and would discuss all the events of the world, whatever had happened during the day. Obviously George was extremely proud of Conrad, and Conrad was trying to live up to his father's expectation of him, which had probably been seriously tested and disappointed in his school career."

Completing his studies at Carleton in 1965, Black registered at Osgoode Hall Law School, but dropped out. White remembers that his friend "had now come a cropper in his first year at law school, and I think he was a little displeased by the way he had been treated by Osgoode Hall, and he wasn't inclined to go back on bended knee and ask to be re-admitted. And he said to me one day that he had had it with this country, that he couldn't stand the Canadian winters, they were too cold and disagreeable, and Osgoode Hall had dared to flunk him, and that he was leaving, and he was going to go to Tulane University in New Orleans, which was as far south as he could get in the continental United States, where at least it would be warm, and he would do of course what he would want at Tulane. I said to him,

'Look, don't be silly, there's no sense going off half-cocked just because you flunked your year.' I had previously flunked a year at McGill, and knew sort of the type of reaction that that creates, and I said, 'Why don't you take a year off?' "

In 1966, Conrad Black took White's advice. As he looked back over his early years, he realized that he was being thwarted — by his own actions. "I was floundering around like a dilettante, vicariously reinvigorating myself reading the lives of great men," Black later wrote. He accepted White's invitation to move to the White family cottage in Knowlton, in the Eastern Townships of rural Quebec. The journey represented the new beginning Black had always craved. In Quebec, he would still be a romantic rebel and moody intellectual — but finally he would become his own man.

The Canadian Press/The Globe and Mail/Tibor Kolley

CHAPTER FOUR

THE QUEBEC YEARS

AN HOUR'S DRIVE EAST OF MONTREAL, sitting discreetly behind a white picket fence on the north shore of Brome Lake, is a private refuge that includes a pale blue clapboard cottage shaded by luxuriant pines and maples, a barn and paddock where a prancing chestnut thoroughbred can sometimes be seen and an old converted boathouse along the waterfront. On most summer days, Brome Lake is a glittering sapphire nestled in the fragrant green forests of the Eastern Townships. Its frothy gold-tipped waves roll ashore prodded by a gentle breeze from Mount Sutton to the south.

But the change of seasons in Quebec is dramatic, and when summer fades, furious autumn storms strip scarlet leaves from trees and churn the muddy lake bottom, sending rollers thundering to shore. And in winter, like a dying giant, the lake shrieks and moans as ice thickens on the surface, sealing the waters beneath until well into spring.

Jonathan Robinson, a member of Quebec's legislative assembly and minister of mines under Quebec premier Maurice Duplessis, once owned the property. Robinson's greatest political achievement was doubtless the opening up of Quebec's northern territories to mining interests — a move that later proved a bonanza for Hollinger Mines, the corporate ancestor of Conrad Black's media empire. When Robinson died suddenly in October 1948, the entire provincial cabinet arrived on Brome Lake by float planes for the funeral. Soon after, the White family acquired the property.

In 1961, from this new base, Peter White had begun re-inventing the local newspaper, the *Eastern Townships Advertiser*, from a cottage country summer paper to a thriving weekly. Conrad Black's first venture into the newspaper business was ownership, with White, of this and a second paper, *L'Avenir de Brome-Missisquoi*. "The consideration for this investment was nominal and consisted of a balance of sale determined by subsequent earnings, just under $500," Black wrote. "Peter and I never entirely agreed on that figure but we resolved the matter by my taking a rug from the cabin I rented from him."[49]

Describing his 1986 merger of Hollinger and Sterling Newspapers, Black claimed "we had started nearly twenty years before, with $18,000, which came from the *Knowlton Advertiser* (the enterprise in which I purchased a 50 per cent investment in 1967 for $500 less a cheap rug, ultimately my only investment in Sterling or Hollinger)." Heward Grafftey, Progressive Conservative Member of Parliament for Brome at the time, saw a lot of the young Black and said his "attempt to portray himself as something of a Horatio Alger character who rose from the meager beginnings of the *Knowlton Advertiser* weekly newspaper he started with Peter White never washed with me. While he was still in his early twenties, Conrad would arrive at our door in a black Cadillac sedan. He was obviously well off and would soon inherit millions from his father, George Black." And Black's cousin Ron Riley said the idea "that he started everything from a $500 investment is a bit exaggerated. He started with a minority position in Argus — he was a 20 per cent player."[50] A 20 per cent player, it was true, but only at his father's death, in 1976.

Somehow, in the telling, that $500 investment was eventually transformed into a single dollar. When Black's brother, Montegu, died of liver cancer in January 2002, the *Daily Telegraph* obituary claimed that "Conrad paid his friend Peter White $1 for a half interest in a rundown weekly newspaper in rural Quebec, the *Knowlton Advertiser*. Conrad ran it, writing most of the copy, collecting the advertising and delivering many of the copies."

Conrad Black lived in Quebec from 1966 to 1974. The eight years he spent there were formative, probably the most important of his life, for it was in Quebec that he affirmed and perhaps even reinvented his personality.

He became a man of letters, a historian, a newspaper editor and publisher, a political networker par excellence and an emotional, hard-core conservative. He narrowly survived a car accident, confirming his belief that he had a destiny to fulfil. It was also in Quebec that Black first embarked on "the path to Rome," ultimately converting to Catholicism in 1986. He earned a law degree at Université Laval in Quebec City in 1970 and went on to complete a master's in history at McGill Univeristy in Montreal in 1973. Black liked the idea of *la bonne entente*, bringing English and French Canadians closer together, so he applied himself to mastering French. Quebec was also, for him, a foreign society, and his irrepressible curiosity was soon aroused by the unwritten codes of French Canadians, by their hopes and sorrows, virtues and blind spots. He was good at making beautiful French-speaking women laugh — even the English-speaking women of Montreal didn't seem to know or care about his Establishment connections in Toronto. Jean Riley, the wife of Black's cousin Jeremy Riley, said for the first time in his life Conrad felt free.

"I had read the Quebec press carefully during my years in Ottawa," Black later wrote. "Quebec politics and the quality of Quebec political leadership were the best in the country, and I had returned from Europe to relaunch myself and discovered that my former sub-tenant Peter White was Premier Daniel Johnson's executive assistant. I telephoned him and said that if it was my lot to be in Canada, it must be in Quebec and it was not one minute too soon to invoke the Union Nationale's legendary penchant for patronage. Quebec was the only part of Canada that appeared to have any sense of mission or even purpose, and in the Lesage-Johnson era, before nationalism turned to separatism, pursued it with great panache."[51]

White, in turn, offered Black his first business opportunity. The *Eastern Townships Advertiser* was not a great newspaper, but it was a newspaper — a perfect platform for Black to express himself. White was plugged into the Union Nationale establishment. In one of his first editorials, in 1961, under the heading "French spoken here," White wrote: "Nos hommages aux Canadiens français, à l'occasion de leur fête nationale. We believe, in other words, that the 'true Canadian' will be the Canadian who sees the advantages of a two-nations country such as Canada; the Canadian who is proud of the fact that he must learn two languages, not apologetic about it. When this pride in difference is a true force, we won't have to ask ourselves questions we will never be able to answer." That youthful openness to Canada's linguistic duality was typical of the newspaper.

Arriving in Knowlton in 1966, Black was determined to be his own man and pay his own way. The transition from father's son to self-reliant young man "roughing it" was a difficult one. His first home away from home was the humble, converted boathouse on White's Brome Lake property.

"I was trying to inspirit myself with the salubrious qualities of the Canadian winter, which I got a pretty full blast of in that little cabin," said Black. His high-school friend Brian Stewart visited often. "Conrad was living in a very small, one-room cottage on about fifty bucks a week. He told me he wanted to live on what he earned through the *Advertiser*. He was living out of tins, devouring books until three, four or five in the morning, and would quite often forget about lunch or dinner."

White remembers that Conrad "had found a pickaxe around the property, and he would go out in the morning and break up the ice that had formed right in front of his little cottage. Sort of like King Canute, figuring that he was going to prevent the lake from freezing. He learned a great deal. He wasn't a very practical person. He had been brought up with servants. He didn't even know how to use a can opener when he first arrived. We had to demonstrate that to him, and he learned that you can't get anything done unless you keep some kind of regular hours, and you prosecute your business with some diligence, which he had not been used to doing."

Black was trying to affirm his personality and integrate his experiences and impulses into a coherent system of belief. He read voraciously, searching for role models. He devoured books, including Joseph Conrad's *Youth*, a late-nineteenth-century tale of doom on the high seas; his *Almayer's Folly*, about a Dutch trader who cursed his more successful Muslim rival across the Malayan waters (Black drew a parallel between himself and the well-heeled owner of the Montreal *Gazette*, John Bassett, who lived across Brome Lake); and the 1915 two-volume *Life of Lord Strathcona and Mount Royal* — the rather uncritical romantic account of the life of the Scottish fur trader and robber baron.

Brome Lake provided a visual equivalent of the rich imagery in Black's readings. He could picture Joseph Conrad's sailing ships drifting silently along the luminous, glassy surface or, in winter, imagine Lord Strathcona's dogsled belting across the blinding ice sheet. Black's penchant for allegory worked on a personal level as well.

"Strathcona endured long bleak winters of solitude," according to Stewart. "Conrad identified with that lonely existence. He was taken by the loner personality. Since he bought the newly renamed *Knowlton Advertiser*, he has never been out of controversy. He sees himself as a lone battler." Strathcona's career bears comparison with Black's. The Scotsman lived in a snowbound Labrador trading post, became one of Canada's leading parliamentarians and railway tycoons and raised a regiment during the Boer War, before serving as Canada's High Commissioner to London. "The man had spent thirty years in Hudson Bay," said Black. "He was an astonishingly tenacious man, and lived to be ninety-five, and was one of the founders of Canadian Pacific Railway in his fashion. He is one of the great figures in Canadian history, certainly."

Through his work at the newspaper, Black soon came to understand local politics. "He knew all of the councillors of Knowlton," said Stewart, "soaked up all the local news. He had this incredible memory. That was his father's doing — playing intellectual games, like chess, remembering names and dates." Black became friends with the late Jonathan Robinson's son, also named Jonathan — a prissy Catholic priest and secretary to

Paul-Émile Cardinal Léger, archbishop of Montreal — as well as Heward Grafftey, the local Conservative MP, whom he supported for a time.

The newspaper featured ads for Clairol, which ran a factory nearby; articles about the region's Loyalist heritage (the Loyalists had settled the Eastern Townships in the eighteenth century after fleeing the American Revolution); and articles about water pollution and the need to scrutinize plans for the development of nearby ski hills and tourist centres. The newspaper also reported local sightings of bears. Black, who considered himself a man of the world, was probably frustrated writing editorials about the administration of the Knowlton dump and praising "the imagination and altruism" of the Knowlton Lions Club.

Although Conrad's brother, Monte, was working full-time for a Montreal brokerage firm as an analyst, he served as the *Advertiser's* finance editor, and contributed business articles and essays to the paper. At home in Ontario, the mischievous Black had enjoyed a bit of debauchery and living up to his reputation as the misunderstood rebel. But in Knowlton, he had chosen a more disciplined life and had made it work for him. In early 1967, he dated for a time a vivacious Montreal girl — Wilda Lossing — who worked at McGill University's Redpath Library. She later went out with Conrad's friend, Brian Stewart (but died tragically a few years ago).

Black's Quebec period coincided with a turning point in Canadian history. As the once oligarchic Anglo business elite of Montreal lapsed into inertia through the 1960s, French-speaking Quebeckers resolutely threw off their subservient minority status. Provincial Crown corporations such as Hydro Quebec and a cocky new francophone political and financial bourgeoisie rose to prominence. The World's Fair in 1967 — *Exposition universelle* — was a magical, superbly organized event staged in Montreal to celebrate Canada's first century as a Confederation free of British colonial rule. "Expo 67" became a celebration of French Canadians as much as anything else — of their coming of age — and wowing the world with their exuberance, flair and know-how. In just six months, Montreal attracted more than fifty million visitors, more than all the visitors to New York's two-year-long world's fair earlier in the decade. Black tried to date the pretty French-speaking hostesses on the spectacular mid-river exhibition site, usually without success.

In an era of mass protest and ethnic rivalry, Montreal was also living on a political knife-edge. Many terrorist bombings and politically motivated bank robberies had interrupted the serenity of Montreal life since 1963.

Two political paths were open to French-speaking Quebeckers. One led to Ottawa, where Prime Minister Pearson's Quebec lieutenant, Pierre Trudeau, and other progressive young Quebec politicians pushed to make government institutions officially bilingual, to build up the welfare state; and to trounce Quebec nationalism at every opportunity. The other path led to Quebec, where a succession of nationalistic premiers, including Daniel Johnson and Jean-Jacques Bertrand of the Union Nationale (and later Robert Bourassa of the Quebec Liberals and René Lévesque of the Parti Québécois) promoted the defence of a French island nation awash in North America's sea of English-speakers. Quebeckers prudently explored both alternatives, never really committing themselves to either, and certainly never (quite) to Quebec independence.

Their testy ambivalence had the unexpected effect of allowing Quebec disproportionate political power from the 1960s through to the 1990s as the dramatic question of Quebec's fate periodically monopolized Canadian politics.

"The political turmoil in Quebec in the 1960s gave Conrad a permanent garrison mentality," said Brian Stewart. "He had passionately believed in the America of Roosevelt and Johnson. But then he saw the tumultuous animosity of Quebec at the time — the vilification of English Canada. It gave him a sense of what social disorder and the liberal left could lead to. This made him into a highly emotional conservative. He saw street demonstrations, anti-American protests, pot smoking and swearing as something he did not want to have anything to do with."

Stewart and Black had been shocked by what they saw of the Philadelphia race riots in 1964. But the incident had not altered Black's attachment to liberal values. He witnessed the unruly masses once again during French President Charles de Gaulle's visit to Montreal in July 1967. He stood in the square opposite city hall, as a boisterous crowd of Quebec nationalists cheered for Premier Johnson and the visiting president. Then de Gaulle moved up to the microphone, stretched out his arms to the crowd as if he could touch them and, with sovereign dignity and a stifled sob, cried: "Vive Montréal . . . vive le Québec . . . et vive le Québec libre!" It was a defining moment in Quebec political history, giving credence to the struggle for national liberation and strengthening the determination of French-speaking Quebeckers to never again be treated like second-class citizens. (It also outraged many Canadians — English and French — whose fathers, brothers, sons and husbands had left their blood on French soil in two world wars.)

On July 28, 1967, Black published an editorial expressing his lasting admiration for de Gaulle despite the provocative speech in Montreal. True to form, he idealized de Gaulle's historic role while disdaining the Quebec nationalists who cheered him.

Black acknowledged de Gaulle as the solitary wartime hero — a defiant man of faith embodying the soul of his nation and planning his triumphant return. Then Black attacked. "In service to what he perceives to be the greater goals of France, he has often descended to squalid expedients, and has seemed recently to be concerned with little else," he wrote. "He apparently thinks that French Canada will gravitate toward Europe, while English Canada must pass entirely into the orbit of the United States; that Canada therefore is something of an anomaly to be treated with benign indifference while Quebec nationalism is openly encouraged. Hence his performance at Montreal City Hall before a flea-bitten rabble of screaming separatists . . . was surely one of the most monstrous discourtesies in the history of diplomacy.

"President de Gaulle's purposes, amounting to the dismemberment of Canada, and pursued despite his presence here on a state visit commemorating 100 years of Confederation, dovetailed conveniently with Premier Johnson's not discreditable desire to remind English Canadians of the continuing constitutional crisis. [Prime Minister] Pearson's admirable rebuke showed not only that the General makes mistakes, but that in this year of surprises Canada was the scene and subject of a truly gross one."

The evening after the editorial appeared, Brian Stewart told Conrad Black that half the countries of the world, including the United States and Britain, envied Canada for its ability to embarrass de Gaulle. Black felt it was a turning point in his life. "It had finally dawned on me that I had been a rather silly and indiscriminate rebel, the student equivalent of an armchair revolutionary — a political type I was finding increasingly distasteful as the Vietnam era unfolded. I concluded that there were higher and more useful callings than invoking great names like de Gaulle's in bucking the false disciplines of the Canadian Establishment, an unintimidating and not overly sinister entity that for tactical reasons at least, was better joined than fought."

So what was Black to do? "Well, he hadn't really decided," Peter White recalls, "he thought maybe he should continue the study of law. He didn't want to go back to Osgoode Hall because he would have had to go back with his tail between his legs, which he wasn't prepared to do. He was toying with the idea of going to the States or somewhere else. And I said, 'look, what you ought to do is: you've been here in Quebec for a year, you've learned a fair amount about this province, you've become interested in the local politics — why don't you go to Laval and take a law degree there?' And so he said, 'All right, let's do it.' "

The deadline for applications had passed, but White used his influence with the dean, Louis Marceau. "I said, 'Louis, there's this very bright young man who wants to apply, and I recommend that you accept him. Can you make an exception even though he's so late in applying?' So we got him in."

On September 15, 1967, Black appeared in the *Eastern Townships Advertiser* for the last time as publisher/editor and was soon perfecting his French, studying law in Quebec City and going out in the evenings with fellow students Jonathan Birks and Daniel Colson, who remained lifelong friends.

Jonathan Birks, heir to a jewellery store fortune, said Conrad's apartment "was stacked high with newspapers. He had a black and white photograph of de Gaulle on the wall. If you watched him read, he was engrossed in whatever he was reading. You could fire cannons off, and he wouldn't hear them. We used to go to a greasy spoon beside my apartment on rue Mayrand, where our favourite meal was chocolate milkshakes with bacon-and-egg sandwiches. He sometimes wore bright yellow pyjamas and red slippers and once opened the door for me holding a coffee mug. He told me he had cereal first in the mug and left a little milk to have it with coffee afterwards . . . . If my phone went off any evening after eleven o'clock, it was Conrad. He could work straight through the night studying for exams."[52]

Colson remembers Black at Laval as a brilliant student who displayed a mischievous sense of humour at parties and in drinking sessions and who enjoyed political sparring with Quebec nationalists. "Most of us students lived in the older section of Quebec City in accommodation that could generally be described as historic. Conrad was closer to the university in a very comfortable penthouse in a modern building looking over the St. Lawrence River. I think he was actually the only person in the law school who drove around town in a Cadillac, while the rest of us were driving ten-year-old, beat-up jalopies — or hitchhiking to class." (Black says it was a Buick.) For one of their courses, Colson and Black co-authored a paper on the effectiveness of equalization grants in the United States and Canada. Conrad's work was so lengthy and well documented that the two were called before their professor, who thought the work had been plagiarized.

"Little did he know who he was dealing with until he had a chance to sit down with Conrad and be easily impressed by this person who had an encyclopedic knowledge of the U.S. government and political systems," said Colson. "That was the end of that discussion. We did rather well on that paper."[53]

Colson later went to work for the prestigious law firm Stikeman Elliott. By the 1990s, he was devoting most of his time to negotiations on behalf of Black, who would later appoint him deputy chairman of the Telegraph Group.

Black enjoyed going out with francophone women in Quebec City and Montreal. His main girlfriend in 1972–75 was Monique Benoit, a translator. They spent three years together (she kept her own apartment), and they remained on good terms afterwards. In the late 1970s, she translated the first edition of Black's biography on Duplessis into French.

During his first year in law at Laval, Black was shocked by Lyndon Johnson's announcement at the end of March 1968 that he would not seek re-election. "I had a ghastly feeling that not only the communists but the radical chic quislings who had kidnapped American liberalism and lionized Ho Chi Minh, who had exalted the Vietcong and debased American martial traditions and strategic interests, had won. Everything I politically believed in, including traditional and tolerant liberalism, was being desecrated by cowards and hucksters."[54]

Black was undergoing a transformation, moving gradually from gentle 1960s liberalism to hard-core 1970s conservatism, and the transformation took place on multiple levels.

After his first year at Laval, he went to Argentina, where he was fascinated both by the beauty of the women of Buenos Aires and by the country's politics. He wrote a piece for the Montreal *Gazette* on General Juan Carlos Onganía, the country's puritanical and pompous dictator who in 1970 was deposed by his fellow generals and pitifully thrust into a cab without enough in his pocket to pay the fare.

Broadcast journalist Larry Zolf met Black in the late 1960s and remembers him as a hero worshipper. "I can still see Conrad Black now. He was wearing some kind of a Bay Street cowboy ensemble. He had massive sideburns and sported a very expensive pair of Los Angeles–made calfskin boots. He also had the largest stand-up brush-cut east of the Kootenays. . . . Black and I were having our first lunch together at Wellington's [a Toronto restaurant]. Black assiduously began to talk of his heroes—Maurice Duplessis, Benjamin Disraeli, Napoleon and, of course, Wellington. Not only was Black waxing full of hero worship, but he started a kind of quotes game at 10 bucks for every quote not guessed. When I owed Black $50 I told him I had a quote he'd never guess and I'd like to go double or nothing. He obliged me. I then gave him this: 'It behooves one who has supped at labor's table to curse with fine fervor and equal impartiality both labor and its adversaries when they are locked in deadly embrace.' Black took less than ten seconds to reply. 'John L. Lewis, leader of the Mine Workers and founder of the CIO.' It was in a Labour Day speech in Pittsburgh, said Black. Lewis was attacking Roosevelt for condemning both labor and management for the sit-down strikes of 1937. There I was in Black's debt for $100. But Black waived payment."[55]

During the summer of 1968, Black and White tried to buy the Sherbrooke *Record* from John Bassett. They finally succeeded in July 1969, paying $18,000 for the money-losing paper in the run-down former industrial city in Quebec's Eastern Townships. They brought in a friend of White's, David Radler, to manage the operation. The fact they were able to make a success of this small country newspaper in a rapidly declining and greying market (for decades, the anglophone population of the Eastern Townships had been dropping faster than the francophone population) is a tribute to their business acumen. Brian Stewart remembers: "I was in love with my work at the Montreal *Gazette*, covering city hall. Black, White and Radler bought the Sherbrooke *Record* in 1969, and I remember Conrad asking if I wanted to take over the paper — and I said to him, 'No, I am very happy where I am, and besides I know nothing about business.' The prospect of going to Sherbrooke did not appeal to me. My father, who was president of Simpsons (a Montreal department store), thought Conrad was absolutely brilliant and would go on to be a very successful businessman, and I should think twice before saying no. I was not ready to settle down, and money was not that important to me."

David Radler was a short man who waddled like a penguin, sometimes gasped when he talked and had a shock of crazy black hair. He was from a social background unlike Black's. Radler remembered eating hot dogs as a child at Jarry Park in Montreal, while watching the Montreal Royals play — the only team in professional baseball that would allow the black American legend Jackie Robinson to play. His father was a

Jewish Montreal restaurant owner who went on to manage the Fontainebleau Hotel of Miami, featured in the James Bond thriller *Goldfinger*. Radler was a numbercruncher who took pride in his penny-pinching management style — he arrived at the *Record*, counted the desks and immediately started laying off some of the thirty-two employees. Charles Catchpaugh worked at the *Record* and had regular run-ins with his new boss. "I used to tell David Radler that he would skin a fart just to get the grease."[56] Radler slashed expenses and boosted profits. Years later, a reporter visiting him in his Vancouver offices noted that "lunch at the paper-littered desk — only a constantly used calculator was not buried — was two hot dogs with lemonade and two cardboard sandwiches for his visitors, bought by his secretary for less than $5 in Eaton's basement cafeteria." An editor told the reporter Radler "is so tight, he squeaks."[57]

In the late 1960s and early 1970s, Black and Stewart had a circle of Montreal friends that included Nick Auf der Maur, a rumpled, hard-drinking, chain-smoking radical journalist of Swiss Catholic parentage with a flair for human interest stories and scandal. Auf der Maur regaled friends with stories of his mid-1960s punch-up with beat author Jack Kerouac, or the time he squeezed the butt of Russian ballet dancer Rudolf Nureyev or the time he encountered the "crazed" Libyan dictator Moammar Gadhafi. Nick could be found many afternoons in Montreal bars such as the Boiler Room, Grumpy's or the Sir Winston Churchill Pub. In these settings, he was sometimes fuzzy about details but he was nonetheless busy researching hard-hitting stories about Irish-Canadian gangsters or corrupt municipal politicians.

Auf der Maur appealed to Black because he was a bohemian, an entertaining raconteur and a radical with a heart and a sharp mind to match, who could tell him about the huge cultural changes taking place, like the sexual revolution depicted in such popular films as *I Am Curious (Blue)* and *Quiet Days in Clichy*. Audiences silently watched random sexual encounters in pointless films with little or no plot — but compared to movie audiences of the 1950s, by the late 1960s, movie audiences were becoming voyeurs, simply watching other people defy conventions. Auf der Maur told raunchy jokes about sex, drugs and rock 'n' roll, and was completely unlike Black's staid private-school classmates back in Toronto. Black later recalled that "Nick always made me feel young."[58] If Melissa, the daughter Nick had with his wife, Linda Gaboriau, grew up to be one of the world's leading bass guitar rock stars, it was no accident. He was plugged into a creative and subversive crowd — nothing like the horsey set of Toronto.

Through Nick, Conrad Black got to know Quebec's fiery union leader Michel Chartrand as well as the separatist poet Gérald Godin.

Conrad Black became publisher of the *Record* but not its chief operating officer. He had always been the ideas man. Within one month after taking over the *Record*, he wrote a 5,893-word article entitled "A Year after Chicago: Homage to LBJ," published on the former president's sixty-fifth birthday.

The article stands today as perhaps the most important and revealing piece Black ever wrote and represents his definitive break with liberalism and his identification with presidential power. The caption under an accompanying portrait of LBJ — a caption no doubt approved or written by Black — said simply: "A great man much reviled." The article sounded like the first phase of tragedy described by the literary critic Northrop Frye — the stag unjustly brought down by the wolves. LBJ was the righteous hero whose memory deserved to be cherished, whose reputation, restored. Black was inventing a new role for himself — the redeemer of fallen giants. I wonder whether he thought he'd ever be a fallen giant himself, praying for redemption.

The article's subtext was that Black was affirming his place as a newspaper proprietor and historian — not a mere journalist. The article highlighted the major accomplishments of Johnson's long career, including his push for aid "to embattled Britain and peacetime conscription in 1940 and 1941, and large post-war foreign aid programs, starting with the Marshall Plan." Black also credited Johnson with engineering "the downfall of the immensely distasteful Senator Joseph R. McCarthy . . . the dissolution of his witch-hunting committee in 1954" and securing passage of important civil rights legislation — the first in eighty years.

"Never has a President been sworn in who was better qualified by experience, and never in more tragic circumstances, than Lyndon B. Johnson, hastily inaugurated at Dallas airport on November 22, 1963, following the assassination of his popular and talented predecessor," wrote Black. No doubt recalling the 1964 Atlantic City convention he attended with Brian Stewart, Black praised Johnson's "Great Society" program as "a concentrated attack on all the roots of dispossession and under-privilege in America" rivalling Roosevelt's New Deal. "And when current emotionalism subsides, LBJ will take his place beside FDR in the pantheon of American reformers."

The tone of the article turned into a rant when it touched on Vietnam, condemning "the hysterical and apocalyptic . . . to whose uninformed tongues the tedious refrain of genocide, war criminals, etc. comes automatically. . . . At no time did the War absorb more than 15 per cent of federal government expenditures. The loss of 34,000 men over 7 years is of course an immeasurable tragedy, even in a country which loses over 50,000 dead a year on its highways." From a newspaper office in the remote Eastern Townships, it was easy to make such a statement. Black wasn't risking anything. He conceded that it had been a mistake for Johnson "to send 540,000 soldiers to a foreign war without express Congressional authorization. He could have obtained such approval in February 1965, almost unanimously, and a man of Johnson's experience should have known better than to embark on that enterprise on such vague authority as the Gulf of Tonkin Resolution, which only urged him to take the steps necessary for the defence of American interests."

While slamming an assortment of liberal critics of the president as whiners and snivellers, and Johnson's Democratic rival Robert Kennedy as a seductive young rival, Black launched a vitriolic attack on those who dared protest the war. "The campaign of youthful vilification against the President reached a sickening climax in Chicago last August," he wrote. "The President was in Texas celebrating his birthday, but this did not prevent thousands of youths from marching around Grant Park shouting the ultimate obscenity at Johnson, and finally feeding a birthday cake to a pig in commemoration of his anniversary. Johnson said only that if he were a young person he would probably feel like protesting too; a less patient and dedicated man, when taunted incessantly with the chant 'Hey, hey, LBJ, how many kids have you killed today?' might have been tempted to reply: 'None, unfortunately.'

"Johnson's abdication," Black solemnly concluded, "like that of Cincinnatus, was a classic example of the voluntary surrender of great power, a very dramatic act, in history as in the theatre. All knew that a titan had passed whose like would not be seen again. His talents, his ego, his compassion, determination and capacity for work were, like his services to the nation and his much-caricatured ears, very prominent."

Johnson's abdication marked the end of Black's liberalism, but also the end of liberalism in the United States.

"American liberalism was held unreasonably to blame for the Vietnam war, the revolt of youth and the race riots," the late Pulitzer Prize–winning historian and Kennedy biographer Arthur M. Schlesinger, Jr., told me in 2004. "It was a terrible time, with the assassinations of John F. Kennedy in Dallas and Robert F. Kennedy in 1968. American liberalism has not taken back this ground since then. Jimmy Carter was a right-wing non–New Dealer; Bill Clinton, who would have been a New Dealer, was handicapped by his behaviour."

Black didn't think much of most journalists and believed the *Record* should be run with as few of them as possible. It was a position he, Radler and White included in a 1969 brief to the Special Senate Committee on the Mass Media. Presented by Black, the brief said there were not adequate safeguards to ensure that journalists vested with "influence and heady individual exposure . . . are intellectually and psychologically qualified for their positions. My experience with journalists authorizes me to record that a very large number of them are ignorant, lazy, opinionated, intellectually dishonest and inadequately supervised. The profession is heavily cluttered with abrasive youngsters who substitute 'commitment' for insight, and to a lesser extent, with aged hacks toiling through a miasma of mounting decrepitude. Alcoholism is endemic in both groups."[59]

In his presentation, Black criticized the excessive concentration of media ownership in Canada and the anti-Americanism and leftist mindset of many journalists — confirming his own dramatic and ongoing shift to the right.

Black noticed that the English-speaking community of Montreal had lost its creative edge and was gradually falling into the symbolic role assigned to it by Quebec nationalism, the role of a privileged minority living in the past. He paid more attention to a rising French-speaking tycoon from the northern Ontario mining town of Sudbury. Paul Desmarais had started out with a bus line in Sudbury, at one point staying solvent by paying employees with bus tickets. He had overcome compulsive shyness to build up Power Corporation, a prodigious holding company based in Montreal with interests in paper, glass, newspapers such as Montreal's *La Presse*, sheep ranching in Australia and Canada Steamship Lines.

He was a new kind of business tycoon for Canada. He had a private projection room installed in his Ramezay Road mansion in Westmount so he could sit in privacy, watching his favourite film, *The Godfather*, over and over again. He joked with friends that he would make offers they couldn't refuse, just like Marlon Brando's Don Corleone. Desmarais liked the company of intellectuals — he often drove down to the Mount Royal Club in his black Mercedes 600 to drink Moët et Chandon with Québécois novelist and *La Presse* publisher Roger Lemelin. But he was not an intellectual himself: his bookshelf had only a handful of volumes — Dale Carnegie's *How to Win Friends and Influence People* and biographies of Napoleon and Roy Thomson. Instead of reading books, he read people. He let them talk, and then sized them up. There was something brooding and grandiose about this Franco-Ontarian with his towering height, aquiline nose and occasional long silences. Driving among the rolling hills of Quebec's Charlevoix county in the early 1970s, playing an eight-track cassette of Wagner's *Tannhäuser* and munching on cheese curds, he liked to expound on the importance of establishing corporate dynasties and the appeal of doing business one day in Mao's China. He hoped to become a global tycoon and statesman, much like Thomson. Even though he bought E. P. Taylor's minority shareholding in Argus Corp., the shares did not hold voting rights. In the early 1970s, the Canadian Establishment still considered Desmarais a corporate outsider.

In the early 1970s, Black, Radler and their associates, financed by bank loans of $6.7 million, purchased twenty-one newspapers in rural Canada, from the *Alaska Highway News* in British Columbia to the Summerside *Journal Pioneer* in Prince Edward Island. The group of properties became Sterling Newspapers, and in May 1972, they offered to sell the lot to Paul Desmarais at Power Corporation. They wanted $6 million, but Desmarais would go no higher than $2.5 million.

Black and the others held on to Sterling, implementing a strategy of severe cost-cutting to make the papers profitable. As publisher of the Sherbrooke *Record*, Black cut the editorial staff to a minimum. Alex Radmanovich, editor in 1973–74, recalls speaking to Black by phone "on a very regular basis. I was running the paper. He was never arrogant toward me and always treated me with the utmost respect. He always came across as being very sincere. Bringing out the paper every day was no easy task. I had a full-time reporter, a stringer, and a women's editor who did layout. I figured I could do some layout myself and free up that person to be a reporter. Conrad called to say, 'You've just proved to me I didn't need a women's editor.' So because of my efficiency, I had to fire the women's editor. . . . He's a very aloof person. He doesn't give a fuck. He lives in a bubble, that's how he lives his life."[60]

In March 1970, near the end of his time at Laval, Black went through a period of serious physical and mental distress. "I began to experience worrisome symptoms of tension," he wrote. "Indigestion, claustrophobia in restaurants, airplanes, and other confined spaces, fitful sleep, sudden attacks of perspiring and even hyperventilating, all new to me, began to occur with increasing frequency." His father arranged a consultation with the psychiatrist-in-chief at the Clarke Institute of Psychiatry. Thanks to psychoanalysis, he realized he was suffering what he describes as a "diffuse, paralysing, strangling terror of a full seizure of anxiety."[61] His symptoms fit a form of anxiety disorder known as a "panic attack," defined as "a discreet period in which there is the sudden onset of intense apprehension, fearfulness, or terror, often associated with feelings of impending doom. During these attacks, symptoms such as shortness of breath, palpitations, chest pain or discomfort, choking or smothering sensations, and fear of 'going crazy' or losing control are present."[62]

Brian Stewart remembers things differently. Black came to see him in the newsroom at the Montreal *Gazette*, and said he was suffering from serious depression.

The attacks led Black to an inward spiritual search. In his autobiography, he said there was a kindling of "a latent religious sense, never to be endowed with fervor or even much piety, much less sanctimony." During "the most difficult bouts of nervosity," he said, his desperate, silent prayers "incited me to read some theology, especially the masterfully elegant and persuasive Cardinal Newman."[63]

Black found the experience of psychoanalysis so interesting that for a time he considered becoming a psychiatrist. He may simply have been overwhelmed by the stress of having so many different experiences at once — surviving a major car accident; reviving the fortunes of a newspaper in which he had a considerable financial stake; completing a law degree in a language that he was still mastering; seeing his hero Lyndon Johnson go down before anti-war protesters; and wondering how the Canadian federation would survive a wave of protest and bombings in Quebec.

Thanks to the fawning LBJ article, Black managed briefly to meet the former president, a connection he used to arrange a visit to Vietnam in September 1970. He wanted to see something of the war first-hand in the land Graham Greene had described as "the gold of the rice-fields under a flat late sun: the fishers' fragile cranes hovering over the fields like mosquitoes: the cups of tea . . . the mollusc hats of the girls repairing the road where a mine had burst: the gold and the young green and the bright dresses of the south. . . ."[64]

That wasn't exactly the scene that greeted the twenty-six-year-old newspaper proprietor in humid, battle-weary Saigon, with its faded French colonial charms, continuous and noisy helicopter over-flights and the shrill gossip of hard-drinking war correspondents. He said he was on a "fact-finding tour" and used his position as a pro-American newspaper publisher to open doors. Scoring a scoop of sorts, he arranged a lengthy interview with South Vietnamese President Nguyen Van Thieu,[65] who predicted the Paris peace talks would fail, the war would be reduced to a minor frontier skirmish within three years and reunification of the north and south was only a long-term possibility. He also questioned the U.S. decision to halt the bombing of the North.

"Thieu said he agreed with such experts as Gen. William C. Westmoreland, former head of the U.S. forces in Vietnam, that North Vietnam was on the verge of a general collapse when the then president Johnson partially halted bombing in April, 1968," wrote Black. "He said he opposed the bombing halt or any other unconditional concession to the North, unless it led quickly to peace. But Thieu also expressed gratitude and admiration for Johnson, saying he was 'in large measure, the saviour of the freedom of Vietnam.' "

For the first time in his life, Black was enjoying the role of political insider. Thieu, for example, told him that President Kennedy had been behind the assassination of Ngo Dinh Diem — a scenario that was widely believed but had never been publicly confirmed. Henry Kissinger wrote many years later that the U.S.-led coup against Diem in 1963 weakened South Vietnam and strengthened the communist North.[66] Starting in the 1980s, Black's close association with American neo-conservatives was a logical maturation of the political views he developed observing seminal events in the United States and Vietnam in the previous two decades.

One of the most interesting discoveries during his travels was foreign women. "Hong Kong was a fantastic city. The women, Western orientals in dress and manner and bilingualism, were the most beautiful of any city I had visited — except Buenos Aires and Budapest."[67] While travelling in Southeast Asia, Black learned that in Montreal the Front de Libération du Québec (FLQ) had kidnapped — and were holding hostage — the British trade commissioner James R. Cross and Pierre Laporte, the Quebec labour minister. On October 15, 1970, the Quebec government asked the Canadian Army to assist local police. The next day, Prime Minister Pierre Trudeau declared the province was in a state of "apprehended insurrection," and he imposed the War Measures Act. First enacted in 1914, this law suspended a whole series of civil liberties and gave the federal cabinet sweeping powers to suppress the media; arrest, detain or deport individuals and confiscate private property. A day after the declaration, the FLQ killed Laporte and left his body in the trunk of a car near Montreal.

During what came to be known as "the October Crisis," hundreds were picked up and jailed, including some of Black's friends. Nick Auf der Maur was among those arrested. Like most of those arrested, he was released without charge. At the time, Canadians overwhelmingly supported Trudeau's actions. But many Quebec nationalists and civil libertarians across the country condemned it as an overreaction.

In many of Montreal's pubs and bars, a fiery separatist could be counted on to make "a colorful, if incoherent, outburst," wrote Black as he busily turned out strongly pro-Trudeau editorials in the *Record*. Like many Quebeckers, he found the crisis deeply troubling and potentially explosive with students and unions — the "rabble," as he called them — demonstrating in favour of the FLQ.

John Turner, federal justice minister at the time, told me in early November 1970 that Montrealers had experienced "a climate of fear" in the days preceding the proclamation of the War Measures Act and people were concerned that society might not be capable of protecting itself. He said the government knew there was a risk that Cross and Laporte could be killed. "But if we had exchanged Mr. Cross and Mr. Laporte for criminals . . . then where would it have stopped? We free twenty-seven of what they like to call 'political prisoners' but what I like to call 'criminals' for Mr. Laporte and Mr. Cross, and then what happens? More crimes are committed, further exchanges, and it goes on and on until the freely elected government of the people has lost control. This was a test case. We were the first government in the world to hold the line and say 'no.' And for this the Canadian people have received, I think, the admiration of the British government, which has been closely in communication with us."[68] Cross was eventually released in return for the safe passage to Cuba of several FLQ members.

By the early 1970s, Paul Desmarais was toying with the idea of building a 100-storey office tower on the site of his bus terminal at the Berri-de Montigny metro station. But he abandoned the idea, partly because of the October Crisis — it turned out the FLQ had put him on a list of people to kidnap. For years afterwards, an overweight Montreal police constable named Roma sat in an unmarked car farther up Ramezay Road, watching everyone coming and going, to keep Desmarais secure.

A year after the October Crisis, Conrad Black had recovered from the shock and was integrating his personality and belief system. He would be an enterprising business proprietor and hopefully an important one — but his mindset would turn to religious and political models of the past, to values and social institutions in decline and just about to disappear.

Peter White said he was always very conscious that Black "is attracted to people that he considers great and interesting. . . . So I invented the word *magnophile.* . . . Conrad was a magnophile, and he still is . . . if that's the study of leadership, then he was doing that."

Black's family was not religious. In the 1950s, the Blacks and Rileys, like many Protestants of their class, considered religious faith to be a personal extravagance, akin to unseemly public demonstrations of emotion. Black had frequent discussions about religion during the 1960s at Métis on the Gaspé coast with his cousin's French-Canadian wife, Jean Riley, who felt her Catholicism was spiritual while Black was more interested in history.

In Quebec, Black saw that the Catholic Church still played a significant role in the province's politics with people such as Pierre Trudeau on the left and Daniel Johnson, Sr., on the right, entwining political and social philosophy with their Catholic faith but not taking the teachings too literally and maintaining a healthy balance between intellectual rigor and joie de vivre. Some of Quebec's conservative nationalists were also Roman Catholic: they favoured gradual reforms, weren't particularly anti-English or prone to violence and radiated an attractive *ancien régime* quality. Black found the combination of *ancien régime* religion and politics intoxicating. He began flirting with his own kind of radicalism.

Periodically through his life, Black developed filial relationships with older men, from English Canada's Bud McDougald to America's Richard Nixon and Britain's Lord Weidenfeld, latching on to the grandeur and experience of his mentors in the hopes some of it would rub off. These were men who could open their mythical private world to him and share experiences, insights and the forgotten grandeur of their earlier years. It was like casting stones into the water and regretting the way the ripples vanished. Perhaps without realizing it, these men were like surrogate fathers to him.

The first of these filial relationships was with Cardinal Paul-Émile Léger, Catholic archbishop of Montreal. Black was introduced to Cardinal Léger by the prelate's secretary, Jonathan Robinson's son Father Robinson. Black described Léger as "a formidable presence, trim, of medium stature, with silver hair combed straight back under his biretta, and deep, dark quintessentially French-Canadian eyes squinting and flashing with an intensity that faithfully reflected the powerful and original activity of his mind. His most outstanding characteristic was, and remained right to his death (in 1991), his rich melodious gift of speech in conversation and oratory that conferred upon him, at least in French, an almost infallible eloquence."[69]

Léger's career spanned several decades, from humble origins in

Valleyfield, Quebec, where he aspired to be a railway engineer before entering the priesthood. Then it was missionary work in Japan before the Second World War and finally, after the war, his appointment as director of the Canadian College in Rome where he became a confidant of Pope Pius XII. Returning to Canada in 1950, Léger replaced the progressive Mgr. Joseph Charbonneau as archbishop of Montreal. Three years later, Léger was made cardinal. Arriving at Montreal's Windsor Station following his voyage from Rome, Léger cried exultantly to the huge welcoming crowd: *"Montréal, ô ma ville, tu as voulu te faire belle pour recevoir ton Prince!"* — "O Montreal, my city, you wanted to be at your most beautiful in order to receive your Prince!" Léger later came to regret this bizarre triumphalist outburst.

Black was well aware that the Vatican was a sovereign state ruled by the Pope, an absolute elective monarch. The College of Cardinals formed the Vatican's Senate, and each cardinal was a prince, able to vote for a papal candidate during the Conclave. It was even said that Léger had almost been elected Pope himself, in 1964. Léger offered a unique insider's view of the world's most secretive monarchy. His stories gave Black an intoxicating taste of power. So this is what it meant to be a king-maker.

The advent of the Quiet Revolution, a period of intense secularization of Quebec society, coupled with the cardinal's long absences during the Vatican Council of the early 1960s, weakened his hold on the archdiocese. And by the time Black met him, Léger was struggling to find a role for himself. He established a charity to help the poor of Montreal, but it was not well managed during his lifetime. A group of friends purchased a Westmount mansion for Léger at 3165 Ramezay Place. It was an unattractive white-brick building in the shape of a shoebox, with a three-car garage. A few doors away was the mansion of financier Paul Desmarais. Both properties had belonged to Black's aunt, Margaret Riley. Léger left the mansion and Montreal a year later to look after lepers and orphans in Cameroon, where he lived in a ramshackle trailer. The adjustment was as difficult for him as it was for the bishops and priests there who were not sure how to behave around a missionary with direct access to the Pope.

Brian Stewart remembers Black telling him about the cardinal at the time: "Here was a man who was a prince of the Church, who stood for grandeur and history, but he was also a man who stood for the poor and the downtrodden, by living with lepers in Africa."

Léger's biographer, Micheline Lachance, said the cardinal "had spent his life torn between humility and the lustre of wealth. He would love to have been humble, as a priest once told me. Cardinal Léger liked being close to rich and influential people. He spoke to me about Black. Their relationship was filial, but he felt Black had been wrong about Duplessis in several respects. He considered Black an interesting young person, but not much more than that."[70]

But Black cultivated the relationship, travelling to Cameroon in 1971 to interview Léger for his Duplessis book, offering fund-raising help; and preparing a document nominating the cardinal for the Nobel Peace Prize. (Coincidentally, the English Catholic intellectual Malcolm Muggeridge, whom Black greatly admired, was developing a similarly high-profile friendship with Mother Theresa in Calcutta.) "Thanks to your good works and the attention attracted by your personality, your undoubted genius, and the extraordinary achievements of your career so far, you enjoy the heart felt affections of the collective spirit of the world," Black wrote after visiting Léger in Cameroon. "Unfortunately, this is the only asset your organization possesses, and it is with inexpressible but nonetheless real sorrow that I noticed how the huge structure [of Léger's charity] had become unstable and even precarious. I urge you to bring about essential reforms ... to ensure that your admirable activities may continue, and you may continue to enjoy a massive, spontaneous and richly deserved reputation."

Black offered financial expertise and impressive contacts, but no more than $500 in cash.

In the same letter, Black proposed using Léger's charity to acquire the Ottawa newspaper *Le Droit*. Despite "the slanderous campaign that has been directed at you, and the gulf separating you in various respects from several members of the Quebec clergy," wrote Black, "would you be interesting in buying the

Ottawa newspaper, *Le Droit*? *Le Droit* has an admirable history of defending the interests of Franco-Ontarians. This newspaper, which has a higher circulation than *Le Devoir*, currently belongs to the Oblate Fathers. It could be purchased, possibly in the name of our French language publications on [Quebec's] North Shore, and of Cardinal Léger et ses Oeuvres [Léger's charity]. We could clear the money through your organization and grant you a percentage. This would require neither capital nor any risk on your part. It goes without saying that we would maintain the raison d'être and the good reputation of the newspaper, putting in an assuredly more efficient administration than the current owners have in place. (I have taken a very close look at the finances.) The advantages for you would be to stop the rumors currently circulating about the financial basis of your organiza-tion, rumors that are being spread as you know by a number of slanderers. Moreover, those who see themselves during your absence as your adversaries would doubtless be impressed to witness the transmission of such a well known and influential newspaper into hands which would include Your Eminence."

The scheme might have provided tax advantages and the leverage Black would need to win *Le Droit* from the Oblates, and it might have resolved the Léger charity's financial prob-lems. But Léger didn't follow up. He continued his missionary work in Africa for several more years while Black remained on the board of directors of the cardinal's Montreal charity.

In the aftermath of the October Crisis, Black was beginning to form an elitist view of the Catholic Church, a view of princes and popes and historical grandeur, as if Rome were the insur-ance policy of Western civilization, as if a return to the faith could protect Quebec from its ongoing linguistic and economic conflicts and salvage something of its age-old anti-modernist character. Black was also studying Quebec history in search of a formula that would encourage the development of society in a measured, constructive way while safeguarding order and the rule of law.

As his business interests grew, Black felt constrained in Quebec. Perhaps *la bonne entente* was not to be. In the early

1970s, the English and French of Quebec seemed like "two scorpions in a bottle," as the separatist René Lévesque used to say. Anglophone Quebeckers were leaving the province by the tens of thousands, and Montreal, once the financial capital of half a continent, was in fiscal crisis and becoming increasingly neurotic and self-absorbed as investors fled or avoided the city altogether.

"I think the ambivalence of the French Quebeckers about their political status has caused the city to pay a terrible price," said Black. "I think it used to be a very stylish place, and a very interesting mélange between a largely English-speaking continent and the overseas culture of the French, although the Quebec variant is not entirely representative of France. . . . It had a certain panache of its own and an unselfconscious blending of these different elements. . . . Montreal is like a woman who has faded a bit, and you can see that once upon a time, she was a good-looking woman, and still has traces of it, but her clothes are twenty years out of date, and she is slightly down at the heel. . . . There is a certain amount of tension between the French and the English. The English-speaking people are in general rather a detritus of a former, much stronger community, and the French Canadians have gone about as far as they can, threatening to set up their own country, which they are in fact not going to do. And the whole script has just got very, very tired. It's just like a play that's run too long. And a play that has gotten pretty shabby and run down."

In May 1971, Naomi Griffiths, Black's former history professor at Carleton University, told him about a history seminar devoted to the late Maurice Duplessis, Union Nationale leader and premier of Quebec from 1936 to 1939 and again from 1944 to 1959. There was something paradoxical about this much-reviled conservative Quebec politician, who built more new schools and universities than any Quebec premier before or since but claimed never to read books, courted English-Canadian and American industrial magnates but identified with the poor and downtrodden to the point of offering them cash out of his private safe, and developed an elaborate network of patronage and influence.

For Black, the conservative contrarian, Duplessis had the additional advantage of being a colourful rogue, a supporter of the corporatist view of society and champion of collective rights and a man not above political thuggery. In writing about Duplessis, Black returned to one of his favourite roles — the redeemer of fallen giants.

Duplessis was an extremely controversial figure in Quebec history. His name was synonymous with *la grande noirceur* — best translated as "the Age of Darkness" — a period of autocratic political rule that, according to the traditional view in Quebec, was followed by the Quiet Revolution — the rapid secularization and democratization of society. This era began in 1960 and was due largely to the heroic efforts of federalists such as Pierre Elliott Trudeau and Gérard Pelletier and Quebec nationalists such as Jean Lesage and René Lévesque.

Trudeau was a strange bird — a multi-faceted, articulate narcissist who had become the archenemy of Quebec nationalism. There was something of the bourgeois dilettante in this man who lived with his mother until he was into his forties but was a fervent lover of far younger women and possibly, it was whispered, of men. Few people knew that he had indulged in fascist fantasies of absolute power during the Second World War, meeting with rich friends in Outremont and mapping out a *coup d'état* that would have made him a New World Mussolini.[71] Nothing came of the plot, and many of his later attacks on Quebec nationalism, equating it with extreme right-wing ideologies, could have been projections of his own youthful fascism. By the 1950s, at the helm of the influential political journal *Cité Libre*, Trudeau had undergone a conversion to a Jeffersonian kind of liberal democracy. English Canadians loved him, making him the subject from 1968 to 1972 of "Trudeaumania" — a virtual personality cult with some fascist overtones. For who else but the complex Trudeau could be the very incarnation of a mosaic of diversity like Canada? He had flair, he was sexy, he was a brash, bold leader who could put Quebec in its place.

Beginning in May 1971, Black developed a second filial relationship — this time with an aging, controversial but popular historian, French-born Robert Rumilly, who had known Duplessis well and was writing a biography of him. The relationship was in many respects a surprising one. Black was an admirer of Franklin Roosevelt and Charles de Gaulle, of parliamentary institutions and the rule of law. Rumilly was anti-Semitic to the core, an ardent admirer of French fascism, an intellectual Janus who wrote scissors-and-paste chronicles of Quebec history (usually commissioned by municipalities and nationalist organizations and based almost entirely on newspaper clippings) while maintaining — in private and sometimes in public — a lifelong commitment to his fascist friends.

This was very strange company for Conrad Black — whose family had been staunchly on the side of the Allies during the Second World War. One of his mother's brothers had been killed in action in Italy, and his father had played a significant role in the war effort as a senior government bureaucrat and president of a Montreal company manufacturing aircraft propellers. The whole point of the Spithead coronation naval review in 1953, which Black had witnessed as a child, was to show the world that Britain had triumphed over the destructive forces of Hitler, Mussolini and Japanese militarism.

There was no secret about Rumilly's lifelong support for fascism. Rumilly was a thin, bitter old man with nasty eyes peering through thick glasses. He was the leading organizer of the "Vichy Rat Line" to Quebec after 1944, which enabled Vichy fugitives to slip out of liberated France, where they faced prosecution and possible execution for treason and war crimes. Sometimes provided with false papers by the Vatican and disguised as Catholic priests, they travelled to Argentina, Brazil, Spain . . . wherever a friendly right-wing regime would take them in.

Thanks to the active intervention of Rumilly, Jacques de Bernonville — a member of the 1930s French right-wing terrorist group La Cagoule and a close associate of the infamous Klaus Barbie who crushed resistance in Lyon during the war — found refuge in the arch-conservative province run by Duplessis, along with a number of other Vichy war criminals. Rumilly was chief propagandist, both for these fascist fugitives and for

Duplessis. In the Rumilly papers at Quebec's national archives in Montreal, a 1968 letter from Bernonville shows they remained close ideological allies more than two decades later:"It is dreadful to think that History will only be written by our enemies. And legends will always be more powerful than the truth."[72] Bernonville, who freely joined the Waffen SS during the war, conducted an extensive Vichy census of Jews and their property and was condemned to death in absentia for organizing massacres of resistance fighters, torture and other war crimes. An unknown assailant murdered him in Rio de Janeiro in 1972.

According to Black's former professor Naomi Griffiths, "something many people long for, and Conrad is too intelligent to be seduced by, is a desire for order, with recognized leaders and a single ideology." But the ever practical Black, despite his very different ideological views, wanted to understand the historical basis of conservative nationalism in Quebec.

And who better to help him find answers than Robert Rumilly? In his memoirs, Black recounts driving Rumilly around rural Quebec in a Cadillac Eldorado over a one-year period, meeting aging "survivors of the old Quebec," from Archbishop Georges Cabana to the Dominican anti-Duplessis scholar, Father Georges-Henri Lévesque. These encounters gave the twenty-seven-year-old Toronto patrician-turned-scholar a feel for a bygone era when Quebec society was dominated by three institutions: the French-speaking provincial government, the arch-traditionalist Catholic Church and the largely English-speaking old-boy network tightly gripping the province's business interests. The Duplessis system relied on two communities—ultramontane Catholic bishops, who provided much-needed legitimacy with their pervasive religious control over much of Quebec society; and English-speaking industrial magnates, who provided most of the cash needed to operate the patronage system. Black spent time getting to know both of these communities, which had been severely compromised by their association with Duplessis and had lost their grip on the province after his sudden death in 1959.

After his first encounter with Rumilly in 1971, Black wrote a courteous note in French, which is filed among Rumilly's papers in the Quebec national archives — along with Rumilly's extensive correspondence with leading politicians, littérateurs and fellow right-wing ideologues and fascists. Included in the files is a letter from an organization in France dedicated to defending the memory of disgraced Vichy leader Marshal Philippe Pétain. Even as late as the 1970s, Rumilly was unwilling to let go.

Black's letter, one of several in the file, offers Rumilly "my profound thanks for your hospitality, help and wise counsel. It is with considerable pleasure that I look ahead to our next meeting." Later in 1971, convinced that he was on to something, Black entered the master's program in history at McGill University in Montreal. The two-year course of study required him to develop a thesis. He set out to write a revisionist political biography of Duplessis, an experience that also helped him question and deepen his newfound commitment to conservatism.

This put Black at loggerheads with his old friend Nick Auf der Maur (born to Catholic parents, for whom "Duplessis represented a reactionary, insular, church-dominated society" in which "the intellectuals were in the opposition").

The thesis was later expanded into a book, which has gone through two editions. In Quebec it was considered something of a novelty since it was written by a Torontonian (translated into French by his former girlfriend Monique Benoit).

Based on countless interviews with eyewitnesses as well as exhaustive research in published and unpublished records, Black's book, a journalistic history, was the result of a negotiating coup — the first anglophone ever to gain access to the tightly held Duplessis archives. Black made clear that his research was based essentially on the Duplessis papers and his friend Rumilly's history of Quebec. Black formed an intellectual alliance of sorts with Rumilly, tapping into his musings and memories, and those of his elderly contacts around the province. On the first page of *Duplessis*, first published in 1977, Black thanked his "friend" Rumilly for his help and wrote: "I shall always count it a pleasure to have known so well this most prolific historian and interesting companion."

At McGill, Black chose as thesis adviser a former teacher from his Upper Canada College years, Laurier LaPierre. The choice seemed a peculiar one, since Black later wrote in his memoirs that LaPierre had often caned boys at the school and was "one of the most enthusiastic flagellators of the time. . . . Many years later when we became friendly radio debaters in Montreal and he sponsored my thesis at McGill, and still later when he publicly declared his homosexual proclivities, it became possible to imagine some of the socio-economic and psychological displacements that must have motivated this penniless young French-Canadian socialist to assault so violently the comfortable derrières of Upper Canada's scions."[73]

By 1971, LaPierre was a leading authority on French Canada's political history, from an ideological horizon far from Black's own — LaPierre was close to Pierre Trudeau. He was also a broadcaster, whose attendance at McGill's history department meetings was spotty and who didn't devote as much time to his academic work as he might have. Black and LaPierre met regularly in the Leacock building on the campus — a mouldy, airless concrete bunker housing history department offices and classes. LaPierre, today a Liberal senator living in Ottawa, supervised the research and writing of Black's M.A. thesis and was impressed by his ability to charm and cajole Auréa Cloutier, Duplessis's former secretary, into granting him access to the private papers.

Brian Mulroney remembers running into Black at a restaurant in Quebec City while he was doing research for his thesis: "And there was Conrad, off in the corner, with this lady. So I went over to say hello . . . and I asked him who the lady was. She was one of Duplessis's secretaries or assistants [likely Auréa Cloutier]. Here he was on a Saturday night in Quebec City, or whatever it was, in the Continental having dinner with her, so as to elicit interesting information. That is the way he did it. He worked very hard at it. It was quite an accomplishment."[74]

Black compiled an enormous mass of documentation, stored in his Montreal apartment. Henry Aubin, an author and Montreal *Gazette* writer, met Black in the early 1970s when Black was living in suite 1802 of the Vatican-owned Port Royal apartment building on Sherbrooke Street, within walking distance of McGill University. A heap of Duplessis papers was piled up on Black's dining-room table. "His apartment was so eclectic, sumptuous, but with many objets d'art," said Aubin. "Facing the mountain there was a classical statue [a torso] — all in very good taste. There were plants. It was Baroque, there was something everywhere — his Duplessis book is Baroque, too."[75]

Peter White believes Black studied Duplessis — the master — as a model from whom he could learn about manipulation of power, just as he learned about business from his mentor Bud McDougald, chairman of Argus Corp. McDougald, said White, "was very Machiavellian and Byzantine in the way he just governed everything from the centre of the spider web, and he's very much like Duplessis in that sense — playing one rube off against the other, and shoring up so and so. . . . Conrad sort of learned that form of power, certainly both from Duplessis and McDougald." For Black, Duplessis belonged to that elite group of leaders who operated above the normal conventions of society — and the law. "Duplessis's legacy includes his personality," Black wrote. "Like Marshal Pétain, he made to the state the gift of his own person and his own personality, which has not ceased to be a legendary one."[76]

It was essential for Black to stay on good terms with Rumilly since both were working on Duplessis biographies. Rumilly's two-volume biography came out in 1973 — a fascist tome praising the regionalist movement led by Mistral in Provence, as well as Charles Maurras, Marshal Pétain and the Portuguese dictator António Salazar. It transposes France's right-wing ideology onto Quebec, devotes several hundred pages to Quebec's isolationist and anti-conscription movement during the Second World War and includes only a few sentences, largely sarcastic, about the Allied war effort and "propaganda" that was needed to defeat Nazi and fascist alike. The biography disparages Jews, Freemasons and other groups of supposed social outcasts whom Rumilly portrayed as conspirators seeking to twist the rules to destroy hearth, faith and fatherland.

But Black's perspective was different. According to Pierre Godin, a noted Quebec historian and biographer, Black and

Rumilly took divergent views of Duplessis. "Rumilly must have seen in Duplessis, in his way of managing the province, a father figure, the incarnation of the ideal of a fascist leader. Duplessis was not a fascist, however. He was authoritarian, a neo-conservative and a corporatist. But when Duplessis lost the elections in 1939, he accepted the will of the people. Black found that the former Quebec premier was on the same wavelength. He was a neo-conservative, someone from the same ideological horizon. Black had to be in agreement with the conservative vision of Duplessis regarding the role of the state and the government."[77]

Black's portrait of Quebec society is essentially faithful to the corporatist model popular in Quebec at a time when political leaders of all stripes praised Mussolini, Franco and Salazar and their division of society into distinct corporations, which could be handled at will. He skilfully synthesizes the history of Quebec in the late 1930s in broad brush-strokes: "Traditionally, everything was decided by the Church hierarchy, and particularly the Archbishop of Quebec; the Anglo-Saxon business leadership; and the government" which played a role similar to that of business in the English-speaking provinces. "The position of the Prime Minister of Quebec was unique as the secular leader of the French-Canadian nation. Seconding these triumvirs — of state, Church, and commerce — were the Caisses Populaires and agricultural union leadership; the Chambers of Commerce; and the associated Catholic, service, parish, co-operative and labor groups. Into this cosy, highly structured realm, the secular labor movement erupted with no great discretion, pushing the Catholic unions before them in the stridency of their demands, as the Huns had pushed the lesser barbarians before them across civilization in the fifth century."[78]

In *Duplessis*, Black evokes the main actors in Quebec's political drama: the verbose, ambiguous, inventive politicians; the austere ultramontane prelates; the cigar-chomping industrialists after the best deal; the sensuous available women like moths attracted to the flame of power, their lissome bodies slipping out of silk dresses as they clung to weary politicians; the journalists it was so easy to corrupt with cash-filled envelopes, offers of access, or modest public relations contracts; and the brutal thugs, ready to whip out pistol and baseball bat to intimidate voters and strikers. Some thugs even kidnapped opposition candidates on behalf of Duplessis. While English-speaking business leaders abundantly greased the wheels of the Duplessis patronage system, the middle- and upper-class anglophone electorate stopped voting for his party after 1936. This kind of fundamental cleavage in anglophone society had rarely been seen. Among French-speaking Quebeckers, meanwhile, the slow pace of electrification outside the province's cities meant that until the late 1940s and early 1950s many rural voters had little access to information beyond what the parish priest told them. And almost all Quebec daily newspapers, with the exception of *Le Devoir*, had been co-opted by the provincial government.

Black treated patronage on a partisan basis, ridiculing patrician Liberal patronage but forgiving Union Nationale patronage as a legal and useful instrument of influence. He wrote that Montreal industrialist J. W. McConnell had delivered cardboard boxes full of cash to Duplessis — $50,000 in 1952 and $100,000 three years later — just part of an estimated $100 million (in 1950s dollars) received by Duplessis in kickbacks, political contributions and gifts, including works of art, during his long reign in Quebec. (In 2007 dollars, the amount of graft under Duplessis might have amounted to more than $790 million.) His art collection, valued at $15 million in 2007 dollars, has since been donated to a Quebec City museum. Black describes the paintings as slightly better than those found "in a good haut-bourgeois Quebec home in the 1940s and 1950s. . . . Well, he wasn't a man of particularly insightful artistic taste . . . he wasn't terribly original." Media and other critics, including progressive Catholic clergy, at the time considered Duplessis patronage to be an immoral subversion of democracy. The cash contributions from McConnell alone were the equivalent of sixty times the $2,500 average annual income of Quebeckers in 1955.

Missing in Black's *Duplessis* is an investigation of the corporatist, if not outright fascist, ideology of many leading Quebec politicians, usually based on the ugly foundation of anti-Semitism. He also failed to mention significant events prefiguring the Quiet Revolution, such as the 1948 *Refus global* of the artist Paul-Émile Borduas, which rejected the post-colonial status of Quebeckers under the thumb of priests "in soutanes who were the sole guardians of faith, knowledge, truth and national wealth"; and *Les insolences du frère Untel* — describing the tyranny of the Church, based on paternalism and moral slavery, as well as the intellectual paralysis of poorly educated, inarticulate and ever-fearful French Canadians. Black's motivation in writing about Duplessis was very different from Rumilly's. They both wanted him rehabilitated, but Black hoped the newly restored reputation could be a spring-board to rebuild the Union Nationale as an alternative to the rising nationalism of Quebec's main political parties — the Liberals under Robert Bourassa and the Parti Québécois under independence-minded René Lévesque.

Despite Rumilly's fascism and anti-Semitism, LaPierre, who met him several times in his later years, said he was "a great popular historian and made extensive use of provincial and local newspaper clippings conserved in seminaries. He made a record for the first time of our political and social life, and to a certain degree of our religious life. He told a good tale, he was a good raconteur."

Black said Duplessis "was this huge figure in Quebec and Canadian history, who was, in the years that I was familiar with, almost universally disparaged. And yet, he had been tremendously successful. Premier Daniel Johnson [senior], whom I knew and for whom I had great respect, spoke of Duplessis with tremendous reverence. And that was the first thing that gave me to understand that, possibly, this man had been short-changed historically. . . . And I thought it was a chapter that had not been addressed properly, so I was interested in looking into it."

In challenging the "heroic" account of the Quiet Revolution, Black sought to resurrect the reputation of Duplessis by showing that he had masterfully exercised power, laying the foundations for Quebec's modernization and industrialization. Some of the leadership qualities Black most admires — in politicians or ecclesiastics — include "cool-headedness, ingenuity in devising innovative ways of getting out of difficult situations, or making the most of difficult situations, courage, the ability to inspire others. . . . These are all characteristics of leadership, and I admire all of them."

"With all due respect, a great part of the so-called Quiet Revolution was secularized education with essentially the same people teaching the same curriculum to the same students in the same buildings. But they [nuns and priests] secularized themselves and cost the province a great deal more money. And then taxes went up, and the deficit started, and the whole thing changed. Therefore, I think that Duplessis is responsible for a great deal of the Quiet Revolution, and a good deal of the rest of the Quiet Revolution is essentially a fraud, and nothing to be very pleased with." (Black means that Duplessis was largely responsible for the positive achievements associated with the Quiet Revolution, and the part of the Quiet Revolution that he was not responsible for is not worth remembering.)

Black's relationship with Rumilly couldn't really last, since their motivations were quite different. Rumilly's true attitude to Duplessis is expressed in a letter the historian wrote on December 14, 1971, to the Vichy war criminal Jacques de Bernonville, then living in Rio de Janeiro: "My dear friend, I am happy to know that you are finally in a place you find agreeable. What you tell me about the 'ex-fatherland' [France] does not surprise me. Have you not been imprudent [Bernonville had risked arrest in France, by travelling there incognito to see his family]? As for your petition, I have put one of my judge friends, who is very respected, on the case with me. We have gone from one person to the next, without obtaining any result. I am working incredibly hard, it is like a virus, and I enjoy it. With a certain success besides, which is proved by the hatred of leftists. I am correcting the proofs of the third volume of my history of Montreal, there will also be a fourth and possibly a fifth volume, and I am also working on a monumental history of Maurice Duplessis and his time, with the help of the Duplessis papers, which the family, trusting nobody but me, has sent me. Things are going so badly that people are now beginning to say: 'there's a man just like Duplessis' — who now has the reputation of a quasi dictator 'such as we need.' Our separatists, much influenced by the revolutionary spirit, are chasing capital away. One

by one, discreetly, the big companies are transferring their headquarters to Toronto. We are still in good health. The surviving
group of your friends send their regards." An extract from the
letter was reproduced in a Rio newspaper after Bernonville was
murdered in 1972 and was entered as evidence in the inconclu-
sive trial that followed. Black would not have known about this
letter at the time it was written.

When Black left Quebec in 1974, he kept contact with Rumilly,
and sometimes shared his shrill views of the Quebec situation.
In a letter dated February 27, 1976, Black wrote: "I do not for a
moment want to give you the erroneous impression that I have
lost my personal affection for Quebec. Far from it. But one has
to be realistic. The last sixteen years of equivocation have been
terribly damaging for the Quebec both of us have known and
loved. Let's hope the next sixteen years will be more fruitful,
because if the current trend continues, Quebec will only know
the chaos, fanaticism, and build-up of nightmares you described
in your slim volume, *Quel monde.*"

Black's statement was astonishing, since *Quel monde*, published in 1965, is one of Rumilly's most hate-filled, racist pam-
phlets. "Civilization is the work of the white race and the other
races deploy their greatest efforts to imitate it," Rumilly's pam-
phlet reads. "Racism consists essentially in the rejection of inter-
breeding. This is [due to] the normal desire of a race to conserve
its original traits, its unique character. The awareness of race is
deeper and more powerful than national consciousness. Leave
two white men, belonging to enemy nations, among yellow or
black people, and you will see them immediately join in soli-
darity and brotherhood. There is naturally a hierarchy of races,
and it is normal that the white race should seek to perpetuate
itself. To acknowledge this does not in any way imply animosity
or contempt towards colored races."

Did Black flatter Rumilly about the *Quel monde* diatribe as
the price of maintaining continued access?

In June 1976, three months before his book was to be published, both of Black's parents, who had been in a long and
painful physical decline, died within ten days of each other. In

September of that year, Black sent a postcard to Rumilly from Paris: "Owing to the problems and even the anxiety caused by these events, I decided to leave Canada for a few weeks. My book will be out in three weeks. I hope all is well with you. I look forward to seeing you again, after this long separation — if I may use a word which I greatly regret. Best wishes, yours ever, Conrad Black."

But when the book was published, Rumilly disapproved of Black's portrayal of Duplessis and abruptly ended their relationship. The book was largely positive, but the ending was not so kind: "Maurice Duplessis was a paradoxical figure — gregarious and aloof, generous and cruel, all-forgiving and vindictive, a fanatical upholder of Parliament and the courts and the rule of law who did not hesitate to bend them to his own purposes. An avid devourer of bulky legal and theological tomes and political biographies, who would claim to some that he had never read a book, Duplessis remained a mystery even to his closest associates. . . . His mastery of procedure, pugnacity, quick-wittedness, and almost watertight memory made him tremendously effective."[79]

Listing Duplessis's negative traits was probably intolerable to Rumilly, who, after all, came directly out of the Maurassien tradition of right-wing propaganda and absolute, unquestioning obedience to a single, all-powerful leader.

Perhaps Rumilly was also upset that Black had dared describe the great leader's physical affliction — "hypospadias" — a malformation of the penis in which the orifice is located on the side of the shaft, rather than at the tip.

"I wouldn't call it a deformity," said Black. "That's a condition that affects a very substantial amount of men. I think as a percentage, it's not high, it's something like 1 per cent. But it wasn't a severe case of it, and all I said was that it might have had psychological implications, but if people were shocked by that, I must question their judgment. It was treated most delicately, right at the very end of the story, and all I said is that it might have psychological implications. And it was sort of in the interest of full disclosure."

Disappointed by Rumilly's reaction to his book, Black

scolded his old friend in a blistering letter dated December 17, 1976: "In the normal course of my career, I am used to disappointments, desertions and even defamation. But I would never have imagined that my old ally in the cause of justly recovering the reputation of Maurice Duplessis could be guilty of such an injustice towards me. In Montreal briefly this week, I vigorously defended myself against the accusation of certain journalists that I had whitewashed the career and personality of Duplessis. . . . I am conscious of having faithfully fulfilled my duty of presenting historical facts as they were, and in so doing, of having fought and even converted several people who had sullied the name of Duplessis. Your copy of the book . . . is too big to be mailed, so it will be delivered to you by T. Eaton Co. of which I am a director. I had expected to hand the book to you personally at the Canadian Club. You owe me an explanation. In the meantime, I still consider myself well disposed towards you, mindful as I am of the cause, which has united us for almost six years, right up to last week."

The split with Rumilly was no doubt painful for Black, but the filial relationship he had developed was circumstantial, even opportunistic, bound to expire once their respective interests diverged. Rumilly did not keep a copy of his reply to Black's sharp letter. But he did keep a final letter from Black, dated January 5, 1977: "I still consider myself 'an admirer and champion of Duplessis' as you [formerly] indicated. In reading my book, you will doubtless reach this same conclusion. It is disagreeable to be accused by you of showing hostility towards Duplessis, and to be accused by the adversaries of Duplessis of having whitewashed and practically beatified him."

By the early 1970s, Black had reasons to return frequently to Toronto — his parents were not well and many large corporations had moved their head offices to Toronto. Now Black was considering his own move. In the spring of 1971, he met "the legendary Lord Thomson of Fleet at a Canadian business function, and he gave me his 'rules of thumb' starting with his policy that all building alterations had to be approved personally by him and if it was proposed to make a publisher's office larger than the men's washroom, Roy fired the publisher."[80] In some respects, Black modelled his future career on that of Roy Thomson, the Ontario radio station owner who went on to control the *Scotsman* and *The Times* of London before diversifying into North Sea oil and the travel industry and gaining a seat in the House of Lords.

Finally, in 1974, Black made the decision to leave Quebec. He said *adieu* over the airwaves of a commercial radio station with an emotional, highly personal attack on everything he had come to dislike about Quebec.

"There was a sense of personal rejection when he slammed the door on Quebec," said Brian Stewart. "He had come from Toronto, gone to Laval, learned French, become an authority on Quebec politics, developed businesses. He felt 'no good deed goes unpunished.' And if that was the way it was in Quebec, he would never be accepted. He admired the old builders of Anglo Montreal, but felt the new leaders were going down the road of appeasement that would only feed the demands of separatists."

Black felt betrayed by the province that had offered him a new beginning, but after eight years, he had outgrown the role he had invented there for himself. Perhaps Quebeckers refused to read from the radically conservative script Black was writing for them — they didn't want to re-elect the corporatist Union Nationale, return in droves to mass in rural parishes and leave the *ancien régime* trimuvirate of French-speaking politicians, Catholic ecclesiastics and English-speaking business magnates to run things in the province.

From his new home in Toronto, Black continued to want to apply lessons of the past to solve the problems of the present. He had played the redeemer of fallen giants in the cases of LBJ and Duplessis. He wanted to be a kingmaker like Cardinal Léger. Now he was trying to be a backroom boy, a Machiavellian with a pragmatic understanding of power who could quietly pull the levers behind the scenes. He wanted to replace the new and threateningly subversive separatist nationalism of Quebec with the comforting old conservative nationalism. He tried to interest Pierre Desmarais II, a successful businessman and chairman of the Montreal Urban Community, in running for the leadership of the Union Nationale. Desmarais declined for family reasons, although he and Black later became business associates with Desmarais running UniMédia, Black's French-language newspaper chain.

In mid-1976, mourning the death of his parents and the end of his friendship with Rumilly, Black, now firmly rooted in Toronto, was closely watching the dramatic political changes in Quebec. The Parti Québécois was ahead in the opinion polls and was boasting that, once elected, it would hold a referendum on Quebec independence. Although Black was busy promoting the Union Nationale, his critics considered that a split in the problem federalist vote (between the Liberals and the Union Nationale) would be a serious mistake. "If we turn our backs on the Liberals," the business leader Charles Bronfman sputtered, "we are committing suicide. It would be worse than a disaster, it would be criminal — putting spears and daggers into our own backs. The election is the referendum [on separation] . . . the referendum on whether we live or die . . . because they [Parti Québécois] are bastards who are trying to kill us."

On November 15, 1976, the Parti Québécois, under René Lévesque, won a large majority in the provincial legislature — grandly rebaptized the Assemblée Nationale. A few months later, the historic and controversial Bill 101 was tabled and passed.

"I think it was a most significant event in Quebec history," Camille Laurin, architect of the bill, told me in 1990. "It was a natural thing to happen because, after all, in 1976, there was a French nation in Quebec — by the numbers, by the strengths of the culture, by the desire to maintain a linguistic and cultural identity." On the other side, he said, were considerable obstacles to the francophone dream, including "the omnipresence of English" as the language of science, technology and business. There were also the numbers. French-speaking Quebeckers were a small island in a sea of 250 million Americans and 20 million English-speaking Canadians.[81]

Also known as the Charter of the French Language, Bill 101's purpose was to protect and promote the French language in

Quebec by requiring all companies with fifty or more employees to function in French only; banning all languages other than French from all commercial and traffic signs; and decreeing that the children of the francophone majority and the children of immigrants could no longer attend English public or secondary schools (although some English instruction remained compulsory in the French school system).

"I think the Quebec government had a right to act," said Laurin. "It was a deeply thought-out law, and I think this may be the reason why it was so widely accepted by the French-speaking people of Quebec at the time, and this approval has [been] maintained ever since."

Although Black took the electoral results as a disaster, he was determined to rebuild the Union Nationale from his base in Toronto. It was a dream that soon died, never to be revived. His time with Duplessis was now officially over, but he at least had plenty of copies of his book available to impress his powerful friends. Henry Kissinger proudly displayed his signed copy to me in his office library on Park Avenue in New York. "Here is my friend Conrad's book on Duplessis," he said. He didn't say whether he'd read all 680 pages.

Putting Duplessis, his Quebec years and writing behind him, Black was soon fully occupied building a financial empire in Toronto. Writer Henry Aubin recalls a chance meeting with Black in Montreal in the mid-1970s: "We left the building together in a taxi. During that taxi ride, I asked him what he wanted to do with his life, since he obviously had so much potential."

"I want to make money," said Black. "I can do so much more with money . . ."

Black left the taxi in front of a bank building at the corner of Peel and Dorchester. He told Aubin he was meeting his lawyer, Brian Mulroney — who would become prime minister of Canada within a decade.

CP PHOTO

CHAPTER FIVE

MACHIAVELLIAN, BACKROOM BOY, KINGMAKER

ON THE NIGHT OF JULY 24, 1974, Conrad Black's sleek black Cadillac Eldorado sped through the darkness of Highway 401 as he crossed the great emotional divide between Quebec and Ontario and headed home to Toronto. He was now twenty-nine. His Quebec diet of chocolate milkshakes and bacon-and-egg sandwiches had left him noticeably stocky in his tight-fitting, three-piece pinstriped suits. He gripped the steering wheel with his big, stubby fingers, pondering the future. It was a long, monotonous drive.

So much had happened over the last eight years. His time in Quebec had been an interlude, a safe space in which the young Torontonian could prove himself, conquer his demons and insecurities and acquire professional and intellectual achievements, far from the watchful crowd back home. He had hoped to emerge from the gloomy shadow of his father, set things right for the Black family and become his own man.

But the achievements did not really satisfy him. Let others be dazzled by his law degree from Laval, conversational French, master's degree in history from McGill, growing chain of newspapers and impressive array of political contacts in Quebec and Ottawa. The scar on his forehead (from his car accident) and his fingers jabbing the air gave him an air of toughness. His social standing and growing fortune helped to create distance.

Black had developed new emotional needs over the last eight years, and these needs could be disturbing. Like the anxiety attacks. "Incidences of anxiety became steadily less frequent and less severe, and none occurred after a bout in 1973," he said. According to his Laval classmate Jonathan Birks, Black hated to fly and got terrible nosebleeds on long-haul flights (Black denies this). He couldn't be just himself — just Conrad. There was something voracious inside of him, a singleness of purpose, an appetite that could not be satiated, a void which that could not be filled. Peter White's label of "magnophile," was certainly appropriate because at the first sign of greatness in other people, Black began strategizing to transfer some of that greatness onto himself. He had begun to weave a self-aggrandizing personal narrative, in solitude, capturing symbols of grandeur and fusing himself to them. It was better for princes to be feared than loved, Machiavelli had written. And Black had every intention of being a leader — a feared leader if he could not be loved.

With so much on his mind, he rear-ended another car along the 401. Fortunately, not much damage was done.

It was in Quebec that Conrad Black developed the habit of latching on to older men, flattering and coaxing them to the point where they accepted to serve as mentors and share confidences with him. These relationships allowed him to enter the private universes of elderly men with rich historical memories. Their memories somehow became his own, as if the film of their life were projected onto a giant screen. He paced back and forth in front of their screen — he felt he had a special rendezvous with their historic destiny.

These relationships quickened Black's appetite for grandiosity. In this lonely, half-imagined interior world, Black relished the roles he created for himself. He was an omnivorous entrepreneur-intellectual. He was a romantic rebel who had never failed at anything. He had gone from being a generous, early 1960s liberal to an emotional conservative, a fighter boiling with rage, in cycles of frustration and aggression, thrusting his sword at the world. He was an eyewitness to historical greatness who knew the private vices behind the public virtues of leadership. He just knew, because he had studied the art of power. The end justified the means. Leaders were a cut above normal people. Leaders had rich, full-colour personalities and lived out a passionate life against the magnificent pageantry of wealth and power. Normal people were like two-dimensional cartoons, in varying shades of grey. They were awkward, unsophisticated and simply existed to be played one off the other.

Black's departure from Montreal followed the pattern of departures in his life. In a fiery outburst, he slammed the door on Montreal for refusing to be everything he had wanted it to be. But deep down, he knew that his economic interests were back in Toronto, which had replaced Montreal as Canada's business capital.

As Conrad Black and his brother Monte witnessed the declining years of their parents, they pondered how to maintain the family's position in Argus — soon to be in the throes of a struggle over succession. At the same time, Black was renewing contact with the old Toronto Establishment families — the Eatons, the Bassetts and the Westons. He was no longer the notorious boy who had been twice expelled from exclusive private schools, nor did he need the protective cocoon of the old boys' network. He was a force of nature, his piercing eyes darting right and left as he analyzed, assessed, sized people up. In contrast, his cigar-chomping, athletic brother Monte seemed jovial, fresh-faced and untroubled.

Black rediscovered selected, well-heeled friends from his youth, and sought out radical journalists such as Larry Zolf — men with well-defined, contrarian views who were fun to spar with from time to time. He needed the intellectual give-and-take — a break with the traditional image of Toronto's austere financial elite.

He was close to his parents, but he didn't want to be like some of the millionaires' sons he knew — poor little rich kids dependent on regular remittances, guilty about all that unearned wealth, hiding their futile lives behind a facade of extravagance. He had seen for himself many times evidence of the adage "shirtsleeves to shirtsleeves in three generations" where kids grew up to be a substantial drain on their family wealth — the middle generation not working for a living, creating nothing, spending everything and leaving nothing for the next generation.

Black developed his own work ethic. He was more interested in associating with powerful builders of wealth such as his father's former associate Bud McDougald, Canada's little-known mastermind of finance. There was something dark and muted in McDougald's face, as if this stooped, elderly man bore a mask. Black remembers McDougald as "a dapper, elegant, droll, cunning, feline man, almost completely uneducated, proud of his ignorance, an entertaining if languorous raconteur, and a childless teetotaler."[82]

Black was present at a Toronto meeting on May 30, 1969, when the Ravelston Corporation was formed as a holding company with a controlling interest in Argus. Two years later, he gained McDougald's support in a failed bid to take over the *Toronto Telegram*, which the proprietors — the Bassett family — decided to wind down instead.

McDougald was the leading shareholder of Argus Corporation, whose headquarters at 10 Toronto Street occupied a former branch of the Bank of Canada, built in 1852 as a post office. Argus acquired the neo-classical building with its stoic columns and polished brass door handles in 1959, redecorating it in the style of a nineteenth-century London merchant bank. On the walls inside were undistinguished eighteenth-century Dutch seascapes (this was before Black installed one of the huge pop art Andy Warhol portraits of himself). Velvet swag ropes led up the winding staircase to the executive suites. Marble floors, Georgian mouldings and a signed portrait of King George VI in a gleaming silver frame completed the decoration.

In the shadow of Toronto's glass, steel and concrete business towers, Argus managed its charmingly static portfolio of investments. In 1970, they included 13.4 per cent of BC Forest Products, 24.8 per cent of Dominion (a grocery chain), 16.9 per cent of Domtar (pulp and paper), 20.3 per cent of Hollinger Gold Mines, 15.7 per cent of farm equipment manufacturer

Massey Ferguson and 48.0 per cent of Standard Broadcasting. Apart from a disposal of its interest in BC Forest Products, these percentages had changed only marginally by 1976. Although these were all minority shareholdings, by the sheer force of his personality (and some strategic manipulation), Bud McDougald controlled the destinies of these companies, which in turn supplied a steady flow of dividends to the partners in Argus, including McDougald himself, George Black, E. P. Taylor, General Bruce Matthews, Colonel Maxwell Meighen and Alex Barron.

Peter C. Newman was likely the first journalist to interview McDougald, at Green Meadows, his magnificent estate in the Toronto suburb of Willowdale. "I remember visiting his house for the first time, and he showed me around his thirty-five-car garage. He even had a car made entirely of tulipwood, built for King Alphonso XIII of Spain. A lot of people think that I get interviews with these people very easily, but I don't ... I phoned him and I wrote to him and asked him for an interview, and he said he didn't speak to journalists. And that was that. It was true. There were no clippings of him ever having talked to a journalist even though he was a very important industrialist at the time. He controlled companies worth about $1 billion. So I had lunch with his friends. I found out who his friends were, and I told them I was writing a book on the Establishment. I wanted an interview with Bud McDougald, but he wouldn't talk to me. I said I was going to write the book anyway, and I was going to describe his $10-billion empire. Or sometimes I said a $100-billion empire, and they got very nervous of course. I knew that as soon as the lunch was over they'd be on the phone to McDougald saying that there was this crazy out there saying he was worth $100 billion and he had better do something about it.

"It worked. Eventually he saw me, and we had a real interview — quite a few of them actually. He had never talked to a journalist, so when I asked him a question he answered it rather than acting like a politician, who can talk all day about nothing. A favourite quote from McDougald, when I asked him about his education, was: 'Well, I left school at fourteen. I have

regretted it all my life.' I had an image of all the great facts that
he had missed, great books that he had missed, and he continued: 'Yes, I have regretted it all my life. I should have left at
twelve.'"[83]

McDougald loved to visit London, where he would travel
around in a Phantom VI Rolls-Royce, stay in a permanent suite
at Claridge's and call on the dukes and marquises of his circle of
friends. He boasted that the Turf, the exclusive club where he
took lunch, had sixteen dukes on its membership list. He raised
thoroughbred horses at private stables in the Cotswolds, rolling
hills on the way from London to Oxford. He had a hacienda at
640 South Ocean Boulevard in Palm Beach, the exclusive win-
tering ground of America's billionaire class, on a thin sliver of
land on Florida's Gold Coast. The mansion boasted eighteen
bathrooms and had previously belonged to the legendary
DuPont family. Bud loved belonging. He loved the seafront
cocktail parties with leading bankers and their glittering and
usually far younger wives; the gleaming white Mediterranean
luxury palaces with their tiled roofs on oversized lots; the private art collections and armies of liveried servants; the manicured gardens of cabbage palms, red hibiscus, coral honeysuckle
and dune sunflowers set around rippling turquoise swimming
pools.

"I grew up in a time when they didn't have capital gains tax,"
McDougald said in a 1970s interview. "They didn't have all this
terrific inflation. They didn't have all these other things — these
interferences. I grew up in a free world."[84] In the mid-1970s,
McDougald was worth $250 million — $988 million in 2007
dollars.

McDougald and his associates were leading members of the
Canadian Establishment. The public knew little of their business
interests but did know something of their lifestyle. They were
gentlemen in top hats and morning coats with wrinkled, chain-
smoking wives. They were chauffeured around in black Rolls-
Royces (lent on occasion to visiting royalty), and they escaped
Canadian winters to walk barefoot on the sand of their exclusive tropical paradises.

A lot of hidden value was locked up in Argus, which controlled assets of $4 billion. By the time Conrad Black returned to Toronto in 1974, several high-profile players hoped to seize control of the company, including Toronto's Hal Jackman and Montreal's Paul Desmarais. Jackman was a patrician, heir to the Empire Insurance Company and Algoma Central's railway network and fleet of Great Lakes bulk carriers.

"The future of Argus Corporation was a race between the natural erosion of the businesses and McDougald's undertaker," Black later wrote. "If the mortician preceded the liquidator, we would have a chance, possibly a great chance. . . [My] father was too out of touch and physically immobile to be either an operator or a stylish and dynamic market player. He didn't know the current crop of financial stars and the market and professional advice he was getting was not at the cutting edge of what was available."[85]

Black developed a filial relationship with McDougald, who considered him a potential successor. He listened to Bud's endless stories of empire-building, taking mental notes. He modelled himself as a businessman on McDougald far more than on his own father, and the childless Bud sometimes joked that Conrad was like a son to him.

McDougald was a Machiavellian who did things with flair. In a later interview with CBC television host Adrienne Clarkson, Black remembered that McDougald "tended to divide the world into friends and adversaries. He was a man of unshakable loyalty to his friends, but was capable of quite a high degree of unsentimentality toward adversaries. He had a profound conviction of the worthwhileness or correctness of those standards that he was endeavouring to maintain, which in large measure he embodied as an individual. That was part of his strength. He was a person of style, almost ostentatiously unashamed of his own success and of his own championship of his view of society, his idea of how to direct events."[86]

In 1975, McDougald and the Blacks worked together to fend off an attempted $150 million takeover of Argus by Desmarais, who had bought out the stock of one of the founding partners, E. P. Taylor, which won him a lot of preferred shares but very little voting stock. Desmarais was thwarted in his moves on

Argus. As Black later put it: "McDougald was a toady, a snob, a bigot, an elegant anachronism and an unlearned reactionary, but he was also tough, purposeful, and crafty and he was a good deal more adept at public controversy than Desmarais. . . ."[87]

On New Year's Day 1976, Black sent greetings from Hamilton, Bermuda, to Robert Rumilly: "I have spent two weeks in Bermuda with my family. We are sheltering here, from the disagreeable Canadian temperatures, which we have read about in the newspapers. I would like to wish you Happy New Year, and I expect to be back in Montreal soon. I will call you and I long to see you again. So, the year of the publication of my book [on Duplessis] has finally arrived. Best wishes to you and Madame Rumilly."

Michael Meighen, whom Black had once supported as a federal Progressive Conservative candidate in Quebec, was also vacationing in Bermuda with his family that Christmas. "They [the Blacks] were staying at the Hamilton Princess, while we were at the Coral Beach," he recalls. He noticed Betty Black was physically wasted, her skin yellowed from disease.[88]

Then in a letter from Toronto, on February 27, 1976, Black confided to Rumilly: "Both of my parents are gravely ill; my mother has pretty well generalized cancer, and my father is suffering from respiratory problems and arthritis. My mother will not be getting better, despite the indescribable courage she has shown in the face of this situation. My father is better, but his condition is nevertheless very delicate. This situation saddens us profoundly, but also imposes very heavy obligations on my brother and myself, to tidy up the estate and transmit shares etc. between ourselves so that the inheritance is wisely divided up. Particularly important in this regard is our strategic block of shares in Argus Corporation: 230,000 common shares and 561,000 [class C] preferred shares, the largest single block held in the company by a single person or family.

"My brother and I have acquired the majority — in fact, almost all — of the shares of Draper Dobie just as it reached a turning point on the stock market. As for our newspaper business, it is with a certain pride that I can tell you our net profit over the last six months of 1975 reached $679,884 which puts us in sixth place in this industry in Canada, behind Thomson, Southam, F.P., Toronto Star and Power Corporation, but ahead of Péladeau [Québecor].

"Which explains, Monsieur Rumilly, that I have been extremely busy and I wanted to wait for the time when I would best be able to respond in a manner worthy of your letters and of the particular attention which I give both to you personally and to our common cause. It is only the above-mentioned circumstances, which have kept me away from Quebec. The trip to Bermuda, for example, was nothing more than an attempt to stabilize the worsening health of my parents."

Conrad's mother, Betty, died on June 19, 1976. Conrad later wrote that his father "wasn't robust enough to go to the funeral, but went to within sight of the graveside, which he viewed through dark glasses from the back of his car like a Mafia gang lord, driven by his multi-purpose Catalonian houseman." Black recalled he was "extremely worried about his [father's] physical and psychological condition. The death of my mother had been a crushing, excruciating experience. All my father's tendencies to melancholia and loneliness could be expected to be accentuated, as well as his sense of helplessness at his immobility and poor eyesight." Within days, Conrad's brother Monte felt their father had lost the will to live. Although Black was suffering from a severe cold at the time, he called on his father to cheer him up. Father and son spoke a long time.

George Black expressed an exasperated sense of futility. "Life is hell," he said and exhorted his son to remember that "most people are bastards, and everything is bullshit."[89] From the garden room, Conrad watched his father move up the circular stairs in the front hall. "He had a formula he had developed over many years when he retired very late of declaiming Shelley's *Ozymandias*, matching lines to steps. I was thinking of this, though he didn't do it in daylight hours, but I had accompanied him as a steadying hand many times, when there came the unnerving crack of straining and breaking wood, followed by the descent of my father backwards through and over the bannister to the floor about ten feet below." "My father," Black recalled, "when he came round a bit, spoke of having lost his balance on the stairs and of having no desire to live."

Later, at Scarborough General Hospital, they "had a little conversation, one more effort to bridge the gap of years and pathos that separates a man from his son." After his father's death, "the coroner's report, obligatory where death was not from natural causes, spoke of 'an accident in the house,' which, it was suggested privately, might have been caused by an arthritic seizure in the knee causing him to fall through the bannister. Obviously I would prefer to take that explanation over a self-inflicted cause, but his life had drained away, almost as cruelly and over a longer but less precisely diagnosed time than my mother's. . . ."[90]

The final lines of Shelley's poem are poignant: "My name is Ozymandias, King of Kings/ Look on my works, ye Mighty, and despair!/Nothing beside remains. Round the decay/Of that colossal Wreck, boundless and bare/The lone and level sands stretch far away."

It was the sort of rhythmical, gloomy poem that a man might recite, trying to find his way home, trying to get in a last laugh at the vanity of the world. Conrad had gone to console a man who had simply lost the will to live, only to witness the final, bitter scene of his father's personal tragedy. Questions remain after many coroner's reports. Conrad Black's own account of his father's death opened the door to the possibility that his father's fatal injury could have been self-inflicted. With unusual candour, Black opened that door publicly . . . only to close it once again.

In *A Life in Progress*, Black wrote: "My father used to cite the French philosophical aphorism that life leads 'to suicide or the foot of the cross.' I believe the choice need not be so stark, but he and others of my acquaintance who avoided any serious intellectual effort to reconcile themselves to the unkind limitations imposed in the nature of life, paid a heavy price in mental strife."[91] George Black had been in a deep depression as his wife lay dying and had rejected his son's pleas to seek psychological counselling. Black may have concluded that a solid spiritual grounding would have mitigated his father's "mental strife" and allowed him to better cope with his wife's death.

According to Montreal billionaire Stephen Jarislowsky, chairman of one of Canada's largest investment counselling firms, Jarislowsky Fraser Limited, and a former Southam and *Telegraph* board member, Conrad Black has long suffered from manic depression but has managed to hide it well. "Ask David Radler," Jarislowsky told me, "he can tell you all about it."

The almost simultaneous death of his parents came as a cruel blow. Black remembered the family's voyage on the *Queen Elizabeth* when he and his brother were boys. That voyage was a well of happy memories, from the time when his father was still riding on the crest of the wave in the corporate world. Even the *Queen Elizabeth* was gone, gutted by fire in Hong Kong, in 1972. The hulk smouldered for an entire week, stood in as an improbable MI6 headquarters in the James Bond film *The Man with the Golden Gun* and was then scrapped.

Over time, the *Queen Elizabeth* voyage came to represent something innocent and vital that Black had lost, back before all the suffering and despair of later years — like the old wooden sled in *Citizen Kane*, which symbolized the lost innocence of the fictional tycoon's youth. Throughout the film, reporters are trying to figure out the meaning of *Rosebud* — the last word Kane said before dying. In the final scene, when the sled is consigned to the flames, the answers suddenly appear — the painted name Rosebud bubbles, blackens, then vanishes.

Everything was vanity. Black felt his father had been humiliated, manipulated, turfed out by the old guard, denied his rightful place in the Establishment. And he was determined to avenge these wrongs and set things right. He couldn't redeem his father — it was too late for that — but he could honour his father's memory and complete what his father would have begun.

The Black brothers organized a spectacular Establishment funeral at Toronto's Grace Anglican church, with Bud McDougald as chief pallbearer and a succession of other tycoons in assorted official roles. For family dynasties, funerals mark the transition of ownership to the next generation, and it was a given that the Black brothers would be named to the board of Argus, filling the vacancy left by their father. As the mournful Anglican priest droned on, Conrad Black remembered the bitter spectacle of his father's last years — a convivial man withdrawn into himself after being betrayed by others; a man whose sharp intellect had been blunted by suffering and melancholy.

It was about this time that Black discovered conservative German thinker Oswald Spengler's *Decline of the West*, a gloomy, weighty work running to a thousand pages in the English translation and published during the First World War. Black identified with Spengler's profoundly melancholy take on conservatism; the way he reached beyond chronology in search of larger patterns and analogies — a kind of truth that was more poetic than factual. He shared Spengler's narcissistic belief that the decline of civilization could be reversed when lonely historical figures willing their way to power came along and realized their destiny. It seemed a valid explanation of the courage Black had long admired in de Gaulle and Churchill.

Most pleasing to Black was Spengler's understanding of the warlike character of newspaper empires: "The press campaign appears as the prolongation — or the preparation — of *war by other means*, and in the course of the nineteenth century the strategy of outpost fights, feints, surprises, assaults, is developed to such a degree that a war may be lost ere the first shot is fired — because the Press has won it meantime. . . . What the Press wills, is true. Its commanders evoke, transform, inter-change truths. Three weeks of press work, and the truth is acknowledged by everybody."[92]

And Spengler acknowledged that a sharp mind can be just as effective as a military machine: "Politics and trade in developed form — the art of achieving material successes over an opponent by means of intellectual superiority — are both a replacement of war by other means."[93]

In addition to Spengler's apocalyptic pessimism, Black applied Darwinism in his approach to business. "You do have the Darwinian rule of the fittest do better and the less intelligent investors do worse," he said, "and in the end, smarter investors have a better sense of timing of when to buy and when to sell and a better sense of a quality investment, of where to put their money."

Black felt a need not just to triumph but to explain to a willing audience how he was triumphing. He took Spengler's melancholy and grandiose focus on great historical personalities, threw in Machiavellian strategy and added Darwin's belief that there was something inevitable in the triumph of the stronger over the weaker. But there was more. Joking in the late 1970s with Peter C. Newman, Conrad Black said, "Hal Jackman and I agree that we're basically more Nietzschean than Hegelian."[94] Nietzsche believed that superhumans of prodigious intelligence and willpower loomed above society — they were amoral because the normal rules of conduct did not apply to them. This hodgepodge of ideas justified doing whatever Black needed to do on his road to victory.

Shortly before Bud McDougald's death in March 1978, he suggested to Conrad and Monte Black that they should be vice-presidents of Argus in the future. But at McDougald's funeral at St. Michael's Catholic Cathedral in Toronto on the Ides of March, a palace coup was brewing among the older surviving partners at Argus, who were determined to edge the Black brothers out of any management role.

Also at the funeral was a film crew gathering material for a documentary to be presented by Patrick Watson and aired by the Canadian Broadcasting Corporation. As ashen figures marched solemnly beside the coffin, the music playing under the televised funeral sequence was vaguely reminiscent of *The Godfather*, combining a weeping cello with a harpsichord and tolling bells. There was a frozen shot of Black in the crowd, perhaps reflecting on the loss of the surrogate father that McDougald had been to him.

"Whatever purification and healing the Lord demands of Bud," intoned the soft-voiced celebrant, "may we, his brothers and sisters, call in confidence on Jesus our Lord to unbind him and let him go freely into the kingdom of Heaven."

"The death of Bud McDougald precipitated a power struggle at Argus," said Michael Gerard, director of the documentary. "Black had always been late for meetings. He was late for a key meeting at Argus [nine days after McDougald's funeral], and discovered all the key jobs at Argus had been divvied out."[95] In fact, Matthews, Meighen and their associate Alex Barron had decided to keep control of Argus for themselves. "That they wanted to take all the top jobs for themselves and make themselves chairmen of all the affiliated companies, with all the emoluments thereunto appertaining — that didn't rankle with us, as long as we got some recognition," Black told Watson.[96]

Gerard and his crew were privy to one of the most colourful and even comic transitions of power in the history of the Canadian business. "We just happened to be there when he was taking control of Argus," said Gerard. "We found that Establishment figures still had their virginity and tended to be quite unguarded and honest — they had no media training. The old guard of the company, Colonel Meighen and others, felt Black was young and was 'rushing defences.' Conrad was always haughty — that's his style — but probably less in those days. He was growing into the role of prince-tycoon. In those days, he was still carrying plastic shopping bags up to his office."

While studying his options, Black noticed that a little-known provision in the original Ravelston agreement allowed any three partners to buy out the fourth partner. Given that Bud McDougald's will allowed his widow, Maude Smith McDougald (nicknamed Jim), to dispose of his shares sixty days after his death, and that she and her sister Doris Smith Phillips, who had been widowed fourteen years earlier, had 47.3 per cent of the stock of Ravelston between them, Black realized all he had to do was to make the right offer and snatch up their shareholding, adding it to the 22 per cent owned by the Riley-Black family holding company, Western Dominion, then serve a Compulsory Transfer Notice on Colonel Meighen to acquire his 26.5 per cent. Black concedes today that "it is very hard to fight it out in the court of public opinion, when still recently bereaved septuagenarian widows" told their story.

Part of his strategy was to quietly secure control of Crown Trust, the firm that held the widows' portfolios, which might make it possible to take pre-emptive action in the event that the women changed their minds.

As Maude McDougald explained to Patrick Watson, "Exactly sixty days after the funeral, we came down [to Palm

Beach] and the next thing we knew, [Conrad Black's] lawyer, Lou Guolla, a very good lawyer [came to see us.] He said, 'I've got these things I would like you to sign, and it is what Bud would want and it is what I certainly advise that you do.' And I said, 'Well, Lou, you wouldn't say it unless you knew it was right.' And he turned back all the sheaf of papers and my sister and I, like absolute idiots, birdbrains, signed and signed without reading at all." To many television viewers, it seemed an archetypal story, a morality tale, with the ruthless young capitalist snookering the defenceless widows. The story of "Black versus the widows" has been added to the dark legend of Conrad Black. McDougald appeared distraught on screen, scattered, inarticulate, spoiled by a bevy of liveried servants responding to her every whim. One imagined her under the thumb of a domineering, manipulative husband, unable to make any decisions in her own right. Maude McDougald confessed to Watson, "It's our own stupidity, really. I don't think we can blame anyone but ourselves for being so stupid."

But many questions were left unanswered. Was a woman who had inherited the equivalent of hundreds of millions of dollars really defenceless? Weren't the sisters (one of whom was clearly in mourning, while the other was not) properly advised, and weren't they responsible for what they signed? Wouldn't they have sold to someone in any case? Was the price Conrad Black offered for their stock adequate? Ron Riley, who served on the board of Western Dominion and assisted Black in the negotiations to acquire the McDougald and Philipps stock, believes the price paid for their shareholding — $18 million ($56.1 million in 2007 dollars) — was a good one at the time.

Shortly afterwards, Maude McDougald and Doris Philipps changed their minds, renounced their agreement with Black, and threw their lot in with another investor, John Prusac. After three months of acrimonious corporate infighting, it seemed the widows had tried to snooker Black and had failed. . .with Michael Gerard's cameras rolling the whole time. "It gave complete control to Con Black and the others," Maude McDougald admitted, during a confused snippet of an interview ["instead of . . . we would have had control, my sister . . .

the voting shares. . ."] with Patrick Watson doing his best to prompt her to form complete sentences.

"According to her," Gerard remembers, "her lawyer, who was also Conrad's lawyer, handed her a whole sheaf of papers to sign, including one agreement that would give Black a larger pool of votes. She was unhappy about it. A couple of other people tried to help out, like General Matthews, the other was a real estate man [John Prusac]. She was helpless and flailing around: a straw in the wind anyone could bend. She said she didn't read what she was signing, but we can't say he snookered her. We were doing a story about people; we just said she felt the way she felt. We didn't try to judge her."

The television documentary had started out as a film about Argus, with Conrad Black playing a relatively obscure role. As they watched this early version of a TV reality show, millions of viewers wondered which board members would get voted off. In the end, after all the venerable old guard had been booted out, Black, the young pretender, was the improbable survivor — a tribute to his tenacity and boardroom strategizing.

Black was shown chairing board meetings, chortling at his own bons mots about Charles de Gaulle and re-enacting Napoleonic battles with Hal Jackman's collection of toy soldiers.

Michael Meighen, who is now a Canadian senator, recalls of Black: "Our paths crossed when he took over Argus Corporation, where my uncle Max had been a partner of Phillips and McDougald. Conrad became *persona non grata* in our family. It was felt he had taken advantage of the widows, that he had bamboozled them. Max felt Black had rushed his fences. My dad felt Black had not been terribly forthcoming with the widows." Despite the falling out, Michael Meighen and Black remained friends.

By July 1978, he Black had acquired control of Argus Corporation, kicked his erstwhile opponents upstairs (or, more accurately, out into Toronto Street), and laid the foundation for his corporate empire. On learning Black had won out over the widows, Hal Jackman told him he was "the young Bolingbroke who in the first act of *Richard II* arrived with 20,000 soldiers to repossess his father's estates, and in the last act is crowned King of England. Congratulations. This has been high drama."[97]

In the summer of 1978, Conrad Black, now securely installed as president of Argus — with brother Monte president of Ravelston, and Nelson Davis and Hal Jackman each with 16 per cent of Ravelston stock and Ron Riley with a further 10 per cent — dramatically increased his personal wealth and became a commanding presence in Canada's business capital.

Seizing control of Argus gave Conrad tremendous financial power. He was now said to be worth $50 million — $156 million in 2007 dollars. He lived in his parents' Georgian home in the Bridle Path district, with its garage fit for seven cars, including two Rolls-Royces. He was now a thirty-three-year-old celebrity, and he played to the gallery. "Nowadays, Black takes a certain malicious pleasure in picturing himself as an old-style, rapacious, Hearstian tycoon," noted a reporter for the *Toronto Star*. He was described as Canada's most eligible bachelor, one of the world's richest men (surely a gross exaggeration), a brainy, feisty media tycoon with a photographic memory, the contrarian biographer of Maurice Duplessis. "I'm not interested in any electoral position except that of prime minister," Black said. "I'm a rich man and I'm not ashamed of being wealthy. Why should I be? I made all my money fairly."

"The thing about Conrad," said his Montreal drinking partner Nick Auf der Maur at the time, "is that he could have been a coddled, pampered, coupon-clipping kid cracking up cars everywhere. But he's different. He was more disciplined."[98]

Beyond the public bluster, Black had routed the old guard at Argus and had avenged his father. But he was still not satisfied.

In the months leading up to the Argus takeover, Conrad Black had been carrying on an affair with Shirley Gail Walters, corporate secretary of Western Dominion and a close colleague. Shirley was a charming twenty-seven-year-old Catholic divorcee from Montreal, tall and slim, with short brown hair and blue eyes. She was more down-to-earth than Black. She grew up in a modest clapboard-and-brick duplex in St. Laurent, a lower-middle-class district. She graduated from Malcolm Campbell

High School, where she took extra courses in business administration. She worked for a stock brokerage in Montreal, transferring to the firm's Toronto offices at the age of twenty-one. Shirley was not an heiress or a horsy Establishment figure. She was a homemaker — grounded in reality — who proved a positive counterbalance to the sometimes excessive Black.

Black said their first date was in May 1978: he listened on the car radio that evening to a speech given by Quebec premier René Lévesque to the New York Council on Foreign Relations. Shirley was simple, unsophisticated, full of fun, with no interest whatever in high society. With a baby on the way, they were married in Grace Church on July 14, a few weeks after the Argus *coup d'état*.

"The day before his wedding, Conrad Black was elected president of Argus," one reporter noted. "Walters wore a skirt of off-white silk crepe, which fell below the knee, and a round-necked long-sleeved top of the same material," wrote another. "The first part of the reception was held on the patio of Black's mansion, overlooking lush manicured lawns and a swimming pool. There were hors d'oeuvres of steak tartare, shrimp, paté and lobster, with champagne to go along with it." Dinner was catered by the deluxe Winston's restaurant of Toronto and consisted of lamb chops, salad and vegetables, with the ritual wedding cake afterwards.[99]

The wedding reception was not a society event. Few people were aware that Shirley was expecting. In August, the newlywed couple spent their honeymoon in Nantucket. That winter, for the first time, they fled the snows of Ontario for Palm Beach.

Over the years, Black had had many romantic interests — from Caroline Dale Harris to Lynn Sifton, Wilda Lossing and Monique Benoit. During his world travels, he discovered that the women of Hong Kong, Buenos Aires and Budapest were strikingly attractive. And if this unusual comparison was worth mentioning by him, there must have been some first-hand research behind it. These various relationships and dalliances were of many sorts: infatuation; unrequited love; going out with the "right sort of person" in Toronto; rebelling and hanging out with Montreal Bohemians instead; enjoying some sport abroad;

and maintaining intellectual companionship once the bloom of mutual attraction had faded.

All the while, Black seemed a serial monogamist, destined ultimately for marriage. He had in mind the example of his parents, who were so close they ended up dying within two weeks of each other. As a young tycoon taking Toronto by storm, Black could command a good deal of female attention — buxom gold-diggers dressed to kill; political groupies; Establishment women willing to forgive his sometimes checkered past now that he had "made good"; and tantalizing decorative snobs prepared to insert themselves into a tycoon's life if only they could spend some of the man's money. It had all become so easy — too easy.

He had picked up experience and self-assurance along the way and could see the difference between a "squeeze" and a more serious woman. Shirley attracted him. And more than that, he felt she suited him. Yet Black was awkward in describing his relationship with Shirley to others. He once told a friend "there was a certain parallel between my romantic career and Duplessis's. There were a good number of one-night stands and a few liaisons that had a certain quality of seriousness to them, but until Shirley, none with matrimonial intent."[100]

In fact, there was *no* parallel between Black's romantic career and that of the late Quebec premier. Duplessis was a loner; he had suffered from a malformed penis that likely prevented him from having sexual relations; and besides, he had never shown any taste for marriage, while maintaining an official rather shallow religiosity.

Conrad and Shirley Black would have three children — Jonathan, born in 1979, Alana, born in 1982 and James, born in 1986. In 2007, these three faithfully attended Black's criminal trial in Chicago — making an appearance almost every day.

On August 24, 1978, the Canadian Press announced, "Three partners invest $20,000 then sell out for $20 million." It was understandable Black did not take his young bride on a real honeymoon, because he, David Radler and Peter White were just completing the sale of their chain of newspapers to Maclean-Hunter. Radler proudly told the CP reporter that "the

Sherbrooke Daily *Record* was losing money at the rate of $100,000 a year when we bought it in June 1969. In four months we made a profit and never looked back. And we never put another cent into it. All the purchases in the West were bank loans and the vendor taking paper (promissory notes)."

Black's marriage nudged him closer to Catholicism. Gerald Emmett Cardinal Carter, the archbishop of Toronto, met Conrad Black in 1978 and they were soon good friends. Unlike the unpredictable Léger, who was ambivalent about wealth, Carter was worldly, political and very comfortable in the company of the rich and famous. He enjoyed networking and officiating at extravagant celebrity weddings in Toronto (delegating to his priests the less glamorous task of marriage and annulment counselling afterwards). Carter was also a strong defender of the right to a Catholic education in Ontario and devoted considerable time and energy to improving race relations.

"Despite the differences in our ages, professions, and background, or possibly in part because of them," Black wrote in 1993, "our relations are intimate and without rancour. His culture, from Irish folkways to Thomist theology, is inexhaustible; his humour vivacious but gentle. He is one of the very few people I have ever known who successfully combines worldliness with idealistic sincerity. He is always confident but never arrogant, serene in the face of his declining years and life's approaching end."[101]

Black's filial relationship with Carter provided the convert-to-be with inside knowledge of Vatican politics at the high point of the Cold War.

A charismatic, intense, highly intellectual Pole, Karol Wojtyla had stood up to Soviet Communism while serving as archbishop of Kraków. In 1978, as the first non-Italian in four centuries to occupy the Holy See, he became one of the pillars of resistance to the Soviet Union, mobilizing millions of Polish Catholics in their peaceful and ultimately successful opposition to Moscow.

In his private chapel in Castel Gandolfo, the papal summer residence originally built by the Roman emperor Domitian,

Pope John Paul II would kneel at his prie-dieu. There was, in his person, something of the historical grandeur and dignity that Black had long admired. Above the altar was an icon of the Black Madonna of Czestochowa, and John Paul would glance up at the painting several times while praying. The windows looked out on the Lago di Albano, where pink dawn was breaking. On either side of the altar were vases in the shape of cut-off grey granite columns, and the floor had huge squares of red-and-white marble. The altar itself was marble and featured inlaid marble blocks in the shape of chalices. The Pope was dressed all in white, his head cupped in his hands. He seemed wholly turned to God. He also seemed to be suffering, as if the entire weight of the world and the Church's own imperfections pounded down on his shoulders.

John Paul II had exactly the spiritual qualities that Black admired — a faith that could move mountains, a single-mindedness of purpose and a masterful sense of *realpolitik*. Josef Stalin had once mocked the Vatican, wondering aloud how many divisions the Pope had. The Slavic Pope proved that the Vatican had far more than divisions. Black was fascinated by the charisma and courage of John Paul II, who could draw together Eastern European crowds in the millions, leading them in spasms of song and prayer. The Pope also scolded the West for its materialism and loose sexual mores. He was a vital new force for conservatism.

Machiavelli had dedicated his most famous work, *The Prince*, to Lorenzo de' Medici, the nephew of two popes. He was torn between disdain and admiration for the Church. The book had revolutionized strategic thinking, the Vatican adapting Machiavelli to its own purposes. The Vatican was arguably the world's most powerful corporation. Its financial arm, APSA (the Administration of the Patrimony of the Holy See), held significant investments in many industrial corporations, including IBM, General Motors, General Electric and other multinationals fully integrated into the military-industrial complex. These corporations supply and produce computer hardware and software for the Pentagon, nuclear missiles, spy satellites and a wide variety of modern weapons. Most Catholics were unaware of the scope of the Vatican's investments; Black found the behind-the-scenes perspective of Cardinal Carter compelling.

Black proclaimed the rebirth of the right during an address to the spring convocation of McMaster University in June 1979. In a bombastic speech peppered with historical references, he declared his sense of revulsion over the "unrest and the rise of the counterculture, manifested in protests against the Vietnam War, a resurgence of socialism among students and attacks on the Establishment." Capitalism had led compulsive and garish consumerism, raised material expectations, created economic inequalities and provoked political agitation. "But that has changed with the emergence of a renascent intellectual right . . . producing the re-emphasis of the proprietor in Canadian business."[102]

It was time to turn the clock back: government should be downsized, individual liberty maximized. Let market forces work out who the winners and losers were. Black had taken his bad-boy image to a new level, and had now found a soapbox to trumpet his neo-conservative view of the proprietor, who invested capital, took risks and was entitled to the spoils, in the style of late-nineteenth-century and early-twentieth-century tycoons from Baron Strathcona to William Randolph Hearst. He was taking the cunning business practices of Bud McDougald and the old guard at Argus, combining them with his meticulous study of Duplessis, and shaping a private ideology that was radical, conservative and self-serving.

The pattern of Conrad's personality had been set long before. He had been a turbulent child, according to his own cousins and early friends; he had experienced more than the usual growing pains, such as expulsion from two private schools; and then he had tried during the Quebec years to maintain his many interests simultaneously, from history to law to newspapers to business to flirting with the French-speaking beauties of Montreal.

We become what we are. Aspects of Conrad's later personality were clearly visible in his younger years — that sense of being far older mentally and emotionally than his chronological age; of seeking to redeem fallen giants such as his father; of taking an acid, inquisitorial look at the world's failings and making sweeping judgments; of compulsively trying to find links between world historical personalities from Napoleon to Franklin Roosevelt and himself; of playing with words, even to the extent of dropping broad hints that he was a Nietzschean superhuman, the fittest to survive along Darwinian lines, a Machiavellian master of the craft of power or a grandiloquent Catholic in a position to philosophize about our age. There was also the other side to his personality — the sombre moon stealing its silent way across the sun — the self-destructive urge to humiliate, make it personal, take vengeance, that sometimes rubbed out his more substantial accomplishments.

Ever since childhood, Black had been acutely aware of the importance of belonging — of networking. His mother's family, the Rileys, were a handsome, self-confident, athletic and competitive group — an industrial tribe with their own coded language and social conventions. "Con," as his family called him, eventually expelled from two exclusive private schools, simply didn't fit in. One would be hard-pressed to imagine him turning up at class reunions and, over drinks, fondly remembering sadistic masters and bratty classmates while listening to old boys' ringing appeals for donations. He was more interested in networking in the wider world than he was in the old school tie. Jean Lafferty Riley, wife of his double first cousin Jeremy, remembers that Black did not share the "parochial" mindset of many Torontonians at the time. When he made the move to Quebec, Black was fascinated to discover richly layered networks that he could join on his own terms. And it was there that foundations for his own network were laid when he developed lasting friendships and associations with Peter White, Daniel Colson and David Radler. Black was very much the leader, developing the vision, the ideas, the connections, while the others helped execute his plans and awaited his next inspiration.

During his Quebec years, Black overcame his native shyness, becoming at times an extrovert who craved social stimulation, a man whose memory, skill at wordplay and taste for extravagance and provocation could make him the centre of attention. Behind the social veneer, however, Black seemed to long for the approval of accomplished men who commanded networks of their own, whether commercial, political or ecclesiastical. Black was not shy about approaching these older paternal figures and engaging them in sophisticated conversation about their own views, possibly as a way of jump-starting his entry into their world. Some of these men — Bud McDougald, Robert Rumilly, Cardinal Léger, Hal Jackman, Cardinal Carter, Henry Kissinger — became, for a time, mentors to Black, no doubt attracted by his brash intelligence and his flair for taking other people's ideas and recasting them in his own exuberant language.

During the late 1970s, after he took control of Argus Corp., Black built up an impressive network in Toronto. His 1993 autobiographical account of these years contains a dizzying number of names of prominent people, from Fiat chairman Gianni Agnelli to U.S. banker David Rockefeller. After a few false starts, Black was poised to take up his rightful position in the Canadian Establishment. In the years that followed, he named an extraordinary number of accomplished non-financial people to the boards of the companies he controlled, including retired cabinet ministers, generals, judges, cardinals, ambassadors and at least one former spymaster. Black surrounded himself with men who wielded power and who could offer him business intelligence and historical insight. Stephen Jarislowsky and Hal Jackman, who were close to Black during the 1970s and 1980s and served on several Argus and Hollinger boards, now criticize Black for the high-profile appointments.

Peter C. Newman explained the importance of networking in Black's life: "Conrad Black's ascendancy within the Canadian Establishment can be explained partly because he is so acutely aware of what is happening in the country and world at large. He avidly studies the forces that bestow and rob institutions of their authority. This is in marked contrast to the practices of Canada's Establishment, many of whom are out of touch with prevailing realities. . . . Having examined and documented the manipulative techniques of the late Maurice Duplessis, Black understands power and how it can be protected. . . . He is close to the powers that be in Washington, where he is on intimate terms with *two* former directors of the Central Intelligence Agency and with Thomas O. Enders, former ambassador to Canada and currently Assistant Secretary of State for Inter-American Affairs. He knew the late David Bruce, ambassador *extraordinaire*. He is friendly with Henry Kissinger, Malcolm Muggeridge, Andrew Knight (editor of the *Economist*), Marietta Tree (who's been called the salonkeeper of the liberal wing of the Democrats), and Leopold Rothschild, and claims Sir Sigmund Warburg as his most influential financial mentor. At home [in Canada], such Ottawa luminaries as Michael Pitfield, Clerk of the Privy Council, and Energy Minister Marc Lalonde are in regular contact with him, even at his winter retreat in Palm Beach."[103]

As a winter resident of Palm Beach, with a \$35.5-million home on Ocean Boulevard, Black spent a fortune trying to keep up with Donald Trump (whose mansion was worth \$125 million) and pop star Rod Stewart as well as the Fords, the Pitts and other old-money families. The billionaires' enclave, with its charming tile-roofed haciendas, turquoise swimming pools and eucalyptus gardens, has been described as "America's richest sandbox . . . the last place in America where celebrity per se doesn't count . . . It's about money, money and more money."[105] One of the hallmarks of Palm Beach is conspicuous consumption. Money is raked into huge piles and burnt, like autumn leaves. "I feel like a court painter living in Versailles," said Tania Vartan, a *trompe l'oeil* artist who hand-painted the dining-room wallpaper in Black's oceanfront mansion. "People love to decorate down here. One house is more beautiful than the other. It's an enchanted world, a microcosm of highly civilized people who are only interested in being surrounded by beautiful objects and a beautiful environment. They already have the money. These are the spenders. These are the Medicis. Yes, it can be stifling. You have to have a strong sense of humor. And irony."[106]

In an article entitled "The Eminence of Excess," readers of the *New York Times Magazine* got a behind-the-scenes look at jet-set architect Thierry Despont, who had built lavish homes in Washington State for Bill Gates, in Toronto for Conrad Black, and in Palm Beach for apparel billionaire Sidney Kimmel, whose long driveway consists of five hundred thousand hand-set pebbles leading up to "an immense limestone palace."[107]

That was the essence of Black's networking — studying the nature of power, using his corporate position to gain access to privileged information and advice, and entertaining in his mansions in London and Palm Beach — where he developed a loose network of international jet-setters. Other networks came out of the Bilderberg conferences and contacts with Catholic intellectuals, Canadian Conservative politicians, British Conservative politicians, and U.S. Republicans and neo-conservatives.

Thanks to the best-selling reportage by Peter C. Newman, Canadians were beginning to realize a secretive class of millionaires and billionaires exerted considerable influence over the county's politics and financial life. The public wanted to know more about this ruling class that had always been there but was largely invisible.

In the meantime, Conrad Black was evaluating the sorry state of Argus Corp.'s holdings. His approach was to serve the interests of Argus first and those companies Argus had invested in second. The two interests were not always compatible. Massey-Ferguson was the pride of Canadian industry, a storied company that had exported farm machinery all over the world and produced aircraft parts during the Second World War. But in the year ending October 31, 1978, it recorded the largest loss in Canadian corporate history — $257 million—laying off one-third of its worldwide workforce and writing down $600 million in assets (due to the sale of unprofitable operations). The problems at Massey were extremely complicated. Over the years, the controlling partners of Argus had not taken much interest in the challenges facing the company. A combination of rising interest rates, poor weather conditions and disastrous agricultural yields meant that Massey's global clients — farmers — were in no position to buy new equipment. Black had gained a good deal of notoriety by taking over Argus at such a young age. But "his ideas of what could be accomplished were rooted in his own experience of small business," wrote Peter Cook, a journalist who became the editor of Black's columns at *Report on Business* magazine in 1985.[108]

Once Black took on the role of chairman of Massey, he enjoyed speaking to journalists about his new ideas and strategies. But his public pronouncements were more philosophical than financial and did little to reassure investors.

The moves led to a small operating profit in late 1979. But then, in early 1980, the company suffered a catastrophic reversal of fortune. Grain markets crashed; oil prices surged; the dollar fell on foreign exchange markets; inflation shot upward and interest rates began their inexorable climb. Massey's short-term debt had become unmanageable. The company faced the real possibility of going bankrupt. Things had reached the point where Massey needed an injection of equity in order to survive — but that equity would have to be guaranteed by the federal government. This raised a difficult issue for Black. How could he hold his hand out to the federal government on behalf of one of Canada's most famous multinationals when he had gone on the record so frequently expressing his disdain for the interventionist state of Pierre Trudeau?

The following year, Black suddenly transferred the Argus block of shares in Massey (worth $30 million — or $70 million in 2007 dollars) to Massey's pension funds, making it easier for the struggling company to receive government assistance. But it also meant Argus was abandoning the money-losing company.

"For a self-appointed spokesman for free enterprise like Black to withdraw from Massey was to admit that something very fundamental had gone wrong," wrote Peter Cook. "He was, after all, declaring that a great Canadian company — with 133 years of history behind it — would be better served by putting itself in the hands of governments and banks than by enjoying the continued participation of its largest private shareholders. Tactically, he may have acted in the best interests of himself and his friends who ran the re-named 'Hollinger Argus.' But the precedent of admitting defeat and leaving the problems to be solved by others, was hardly a helpful one."[109]

Black's move was harshly condemned in the Canadian financial press. But Argus had a minority interest in Massey, and Black could not be held responsible for the disastrous erosion of

Massey's business. Despite its impressive $3 billion of annual sales, the company had been mismanaged for years, and Black's predecessors at Argus had shown no particular interest in the company. Black was not the right person to negotiate government assistance in any case.

The way Black had treated the widows in his takeover of Argus had set tongues wagging. Now he was dismantling Argus, dumping a company that was as important to Canadians as General Motors was to Americans. Whatever ideological justifications he might offer for his actions, he struck many people as a self-involved corporate manipulator, someone answerable only to himself, who had few if any responsibilities toward his employees.

After the transfer of the Argus shares to the Massey pension fund, Black became increasingly interested in a Calgary-based oil and gas company called Norcen Energy Resources, using it as a vehicle to look for investment opportunities in the United States.

He enjoyed the oceanfront palazzos of Palm Beach, the social pecking order, the gossip, the extravagantly beautiful women in their Ray-Bans and skimpy bikinis. It was in Palm Beach that Black found a fabled setting to develop American political contacts. That is where he first met Ronald Reagan, who gave a speech to a staunchly Republican, ultra-rich audience. After the speech "a mighty procession of Palm Beach's most ostentatious automobiles awaited at the front of the Breakers Hotel," Black wrote. "As far as the eye could see were Mercedes Benz 600s and 900s, Rolls-Royce Phantoms, Silver Clouds, Corniches, Shadows, and Spurs, many elongated or transformed from saloons to dropheads in proof of their owners' ingenuity at devising methods of spending an additional $100,000 on a $200,000 automobile."[104]

Black considered Reagan a man who "had the intuition of what the people wanted, and the mastery of the technique of moving public opinion towards him. After Vietnam, Watergate, and the inanities of the Carter era, the presidency had to be restored to a position of natural leadership, and the United

States, which had suffered the most precipitate decline of influence of any great power since the fall of France, was to be restored to its rightful place of world leadership."[110] It was the beginning of a long friendship.

Black also got to know Henry Kissinger, who shared his passion for history and sympathy for Richard M. Nixon. For many people, Nixon was Tricky Dick, a ghoulish and paranoid dissembler who deliberately broke the law. (In the leadup to the 1972 presidential election, the Committee to Reelect the President worked hard to keep Nixon in power. As things turned out, the committee's acronym — CREEP — was an ironic choice, given the committee's role in the Watergate scandal.) But Black had always believed Nixon had hidden virtues that could have redeemed him if only they had been more visible. Kissinger, who had been Nixon's and Ford's secretary of state and national security advisor, said he often shared with Black his insider knowledge of world affairs. Black, who later cultivated Nixon's friendship, wrote of the former president as "a figure of transcendent durability, startlingly intelligent, surpassingly skilful in his analysis of international affairs and domestic politics, 'his soul serene, all passion spent,' and especially a considerate, courteous, unselfconscious, humorous, even pleasant, or at least generous man."[111] In March 2007, Black published *The Invincible Quest*, a biography of Richard Nixon.

Although notoriously thin-skinned, Kissinger was ruthless. A short, grasping man with curly hair, he had fled Nazi Germany in 1938 on account of his Jewish ancestry. He never managed to throw off his German accent. While attending night school in New York, he worked in a shaving-brush factory by day. He helped the U.S. Army round up former Gestapo agents in Germany after the war. He wrote a brilliant doctoral thesis at Harvard, expressing his admiration for Prince Metternich, the early-nineteenth-century Austrian master of *realpolitik*, although the thesis had obviously been touched up by an editor with a far better command of English than the author. Henry Kissinger aspired to play the same role in the twentieth century. He made up for his diminutive stature through intellectual power and sheer brutality. During the 1960s, he made a name for himself as a Cold War strategist and adviser to Nelson Rockefeller. He was an unlikely match for red-headed girlfriend Jill St. John, a beautiful Bond girl with a 36-22-35 figure and an IQ of 162. She played a ditz in *Diamonds Are Forever*. Kissinger is reputed to have told her, "You don't think power is the ultimate aphrodisiac? Wait till you see me nekkid." Kissinger was a master manipulator, a man who organized South American *coups d'état* as willingly as he pushed détente with China and the Soviet Union and sent B-52s over Cambodia. He had left a long trail of corpses behind him.

Kissinger's 1957 work, *A World Restored*, a historical study of Metternich's diplomacy from 1812 to 1822, was one of the most compelling examinations of political manipulation and networking. He recognized Metternich's ability to combine psychological insight, conservatism and tact to dominate every negotiation in which he participated "through an almost uncanny faculty of achieving a personal dominance over his adversaries and the art of defining a moral framework which made concessions appear, not as surrenders, but as sacrifices to a common cause." Moreover, Kissinger wrote, "so agile was Metternich's performance, that it was forgotten that its basis was diplomatic skill and that it left the fundamental problems unsolved, that it was manipulation and not creation."[112]

In *A World Restored*, Kissinger quotes Metternich comparing himself to spiders at the centre of their webs, which are "beautiful to behold, artfully spun and capable of resisting the light attack of a breeze, but not a gust of wind." Kissinger said this "ironically whimsical aphorism reflects the essence of the 'Metternich system'; the policy of enmeshing the opponent by his own moves, of frustrating him with invisible bonds, and dependent on the myth that the 'rules of the game' prevented the adversary from sweeping the web away in a moment of impatience. By these tactics Metternich had achieved extraordinary successes."[113] But a gust of wind could blow the web away.

"Well, the night before he left office," Kissinger told me in his Park Avenue office, "I was meeting with Nixon. And I said to him, 'History will treat you more kindly than our contemporaries did.' And he said, 'That depends on who writes history.'

And there's a lot in that. I am beyond the point in my life, where I can affect the judgment in history. . . . It depends so much on the circumstances of the time. I've tried to leave as accurate a record based on as many basic documents as I could, to permit people to judge it. But, you know, I've left a record of all my negotiations, of all my staff meetings. You can't fake those. You can't retroactively make them look better or worse."

Black wanted to be at the centre of the web, just like Metternich, Duplessis, or McDougald before him. His conversations with Kissinger offered an escape from Canada's English and French parochialism and access to an eyewitness and participant in world events. What Kissinger said mattered. Black was thrilled with his prestigious American connections.

But as his business interests expanded in the United States, he soon discovered ominous realities — hardball litigation and strict regulatory enforcement. The first investment Black sought through Norcen in the United States was with the Hanna Mining Company of Ohio, which controlled the Iron Ore Company of Canada and operated a joint venture with Hollinger Mines in Labrador. The president of Iron Ore was Black's friend Brian Mulroney, who aspired to be Progressive Conservative leader and prime minister of Canada.

In August 1981, Black informed Hanna's vice-president of sales, George Humphrey, that Norcen would soon be buying shares in Hanna. According to the minutes of a Norcen board meeting in September, which Black signed, "U.S. Acquisition: [Norcen president] Mr. Battle stated that the Company, subsequent to telephone contact with the members of the executive committee, had initiated through stock market transactions the acquisition of 4.9 per cent stock interest in a U.S. company listed on the New York stock exchange with the ultimate purpose of acquiring a fifty-one per cent position at a later date."

Under U.S. securities law, a public company planning to make a significant purchase of stock in another public company had to make its intentions known, by filing a Schedule 13-D with the SEC. In November, Norcen's 13-D Schedule stated that its objective "was to acquire an investment position in Hanna. Norcen intends to review its investment position from time to time. Depending on such review, market and business conditions and other factors, Norcen may seek to acquire further shares of Common Stock or may sell shares of Common Stock."

After increasingly unpleasant negotiations between Black and Hanna executives, Norcen made a public offer for control of Hanna in April 1982 at almost twice the going price of its stock. Shortly after the offer was announced, Hanna filed a suit in Ohio against Norcen, Conrad Black, his brother, Montegu, and others for fraud and racketeering, on the grounds that they had not accurately announced their intentions when they filed the 13-D Schedule with the SEC. Hanna did not want to be subject to a larger takeover bid from Black, and had been pressing him for some time to sell off the shares he held. Hanna was also behind a ten-month police investigation into Black and Norcen in Ontario. The investigation went nowhere. Journalists Ian Austen and Linda McQuaig wrote a two-part exposé in *Maclean's* magazine asking whether Black had intervened with authorities to put a stop to the investigation.

"Our story involved looking into all of that case and the question as to whether Black had intervened with political authorities in Ontario," said McQuaig. "The Ontario Securities Commission and the Toronto police investigated with the view to possibly laying criminal charges. We were looking at how Black had contacted Roy McMurtry, then Attorney General of Ontario. We spent months working on it."[114]

McQuaig and Austen wrote in *Maclean's*: "The attorney general is adamant that the Black case was handled like any other. 'What has concerned me,' [Roy McMurtry] said, 'is the suggestion . . . that Conrad Black, because of his prominence, would be able to influence the course of any police investigation. The hint that that could take place I find quite offensive, because the integrity of the criminal justice process to me has to be a number one priority.'"[115] During court testimony in Ohio, it was apparent that Hanna executives had at first believed Black's assurances he had only acquired the stock for investment purposes. But as Hanna and Norcen executives staked out increasingly trenchant positions, Black testified, "we were somewhat flabbergasted at the militancy of [Hanna President] Mr. [R. F.]

Anderson's request that we not buy any more shares." When the Norcen minutes were entered as evidence of its secret intention to make a bid for control of Hanna, Black's defence was that there had never been any intention to make a bid for control prior to the day the bid was made. But U.S. district judge John Manos concluded Norcen's "construction of the record is strained and unpersuasive." He said the evidence established conclusively that Norcen contemplated a takeover of Hanna as early as November 1981, "if not earlier." Hanna was granted an injunction restraining Norcen from further stock purchases; and the SEC charged that the company and Black had violated anti-fraud provisions with "fraudulent, deceptive and manipulative acts and practices before such offer commenced"; misrepresented the facts in their Schedule 13-D filing; and issued "untrue statements of material facts. . . ."

When Black was accused of racketeering in the United States and subjected to a securities investigation in Canada, Cardinal Carter offered his help and support. Did he provide a lofty moral justification for Black's business dealings? In his eulogy at Carter's funeral in April 2003, Black revealed the cardinal's unusual offer: "When my associates and I were the subjects of a spurious securities investigation in 1982, I mentioned to Cardinal Carter that we had discovered illegal intercepts of our office telephones, presumably from the Crown Law Office. I wondered if the next initiative from that quarter would be a search warrant on my house, though I accepted that perhaps I was becoming paranoid, since I had done nothing wrong. My concern was that they would seize personal correspondence and records having nothing to do with what they were supposedly investigating, and leak material to the press, behaviour for which there was some precedent. The cardinal reminded me that 'even paranoids have enemies,' and invited me to leave anything personal I might be concerned about at his house. 'I doubt that even the most zealous headline-seeker would try to search your house, but if they try that on me, we can flee together.' "

Despite the cardinal's support, a cloud had started building up over Black. He had been charged with serious securities violations by an agency of the American government. The violations involved fraud, deception and lies. Black was required to sign an agreement "without admitting or denying any of the allegations of the Complaint," confirming his consent for a permanent injunction against him, "enforceable by contempt proceedings" if he violated regulations in the future. But Norcen was allowed to hold on to the 20 per cent of Hanna stock it had purchased.

Black had a totally unrealistic view of power relationships in the United States. There was something infantile about his misjudgment, as if he believed he could take on the world's number-one superpower head-on. Nevertheless, it became a habit that would come to haunt him in future years.

Despite the controversy surrounding him, Black was consecrated as *The Establishment Man* in Newman's 1982 book of that name. His public pronouncements, by turns outrageous, dramatic and boastful, were often exercises in self-parody. He was ruthless; he was exploitative; he was meticulous in his study of other people, adjusting his vocabulary to suit theirs, lining them up as his instruments.

He also knew the value of moral discourse. He told Newman he was perplexed "at the erosion of conviction and the gradual descent of our society into moral torpor. I'm reduced to reading Oswald Spengler, whose theme is that the decline of civilization is as likely as the turning of autumn leaves. Still, the emergence in the West of a renascent intellectual right — rigorous and articulate — has been a long time coming. It has been followed, as such developments usually are, by a move to the right in the politics of Britain and the United States. The re-emphasis of the importance of the *proprietor* in the Canadian business scene is part of this same trend."

As he contemplated the state of the world, Conrad Black was convinced the newly invigorated intellectual right could reverse the decline of the West. He spoke as if he stood above public morality — he could pontificate about it with a strange sort of detachment. Perhaps it was that Nietzschean side of his, the one that permitted superhumans towering above their era to be amoral. He had finally become a king maker, a redeemer of the fallen, a backroom boy, navigating in the secretive world of proprietors, where everything was about winning. It was okay for leaders of superior intelligence to make sweeping moralistic judgments about society down below.

Barbara Amiel was not the type of woman to be happy with domestic life, homemaking, child raising — or being someone's trophy. She was sassy, provocative, articulate, ambitious and self-reliant — a passionate woman in stiletto heels whose life had alternated between personal hardship and soaring, self-imposed political missions. She liked writing about sex from the male point of view, while ridiculing feminists, which gave some of her columns a mischievous flavour.

In 1977, Barbara Amiel met Conrad Black at a Toronto dinner party. They were both in states of transition at the time. In 1979, she divorced from her second husband, George Jonas, although they remained close intellectual partners. Her 1984 marriage to cable television owner David Graham took her to England. The marriage ended four years later.

When she published her tell-all biography in 1980, she thought of calling it *Fascist Bitch*, mocking the nickname she had been given by some of her journalist colleagues in Toronto, but the publisher decided that *Confessions* would sell better. In those years, she was variously called "the toast of the nuke set," "the redneck in a Givenchy dress," "a reactionary Queen Bee," and "the toughest writer and thinker to come along the Canadian pike in a long time."[116] She was also something of a chameleon, able to change her accent from working-class North London to working-class Hamilton, Ontario, to the more refined University of Toronto, and then to genteel, upper-crust Oxford English — her current accent.

She once said she was ashamed of her personal life, she did not particularly like herself. Writing tough columns provided an outlet for her rage at the world.

Journalist John Fraser recounts in *Telling Tales* that he saw her at a Progressive Conservative leadership review convention in Winnipeg in the early 1980s. "There were scrums all over the [convention] floor, but the largest and most active one seemed to be near the west side of the Winnipeg arena. You could tell it was a good scrum. People were five or six thick around the central character or characters; it was impossible from the crush to see who it was. On the outer rim, the gatherers of facts leaned into the crowd to catch the chatter. Some thrust small tape-recorders towards the middle; others were furiously scribbling notes. I drew closer. At the hub of the throng was Miss Amiel, in her ninth designer outfit of the convention. This one was scarlet with a slit down its back that stopped only a provocative millimetre above her trunk and undercarriage. She was in the midst of an editorial consultation with [*Toronto Sun* editor] Peter Worthington that sounded alarmingly like a fishmongers' scrap. I was too far from the centre to get the drift of the debate. All that came through to the backlines were the high frequency expostulations: AMIEL: 'What the hell do you mean . . .' WOR-THINGTON: 'Barbara. For God's sake, if you'd only . . .' AMIEL: 'Don't you patronize me or I'll . . .' WORTHINGTON: 'I'm not patronizing, but you're being silly because . . .' AMIEL: 'Are you telling me that . . .' WORTHINGTON: 'Listen, I'm only telling you that . . .' " Fraser was astonished to realize that in a curious role reversal, Amiel and Worthington were surrounded by Conservative delegates.[117]

They had become the main event. Everyone else was eclipsed.

"Barbara is always influenced by the person she's talking to," Worthington said.[118] "Now she is living to the hilt that role of having money, more shoes than Imelda Marcos, $10,000 clothes, extravagant spending. I think she is quite fragile. She would have made a world-class gossip columnist. She can find out what interests people and what pains them. . . . If she is talking to you, she will bounce your ideas back at you better than you could express them yourself, and you will believe she is smarter than you although she may not be. She is tremendously entertaining and has a mischievous streak in her."

That was the public Barbara Amiel — the attention-seeking celebrity, riding the wave of fame. "Power," she wrote in 1985, "is sexy, not simply in its own right, but because it inspires self-confidence in its owner and a shiver of subservience on the part of those who approach it." Women marry up, she preached, because that is what society naturally expects: "It seems to me that women don't get a fair shake, and it is about time we dismissed those ugly words of criticism (like 'meal ticket' or 'gold digger') that accompany a so-called 'good marriage.' "[119]

This combination of toughness and coquetry was the hallmark of Amiel's style.

In the late 1960s, Amiel joined the drug-taking, laid-back pop culture, hanging out with the likes of Leonard Cohen, Jane Fonda and Alan Alda. But there was something in the self-indulgent anti-Americanism of pop culture that repulsed her as much as did the work of Chinese-born author Han Suyin, a glamorous Communist propagandist in a Dior dress.

By the mid-1970s, according to Christina Pochmursky, a Canadian television newscaster and friend, Amiel "was in the process of creating an identity, a kind of intellectual Madonna. She had to be right up on foreign policy, but she also had to have a very low-cut dress."[120] Her marriage to George Jonas, a Hungarian émigré, gave her an even deeper understanding of the insidious character of Soviet Communism. Amiel and Jonas were intellectual partners and collaborated on a book — *By Persons Unknown*. She learned from Jonas about the "captive mind" — the tight grip that Communism exerted on intellectuals, some of whom voluntarily ceded control of their individual liberty, making fundamental compromises in the interests of personal survival. Amiel took over as editor of the *Toronto Sun* in 1983 and ran columns in the paper by her ex-husband throughout the 1980s. Columns by Jonas have regularly appeared in newspapers controlled by Black. In 2007, the dark, stooped figure of Jonas sometimes loomed at Barbara's side in courtroom 1241 in Chicago, providing her with moral support. It seemed as if Black, in marrying Barbara, had not realized he was also marrying Jonas.

Robert Fulford remembers giving Amiel her first freelance commissions in the 1970s. "I published Barbara Amiel's first magazine article at *Saturday Night*. I found her ambitious and interesting and intelligent and far better read than most journalists. She is as exceptional in her class as Conrad is in his. That they should be together says a lot about them — the fact they chose each other suggests they respond to chords in each other that are deeply resonant. In her book, she makes herself out to be a Marxist as a young person, and then discovering the reality of the world. I think she probably looked with a lot of skepticism on the young people she knew in the 1950s and 1960s, and must have been thinking, 'I don't believe any of this stuff about liberalism and socialism.'"[121]

On a visit to Marxist Mozambique in 1980 with her boyfriend of the time, an upscale travel agent from Toronto, Amiel was jailed because she didn't have the right papers. She survived to tell the tale, which added to the radical conservative aura she was building up. "After we were processed and given our numbers — I was number 975 — we were separated. . . . While my companions were taken into solitary confinement, I was put in a cell with one of the women. Women were a bit of a problem for the prison. We had to be padlocked into our cells, as well as barred in. I'm not sure whether this was to protect us from the other prisoners, the soldiers, or the rampant lusts we were supposed to have. But, like many new socialist regimes, Mozambique is a puritanical and truly chauvinist society. . . Inside my cell was a half-inch thick mat of foam rubber on the concrete floor and a thin blanket. No pillows. No furniture. No books, radios or rehabilitation programs. There were interesting colonies of bedbugs, which had made little honeycombs in the foam rubber, and quantities of mosquitoes, ants and cockroaches. There was a very bright light bulb that remained on all night, and a small, barred opening about eight feet off the floor."[122]

She contracted malaria and typhoid in prison. Her experience of developing-world Marxism was in extreme contrast to her life in Canada. But her rhetoric about Canada underwent a transformation. In a speech to the Empire Club in Toronto in 1982, she denounced the barbarians outside the wall — "a group of quasi-Marxist, quasi-tribal, quasi-theocratic forces that include many African countries and such countries as Iran, Libya and China, who, whether or not they are permanently aligned to the Soviet Union, promote and endorse ideas and institutions designed to propel the entire world back into the

Dark Ages."

Amiel felt Canada was unable to cope with reality and was increasingly undermined from within by neo-Marxist thinking. She criticized as doctrinaire the ideas of Pierre Trudeau and other left-liberal ideologues, claiming they were defeating individual liberty while institutionalizing discriminatory legislation (reverse discrimination), an educational system that did not respond to the real needs of society and economic policies that blocked foreign investment and wasted money trying to promote the equality of Canada's very disparate regions through transfer payments.

She told the Empire Club's high-profile business audience that "those of us who care passionately about what is inside the walls [of Canada], and wish once again to force the people to defend them, can only point these things out. We are haunted by the words of the poet Yeats, 'The best lack all conviction, the worst are filled with passionate intensity. Surely the Second Coming is at hand.' I won't believe it. The best must find conviction, the passionate intensity, the strength. We are a people still of courage, of stamina, of fibre. God help us, the Second Coming is urgent. It is the resurgence of liberal democracy and our willingness to sacrifice something for it, or we will have nothing to bequeath our children but darkness, wailing, and the terrible haunting sounds of oppression and fear."

By 1980, at the age of thirty-nine, Amiel had developed a tough, in-the-trenches neo-conservative image in her magazine columns. But her public image was sterner than reality and there was something raw and subliminal in her sharp message, often delivered in a sexy, suggestive manner. She had everything neo-conservatives liked — a malicious tongue, good looks, contempt for feminism and staunchly radical right-wing views.

Although Amiel had been married and divorced twice, she continued to believe in the institution of marriage. She never had children after the abortion in 1964. "I so loathe the permissive promiscuous society and so long for fidelity, stability and monogamy," she wrote in 1980 "but it is always out of my reach. There is a thing called discipline. I have tried to inflict it on my work. I've tried to inflict it on me. But all that emerges is self-indulgence."[123] She often expressed existential anxiety in her articles, transmuting her personal angst into ideological war, pouring her venom out on the world.

During the Massey give-away and the Hanna problems, Conrad Black had begun orchestrating a severe downsizing of the underperforming Dominion grocery chain — selling off eighty-six Quebec stores and closing nearly a hundred in Ontario, transforming thirty-eight of them into cut-price, non-union franchises.

Hollinger Argus had noticed there was a considerable surplus in Dominion's pension plan, some of which could be applied to paying for the job cuts. In November 1985, Dominion applied for regulatory approval to recover a $60-million cash surplus ($107 million in 2007 dollars) from the pension fund of Dominion Stores employees with the prospect of recovering another $15 million. The final amount of the surplus to be recovered, stated a Hollinger Argus Inc. interim financial report dated November 22, 1985, depended "on a number of factors, including eventual levels of continuing employment by Dominion which will be determined by the nature and extent of future rationalization and winding-down activities." When Dominion employees found out about this, they were horrified to learn that their own pension funds might be applied to the costs of their own job terminations.

The disposal of company pension funds had long been a legal grey zone in Canada. "In the absence of legislated rules," journalist Ann Finlayson noted at the time, "the Ontario Pension Commission had developed guidelines over the years. But it was not easy for employees to determine what they were and how they were applied. As the Dominion employees learned to their outrage, it was difficult even to get through to anyone with authority at the Commission. When correspondence was ignored and requests for information were redirected to the recalcitrant employer who had refused to produce the information in the first place, one fundamental question was inescapable: Whose interest was the Commission protecting — the employees' or the company's?"[124]

After a protracted series of highly politicized court battles, Black and company ultimately settled for half of the pension surplus. This represented a bitter outcome for Black in some respects, although it established an important legal precedent in Canada and served to clarify the thorny question of what could and should be done with a company pension surplus.

The task of managing Dominion's affairs put a strain on Black's business partnership with his brother. Monte "had not always found the role of president of Argus Corporation easy or enjoyable," Black wrote, "and it rarely had been easy or enjoyable. I sustained myself through these tumultuous years with faith in finding a more serene vocation for a repositioned group. He never lost that faith but saw less of a role for himself, and shaken by qualms about his own overlordship of Dominion Stores, and perhaps by the acrimonious end of his marriage [to Mariellen Campbell], elected to take a very handsome profit and carve out a new role for himself away from intense publicity and invidious comparisons with his brother."[125] Invidious because Conrad was known as the brighter of the two — provocative, outspoken, inclined to self-dramatization — whereas Monte was good-natured, loyal and more interested in sports than in ideas. After several years as head of Hollinger Argus, Black had become a very public personality.

In 1978 and 1979, Black had emerged as the boy wonder of Canadian high finance, the eligible bachelor who had seized Argus Corp., the fiery intellectual who proclaimed the rebirth of the right and had global ambitions. By 1985, however, in the space of just seven years, his reputation had darkened. It was now common knowledge that he manipulated companies and people to snag or dump the crown jewels of Canadian finance; he had been charged with fraud, manipulation and deceit in the United States, and had got off with a sharp warning; he showed no compunction about dipping into the pension fund surplus of his employees — the retirement savings of grocers, butchers, clerks and cashiers — who could be shuffled around at will.

Peter C. Newman wrote in a *Maclean's* column, February 18, 1985, that the sale of Dominion Stores "raises pertinent questions about Conrad Black's willingness and ability to hang in and operate functioning companies instead of merely trading corporate blocks and shucking ventures that no longer meet his high profit expectations. . . . Conrad Black has created nothing. In his fortieth year he finds himself comfortable and rich, but surrounded by a rising chorus of voices questioning his future course and asking why he refuses to fulfil the potential for corporate greatness he once inspired among his peers."

But Black was not apologetic and often responded to criticism with deliberately provocative statements. "Greed has been severely underestimated and denigrated — unfairly so, in my opinion," he once told Newman. "I mean, there is nothing wrong with avarice as a motive, as long as it doesn't lead to dishonest or anti-social conduct. I don't think greed, as such, is anything to be proud of, but a spirit of moderate acquisitiveness, is not un-akin to a sense of self-preservation. It is a motivation that has not failed to move me from time to time."[126]

Since his return to Ontario in 1974, he had dealt with the death of his parents, the corporate and legal battles, and the extremely controversial sell-offs of blue-chip companies and the pension grab at Dominion Stores. With a stable home life and most of his corporate re-engineering at Hollinger Argus completed, Black had settled into the new persona of proprietor. But he wasn't satisfied. There was no way to assuage that unending thirst for power and influence. He longed for fresh challenges. Conrad Black welcomed the public exposure that came with his dramatic rise in the corporate world, but he wanted to manipulate his public image.

Spengler offered a solution — if newspaper campaigns were "war by other means," then Black would build up a newspaper empire and get in the last word. The appeal of print was still strong as ever.

CHAPTER SIX

PAPER CHASE

ONCE CONRAD BLACK'S CHICAGO TRIAL got underway in mid–March 2007, we journalists settled into our respective roles.

Jacked up on Starbucks coffee each morning, the media passed through the metal detector in the lobby of the Everett McKinley Dirksen Federal Courthouse. We shared the elevator with defendants in other court cases — nervous Orthodox Jewish businessmen in fedoras and dark suits and gloating black pimps with gold tooth caps, oversized shag coats and chain jewellery. This was another world. The media wanted colour, drama, and impact — after all, Conrad Black had been a press baron, lording it over people much like themselves. But journalists came away from each day's sitting with a mixture of dismay and frustration. This was a white-collar criminal case involving low-key testimony, lawyers meticulously sifting through evidence and engaging in regular procedural wrangles.

Just what was the story? And what would be the outcome? Some media commentators had already made up their minds. Tom Bower, the biographer with malicious eyes, a thin face and prominent front teeth, compared Black to a Nazi. "Are you the same Tom Bower who wrote about Klaus Barbie in the 1980s?" I asked him, at morning break, without saying I was also a biographer. "Yes, I wrote about evil men then." I had read the excerpts from his late-2006 biography of the Blacks in the London *Sunday Times* and was astonished to see him cherry-pick through other people's research and get so much of the story wrong. He exulted each time something nasty was said about Black in court and was one day ejected from the courtroom by a federal marshal for chatting through some important testimony.

On the other hand, Steve Skurka, the Toronto criminal lawyer who often appeared on Canadian television, predicted a clean sweep for Black — acquittal on all counts. Venerable Canadian columnists Peter Worthington and Allan Fotheringham claimed the jurors were stupid, unsophisticated and uneducated. But then they had long known Barbara Amiel, and it was only natural they would tend to minimize Conrad Black's legal woes.

Most reporters attending the trial had a "where there's smoke, there's fire" attitude — if Black had been charged with fifteen counts of fraud, money laundering and obstruction of justice, there had to be something to it. By reporting the daily proceedings, they were simply doing their job. British reporters found that Black's nouveau riche arrogance made a good story, as well as his extravagant lifestyle and apparent contempt for the common people. Just who did he think he was anyway? As a fallback position, in case he was acquitted, they held a second story in reserve — a nasty one about hardball justice in America.

In public, I gave Black a fifty-fifty chance of conviction or acquittal. I mentioned in my reports on BBC World, CBC, CNN International and Radio-Canada that he was innocent until proven guilty. Whether Black was convicted or acquitted, this case raised important questions about due process, the presumption of innocence in the United States today, the right to a fair trial and the ability of an impartial jury to mete out justice. The *Chicago Tribune* and *Chicago Sun-Times* featured daily stories about the declining independence of federal prosecutors, some of whom had been hired and fired at will by the White House on purely partisan grounds. President George W. Bush doesn't care much for the separation of powers (executive, legislative and judicial) that was supposed to prevent the United States from turning into a republican dictatorship. He wants to concentrate as much power as possible in the White House, whatever the effect on the country's democratic institutions.

As part of my research, I had studied the theory of criminal justice and noted that an Italian jurist of the eighteenth century, Cesare Beccaria, had established the principle — now universal — that punishments should be in proportion to the crime. For me, the case raised doubts about the application of that principle as well.

But that was only on the level of criminal responsibility. We were waiting for the documentary evidence and testimony that told the inside story of what had happened. On another level, Black was clearly culpable — he was blameworthy in moral terms for much of what had happened since Hollinger International had been launched as a U.S.-based public company in the mid-1990s. How could he have received tens of millions of dollars and remain unaware of the true character of these payments? How could he have failed to notice the outflow of funds to Radler from the company he controlled? How could he sign quarterly certificates as CEO of Hollinger International vouching for the accuracy of financial disclosures in 2002 and 2003, then simply draw a blank when asked to justify extravagant fees, non-competes, and other benefits paid to himself and his closest associates? If one thing was clear in the criminal case in Chicago, it was that David Radler, Black's closest business associate for almost forty years, had admitted to a major fraud and had agreed to hand back more than $71 million. How could Conrad Black not have known what was going on?

Each morning in Chicago, once the marshals had allowed us into courtroom 1241, the various lawyers filed in. Black's main U.S. defence lawyer, Ed Genson, left his scooter at the door and gingerly limped up to the central defence table, his leg braces checking his movements. He told me at the break one day that he identified strongly with Everett Sloane, an actor who played in the 1947 film noir *Lady from Shanghai*, alongside Orson Welles and Rita Hayworth — because Sloane was cast as Arthur Bannister, a perversely brilliant, handicapped lawyer who walked with a cane in each hand. Black's main Canadian defence lawyer, Eddie Greenspan, came in, settling his bulk into a chair next to Genson. At a break, Greenspan told me he identified with Jonathan Wilk, a criminal lawyer played by Orson Welles in *Compulsion*, a 1959 film about the notorious Leopold and Loeb murder in Chicago in 1924. Wilk was loosely based on Clarence Darrow, who had defended two young men who considered themselves amoral Nietzschean supermen, which gave them special rights to commit the perfect crime of kidnapping and murder. Greenspan told me Welles affirmed his authority in *Compulsion* through his massive physical presence and intimidating stare. I imagined the lead prosecutor, Eric Sussman, as a skinny loudmouth in a T-shirt — the kind of man with a perpetual smirk on his face who would whip drinkers in a pub into a furor then duck outside just as the brawl began.

Barbara Amiel took her place in a row of seats reserved for defendants' families. She wore a new designer outfit each day. Her dark brown hair was always impeccable — no grey roots showed despite her sixty-six years. Her face was perpetually frozen in a forced smile, which she wore like a mask, and she would turn around and flash it at the media. Once George Jonas began sitting next to her, she seemed more like his thirty-year-old daughter than his former wife. Near her sat Alana Black. Her beauty was unique and mysterious, partly because her brown hair fell low over her forehead in bangs. She had an aquiline nose and prominent lips, and a slim figure like a top model. Her face was sometimes caked in foundation to conceal the ravages of insomnia during the trial. Conrad's son Jonathan, a red-haired former fashion model who looked like a more athletic version of Marlon Brando, in *On the Waterfront*, sat nearby. Sitting next to Jonathan was the court artist Verna Sardock, a somewhat distracted middle-aged woman with sparkling eyes, colour sketches of all the key players and charcoal smudged on her hands. Conrad's younger son James, also red-haired although a few inches taller than Jonathan, turned up some days, occasionally refusing to wear a business suit or even to tuck his shirt into his pants. The three showed strength of character — not the brutal strength of their father but an unassuming, supportive presence. Conrad's first wife, Shirley, now renamed Joanna, had to be playing a key role behind the scenes, likely coaching them on how to thread their way past the media into the courtroom, stand by their father, without betraying any emotion on their faces and then thread their way out again.

Conrad Black came into the courtroom, impeccably dressed in suit and silk tie. His hair was silvery white. He was wooden in his movements, somewhat stooped now at the age of sixty-two, worn down by the ordeal but also conscious that everyone was staring at him. He waddled as he walked, thrusting his feet out to each side, then sat down at the central table of the defence team. He sometimes took notes in the courtroom, then would take off his glasses and scowl at witnesses and the jury, or confering with his defence team.

What was he thinking? He described the trial to me as intense, hectic and heavy going, in e-mails now and then. But he always maintained his innocence. "They have nothing on me," he said. "I have done nothing wrong."

Conrad Black was angry about the process — he had been assumed guilty until proven innocent by the Justice Department and most of the world's media. He was convinced his phone had been bugged in Toronto, and before that in New York. He had posted $21 million — the highest bail in the history of American criminal justice. And the FBI had swooped in just when he was ready to collect a cheque for $9.5 million on the sale of his New York apartment, and seized the cheque.

Black often boasted that he was a master strategist, but one huge strategic flaw explained why he was in court in Chicago. In the mid-1990s, the Canadian company he controlled, Hollinger Inc., set up an American subsidiary, Hollinger International. Black then folded Hollinger Inc.'s worldwide newspaper assets, including titles in Canada, Britain, Israel and Australia, into Hollinger International and went public, raising close to $400 million in shares and notes on Wall Street. The influx of new capital diluted Black's effective control of the newspaper empire he ran. The equity interest of Toronto-based Hollinger in Chicago-based Hollinger International declined from 64.2 per cent in 1994 to 30.3 per cent in 2002. But during this same period, Hollinger Inc.'s voting power (through those multiple voting shares) only declined from 94.7 per cent to 72.6 per cent. (Black in turn *indirectly* controlled Hollinger Inc. through his private holding company, Ravelston Corp.)

Placing worldwide newspaper assets under his control in a U.S.-based public company offered advantages. Black noted in the 1995 annual report of Hollinger Inc. that "the Reorganization . . . will complete the emancipation of this Company and its affiliates from the shackles of the holding company format inherited from Argus Corporation. . . . Hollinger International will access the U.S. capital markets in a conventional manner as required to finance expansion or consolidation of existing investments." Some emancipation! Going public in the United States also imposed new responsibilities. It meant that Black was now answerable to American public shareholders, since he was using *their* capital to expand *his* business. They were not investing as an act of charity — they were experienced investors who wanted to make money. They watched Black closely to ensure that he abided by American securities laws for public companies.

But the corporate culture of the controlling shareholders was out of sync with the times. Black carried on with the genteel, self-serving avarice of the Argus old guard of the 1940s and 1950s. "These companies have always been run in the Argus tradition of proprietary businesses where the controlling shareholders take reasonable steps to ensure their comfortable enjoyment of the position they (we, in fact), have created for themselves," Black had written in a memorandum on September 6, 2002, to Ravelston shareholders. "Care must be taken not to allow this to degenerate into decadence, as it did in the old Argus." But he said complaints from disgruntled shareholders over poor stock performance should not "force us into a hair shirt, the corporate equivalent of sackcloth and ashes."

Black seemed well aware of the inherent danger of press barons abusing their power and influence. "If you look at it historically, various newspaper proprietors have clearly suffered megalomania," he said. "So it is something that you want to always be scanning the radar screen to be sure that you stay clear of it. . . . You want to get some sort of balance between a healthy ego on the one hand, and the sense of your own limitations and the propriety of your actions on the other, and there is an element of public trust in the newspaper. If you abuse that, you will not only disserve yourself, you will pay for it. Because the franchise will be damaged."[127]

But in the present-day United States, public shareholders play hardball with their CEOs. Black did not seem to have integrated the fact that going public in the United States required him to play by U.S. rules, whether he agreed with them or not. Even though he was chairman and CEO of Hollinger International, he had not taken the time and care necessary to ensure that various hugely controversial payments were unimpeachable. Payments such as $218 million in management fees paid from 1997 to 2003 to himself, Radler and other top Canadian-based executives; non-compete fees of $90 million paid to the same group in 1998-2001, when they negotiated the sale of assets belonging to the company; plus lavish expenses, advantages and various loans.

The prosecution strategy focused on Black's free-wheeling expenses. An e-mail was read into the record about his use of a corporate jet for a 2001 holiday in French Polynesia with his wife, Barbara. "We just got back yesterday from a shambles of a trip to the South Pacific, where I came down with bronchitis and almost drowned from snorkelling as a result. We felt like geriatric freaks among a sea of honeymooners — loutish young men and their perky wives. Shortly after we arrived on Bora Bora we discovered the island was in the throes of a dengue fever epidemic and we spent the rest of our time there applying insect repellent and sweltering indoors."

It was hard to justify this trip as a business expense. To clear things up with then Hollinger Inc. comptroller Fred Creasey, Black offered to reimburse half the $565,323 cost of the round-trip flight from New York to Bora Bora (which included a stopover in Seattle, to attend performances of the four operas of Wagner's *Ring* cycle).

"Was there any policy in place requiring Conrad Black to

use the company plane for his personal vacation?" asked prosecutor Judie Ruder. "No," replied Creasey. Jurors were shown an e-mail of August 2002 in which Black noted company policy on the use of executive jets should distinguish between "business, quasi-business and nonbusiness expenses. . . . As I have said before, a degree of accommodation with contemporary norms is what we need. We will not abdicate and declare all perquisites to be corrupt."

Arguing for the defence, Greenspan charged that Black's offer of reimbursement was far too high — he was grossly overcharged for his personal use of the executive jet. But it was hard to forget Black had charged holiday expenses to the company in the first place.

There was also the matter of $60 million worth of non-compete payments received in 2000 by Black and several associates when CanWest Global bought the Southam chain of newspapers from Hollinger International for $3.2 billion. Bud Rogers, a New York-based attorney who had long advised the company about sales of publications and disclosure to regulatory agencies, testified that the payments were not properly disclosed to Hollinger International shareholders. Rogers had received a copy of a May 2001 memo sent by lawyer Mark Kipnis to Hollinger's board and audit committee claiming that the non-compete payments were "a critical closing condition" — meaning that if Hollinger did not accept, CanWest Global would withdraw its offer to buy Southam. But the record was not clear who asked for the non-competes and who decided how they would portion out.

Black's defence lawyers claimed that he had been improperly advised by lawyers from Torys, who initially suggested there was no need to disclose the tax-free non-competes in the compensation section of public documents, before doing a U-turn and raising alarmed questions about them later. Beth DeMerchant, then a senior corporate lawyer at Torys, testified via video from Toronto that she had initially "said I would be surprised if it was compensation because it was a non-compete consideration." A fellow lawyer at Torys validated her position. But when pressed by the American law firm Cravath, Swaine & Moore, where

Bud Rogers worked, DeMerchant realized she had made a mistake. She contacted Hollinger executive Peter Atkinson: "I said I was sorry, that there was a problem, and that I was there to talk about it." After studying disclosure rules, she said the proxy circular, approved by the audit committee and board of directors, sent to all shareholders and filed with the SEC, should have disclosed all these payments.

Jurors saw a fax sent from Atkinson to Black saying, "David [Radler] had consistently suggested $19 million for you and $19 million for him in regard to these covenants. Jack (Boultbee) and I suggest $2 million for each of us. . . . We believe Ravelston should be paid $30 million."

The contents of the fax implied that Black and others in the executive suite of Hollinger International had been the ones to divvy up the non-competes — not the purchaser, CanWest Global.

In late April and early May 2007, the prosecution called three witnesses who had served on Hollinger International's audit committee: former ambassador Richard Burt, economist Marie-Josée Kravis and former Illinois governor Jim Thompson. All three had received Wells Notices from the SEC (which indicate that the SEC may bring civil action), as well as threats of government lawsuits against them, heavy fines and possible disbarment from ever serving on corporate boards of directors in the future. Their testimony was considered important since they had approved a raft of rich payments made to Conrad Black and his closest associates.

Burt testified in late April that he had voted in favour of the non-competes because he did not know at the time CanWest Global had *not* made them a condition of closing. Burt, who struck some journalists as a handsome lion with a grey mane, learned initially that Black and Radler were beneficiaries in the agreement and only heard later that the names of Boultbee and Atkinson had been added. Under questioning from the prosecutor, Burt said board directors were asked to ratify a revised deal in 2001 whose terms were very different from the original one they had agreed to.

"It was a terse meeting," Burt testified. "The payments were being characterized in a new way. But there was nothing to be done about it. There was annoyance that the company had been sloppy and was coming back to us for our approval. He added "I had understood CanWest had made the allocations of the amounts but that was now being changed."

Under cross-examination by Ed Genson, Burt was asked whether he had read company documents explaining the non-competes. "As I said several times," Burt retorted, "I missed it. It was incumbent on management to bring those payments to the audit committee — not to put it in a footnote in financial statements 12 or 18 months later."

"Is the fact that Hollinger management were told by lawyers that they didn't have to, does that make a difference?" asked Genson.

"I don't know what they were told," said Burt.

"You were being paid $5,000 a meeting and you didn't read the financial statements, did you?"

"Objection!" cried prosecutor Jeff Cramer, leaping up suddenly.

Then Marie-Josée Kravis, an impressive brunette from Montreal who had made a name for herself as an economist and director of a conservative think-tank before marrying the American billionaire Henry Kravis, testified she had not been properly informed about these non-compete payments, and had definitely not approved them. Defence lawyer Patrick Tuite asked her to explain why she signed Hollinger International's financial statements for 2001 if she believed the information about non-competes was incorrectly stated.

"I missed it," she said.

Tuite noted the non-competes were also mentioned in the table of contents of the same document. "You missed that one too?"

"I did," Kravis answered.

She admitted to having missed many references to the non-competes in company documents and to having memory lapses. Greenspan challenged her claim not to remember getting a package of Hollinger International financial information prior to a 2002 meeting of the audit committee.

"Sir, I can't remember reading something I don't recall receiving," she said.

"We just can't rely on your memory for anything, can we?" snapped Greenspan.

"That is not correct," she snapped back.

Then former Illinois governor Jim Thompson, who had served as chairman of the audit committee at Hollinger International, came to the stand. His cross-examination by Greenspan revealed just how slack the audit committee was in performing its duties. This cross-examination was crucial for the defence, since it underlined that responsibility for various non-compete payments was not Black's alone — it was *shared* with the audit committee:

Greenspan: Any Audit Committee that reports to a Board is reporting to a Board that is somewhat dependent on an Audit Committee who reviews things more closely than the Board; is that not correct?

Thompson: Yes. They review more materials than the Board member does.

Greenspan: In fact, I'm going to suggest to you that you are something like a gatekeeper. You get all of the material; you look at it in whatever manner you choose to; and, you report to a Board; and, you're something of a gatekeeper, correct?

Thompson: Yes.

Greenspan: And that is why the charter requires that financially literate people be on the Audit Committee, right?

Thompson: Right.

Greenspan: It's not a requirement to be a member of a Board, is it?

Thompson: No.

Greenspan: And people like Marie-Josée Kravis and Richard Burt are people — and yourself are people — who the Board thought had that financial literacy and who had that accounting or related financial management expertise, correct?

Sussman: Objection!

Thompson: Wrong.

Sussman: Foundation!

Judge St. Eve: Sustained.

Greenspan: Okay. Let me look at Principle 1, please. (Brief pause.) Principle 1 states, "The Audit Committee" — "The Audit Committee shall oversee the work of management and the outside auditors to endorse the processes and safeguards employed by each," correct?

Thompson: Yes.

Greenspan: And if we can look, then, at the end of the paragraph, it says that it is the — that "Management properly develops the duty of the Audit Board to ensure that management properly develops and adheres to a sound system of internal controls; and, that the outside auditors, through their own review, assess management's practices." Do you see that?

Thompson: Yes, sir.

Greenspan: So, the outside auditors — KPMG — are to review Management's practices, right?

Thompson: Correct.

Greenspan: And you, as the Audit Committee, are to oversee KPMG, right?

Thompson: Right.

Greenspan: So, if we could please look, then, at Principle 2. (Brief pause.) Principle 2. Come to the middle of the paragraph, please.

Thompson: Yes.

Greenspan: And what it says is, "The Audit Committee shall promote a culture that values objective and critical analysis of management." Do you see that?

Thompson: Yes.

Greenspan: Now, do you interpret that by just saying it says what it says and it means what it means?

Thompson: I don't understand that question.

Greenspan: Okay. Well, I'll — you are not supposed to, as I look at this section and just give it its plain reading — "The Audit Committee shall promote a culture that values objective and critical analysis of management," you are not supposed to — just *rely* on management, are you? Isn't that what it says?

Thompson: What it says is that we, in our culture, also value objective and critical analysis of management, not just reliance on management; that we depend on the outside auditors, as well, and their views of management and their practices.

Greenspan: And, then, *your* objective and critical analysis? You do not —

Thompson: Yes.

Greenspan: — *rely* or *just rely* on management; is that not correct?

Thompson: That's correct. We rely on the auditors, as well.

Greenspan: I didn't ask you that. What I asked you was this: You do not do anything but the requirement and the mandate under this charter, which is to analyze management, correct — critically and objectively, correct?

Thompson: You're reading simply one part of Principle 2 and making that the only part. And that's not the only part.

Greenspan: I'm not making it the only part, but is that sentence not self-explanatory?

Thompson: It is to me.

Greenspan: Well, if it is to you, that's why I'm putting it to you. I'm not trying to trick you. That's what it is. Because, you see, if you were to rely on management, then you would be violating the charter. And why should the company pay you a salary or pay you an amount of money in a year if all you're doing is relying on management?

Thompson: I didn't say that. I've never testified that all I was doing — all I was doing — was relying on management. I've previously testified that certainly I relied on management. I trusted management.

Greenspan: Well, relying —

Thompson: That's not all I did.

Greenspan: Relying and trusting management is subject to this particular sentence that says that you should be objectively and critically analyzing management —

Thompson: Yes.

. . .

Greenspan: Let's look at the responsibilities of the Audit Committee, Page 2 of the charter under the heading of "Responsibilities." No. 1 says, "You are to provide an open avenue of communication between the outside auditor and the

Board of Directors," right?

Thompson: Right.

Greenspan: So, that's another duty of the Audit Committee to be that very group that provides an open avenue of communications between the outside auditor and the Board of Directors?

Thompson: Yes.

Greenspan: In other words, it's your job to meet with KPMG and report to the Board of Directors, correct?

Thompson: Correct.

Greenspan: And can we go to Page 3, please, and I want to focus on Section 7(a). (Brief pause.) 7 requires you to review with management and the outside auditor at the end of the audit: "(a), the corporation's annual financial statements and related footnotes," correct?

Thompson: Correct.

Greenspan: And that section elevates footnotes to charter status equal to the body of the annual financial statements, right?

Thompson: Right.

Greenspan: Footnotes are as important as the text —

Thompson: Absolutely.

Greenspan: — in financial statements, right?

Thompson: Right.

Greenspan: You don't need a charter to tell you that, correct?

Thompson: Correct.

Greenspan: In fact, you were the Governor of Illinois for 14 years and I'm willing to bet you've read a lot of financial statements and their footnotes?

Thompson: Financial statements that are akin to corporate financial statements?

Greenspan: Not akin. Financial statements. Surely, you must have, as Governor, looked at financial statements —

Thompson: Oh, sure.

Greenspan: — in your 14 years?

Thompson: State budget.

Greenspan: And when you look at it, you look at footnotes, don't you?

Thompson: Right.

Greenspan: Now — and, so, you're to review the 10-K [the company's annual report] in the Audit Committee — the financials and the 10-K — the footnotes at the back, the — what they call MD&A, which is the "Management Discussion and Analysis" section of the 10-K. You're supposed to do all of that?

Thompson: Right.

Greenspan: To treat each part as equally important, correct?

Thompson: Yes.

Greenspan: And these are the very reports and disclosures that go to the SEC?

Thompson: Right.

Greenspan: And once you have fulfilled your obligations pursuant to Section 7 of the charter, you then report your actions to the Board of Directors, with such recommendations as the Audit Committee may deem appropriate; and, that's what Section 9 of the charter says and requires you to do?

Thompson: Yes.

Greenspan: Do you see that: "Report Audit Committee actions to the Board of Directors with such recommendations as the Audit Committee may deem appropriate," right?

Thompson: Yes, correct.

Greenspan: And you report to the Board, and the Board relies on your representations in approving transactions and signing off on the company's financials, right?

Thompson: Right.

Greenspan: You would agree that the charter does not cover everything that you're supposed to do as an Audit Committee member?

Thompson: Right.

Greenspan: I mean, there's more to being an Audit Committee member than attending meetings four times a year?

Thompson: Correct.

Greenspan: You reviewed documents that are sent to you in advance of the meetings, correct?

Thompson: Yes.

Greenspan: You reviewed the draft financials with the footnotes, correct?

Thompson: Yes.

Greenspan: You would get e-mails from management, correct?

Thompson: Right.

Greenspan: You would send e-mails to management and others, right?

Thompson: Right.

Greenspan: And if there was something that you did not understand at the meetings or otherwise, you could call management or another Audit Committee member for information, right?

Thompson: Right.

Greenspan: You could have called Mr. Radler if and when you had questions, right?

Thompson: Right.

Greenspan: You could have called Mr. Black if and when you had questions, right?

Thompson: Right.

Greenspan: You had no problem reaching out to them when you needed to, correct?

Thompson: No problem.

Greenspan: And they listened to your concerns, right?

Thompson: Occasionally.

Greenspan: Occasionally, they listened to your concerns. And the first time when your concerns were not listened to, as I'm hearing your answer, did you quit?

Thompson: No.

Greenspan: Because it didn't really matter, did it?

Thompson: What do you mean?

Greenspan: Well, in other words, whatever disagreement you had was not a disagreement that was remotely close to causing you to say, "I'm leaving this Board"?

Thompson: No.

(Greenspan then reviewed different financial statements approved by the audit committee, as well as specific non-compete payments made to Conrad Black and others, which were also approved by the audit committee.)

Greenspan: So, what you have here are the draft financial statements before the February, 2002, Audit Committee meeting, so that you could review them, right?

Thompson: Right.

Greenspan: And yesterday you testified that you did not review drafts of the company's SEC filings paragraph by paragraph. Do you remember that?

Thompson: I did.

Greenspan: In fact, I believe you said you *skimmed* them?

Thompson: Correct.

Greenspan: And that was true for the 10-Ks, the 10-Qs [the company's quarterly financial reports] and the proxies [written authorizations given by shareholders, empowering others to vote on their behalf]?

Thompson: Right.

Greenspan: During the time that you were on the Hollinger International Board, you reviewed those documents by skimming them?

Thompson: Yes, sir.

Greenspan: And you were asked why you skimmed the draft filings and I think the first thing you said was, "Well, first of all, they're very long — a hundred-and-some pages — usually single-spaced," correct?

Thompson: Right.

Greenspan: And if you take a look at the draft financials at Tab 27 — which is all of them in this draft — did you *skim* these draft financials?

Thompson: Yes, sir.

Greenspan: Okay. Well, can you please flip through the draft at Tab 27?

Thompson: Sure.

Greenspan: Have you had a chance to do that?

Thompson: Yes.

Greenspan: And can we agree that there are only 17 pages —

Thompson: Correct.

Greenspan: — of draft financials there?

Thompson: That's correct.

Greenspan: Now, you said earlier that you *skimmed* the draft financials —

Thompson: Right.

Greenspan: — because they are very long? Do you consider 17 pages very long?

Thompson: No. 17 pages are not very long, but the draft — the document I had in my hand when I said that — was 141 pages long.

Greenspan: So, you just told me that you skimmed —

Thompson: Right.

Greenspan: — even this one?

Thompson: Right.

Greenspan: So, then, the answer is whether they're very, very long or very, very short, you *skimmed* it?

Thompson: Right.

Greenspan: Is it not your obligation, as a member of the International Audit Committee, to actually read the financials?

Thompson: Yes, I should have read them word for word. I didn't. I skimmed them.

Greenspan: Hollinger International did not pay you $60,000 a year to go to Board meetings and *skim* financials, did they?

Thompson: No, they paid me for other things than that.

Greenspan: Well, they never said to you, "Please skim this"?

Thompson: They never did.

Greenspan: And as you testified earlier, the charter obliges the Audit Committee to look at the corporation's financial statements and related footnotes; isn't that right?

Thompson: That's right.

Greenspan: And that's what these 17 pages are, right?

Thompson: Right.

Greenspan: The draft financial statements and related footnotes?

Thompson: Right.

Greenspan: I want to look at what you missed in these 17 pages; and, I'd like to go to the last page of this document, which is marked as HLR SEC 17063, the bottom right-hand corner. These are the footnotes to the financial statements, correct?

Thompson: Right.

Greenspan: Let's look at letter (f). And it says four lines down in Footnote (f) — could you please read aloud the second paragraph of Paragraph (f)?

Thompson: Yes. (He reads.) "In connection with the sales of United States newspaper properties in 2000, to satisfy a closing condition, the company, Lord Black and three senior executives entered into non Non-Compete — Non-Competition — Agreements with the purchasers to which each agreed not to compete directly or indirectly in the United States with the United States businesses sold to the purchasers for a fixed period, subject to certain limited exceptions, for aggregate consideration paid in 2001 of $6 million. These amounts were in addition to the aggregate consideration paid in respect of these Non-Competition Agreements in 2000 of $15 million. Such amounts were paid to Lord Black and the three senior executives."

Greenspan: Now, as you read this today, this disclosure says that Conrad Black and others received individual non-compete payments in 2000 and 2001, correct?

Thompson: Yes.

Greenspan: And this is the non-compete money from the U.S. Community sales in 2000, correct?

Thompson: Right.

Greenspan: If you had read it in February, 2002, those words would have been the same words that were there that day, correct? Those words are the words?

Thompson: Those words are the words.

Greenspan: Okay. It would have said the same thing. If you had any questions about this paragraph, you could have asked, right?

Thompson: If I had seen this paragraph, I could have asked, yes.

Greenspan: If you had seen the paragraph?

Thompson: Yes.

Greenspan: Well, what are you saying? That some pages you *skimmed* and some pages you *didn't even look at*?

Thompson: No. When you're skimming a document, you don't necessarily see every paragraph.

Greenspan: I see. I don't — I didn't — understand that. You

mean "skimming" means not that you get the gist of everything in every paragraph, you can actually jump paragraphs?
Thompson: You may.
Greenspan: You may. Are you taught this? Is there some kind of skimming school?
Thompson: No.
(Laughter.)

These witnesses sounded as if they had fallen asleep on the watch. They admitted to having skimmed important financial information, which it was their duty to monitor carefully and critically. I could imagine them jetting to New York for board meetings in the Fifth Avenue offices of Hollinger International, with the Roosevelt letters in gold frames and the signed photo of Al Capone on the wall. Here they perused masses of documentation, laughing at Conrad Black's jokes and insider anecdotes, asking a few questions themselves, then approving the motions outlined in the briefing book.

American Home Assurance and Chubb Corp. — the insurance company providing Hollinger International with D&O (directors and officers) coverage — ultimately agreed to a $50-million settlement with one of the institutional shareholders, Cardinal Capital. The huge payout was associated with the performance, or non-performance, of Hollinger International board and audit committee members.

One of the problems with the criminal case against Conrad Black was that a key party to CanWest Global's purchase in 2000 of the Southam newspapers died October 7, 2003. Izzy Asper, an extroverted, chain-smoking Canadian tax lawyer and media tycoon from Winnipeg, Manitoba, was no longer around to tell his side of the story. Had he insisted on the non-competes when he agreed to pay Hollinger International $3.2 billion for the newspapers? And, if so, had he directed that the non-competes be divvied up among the Chicago-based company, its Toronto-based parent company, Black's private holding company, Ravelston Corp., and Black, Radler and several individuals? And if Izzy had not authorized this breakdown of the non-competes, were Black and his former associates within their rights to divide up the non-competes themselves?

A letter handwritten by Izzy Asper to Conrad Black on April 14, 2003, indicates that Asper saw the non-competes in the context of an ongoing personal commitment from Black, Radler and others: "It was in your New York office during our first serious discussion of the deal," read the letter, faxed from Asper's Palm Beach mansion. "It was of paramount importance to CanWest that if we were to do the deal, we would want an ongoing relationship with you, David Radler and others in the Ravelston group — both in a Board as well as Advisory role — given that you people knew the business and we did not. You graciously agreed to provide that ongoing assistance and it was then that I said that it was axiomatic that we would require non competition agreements for as long as our lawyers believed the law would enforce them." Given its date — close to three years after the non-compete agreement was finalized — Asper's letter also may indicate that Black was trying retroactively to document one of the controversial payments that was feeding Tweedy, Browne managing director Chris Browne's anger.

But five and a half months after that letter was sent, October 4, 2003, I got a somewhat different account from Izzy Asper — just three days before he died. I called him in Winnipeg, as he was moving into his new high-rise condo at 1 Wellington Crescent, at the east end of the same street his house was on. Wellington Crescent winds along the Assiniboine River for five kilometres, from the city's most densely populated neighbourhood, Osborne Village, to the gates of Assiniboine Park, the city's largest green space.

In the early evening Montreal time, I spoke to him for an hour and a half (he occasionally had to hang up and ring me back after directing the movers to place his furniture). He was personable, approachable, nervous. There was something melancholy and detached in his voice, which resonated strangely in the vast empty room where he sat. I could hear the movers mutter among themselves, set boxes down and shift furniture around. I had no way of knowing he would soon be dead. This was the last interview he would ever give.

He knew I was calling to ask about his business relationship with Conrad Black, among other things. I had faxed a letter to his office, then waited. To my surprise, he agreed to give me the interview, at a time when the situation was worsening for Black. He mentioned on the phone that the SEC was sending someone up to Winnipeg the following month, to question him about the propriety of the non-competes paid by CanWest. He was in a hurry and he had a lot to tell.

I could hear him flicking open his gas lighter and puffing on seven or eight cigarettes while we spoke. I felt he had chosen me for the summing-up interview of a lifetime. He was taking stock of his life, sorting out his many possessions into boxes, dividing them into rooms, musing about his earlier years as a lawyer — that was one set of boxes — and then leader of the Manitoba Liberal Party — that was another set. He was obviously in poor health and was often out of breath.

Asper said he had never really been destined for the media business. He would have liked to have pursued a career as a jazz pianist instead. He told me about his future plans for COOL TV, an all-jazz specialty channel, and a human rights museum in Winnipeg. He said how much satisfaction he derived from transmitting his media company to the next generation of his family.

He was proud to have built up CanWest Global as a Manitoban, an outsider and a Jew — someone who did not easily fit into the WASP Establishment circles of Toronto or Montreal. He had come to a turning point in his life. During our conversation, Asper told me to call back if I had any supplementary questions. He was so unlike Black — so unpretentious, direct, considerate. My line of questioning was indirect — I wanted to build rapport, gain his confidence since I had never spoken to him before, get in the real questions toward the end of our interview.

"Does the Establishment really exist?" I asked.

"There are, I suppose, what people would call corporate and social elites," said Asper. "But when you come to business, most of the barriers of the 1940s, 1950s and 1960s have been washed away. There are still barriers to entry based on factors like race, religion, gender and so forth. There may be some snobbery in some areas, but it's nothing like it was. There may be a distinction between creators of wealth and inheritors of wealth, but it is not what it used to be. Philanthropy is a big factor — in terms of earning respect. Success is a very personal matter: some people tend to look at people who are wealthy and ask, 'What else did they do — did they do something useful with it?' My thesis in life has been 'you take risks, you reap rewards, and you have responsibilities as a result.'"

"How did you get to know Conrad Black?"

"I went into business in 1977. Shortly afterwards, in 1978, I had my first transaction with Conrad Black in the Crown Life deal. Conrad operates on the basis that he is the principal 'deal maker,' and once he is confident that a deal has been made, he withdraws and leaves it to his more technical colleagues, like David Radler, to bring it home. Conrad had roots in Winnipeg, but he was reasonably detached from Western Canada. By the time I did that deal with Conrad, he was embedded in Toronto, having just done the Argus deal. He had come out of under his father's shadow and made a startling and amazing move to gain control of Argus."

"How did you take over Southam?"

"Conrad wasn't looking to sell Southam. He wanted to sell the weeklies, the smaller papers, to tighten up and skinny down his operation. Shortly after our discussions began (we did not begin talking about Southam and the *National Post*), we talked about uniting our Internet efforts. He had canada.com and we had global.com. We were being slagged by the analysts and the media because we were not a high-tech company. I had been burned in the U.S. in the 1970s with the pay-TV business. And I was reluctant to go into the Internet unless we could see a solid business and we could discuss, rather than just hope for, client revenues. If, at the end of the day, Internet is just a free ride for the public, then we, the content providers, will stop providing. One of the great things about being older and having experience of trends and fads is that I am more restrained and have a broader base to judge things. Canada.com, when we took it over, was essentially a start-up, but we immediately began a program to merge it all into one, pulling in radio and television and newspapers from all over the world. Conrad hadn't really focused on it. But he knew he had to be there."

"Did Hollinger *have* to sell Southam?"

"The Hollinger people did not act like they were forced sellers — we got a decent deal and they got a decent deal. But the fact is not many other people in Canada would want to have bought it."

"How do you see the relationship between newspapers and the Internet?"

"It can be argued that newspapers are threatened by the Internet, but I don't see it that way. The word is the word, whether in print or on the Internet."

"What is Conrad Black's relationship to newspapers?"

"Conrad is fundamentally an editor-in-chief. He has achieved where he wants to go. He wants to engage in the contest of ideas, and challenge and joust. I used to be a journalist, but I didn't get into business until I was forty-five years old. I never got the chance to do what I wanted to do: public affairs, broadcasting and commentary."

"How much are you worth?" I asked, teasingly. "$100 million?"

"Much more than that."

"$200 million?"

"Oh, much more than that. [A month later, a Canadian rich list set his net worth at $1 billion.] I don't comment on things like that. My net worth fluctuates based on the stock price. All my assets are in CanWest. I was lucky. I was able to establish a charitable foundation that will have legs after I am gone. I am the driving force behind the first human rights museum in the world. Health, human rights, scholarship, education and culture (i.e., arts and entertainment) are important to me."

"Has Conrad left his mark on Canadian journalism?"

"Having done several start-ups myself, I admire people who do start-ups. The *National Post* was a start-up. Whether it will survive — the jury is still out. It is not profitable, and we being a public company have to take a hard-nosed look at things. We have made enormous progress in terms of stopping the losses.

The *National Post* forced the *Globe and Mail* to dramatically improve. Conrad didn't spend enough time to make a solid unit of Southam, which was twenty independent companies that did not talk to each other or like each other. You don't need twenty accounting departments or legal departments to deal with twenty newspapers."

"The concept of national editorials (drafted in Winnipeg and imposed on the satellite newspapers) was not well received in Montreal, for example," I said, thinking of the experience at my old employer, the Montreal *Gazette*.

"All the fuss about national editorials was media hype."

"Do you and Conrad agree on Israel?" I asked, since I was aware that Asper still wanted to buy the *Jerusalem Post* from Hollinger International.

"I discuss Israel with Conrad in the philosophical sense: what are the solutions, where is the U.S. president right and where is he wrong, what should Canada do. My view is that the intifada is not something new — there is an eighty-year intifada. The first major fighting and riots were in the 1920s. It is only because of international intervention that no solution has been found. This intervention is based on each country's self-interest."

"How do you see media coverage of Israel?"

"Almost all the coverage fails to recognize what this is all about: it focuses on the leaves of the tree and not the roots. Forget about the borders, settlements, the fence, refugees and even Jerusalem. This is about the refusal of the Islamic countries to permit Israel to exist. Journalists should understand what has been said and done over the last eighty years, what the strategies are. There can't be a solution until the survival of Israel is assured. Survival is non-negotiable, but for many Islamic leaders, every major event only moves the front of an ongoing struggle against the survival of Israel."

"How do you see Canada's role in world affairs?"

"Canada seems to emulate Europe, as opposed to what the U.S. is doing. That is probably an identity issue — not wanting to seem a pawn of the Americans. Canada is missing a meaningful role. Canada can be a beacon of logic, equity and principle, but Canada has been opportunistic, has maintained the middle of the road, although there may not be a role in the middle. I would like to see Canada be a spokesman at the UN for what is right, not what is convenient. One of the first things [the new Liberal prime minister] Paul Martin should do is re-evaluate the Canadian position on the international scene."

"What editorial positions should the *National Post* take?" This was a key question, since Black had used the *Post* as a neo-conservative instrument to hammer the Liberal government of Jean Chrétien. Some of the *Post's* editorial positions and coverage of politics were right-wing propaganda of a kind we had never seen in Canada, although some journalists had a good deal of latitude to report and investigate from their own perspectives. Asper was more liberal than Black, but from what I could see was also more hands-on in his treatment of journalists.

"The *National Post's* identification with the Canadian Alliance (during Black's stewardship there) was just terrible. The paper appeared to be the mouthpiece for the Alliance, just like *Izvestia* or *Pravda*. I felt the paper should not be a preaching device. I believe a newspaper, in order to be profitable and therefore viable, has to take a stand. The *Toronto Star* represents the centre-left, the *Globe and Mail* is in the middle. The *National Post* has to represent the centre-right. It does not have to be mean or snarly — it has to be cogent."

"What happens when you don't agree with the journalists on editorial positions?" I was thinking back to my own run-ins with the top brass at of the Montreal *Gazette*.

"The question is: who owns the place — you (the journalists) or we (the owners)? I don't mind if journalists are cheeky or sassy. But insulting — no! I read the *National Post* straight through every day, as well as 10 other newspapers."

Asper's answers were frank and refreshing, but I still hadn't asked the $64,000 question — the real reason for the interview.

"What happened with the non-compete fees paid to Conrad Black and several associates as part of the sale of Southam?"

"It is standard practice to pay non-competes," he said. "When you buy a business from someone who is still in the business, you automatically take on a non-compete. I insisted on the non-compete, but Hollinger decided who the non-compete would go to."

Asper had made quite a few remarks about the non-competes since 2000 — but this was to be his last word on the subject. From what he said, it sounded as if Black was the deal maker and Radler the technician who worked out the details; Asper insisted on the non-competes, which he may have considered as a closing condition; but the decision on who would get the non-compete, how it would be divvied up between various companies and individuals, was taken by Hollinger alone.

David Radler' testimony in court was considered all-important, since it could determine the outcome of the trial. He was the key prosecution witness. To a large extent, Black's fate depended on Radler's credibility. Radler had already copped a plea, so the defence strategy was to distance Black from Radler and to portray the latter as a dark horse, a fraud artist who had stolen money from the company, as a man envious of Black's social graces, wealth and intellectual achievements. As prosecutor Eric Sussman led him through his initial testimony, Radler, dressed in a dark grey suit, white shirt and hot-pink tie, described his business relationship with Black.

> **Sussman:** Okay. . . . so, just so we're clear, you are at a restaurant with Mr. White and Mr. Black; is that right?
> (Laughter.)
> **Radler:** Yes, that's correct.
> **Sussman:** Okay. And now, what, if anything — what was the general topic of discussion that you and Mr. White and Mr. Black were discussing at this meal [in 1969]?
> **Radler:** There were probably a lot of things we discussed. There were a number of things we discussed; but, the main focus of the discussion was the potential takeover of the *Sherbrooke Record*.
> **Sussman:** And what was the *Sherbrooke Record* in 1969?
> **Radler:** It was a — an — English language newspaper in a French-speaking town that covered a large geographical area. And it was a potential acquisition. The owner of the newspaper was prepared to sell it.

Sussman: What were your impressions of Mr. Black when you first met him in 1969?

Genson: Objection to what his impressions are! Not relevant! We're talking about 1969.

Sussman: Your Honor, I am simply asking — I'm simply — laying some foundation as to the background and how he started and why he started in business with Mr. Black.

Genson: His impressions in 1969 —

Judge St. Eve: Sustained.

Sussman: Sir, did you decide to go into business and start up this newspaper with Mr. Black?

Radler: It was a purchase, yes.

Sussman: Did you decide to purchase this newspaper with Mr. Black?

Radler: Ultimately, yes.

Sussman: And why did you decide to go into business and purchase this newspaper with Mr. Black?

Genson: Objection! We're talking about 1969.

Judge St. Eve: Overruled. You may answer that.

Radler: Well, I was impressed with Mr. Black's knowledge and his ability; and, I thought he would, you know, be a great partner to have.

Sussman: Now, you mentioned that the *Sherbrooke Record* was an English-speaking newspaper in a French area; is that right?

Radler: That's correct.

Sussman: Just by way of a little background, are there French-speaking areas of Canada and English-speaking areas of Canada?

Radler:. Generally, that's the case, yes.

Sussman: Okay. I didn't know these things. So, I'm trying to make it — take it from there. Now, sir, where was — was this in a particular province, the *Sherbrooke Record*?

Radler: The *Record* was in — it was in — Quebec.

Sussman: Okay. Now, did Mr. White go in on this deal with the two of you, as well?

Radler: Yes, he did.

Sussman: And how much did the three of you pay for the *Sherbrooke Record* in 1969?

Radler: We paid a gross of $50,000.

Sussman: And how much — when you say, "a gross of $50,000," what do you mean?

Radler: We — we — we bought the assets for $50,000, assumed $30,000 of liabilities, which gave us a net of $20,000 that we actually had to put up.

Sussman: Okay. How much of that $20,000, did yourself put up?

Radler: Initially, $2,000.

Sussman: When you say "initially," did that change?

Radler: That changed a few weeks later and I put up $6,666, one-third of the total.

Sussman: Now, prior to you and Mr. Black making an offer to purchase the *Sherbrooke Record*, did the two of you have any discussions regarding this potential purchase?

Radler: Yes. Yes, we — yes.

Sussman: Did you discuss the price that the two of you would pay for the newspaper?

Genson: Objection! Leading! Objection hearsay!

Judge St. Eve: Overruled. I am sorry?

Genson: Hearsay, also, your Honor!

Sussman: I'm just asking whether this was discussed. I'm not asking for any statements.

Judge St. Eve: You may answer "Yes" or "No."

Radler: Yes.

Sussman: Did you discuss the terms of the transaction?

Radler: Yes.

Sussman: And did you discuss the financing of the transaction?

Radler: Yes, we did.

Sussman: Now, how big a paper was the *Sherbrooke Record* in 1969?

Radler: It had a circulation — a daily circulation — of 7,000 or perhaps a little more.

Sussman: Would it be fair to call the *Sherbrooke Record* a community newspaper?

Radler: Yes.

Sussman: What exactly is a community newspaper?

Radler: It's a — it's a — usually a — it could be either a daily or a weekly newspaper, usually published in a smaller town than — I'm going to say smaller than — 50, 60,000 population.

Sussman: Did you — what was the financial condition of the *Sherbrooke Record* when you and Mr. Black began the paper — or purchased the paper?

Radler: It was losing money.

Sussman: And when you first purchased the paper, were you working at the newspaper?

Radler: Yes.

Sussman: And was Mr. Black working at the newspaper?

Radler: Mr. Black came in pretty soon after we — we — we started.

Sussman: At the time, was Mr. Black doing anything else other than working at the newspaper?

Radler: To the best of my recollection, he was finishing law school and perhaps had some exams.

Sussman: Okay. So, during the times that Mr. Black was not working or at law school working on his exams, was he working with you at the *Sherbrooke Record*?

Radler: When — when — he was free, he worked at the *Sherbrooke Record*, yes.

Judge St. Eve: Mr. Radler, can you keep your voice up, please, or speak closer into the microphone?

Radler: Okay.

Sussman: Are you able to hear me okay, your Honor?

Judge St. Eve: Yes, I can hear you.

Radler (moving closer to the microphone): Is that better?

Judge St. Eve: Yes.

Sussman: I think so. Now, how often was the *Sherbrooke Record* published? How many days a week?

Radler: It was a five-day daily.

Sussman: And during the time that Mr. Black was not in school, were the two of you there on each of the five days when the newspaper was published?

Radler: I would say, yes, with — with — with exceptions; but, yes.

Sussman: And did you live in Sherbrooke during those —

that time period — those five days?

Radler: In the five days, we — we — lived in Sherbrooke, yes.

Sussman: And when you say "we," did Mr. Black live in Sherbrooke, as well?

Radler: Yes.

Sussman: Did you — did the two of you — see each other during the days?

Radler: Yes. I hesitated because the day may have started rather late, because it was a night — we put out the paper at night.

Sussman: Okay. And did the two of you work late into the evenings together?

Radler: That's correct.

Sussman: And did the two of you see each other socially, as well as at work, during this period of time?

Radler: Well, we — we were — yes.

Sussman: Well, maybe I should ask the question differently. Did you have a social life during this period of time when you were working at night at the *Sherbrooke Record*?

Radler: Not much of a social life.

Sussman: And to whatever social life you had, did you at times share that with Mr. Black?

Radler: Yes, I did.

Sussman: Now, concerning the running of the *Sherbrooke Record*, did you consult with Mr. Black about the operations of that newspaper?

Radler: Yes, I did.

Sussman: What, if any, consultations did you have with Mr. Black concerning the finances of the newspaper?

Genson: Your Honor, I object! It's general questions going back 30 years. No foundation.

Judge St. Eve: Mr. Sussman?

Sussman: Well, your Honor, I can lay — if I can try to lay foundation, if that's what — I'm just talking very generally.

Judge St. Eve: Okay.

Sussman: But I'm happy to try to lay some more specific foundation, if that's what —

Judge St. Eve: The objection is foundation, in part. Is it relevance, as well, Mr. Genson, or foundation?

Genson: Relevance *and* foundation!

Sussman: Your Honor, I think it's relevant because I think that the course of conduct, in terms of how these two men ran their newspaper operations, I think, is relevant and —

Judge St. Eve: Okay.

Genson: It's 40 years ago, Judge.

Sussman: — and their relationship is certainly relevant over this period of time.

Genson: 40 years ago is a long time.

Judge St. Eve: Objection to foundation is sustained. Objection on relevance is overruled. But I hope you are moving on at some point.

Sussman: I'm going to try to move through this quickly, your Honor. . . . Sir, did you consult with Mr. Black about the expansion and the growth of the *Sherbrooke Record*?

Radler: Certainly, yes.

Sussman: Did you consult with Mr. Black about staffing decisions?

Radler: Yes.

Sussman: And did you consult with Mr. Black about salaries?

Genson: Objection! He's leading!

Judge St. Eve: Overruled. You could answer.

Radler: Yes. The answer is "Yes." Sorry.

Sussman: Now, were you and Mr. Black successful with the *Sherbrooke Record*?

Radler: Yes, we were.

Sussman: Were you able to turn a profit?

Radler: Yes, we were.

Sussman: How long did it take you to turn a profit?

Radler: I believe three months.

Sussman: After you and Mr. Black got the *Sherbrooke Record* making a profit, did the two of you purchase any other newspapers in Quebec?

Radler: Yes, we did.

Sussman: How many other newspapers during the early — late Sixties, early Seventies?

Radler: I believe we purchased three or four newspapers.

Sussman: And prior to purchasing those newspapers, did you consult with Mr. Black about the terms of the transaction?

Radler: Yes, I did.

Sussman: Now, after those first few, did you purchase additional newspapers in Quebec?

Radler: After the first few —

Sussman: I'm sorry?

Radler: Sorry.

Sussman: I think you had me at four or five newspapers in Quebec?

Radler: Yes.

Sussman: Did you continue purchasing newspapers in Quebec with Mr. Black?

Genson: Objection on foundation! I'd like to know when.

Sussman: Your Honor —

Judge St. Eve: Sustained.

Sussman: I will lay foundation.

Judge St. Eve: Lay your foundation.

Sussman: Sir, if you could take us through, as best you can recall today, when you purchased additional newspapers in Quebec?

Radler: Well, in 1970 — or late 1970 — I believe we purchased the first major newspaper in Quebec, which was the newspaper known as *L'Avenir & Sept Îles Journal*, in a place known as Sept Îles, which is 700 miles north of Montreal.

Sussman: And what —

Radler: And, then, there were other newspapers. We had a newspaper in Granby, Quebec, called — I can't remember what the name of the newspaper was, but we had a — we had a — small newspaper in Granby, Quebec. We had a newspaper in Farnham, Quebec, which we — in which Peter White had owned a portion of the paper. And that was brought into the group. We owned a newspaper called the *St. John's News* in St. John's [St. Jean] Quebec. We had a newspaper in Baie Comeau, Quebec. So, we had a — we had a — number of newspapers.

Sussman: Now, during this period of time when you purchased the newspapers you just testified to, how were major financial decisions made with regards to the running of those newspapers?

Radler: Well, they were — they were — jointly made.

Sussman: Were they jointly made with respect to financing?

Radler: Yes.

Sussman: Those newspapers?

Radler: Yes.

Sussman: How about labor negotiations?

Radler: Yes.

Sussman: Marketing decisions?

Radler: Yes.

Sussman: Now, during this period of time, were you and Mr. Black continuing to work side by side at the newspapers?

Radler: When Mr. Black was — was — in town, yes.

Sussman: Were you *equal* partners at this point in time?

Radler: At that point in time, we were.

Sussman: And what were your percentages?

Radler: It would have been 33, 33, 33.

Sussman: And where were you living during this period of time?

Radler: I lived in Montreal.

Sussman: Where did Mr. Black live during this period of time?

Radler: At — depending on the period, at — one point he did live in Montreal, also.

Sussman: During this period where he purchased the additional newspapers in Quebec, how frequently were you in contact with Mr. Black?

Radler: Very frequently.

Sussman: Did the two of you eat together?

Radler: Yes, generally.

Sussman: Were the two of you friends?

Radler: Yes.

Sussman: Did you travel together?

Genson: Objection! He's test- — your Honor, it's leading.

Judge St. Eve: Mr. Sussman?

Sussman: I don't think the question is leading, your Honor, but I can try to rephrase it.

Judge St. Eve: Rephrase it.

Sussman: Sir, during this period of time, did you take any personal trips — what, if any, personal trips did you take with Mr. Black?

Radler: Mr. Black and I went to New Orleans once.

Sussman: And who went with you?

Radler: Just the two of us.

Sussman: Were you looking to buy a newspaper in New Orleans?

Radler: No. We were — we were — looking at New Orleans and looking at the area around it.

Sussman: Your Honor, this might be a good time to stop.

Judge St. Eve: We can break for lunch.

The prosecution wanted to establish that over the years Black and Radler had worked closely — seamlessly — as a team and that they were close friends and partners who enjoyed each other's confidences and discussed business transactions in minute detail. "I didn't make a financial decision without consulting Conrad Black," Radler said. "I have no recollection of selling a newspaper anywhere without Conrad Black."

The first part of his testimony recalled the glory days, when the two men had set out to build what one day became the world's third-largest newspaper empire. But Radler then began testifying against Black, saying that the non-compete fees he received at the time of the sale of Southam to CanWest in 2000, and other newspapers, had been Black's idea. Radler now accepted they were improper, since they had not been properly disclosed to the audit committee, board of directors and shareholders, and he now considered they were wrong. He said he wanted to atone for this wrongdoing.

The jury was not told that Radler and his companies would pay a total of $71 million to settle claims by Sun-Times Media Group, but they did hear a lot about his plea bargain and expected twenty-nine-month prison sentence.

Once the cross-examination of Radler began, I sat in the back row of the courtroom, against the left panelled wall. From my angle of vision, I saw Judge Amy St. Eve at her bench, at the front. To her right, but much closer to me, sat Conrad Black, his full hair snow white, stone-faced as he peered at Radler through his gold-rimmed glasses. To his right, but on a stand next to St. Eve at the front was Radler himself, tanned, diminutive, self-deprecating, sarcastic, tilting his head to one side as he consulted documents and was cross-examined by Eddie Greenspan. To the right were the members of the jury, who listened attentively. Here in one glance I could take in all the key players in this drama.

As one of Canada's top criminal lawyers, Greenspan had long fantasized about pleading a big-time case in Chicago. He was here to impress judge and jury. He told the press this was after all the city of Clarence Darrow, the great criminal lawyer and civil libertarian of the early twentieth century. Henry Fonda had developed a famous one-man show based on Darrow's life, and two great courtroom movies were loosely based on one of his most famous murder trials — Alfred Hitchcock's *Rope* and Orson Welles's *Compulsion*.

But Greenspan's style in the courtroom owed nothing to the real Clarence Darrow. He was heavy-handed and slammed into Radler like a battering ram, repeating the same questions over and over again. If Greenspan could demonstrate that Radler had lied under oath on numerous occasions, denying any wrong-doing initially, then changing his story each time until he finally caved in and copped a plea, then he would undermine this key prosecution witness.

Greenspan went over the transcript of Radler's seventy-six-page statement at an eight-hour meeting with lawyers from Hollinger International's special committee and Richard Breeden on October 21, 2003.

"Now you have told this jury that you lied at that first meeting," Greenspan said at the Chicago trial.

"I was not forthcoming at this point."

"Tell me, Mr. Radler, at what point going into this interview did you decide *not* to be forthcoming?"

"I don't know that I actually thought about it. I just went to the interview."

"Did you personally devise a plan on what you were going to lie about?"

"No, sir."

"Was it spontaneous?"

"As I said, there are instances in this seventy-six-page document which I have not reviewed, where there are statements that are not true."

"Was it easy for you to lie?" asked Greenspan.

"No, sir."

"Did you stutter when you were lying?"

"I told lies."

"Did you avert your eyes when you were lying?"

"I told lies."

"Was there a long pause when you lied?"

"I told lies."

"Did you avert your eyes from the people you were lying to?" asked Greenspan. "So I can take it there is nothing you can tell this jury so they will know when you are lying. I take it we may be looking at you right now and you may be lying."

"False," said Radler, throwing Greenspan off his stride. "I am not lying."

"We have your word on it."

"You have my word on it."

Greenspan smirked. What was the word of a man who had admitted he had lied just about every time — up till now, that is. He tried another line of questioning.

"You did say in this trial that you lied because you were afraid of the consequences. But at no point during the interview [in October 2003] with the special committee did you say that the non-competes were improper, or words to that effect. . . . You testified in this trial before this jury that Conrad Black directed the non-competes be paid to Hollinger Inc. And you testified that the lawyers would want to know who made the decision to make the non-compete payments. . . . But at no time did you tell the lawyers at that meeting of the special committee who made the decision to make the non-compete payments."

Greenspan seemed to be looking for something more, a flaw in Radler's testimony, something to get a hold of. As if he wanted to show that Radler not only lied but lied to save his own skin.

"The reason that you lied to the special committee is you did not want to tell them you were doing anything wrong. You lied to save yourself."

"And others."

"You lied to save yourself."

"And other associates."

"You lied to save Number 1, because Radler is Number 1."

"Yes, for me Radler is Number 1."

"Aren't you doing the same here today — lying to save yourself?"

"No, sir."

"You did not come back the next day and tell the lawyers of the special committee that you had misled them."

"That's correct."

"My question really was that you never told the lawyers of the special committee that the non-compete payments to Hollinger Inc. were improper . . . What you are saying now is you lied to the lawyers of the special committee."

"Uhhh, yes."

"The reason you did this was you wanted to convince the lawyers of the special committee that you had not done anything wrong."

"Myself and others."

"You — David Radler."

"And others . . ."

Radler was subtly gaining the upper hand in the exchange. Greenspan was losing his concentration, so he tried a new line of questioning.

"You did not say, 'I know who took the decision about the non-compete payments and that was Conrad Black.'"

"That is correct. I never told them who made the decision."

"Now you say you did not disclose the payments to individuals to the audit committee because the buyers did not request them and that was improper."

"I also believe they were wrong, generally."

"You knew that the special committee wanted to know who had taken the decision about this allocation."

"Yes sir."

"You knew the special committee wanted to know if the audit committee had approved it and who had taken part in the disclosure process. . . . They also wanted to know if there were other matters they should know about."

Some interesting body language was going on. Greenspan was a stooped hulk of a turtle, absorbed in the documents laid out before him. Radler glanced at the judge while he testified, trying to turn the tables on Greenspan, antagonize him, throw him off balance, trip him up in his exhibits. "If you want to take things out of context," Radler said defiantly, "I guess that's your right. You are manoeuvring all over the place. Can we discuss what I *did* say?"

"I object to that characterization," retorted Greenspan, "and if your speech continues, I will ask Her Honor to get you to stick to your story!"

"Objection to the speech!" chief prosecutor Eric Sussman cried, leaping to his feet.

Judge St. Eve turned to the witness. "Mr. Radler, please listen to Mr. Greenspan's questions and if you don't understand them, you can ask them to be rephrased. I will now ask both Mr. Radler and Mr. Greenspan to leave their speeches for another time."

Greenspan tried another line of questioning. "You start meeting the prosecutors on ten occasions, from December 2004 to June 2005."

"That is correct."

"When you finish what you say are lies to the special committee, then you go over to the prosecutors, the SEC and the FBI. . . . You got a proffer letter on December 9, 2004, correct?" A proffer letter is part of a plea agreement, and offers a witness immunity in exchange for incriminating statements about other parties. "You knew if there was any testimony that differed substantially from the proffer, you could be tried for perjury."

Radler would not acknowledge what was contained in various transcripts — he claimed he had never read transcripts of his own testimony to the SEC and FBI.

"You signed a document about a plea on August 9, correct?"

"I would have to look at the document," replied Radler.

"But until August 16, you had been saying the opposite."

"No, I would have to see the document."

The judge called the prosecution and defence attorneys to her sidebar to discuss points of procedure. Black's family shifted in their seats.

"You have said to this jury," Greenspan continued, "a number of times that Conrad was the chief executive and everything had to be run by him and he told you what to do."

"I said the first two — and I had to keep him informed."

"Is it not the truth that you are *not* Conrad's right-hand man?" This was a new line of questioning. Greenspan wanted to portray Radler as an envious subaltern, a bitter underling who was now stabbing his former boss in the back.

"Sir, I don't know what you mean. Can you give me a definition?"

"Isn't it a fact that you told a journalist at the *Toronto Star*, 'I am nobody's right-hand man.'"

"I don't remember saying that. When was it?"

"August 3, 1996."

"I don't remember ever saying that."

"Isn't it the kind of thing you would say?"

"Objection!" cried Sussman. "I have to object to the form of the question."

"Objection sustained."

"Right-hand man," said Greenspan, "second-in-command. What does it mean? What *can* it mean?"

"It can mean a flunky," said Radler slyly.

"You aren't anybody's flunky?"

"I don't think I'm anyone's flunky, but that doesn't mean someone won't call me that!" kidded Radler. The courtroom burst out in laughter.

"Did you say to the *Toronto Star* in connection with your relationship with Conrad Black that you were nobody's right-hand man and you were irked by the suggestion?"

"I would have to see the article and see the context."

What a waste it had all been, what an abominable waste. In its original complaint, filed on January 17, 2004, Hollinger

International sought to recover more than $200 million in damages, plus interest, from Conrad Black and other defendants. In the months that followed, Hollinger International's special committee continued its investigation of questionable payments, inaccurate financial reporting and alleged self-dealing. Then, in its amended filing of May 7, 2004, Hollinger International sought to recover six times the original amount from Black and several associates. Hollinger International was now demanding recovery of "$484.5 million, including approximately $380.6 million in damages and $103.9 million in prejudgment interest." The company also asserted in the complaint that defendants engaged in a pattern of racketeering activities and it "is seeking treble damages under applicable provisions of the Racketeer Influenced and Corrupt Organizations Act (RICO). The Company's total claim including treble damages is $1.25 billion, plus attorneys' fees." The amended complaint of May 2004 was even more damning than the initial complaint of the previous January. The amended complaint outlined serious new allegations of corruption. And it invoked RICO — a federal criminal statute that, in the view of the U.S. Supreme Court, applies to long-term, repeated and continuous acts that constitute a "pattern" of criminal activity. The complaint outlined a wide range of alleged acts — improper "non-competition" styled payments, excessive management fees, breaches of fiduciary duty in connection with the sale of certain newspaper assets at less than fair value to companies controlled by Black and some of his associates, and bonuses paid by a money-losing subsidiary.

When the complaint under RICO was tossed out, the amount of money in play shrank like a snowball in the hot sun.

Sitting in the Chicago courtroom, Black figured the various litigation and legal fees had cost the companies he used to run $200 million. "They admitted $137 million many months ago," he wrote me once the trial got underway. "Add $25 million for the Canadian Inspector, and sundry Canadian legal costs of another $20 million, and bring it up to date and we will be well over $200 million. They will claim recoveries, as of today, of $95 million. This does not excuse operating losses of over $120 million since 2004, in what was formerly a profitable company.

Breeden has taken $25 million." Black considered Breeden a self-serving parasite acting hypocritically in the name of corporate governance, while the people running his former companies into the ground were no more than charlatans.

In June 2007, Hollinger International, now renamed Chicago Sun-Times Media Group, said it had spent $166 million in just four years of investigations, litigation and lawyers' bills. Of this amount, the legal bills for Conrad Black, other defendants in the trial and other former executives came to $79 million.

Against these expenses, Sun-Times Media Group had recovered $127 million through settlements, including $48 million from David Radler and $30.25 million from the Toronto law firm Torys LLP (mostly through its insurance, although the firm did not admit any wrongdoing).

Black had placed Ravelston into receivership, in the hopes of protecting his most important Canadian-based assets. But Ravelston's receiver, RSM Richter, paid out $6 million Canadian in legal fees, pleaded guilty to one charge in Chicago and paid an additional $7 million U.S. fine, over his objections. He had completely lost control of his public and private finances and had only just survived.

If Black were found guilty on all counts in Chicago, he would have to restitute $92 million, reimburse the legal fees that the Sun-Times Media Group had been covering — and go to jail. But even if he were acquitted, he would still face a $542-million civil suit filed against him by the Sun-Times and a $750-million civil suit filed by Hollinger Inc. of Toronto. A civil fraud lawsuit filed by the SEC against Black in November 2004 was still pending. It seemed he was damned if he lost in Chicago — and damned if he won. Retiring to water his flower garden in Palm Beach did not seem a realistic outcome. True, he had slapped countersuits on many parties, but his ability to defend himself in the future depended on the outcome in courtroom 1241.

The prosecution in Chicago wanted to see Black incarcerated in a medium-security penitentiary such as FCI Otisville. This facility, for more than 1,000 male offenders, is an hour and a half's drive northwest of Manhattan, in the judicial district of southern New York. Black *could* be sent to a place like Otisville, if found guilty, since he gave up his Canadian citizenship to become a British lord and would not, therefore, be eligible for transfer to a Canadian prison. He is a British citizen, and British executives convicted of white-collar crimes in the United States have to serve their time here.

Otisville has guard towers, strengthened perimeters with double fences and electronic detection systems, and guards patrolling with twelve-gauge shotguns and slamming doors on "multiple-occupant cells."

Some of the inmates at Otisville are justifiably notorious. They have little in common with the genteel old guard that Black had turfed out of Argus Corp. back in 1978, or the cardinals, generals and former prime ministers and governors he named to his various boards over the years. The inmates are cunning bad asses who are paying for serious and often violent crimes.

George Jung, the narcotics dealer who claimed to have controlled 85 per cent of America's cocaine racket in the 1970s, was still doing time here. Jung was portrayed by Johnny Depp in the 2001 movie *Blow*, a movie all about Columbian druglords, greed and betrayal. Some inmates at Otisville continued their criminal activities behind bars. Two inmates got additional sentences in 2004 for conspiring to import heroin into the prison, for their own use. Other inmates were found to have used prison telephones to organize murders on the outside — one inmate organized the murder of two witnesses and a judge, and even lined up the guns to be used on the outside during their "execution." Some al Qaeda operatives have been jailed here.

Otisville was hell on earth, but Joe Black made it work for him — the tattooed giant, convicted for a crack conspiracy, scored for prison basketball teams and wrote a novel about his gangsta life called *Street Team*. His on-the-court exploits were written up by Soul Man, the world's leading prison basketball journalist, who asked him once what stuck out in his mind besides the championships, MVPs, scoring titles, Varsity team and All-Star game appearances. "One is when I first came in the system," he said. "I was in prison in Atlanta and I banged it on this tall six-foot-nine Nigerian cat." Joe Black mentioned another time at FCI Otisville where he cleared a shot halfway across the court in the last second, winning the game for his team. "It was all net. The bleachers cleared and about twenty cats picked me up and literally carried me around the gym. Man that shit was bananas."

Inmates at FCI Otisville are allowed to have some money, but it is up to the commissary to provide "a bank type account for inmate monies and for the procurement of articles not regularly issued as part of the institution administration. . . . Family, friends, or other sources may deposit funds into these accounts." Funds can be sent by post or wired to inmates via Western Union. No cash or cheques are accepted.

If Black were found guilty and ended up at a facility like FCI Otisville, he could meet periodically with a Catholic chaplain, who would "oversee inmate self-improvement forums such as scripture study and religious workshops, and provide pastoral care, spiritual guidance, and counselling." He could also seek psychological counselling

But for reasons of security, safety and sanitation, the Bureau of Prisons places limits on the amount of property (jewellery, photographs, books, magazines, and so on) inmates can have and the types of publications inmates can receive. FCI Otisville issues clothing, hygiene items, and bedding, and provides laundry services. Inmates are allowed to buy other personal care items such as shoes, some recreational clothing and some food items through the commissary. Inmates are ordinarily not allowed to own or wear civilian clothing (that is, clothing not issued to the inmate by the bureau or purchased by the inmate from the commissary).

If Black was ever committed to an institution such as FCI Otisville, he would have to work if medically able to do so. He could get work assignments such as food service or in the ware-house, or working as an inmate orderly, plumber, painter, or groundskeeper. He would earn between twelve cents and forty cents per hour for these work assignments. Wages would be higher, if he managed to work in a Federal Prison Industries factory, like 17 percent of inmates, who get from twenty-three cents to $1.15 per hour developing skills in metals, furniture, electronics, textiles and graphic arts.

Inmates are allowed face-to-face visits with approved family and friends and confidential visits with attorneys. But all phone calls are monitored and written correspondence is opened and read.

If Otisville — or a place like it — was to be Conrad Black's fate, I couldn't see him surviving there.

The Canadian Press/Toronto Star/Dave Cooper

CHAPTER SEVEN

THE CROWN JEWEL

IN REDESIGNING THE FAMILY HOME in Toronto's Bridle Path district, Conrad Black lived out some of his grandest fantasies. He wanted a Georgian manor of the type built in Britain and colonial America between 1720 and 1840, with reddish brick exterior walls and painted white trim and cornices around windows that nearly touched the ground, and simple mathematical proportions derived from Andrea Palladio's *Four Books of Architecture.* Black had to coach New York-based architect Thierry Despont. He told the magazine *Architectural Digest,* "Thierry started out being really quite unfamiliar with Georgian architecture but he picked it up very fast. He proved himself a great eclecticist."[128]

This would be a manor house to raise his family, entertain high-powered politicians and businessmen and read. "I'm not a great sportsman," Black told the magazine. "My idea of relaxation is to go into my library and just start reading, and I find the room quite foolproof in that respect. As Thierry was finishing up here [in 1987], he was just starting to work on the Statue of Liberty restoration, and I felt that in the brief overlap I got at least equal time with the world's most famous monument."

Black loved to sit in the twenty-eight-foot-high drum-shaped library, which he considered a "jewel," and peruse his many books of history in front of a crackling fire, far from the pressures of the business world.

Black was now a proprietor, a historian — a man of discernment. He was becoming a kingmaker, redeemer of fallen giants and backroom boy — on a grand scale. Rebuilding the Bridle Path house was a personal statement at a time when others had started to define him — TV director Michael Gerard did his controversial take on Black in a 1980 CBC documentary called *Ten Toronto Street*; author Peter C. Newman followed with his 1982 Black biography *The Establishment Man*; and in 1983, journalists Ian Austen and Linda McQuaig exposed, and to some extent hyped, Black's problems with securities regulators in a *Maclean's* magazine investigative series.

The Bridle Path mansion was not the only way Conrad Black sought to define himself. As he developed his business empire in the early 1980s, he sought new outlets for his political and intellectual interests. His failure to reinvigorate the Union Nationale and his disenchantment with Quebec's conservative nationalists, who lacked a power base, caused Black to lose interest in *la belle province*, and by 1978 he was fully absorbed in the task of taking over and reshaping Argus Corp.

Black's position as business proprietor allowed him access to political leaders in Britain and the United States. Attending the annual invitation-only Bilderberg Group conference beginning in 1981, he mixed with Chase Manhattan chairman David Rockefeller, Henry Kissinger and the U.S. ambassador to the United Nations, Jeane Kirkpatrick. (Kirkpatrick was one of the most strident and compelling of the neo-conservatives. She was fiercely opposed to Soviet communism and expansionism but tolerant of right-wing dictators from Ferdinand Marcos in the Philippines to General Augusto Pinochet in Chile and the apartheid regime of South Africa.) This was a completely different league from Robert Rumilly's fascist ideologues.

By 1985, Conrad Black was a master at hobnobbing with the rich and famous and the politically powerful. He was an accomplished insider at the secretive Bilderberg conferences and the Trilateral Commission. But he did not feel *involved* in world events. His business interests — with the exception of his newspaper interests — bored him. His involvement with grocery stores, mining, petroleum, farm machinery and the like served only one purpose. "I was in those solely for the reason of making some money out of them," he said. "Restructuring them, or managing them up and selling or trading them, or doing something financially — preferably a bit innovative — with them."

Ever since Black had run the *Knowlton Advertiser* and the Sherbrooke *Record* in the 1960s, newspapers had appealed to him, and he had picked up a few in provincial Canadian backwaters. But his dream of becoming a press baron on a grand scale had been thwarted. He failed to purchase the *Toronto Telegram* (which folded in 1971). And in 1979, he had been blocked by Kenneth Thomson in his quest to gain control of FP Publications, which controlled the *Globe and Mail*.

Over the years, at Bilderberg conferences, Black occasionally discussed the prospect of investing in a British newspaper with Andrew Knight, editor of the *Economist* and a member of the Bilderberg steering committee.

Black had always admired Canadian press barons who made it in London. Lord Beaverbrook was the glib son of a Presbyterian minister from Ontario, grew up in New Brunswick, then made a fortune through newspapers. He served as a minister in British cabinets in both World Wars and vigorously promoted the Empire Crusade — an attempt to increase trade within the Commonwealth.[129] He was even mentioned in the newsreel sequence of *Citizen Kane* as a newspaper power to be reckoned with.

Black had also made a close study of Ken Thomson's father, Roy, a snowy-haired, portly man, whose thick eyeglasses made it seem his laughing eyes were peering out from a fishbowl. Black admired the way Roy Thomson, an astute but modest man from Northern Ontario, watched the balance sheet. But there was an obvious difference in style between Beaverbrook, the hands-on propagandist, and Thomson, the cool operator who had made a fortune in broadcasting and North Sea oil, then used it to subsidize *The Times*. Thomson considered the takeover to have been "the summit of a lifetime's work."[130]

To this day, more than thirty years after Roy Thomson's death, Brian MacArthur, associate editor of *The Times,* says: "I bless Roy Thomson's name. He hired excellent editors, spent money, didn't interfere, and let us journalists get on with it . . . something like the *New York Times*, the *Washington Post* or the Toronto *Globe and Mail*. All Thomson cared about was the number of classified ads, and giving journalists the resources to do their job."[131]

Black noted that Beaverbrook and Thomson Sr. had been Fleet Street giants, sending journalists around the world to report on events that mattered, setting a high standard for eye-witness news gathering as much as for writing. They dominated the world's most competitive newspaper market, and that com-manding position gave them access to royalty and to politicians — from mayors to prime ministers. They were sometimes asked to quietly smother stories, but also often had a hand in choosing the country's political leadership.

But he also noted they had received the ultimate honour a Canadian could aspire to — the title of baron, and with it a seat in the British House of Lords. In fact, becoming the owner of a large daily newspaper in London was a virtual guarantee of being a life baron. The trappings of aristocracy had appealed to Black for many years, at least since the coro-nation cruise he had made as an eight-year-old boy. He had grown up in a world of English-Canadian tycoons, like Bud McDougald and E. P. Taylor, who fawned on titled aristocracy. In 1982, four years after Black's take-over of Argus Corp., he applied to the Duke of Norfolk and the College of Arms for a newly designed coat of arms. It seemed a business tycoon's rite of passage, but also a curiously nostalgic gesture, as if he were trying to reclaim something lost from the world of his parents or grandparents.

Black knew that Britain was a country with no written con-stitution, where the chain of command within the government — even in the planning of nuclear war[132] — was subject to interpretation based on historical precedents, and there was usu-ally an informal, gentlemanly character to political decision-making. If only he could become a British press baron. This would give him the social prestige and the neo-conservative soapbox he had long wanted.

Peter Carrington greeted me at his home on Ovington Square in London. The owlish elder statesman had served as secretary-general of NATO and British secretary of defence, and as he ushered me into his living room, which featured portraits of aristocratic ancestors and thoroughbred horses and dogs, he explained that he had two baronial titles, one from Ireland in 1797 and the other (with the original spelling of the family name, Carington) from Britain in 1999.

"Particularly in our constitution," he said, "press barons play an important role in Britain, where, if you have a very big majority in the House of Commons, there are no checks and balances. The House of Lords doesn't matter, and the House of Commons really doesn't matter, because if you have a big majority, the followers always go with the premiers — well, nearly always."

"Newspapers influence the outcomes of elections," said Roy Hattersley, a big-jawed, stooped former minister in the Labour governments of Harold Wilson and James Callaghan, a noted journalist and a life peer. "In a free society, it just happens. Journalists have to be accepted as part of the democratic process. People in political office complaining about journalists are like sailors complaining about the sea."[133]

The British government had the habit of drawing press lords into the circle of power by using the honours system, the often-cynical award of noble titles — one of "the most potent pieces of patronage in a premier's hands," according to constitutional authority Peter Hennessy. A peerage transformed newspaper proprietors into legislators, with the power to debate and vote on bills sent up to the House of Lords from the House of Commons. This fudged their role, from observing events and shaping public opinion to participating in decision-making. They are proprietors, marketing facts and ideas on a grand scale. But they are statesmen too — with a political platform of their own in and outside of Parliament.

Ken Thomson was Canada's last press baron with a hereditary seat in the House of Lords. He was a study in contrast. This mega-billionaire still found time to comfort and walk stray dogs taken by the Toronto Humane Society. He owned media properties all over the world, but he was surprisingly unworldly. In his limousine driving from Rosedale to work each morning, he enjoyed listening to a radio documentary series I had written for the Canadian Broadcasting Corporation on the Sahara — but he didn't realize that the fabled medieval mud town of Timbuktu actually existed! Sitting in a high-rise office on Bay Street crowded with landscape paintings and a portrait of his favourite dog, Gonzo, he told me his father "didn't actually renounce his Canadian citizenship to become a peer [in 1964]. Under the laws of Canada at that time, it was not possible to have dual citizenship, and my father lost his Canadian citizenship when he became a British citizen. That took the decision out of the Canadian government's hands and left it entirely up to the UK government. My father continued to regard himself as a Canadian and hoped to finish his life in Canada, but, regretfully, that did not happen."

In May 1985 came an opportunity that would change Black's life. At the Bilderberg meeting at the Arrowwood resort, outside New York, Andrew Knight told Black that the *Daily Telegraph* was undergoing severe financial and managerial strain. The paper was the English-speaking world's largest-circulation conservative broadsheet. It dates from 1855, the time of the Crimean War. Black's great-grandfather Robert Thomas Riley was the son of one of the founding shareholders. Since the late 1920s, the *Telegraph* had been controlled by the Berry family, industrious Welsh entrepreneurs with a history of coming to the rescue of faltering companies and then building up durable value. William Berry, the first Lord Camrose and one of the pre-war giants of Fleet Street, had promoted high standards of reporting at the *Telegraph*. He had the good sense to oppose fascism throughout the 1930s (unlike his competitor, Lord Rothermere at the *Daily Mail*) and had even employed Winston Churchill as a freelance contributor before the Second World War.

The *Telegraph* broke the one million circulation barrier in

April 1947 — a net daily sale of 108,000 more copies than the *New York Times* and the *New York Herald Tribune* combined. But Camrose's son Michael — Lord Hartwell — a deaf and extremely shy man prone to mumbling, did not have much entrepreneurial flair. His mission was to preserve the value and style of his late father in the newspaper's executive offices on the fifth floor of 135 Fleet Street. "Just as he kept his own offices unchanged, with their 1930s panelling and their ancient Telegraph contents bills for decoration, so he maintained his father's routines to the letter," writes Duff Hart-Davis, the *Telegraph* historian. "A butler dressed in black still guarded the entrance to the fifth floor."[134] Staff members of the old school snapped to attention when they spoke to Hartwell on the telephone.

Hart-Davis explains that Hartwell maintained an antiquated system of management, surrounding himself with venerable gentlemen like himself, and had done little to prepare the next generation — his sons Adrian and Nicholas Berry — for administrative roles. Adrian was more interested in science than administration. Nicholas had shown a keen business sense, but had not been prepared for succession. Besides, in the midst of rapid technological change on Fleet Street and an ongoing war of attrition between newspaper proprietors and print unions, Hartwell had made a catastrophic mistake — committing to costly new printing installations in the east London's Docklands on the basis of overly optimistic projections without properly evaluating the financial risks. The new presses would offer financial benefits to the paper, but the *Telegraph* did not have the financial depth needed to pull it off without new capital.

After lengthy negotiations with several banks during 1984, "a consortium led by Security Pacific, and including the National Westminster County Bank, the Hong Kong and Shanghai Bank and Wardley London, agreed to put up £75 million on condition that the Telegraph raised £29 million from the sale of shares."[135] Given the precarious financial position of the company, N. M. Rothschild & Sons was having trouble raising the £29 million. "The *Telegraph* was bankrupt effectively," Knight told me in a long telephone interview from a ferry dock in the

Hebrides, "and it couldn't raise the money it needed to finance its new presses, let alone survive. Rothschild could not raise all the money needed, so I contacted Black with a view to having him invest in the paper. I had two candidates in mind, Conrad or Kay Graham. I went to Conrad because he was more ideologically attuned to the *Telegraph* and, unlike Kay, was not a friend of the Berry family, so future muddles would be avoided if and when he got control."

The *Telegraph* was the crown jewel of the British press. As Black later wrote, "The key to the *Daily Telegraph*'s immense success was a formula devised by Lord Camrose and faithfully continued by his son, Lord Hartwell, consisting of an excellent, fair, concise, informative newspaper; good sports coverage; a page three in which the kinkiest, gamiest, most salacious and most scatalogical stories in Britain were set out in the most apparently sober manner, but with sadistically explicit quotations from court transcripts; and extreme veneration of the Royal Family."[136]

Beyond the quality and prestige of the title, Black was also interested in the political platform that ownership, even partial ownership, would offer — a platform in a world capital, more than just a cut above Toronto. There was a charming, faded elegance to London, with its palaces and hotels, the bulky black Carbodies cabs and double-deckers lumbering by, the trotting procession of the Horse Guards and richly liveried staff in the clubs. London was a layered city, a visual feast for a history buff such as Black.

There was also the impressive literary tradition of British journalism, such as William Deedes (later Lord Deedes), a former editor of the *Daily Telegraph*; he had been a war correspondent during the Italian invasion of Ethiopia in the 1930s (and a character in Evelyn Waugh's *Scoop*); a parliamentary secretary in Sir Winston Churchill's post-war government; and a cabinet minister under Harold Macmillan. In the 1970s and 1980s, following in the footsteps of Waugh and George Orwell, came a series of adventurers and unusually gifted men — Reuters correspondent Anthony Grey, who was held hostage for two years during the Chinese Cultural Revolution as a symbol of the paper tigers of capitalism; war correspondent Max Hastings, who sometimes scooped the competition by taking a taxi to the front; John Pilger, a rugged Australian whose life mission was to denounce every abuse of power (he attacked the manufacturers of thalidomide as willingly as he blasted Henry Kissinger for the indiscriminate American bombing of civilian Cambodia during the 1970s); and Robert Fisk, who risked his life time and again reporting from Lebanon and throughout the Middle East.

There was, above all, the prospect of a global soapbox, from which to expound what he called rather grandly "integral conservatism," an ideology that aspired to dismantle social welfare, trim down the government and allow proprietors the sort of free rein to run and profit from businesses the way they had in the late nineteenth and early twentieth centuries.

Black relished the negotiating process; the opportunity of gaining the *Telegraph* at a bargain price and releasing the locked-up value. "You have all the different elements there," said Black. "You have possible economic gain, you have human drama, you sometimes have ... the abrupt and almost cruel end of long-standing incumbency, and the rise of new interests, which I suppose I myself represented. You have the unfolding drama, and you are conscious at all times of being in the midst of the drama, whose outcome is hoped-for, but there is a great deal of suspense as you get into these things. A lot of nervous energy is put into it."

But Black recognized the risks as well. Knight suggested that by offering the last £10 million Hartwell needed to complete the share issue, Black could become a major player.

"Andrew," asked Black, "what's the point of me acquiring 14 per cent of a bankrupt paper?"

"They would need more financing within a year or two," said Knight. "Provided you get a lock on their inevitable need for further financing through a pre-emption on any future Berry family rights [in future financings], you'll get control."

Knight was right. "Hartwell could not resist Conrad's price for help," he said.

"Dan Colson [Black's long-time friend and lawyer] drafted a

watertight pre-emption that soon gave Conrad control."

Black did not have time to fly to London for a meeting with Lord Hartwell and his advisers. Instead, Hartwell, managing director H. M. Stephen and Hugh Lawson from the *Telegraph*, banker Rupert Hambro (who was advising Black) and a young executive from Rothschilds took the Concorde from Heathrow to Kennedy to meet Black. The meeting took place in an airport hotel room, which shuddered with each takeoff and landing of a passenger jet.[137] They discussed the Canadian's offer to invest £10 million in the *Telegraph* through Ravelston. Following Knight's advice, Black insisted on the pre-emption on future Berry family rights, repeating himself to make sure Hartwell could understand the full weight of his words. And that is when Hartwell made the second catastrophic mistake of his career. After raising £75 million from the banks, he knew that Black's £10 million would allow him to complete his £29 million sale of shares. He could not imagine ever needing to raise more capital, which was the situation that would activate Black's pre-emptive right. Hartwell simply replied, "I don't think we can resist that."[138]

He had just given up effective control of the *Telegraph*, his family's legacy.

For Black, it was a repeat of the Argus takeover. He later wrote, "I felt at once as I had when the Phillips and McDougald estates entered into the May 1978 Ravelston shareholders' agreement with us. After years of retreat and regrouping an amazing prospect was opening up. In corporate life as in other spheres, Fabian tactics eventually produce results."[139] But a takeover with an important difference — control of the *Telegraph* meant that Black was on his way to becoming the next London-based Canadian press lord, and a baron in the House of Lords.

On June 14, 1985, the *Globe and Mail* published a business story by its London correspondent — Black's old classmate at Upper Canada College — John Fraser. "Conrad Black's controversial purchase of 14 per cent of The Daily Telegraph Group of Newspapers continues to fuel speculation on Fleet Street, as insiders at The Daily Telegraph yesterday confirmed that Mr. Black has an option of first refusal on any future shares the controlling Berry family might sell. Official spokesmen for the Telegraph Group, which includes the prestigious *Daily Telegraph* (daily circulation: 1.2 million), continue to issue contradictory and misleading statements about the nature of the investment. Initially, it was denied that Mr. Black and board chairman Lord Hartwell had come to any understanding on future share purchases. Now there is simply no comment."[140]

On Fleet Street there was speculation that the *Telegraph* was taking an expensive gamble by moving and modernizing its printing operations. *The Times* mentioned Black's great-grandfather and said, "the descendant intends to make up for lost time."

John Fraser would later write in the *Globe and Mail's Report on Business* magazine that at the *Telegraph* "the immediate crisis was averted and one company director told a staff member that the 'most amusing detail' of the deal was that Black thought more shares might become available to him. 'He doesn't seem to realize we will never have a need for him again, especially after we are safely moved into the new plant,' the director was reported as saying. . . .When the deal was struck, managing director Stephen informed Fleet Street that the *Telegraph* had found a happy resolution to its short-term problems. Black was described as 'a wholly passive investor' who had 'no known interests in the newspaper business'. . .That ignorance was comical, though, when it came to the company's books. In fact, it became clear that Hartwell had not the faintest idea of how badly off he was. Much of the financial data contained in the April share prospectus turned out to be calamitously underestimated. The company's true position was desperate."[141]

A new audit of the books showed three hundred phantom employees on full pay and uncontrolled personal spending charged to company expense accounts. Moreover, Hartwell had misjudged his ability to move to the Docklands and acquire new presses with existing resources. "The Berry family needed more finance for the *Telegraph* not within a 'year or two' as I had predicted but within months," Andrew Knight told me. "Michael Hartwell was aging, had failed to bring his very bright children in to help him run the company and couldn't grasp that he would be needing additional financing within a short time. His managers were all his age bracket and yes-men. Not one of them understood numbers as Hartwell's [younger] son, Nicky Berry, would have done had he been allowed to see them."

Adrian Berry, the current Viscount Camrose, remained on the board of the *Telegraph* under Black for several years serving as its science editor and told me he was not involved in the negotiations surrounding the sale of the paper.

In the fall of 1985, Nicholas Berry tried to put together a competing bid for the paper, to no avail. The Australian corporate raider Robert Holmes à Court showed some interest, but backed off when he obtained a copy of Black's pre-emption agreement. Berry holds considerable ill will toward Black to this day. "Conrad Black took advantage of an old man, who happened to be my father," Berry wrote me.[142] "My father, having realized his mistake, behaved like a perfect gentleman. Black went around sneering about him. You may want to conclude from the above that his arrogance is greater than his intelligence."

Black does not think any better of Nicholas Berry. "In the case of the Berrys — that allegation that I put one over on Lord Hartwell was produced by his younger son, but again that is one complete falsehood, and it gets tied up in the politics of the Berry family. It is not for me to comment on how those politics have ramified, but I did nothing of the kind. Mr. Nicholas Berry, the person I am referring to, knows perfectly well that I stipulated a condition for making this an investment. His father knew perfectly well what I was asking for and said, and I quote, 'I don't think we can resist that.' And volunteered, and he had the benefit of counsel, and it was worked out, put down on paper, and signed — he had an investment advisor, the House of Rothschild, and he had legal counsel, and he was clearly of sound mind and continued as chairman of the *Telegraph* for two years afterwards at my request. And he knew perfectly well what he was doing. And the argument that he was soundly, functioning chairman of the *Telegraph* up till the point he took the Concorde for New York and suddenly lost his mind and was taken over the barrel by me, in a manner that was not picked up by his own counsel, or as Nicholas Berry would have it, his

counsel was negligent and Rothschild was really acting for us —
all of this is just nonsense. But again, with things like that, you
are better to let it go, instead of arguing it. In fairness to Lord
Hartwell, he never made that allegation. The allegation was
made on his behalf by his son. I had the impression the relations
were not terribly good anyway. His son partly had a grievance
against his father and partly against me."

In late 1985, as Black was closing the deal — using his pre-
emptive right to future family shares to secure control of the
Telegraph — critical articles began appearing in the British press.
Writing in *The Spectator* on November 23, 1985, Canadian
author John Ralston Saul accused Black of enriching himself at
the expense of the companies he had operated over the years,
including Massey-Ferguson and Dominion Stores. Saul promoted rational politics and ethics in his many writings and
detested right-wing corporatism and nouveau riche capitalism.

"By June 1985 his sole remaining operating company was
Norcen Energy Resources. With nothing left to reorganize, he
turned on his partners — and restructured them out, leaving
only himself, a solitary, rich young man with his reputation
severely undermined in Canada. There was even public talk of
some members of the financial community doubting his intentions so much that they didn't want to do business with him."
Saul speculated that Black "is neither a man to spend $17 mil-
lion for a minority shareholder's seat on a Fleet Street board nor
of a temperament likely to restrain himself from interfering in
every detail of what he owns, it is relevant to wonder what
political views he will bring to the *Telegraph* if he gained control. Mr. Black has the spirit of neo-conservatism running in his
veins. The result is right wing rather than conservative. He is
extremely pro-American and pro-Reagan."[143]

On December 5, 1985, the board of the *Telegraph* agreed to
terms for the rights issue, whereby Hollinger, another of Black's
investment vehicles, would obtain just under £20 million of
stock — 39,901,125 Ordinary Shares at 50 pence a share —
bringing Black's total holding to 50.1 per cent.

Simply put, it was a steal. One of the finest newspapers in the
world had changed hands — for less than £30 million. (Just four

years later, Rupert Murdoch valued the *Telegraph* at £1 billion.) It was in despair that the British historian and journalist Paul Johnson wrote in *The Spectator* in mid-December 1985 of Black's "tragic" takeover, played out in several acts — Hartwell's launching of an ambitious investment program in new presses; his ignoring the talents within his own family; his miscalculation in accepting Black's pre-emptive right to new shares; and, finally, the loss of control by the Berry family. "It has always reminded me of Miss Havisham's wedding-cake," wrote Johnson. "To save it requires great sensitivity and above all respect for the uprightness and loyalty which binds the paper, its staff and its readers together. Simply letting in the brutal winds of commercial change could easily reduce it to dust."[144]

Black had published the conservative syndicated columns of American writer William F. Buckley, Jr. in the Sherbrooke *Record* since the late 1960s. Now he was conferring with Buckley on the best way to establish a conservative publication of his own in Canada.

Black was in the company of people who made a difference on the world stage. He was impressed by the staunch conservatism of Margaret Thatcher and Ronald Reagan. The two leaders were a study in contrast.

Autocratic, ideological, self-righteous, almost manic, Thatcher managed to dominate the old boys' network of government, sometimes slamming her handbag down on the table at 10 Downing Street to cut short ministerial discussion. And she had blocked the final dismemberment of Britain's shrunken empire by fighting off the Argentine invasion of the Falklands in the South Atlantic.

Reagan was anything but an intellectual. In his rambling biblical evocations of America — the "light of the world," a "city set on a hill"[145] — and his call on the American scientific community to develop the Star Wars anti-missile defence system, he demonstrated a fierce determination to restore the prestige of the presidency and the political and military supremacy of the United States.

Thatcher and Reagan celebrated their countries' "special

relationship" and triumphantly upheld the profit motive, while attacking statism, the power of labour unions, the militaristic Soviet Union and the general attitude of defeatism in the West. They represented the flowering of what Black called "integral conservatism." He wanted to join this broadly based neo-conservative movement, now spreading beyond Britain and America. Black would like to have played the sort of gadfly conservative role in Canada that Buckley played in the United States. A graduate of Yale, Buckley had served as a CIA agent, newspaper columnist, author of fiction and essays alike and hard-hitting television host of the public affairs show *Firing Line*. Buckley was a Catholic and self-styled conservative in Oxford-cloth shirts and Brookes Brothers suits. He promoted "freedom and order and community and justice in an age of technology" while slamming liberals for government regulations, restrictions on individual liberty and the detrimental effects of well-meaning but flawed progressive attitudes. (Buckley's promotion of conservatism was a regular, if incongruous, feature of *Playboy* magazine, where his articles on Nixon's 1973 visit to China, the importance of human charity, or the imperative of spying appeared alongside soft-core erotic fantasies, sex advice columns and photo spreads of the girl-next-door as misty-eyed courtesan.)

Canada was undergoing a major transition in the early 1980s, but it was not really fertile ground for the Thatcher/Reagan brand of "integral conservatism." Pierre Trudeau's Liberals had defeated the minority Progressive Conservative government of Joe Clark in December 1979 on a confidence motion, then returned to power with a comfortable majority in 1980. Trudeau had patriated the Canadian constitution from Westminster in 1981 under terms that were unacceptable to Quebec's provincial legislature. The following year he enshrined in the constitution a new "Canadian Charter of Rights and Freedoms."

Trudeau had advocated just such a charter since his *Cité Libre* days in the 1950s. But the charter of 1982 came with a twist — a "notwithstanding clause" allowing provincial legislatures to override, when they judged necessary, the charter's protection of fundamental rights (such as freedom of expression, conscience, association and assembly, and the right to life, liberty and security of the person). The charter marked a shift in Canadian political culture since it encouraged individuals to see their relationship to society in terms of rights. It also contributed to a grievance culture according to which everybody was potentially a victim, or victimizer, of somebody else. Trudeau had accepted the notwithstanding clause as a trade-off to gain provincial support for the charter he had always wanted. But the clause was an aberration: it went against the entire classical liberal tradition since the eighteenth century, which had sought to protect the individual from the arbitrary dictates of the state. Moreover, Trudeau's legacy was to make it practically impossible for the Canadian constitution — the supreme law of Canada — to be amended in the future.

I translated two of Trudeau's books into English and remember introducing him at a *Cité Libre* dinner in Montreal to Professor John Humphrey, who had served as director of the United Nations human rights program from 1946 to 1966, was a close collaborator of Eleanor Roosevelt, one of the authors of the Universal Declaration of Human Rights, and the person who saw the UN's great human rights covenants through to their adoption in 1966. He told me at the time that the Canadian Charter of Rights and Freedoms was a remarkable but flawed achievement, since "the notwithstanding clause gives the state an arbitrary power over the individual, defeating the purpose of constitutionalizing human rights in the first place."

Peter White said that at one point, "Trudeau had offered Conrad a seat in the Senate, and I think Jim Coutts [Trudeau's principal secretary from 1975 to 1981] offered him a safe seat to run for the House of Commons, and a possible seat in the Cabinet, both of which Conrad turned down."

Black disapproved of Trudeau's position on the ideological spectrum. "He strenuously confirmed that Canada was a left-of-centre country," Black recalled. "Not an extreme left-of-centre country, of course, and he wasn't an extreme leftist himself, but a soft-left country, and in my opinion, that's the wrong course. He accelerated the process of the brain drain to the U.S., and the economic disparity between Canada and the U.S. . . .

Trudeau had formidable leadership qualities. He was courageous, he had great style, flair, and the ability to inspire people.
As prime minister, he had the cunning to maintain himself in
that office, although he never had two consecutive majority
elections. But his policy decisions were mistaken, other than —
to a degree — dealing with Quebec. In my opinion, he called
upon the country to pay an excessive price, claiming the rights
of the individual were important — not the rights of jurisdic-
tion — as Quebec leaders from Duplessis on had claimed. And
the Charter of Rights he gave us has been a carte blanche for
judges to cease to be jurists, and become legislators. The results,
in my opinion, have been both confusing and, in many cases,
negative. . . . It isn't a Charter of Rights, it's a Charter of Rights
in each province, as long as the governing party in that province
does not choose to vacate it in that province for any given purpose. And he couldn't have had it adopted on any other basis."

I felt Trudeau had been a bourgeois socialist, a dilettante, a
mother's boy with an outsized libido. A narcissist. A womanizer
with a high opinion of his own style. He sometimes seemed to
play the dandy just to get attention. This was a man who had
sampled everything life had to offer.

There was an aura about him. He dated beautiful stars —
women such as Barbra Streisand, Liona Boyd, Louise Marleau
and Margot Kidder. He was something new to Canadian politics: a jet-setting playboy. "Almost all men who are truly successful with women," Margot Kidder, the stunning brunette
who played Lois Lane in the *Superman* movies, later said about
Trudeau, "share a common trait, and that is the unconscious
ability to make women see the little boy who lives trapped
under the layers of defences, because once a woman has seen
that essence in a man she'll never get over him." She recalled a
let's-pretend-we're-children game Trudeau liked to play, because
of its suggestive erotic overtones. "One of the games he invented
was Playing Indian. 'Shall we play Indian?' he'd suggest on the
weekend at Harrington Lake. You played Indian by skulking
through the woods, trying not to alert your enemy as to your
whereabouts by snapping twigs underfoot or breaking the
branches of trees that hang over the path. The RCMP, lurking at

a discreet distance, would act as if they didn't notice that the prime minister was tiptoeing around with a girlfriend. They'd stand at attention in the woods, pretending they weren't there, pretending they were trees."[146]

In fact, a Liberal senator told me Trudeau had voracious sexual appetites, and that senators and ministers were regularly on the lookout for attractive young women they could send his way. It gave a whole new meaning to the phrase "government procurement."

However, this playboy aura was also carefully cultivated and manipulated by the Liberal Party at considerable personal cost to Trudeau's wife, Margaret Sinclair, and their sons.

In 1984, the federal Liberal Party under Trudeau was a spent force. Trudeau tried to divert attention from his incapacity to develop sound social and economic policies by launching an ill-planned and ineffective international tour, ostensibly in the interests of world peace. By then, the Parti Québécois under René Lévesque was also spent. Lévesque's painful political demise in 1985 can be attributed to his poor record negotiating on Quebec's behalf and his commitment to parliamentary democracy (since he had accepted the right of the Quebec population to say "no" to his goal of an independent Quebec state . . . some of his Parti Québécois colleagues would have preferred a unilateral declaration of independence.) After Trudeau's departure, a caretaker government under Prime Minister John Turner was defeated in 1984, and after Lévesque's departure, Quebec's caretaker, Premier Pierre-Marc Johnson, met the same fate in 1985.

The decline of the federal Liberals and the Parti Québécois signalled an opportunity for the Progressive Conservative Party under Brian Mulroney. In 1984, Mulroney led the Conservatives to the greatest majority in Canadian history — 211 seats in the House of Commons, with the support both of English-speaking conservatives and French-speaking nationalists. Mulroney did not have Trudeau's polish. He tried too hard to be charismatic, to inflate and project his personality. His intellectual background was the give-and-take of labour negotiation. And he often seemed to be angling for some personal advantage. But he represented a sea change in a country that tended to treat the Liberals as the natural governing party.

As Mulroney recalled in an interview with me, "We tried to correct what the Liberals had damaged, and that meant deficit reduction, reduction in spending and privatization, deregulation, free trade, NAFTA and the like — these were, all of them, essentially unpopular [at the time], but turned out to be determined to be in the Canadian interest — witness the fact that Mr. Chrétien kept them all." In effect, while Mulroney had moved the centre of the political spectrum to the right, he was essentially pragmatic. But it was the clear, uncompromising ideological expression of the Thatcher and Reagan brands of conservatism that held the stronger appeal for Black.

Mulroney did not gratuitously stake out a position different from the United States. On the contrary, he developed a close and mutually satisfying relationship with Canada's only geographic neighbour and largest trading partner. Mulroney was markedly different from Reagan and Thatcher on one issue in particular — the need to negotiate a transition from South Africa's apartheid regime to the beginnings of a more multiracial state with democratic institutions representing the entire population.

Black had urged Mulroney to run for the leadership of the Progressive Conservatives in 1976, and they had stayed in touch ever since. His business associate and fellow Ravelston shareholder Peter White served as the prime minister's principal secretary. But Mulroney fell short of Black's ideological expectations. Black disdained what could be called Mulroney's "soft-right" conservatism just as he had detested Trudeau's "soft-left" liberalism.

"Frankly," Black recalls, "Brian had a mandate to go much further to the right than he did. Now he doesn't agree with that, and he defends himself very cogently, and I think we have to make clear that he had the job and not us; it was his mandate, and not mine, and he did what he thought was right, and to a large degree I have to respect that. The fact is, I think he could have led the country to a more integral conservatism. He didn't disturb what we might call the 'Trudeau settlement' very much.

He criticized the notwithstanding clause, but only when he was under pressure because of the Meech Lake Accord and other things breaking down. And in his first budget, he stepped back from any repeal of universality [of social programs]. So in the end, Brian did not conduct a very relentless assault upon the structure of statism, as it had been built up by Pearson and Trudeau."

An opportunity for Black to play the public role of thinking businessman and articulate defender of "integral conservatism" (going beyond Mulroney's views) came in 1985, when the Thomson newspaper the *Globe and Mail* decided to bring out a new magazine, and Black was invited to write for it. Kenneth Thomson knew a lot about Black already: "Conrad always admired The Thomson Corporation and its predecessor companies, including Thomson Newspapers. I remember an occasion when he quoted financial information by memory from Thomson Newspapers' annual report with pinpoint accuracy. I was very impressed with his amazing recall."

The respect was mutual. According to Black, Ken Thomson "has not received the credit he deserves for the colossal prosperity of the Thomson Corporation since he became responsible for it. It's unusual, but not unheard of, to see a career like his father's [Roy Thomson] — from socio-economically humble origins, and then making it. What is extremely unusual . . . is to have such a successful man followed by apparent right of succession by his son, who redoubles that success and then builds exponentially on what he took over. . . . As a newspaper owner, I had the impression that the only newspaper he really enjoyed was the *Globe and Mail*, and his definition of ownership was a very withdrawn one from the paper's operations. He was occasionally criticized quite unfairly in the pages of the newspaper. He was, in those respects, considerably more indulgent and broad-minded than other [newspaper proprietors], including me. But commercially, he has been a huge success, including his departure from the newspaper business."

The person who hired Black as columnist was the *Globe*'s editor-in-chief, Norman Webster, a Montrealer from an old Establishment family who had served with distinction as *Globe* correspondent in China. "We were starting the *Report on Business* [*ROB*] magazine, and we wanted to make the *Globe and Mail* franchise stronger," said Webster. "Magazines have a different personality from straight business reporting. We needed interesting columnists, and Black was a clear choice, as someone who was well known in business and was Canadian and had a lot of interesting opinions. This was a major project for the *Globe and Mail*, and I was very involved initially. We wanted the magazine to be lively and well written."[147]

Hiring Black as a business columnist working for Lord Thomson of Fleet was a clever move. Not only was he opinionated and outspoken, he had a brash entrepreneur's self-confidence and, above all, a robust perspective on Canada's place in the world that would interest the *Globe's* readers.

From the start, Conrad Black's role as a columnist reflected a sort of love-hate relationship with the paper. In 1979, Kenneth Thomson had topped Black's bid for FP Publications, which included the *Globe*. Then, between 1985 and 1988, the *Globe's* *ROB* magazine freed up space for Black's columns. Peter Cook, who had worked in the Far East for Reuters, served as Black's editor. Their paths had already crossed, figuratively, when Cook wrote a book that criticized Black's role during the crisis at farm equipment manufacturer Massey-Ferguson.

"I went round to 10 Toronto Street to meet him," said Cook. "I had written the book on Massey in 1981. He knew me from that, although I had not met him at the time. We had a little chat. He was very pleasant. 'You are my editor,' he said. 'You can do with my copy what you will.' He used to stay up late at night in his mansion, bashing away at an Underwood. I think the letter 'e' did not print properly. But actually, he didn't want a single word of his columns changed. He asked for a pay raise at one point, which amused us a lot. I think he was getting about two thousand dollars for an article at the time."[148]

ROB magazine allowed Black to celebrate his own corporate successes in print, and it got his high-school buddy John Fraser, a *Globe* correspondent in Britain, to write a long, sassy feature about Black's 1985 takeover of the *Telegraph*. Black was a columnist unlike any other. He was an observer and player — a high-profile personality continually scrutinized by the media. His relationship with the *Globe* was turbulent. In 1987, Black filed a $7-million lawsuit against the *Globe* when it published a feature attacking him. The same year, he acquired control of the monthly magazine *Saturday Night* from Webster, his *Globe* boss. The following year, Black became a direct competitor of his employer, when he launched the *Financial Post* as a daily national financial paper.

Conrad Black seemed a phenomenon to many journalists — a man of wealth and power, an iconoclast, actor and master of the corporate takeover. He chided them for their haste in judging, and he mocked their lack of professionalism. There was something forbidding, even Gothic about him, as he brooded about the state of the world — the "decline of the West" as the apocalyptic Spengler had written. And journalists knew he was writing the *Report on Business* columns in the genteel comfort of his multi-million-dollar mansion. Black's domed library, with a secret stairwell leading to a second-storey gallery, was sometimes likened to St. Peter's Basilica in Rome. Word had got around about all those 1825 mahogany Empire-style armchairs and marble-paper-patterned upholstery.

Allowing themselves considerable poetic licence, some journalists saw Black's Georgian mansion as Xanadu, the gloomy castle of Orson Welles's *Citizen Kane*. They compared a caricature of Black with the silver screen's all-powerful newspaper magnate whose name was "loved, hated, feared and often spoken." There were some grounds for comparison between Black and Kane.

Black himself explicitly made the comparison in 1993, joking about the way he had defended the water quality of Quebec's rural Brome Lake in 1968. "Like Orson Welles in *Citizen Kane* saying, 'People will think what I tell them to think,' I launched into a violent campaign against the mis-managers of the dying lake."[149]

In the movie, the tragic Kane was expelled from a series of private schools, got rid of the old guard as he worked his way up the corporate ladder, and ended up in bitter solitude — a man out to dominate a world that could not love him on his terms.

Writing of his first encounter with Black in 1987, *Saturday Night* editor Robert Fulford took the comparison with Citizen Kane a step further, noting that Black was "an extremely uncommon millionaire, not so much in the content of his conversation as in his manner. He was more theatrical than any other businessman of my acquaintance. His personality had a staged, directed feel to it. It was also oddly familiar. Where had I seen it before, a large, handsome man with a supercilious and condescending manner and a baroque vocabulary? Of course: Orson Welles in *Citizen Kane*. I was talking to Citizen Black." Fulford quickly decided that he could not continue as editor of *Saturday Night*, considering what he felt would be Black's hands-on role in editorial decisions.

Journalists such as Fulford could be excused for comparing Black to Citizen Kane — but the comparisons may have originated with Conrad himself. He was the kind of man with surging, grandiose fantasies of power and influence, who dropped clues here and there on the path of reporters following in his wake, to see whether they would take the hint and make the connection. He fed their curiosity, so they could feed his vanity back.

Of course, Kane was old before his time — much like Black. "I don't think of myself as being young," Black told Peter C. Newman in 1982. "David Radler, my partner, claims I have a psychological age of eighty."[150]

For his part, Mark Abley of the Montreal *Gazette* wrote of Black that he could laugh without moving his mouth, his double-chinned face was big although his eyes were small, and he advanced "like a tiger through the jungle."[151]

Norman Webster told me that getting Black to stay on topic was not straightforward. "It is not easy being a columnist. It's got to be interesting. In something like the *Report on Business* magazine, there's got to be substance. I've been in the columnist game for thirty years. I like columns to have information and analysis. Too many columns are just rants, blowing off steam and writing how one feels in general. I had envisaged Conrad writing about Canadian business. But one of his first columns was about capital punishment and abortion, which was a surprise to everyone, including the magazine editor. I said 'let him go and we will see how it works out.' The column turned out to be a combination of Conrad's opinions and some business subjects we came up with. Conrad's column did what I hoped it would."[152]

Black's *ROB Magazine* columns were deliberately provocative and disdainful of political correctness. He stated his views on arms control, banking regulations, Senate reform, civil libertarians, capital punishment, the lost work ethic and corporate concentration — not the usual fare for a business magazine. He put a lot of work into the columns, researching them carefully, reading exhaustively, making connections that most journalists would miss. The writing was done mostly late at night.

Editing Black was a challenge, said Peter Cook. "He used extremely long words and sentences that did not always seem to mean anything. But the articles could be vitriolic. Managing editor Doreen Guthrie and I would try to get back and discuss changes with him. We had small confrontations with him, but we had a magazine to bring out. Besides, if he didn't make sense, that would ultimately be Norman Webster's problem, not mine."

The articles were like the Rabelaisian "verbal tempests" Northrop Frye had written about — "the tremendous outpouring of words in catalogues, abusive epithets and erudite technicalities."[153] Black's writing was not particularly persuasive — it was more a series of peppery self-affirmations. Writing from personal experience gave an added edge to Black's distaste for the media's abuse of power and absence of responsibility. "In Canada," he wrote, "the press is addicted to creating news by the elevation and destruction of reputations. It is easier to manufacture news than to report it." He attacked his employer directly: "*The Globe and Mail* has fatted itself for decades on the very tenuous propositions that it is our national newspaper and that it is a distinguished newspaper by international standards."[154]

Month after month, Black's columns were platforms for his strident neo-conservatism. He urged Canadians to reduce the share of the gross national product consumed by the public sector (as Thatcher and Reagan had done); to "complete the detachment of the public service unions from the industrial trade unions, and to revoke this antediluvian nonsense of the right to strike in public service — and against the public interest"; to reward merit and innovation in the business world rather than seek "another outlet for our dreary national tendencies to punish success, promote mediocrity, encourage envy and resentment of economic success, and exalt mindless official meddlesomeness"; to stop "the Canadian media's unshakeable predilection to destroy almost anyone who actually does anything"; to appreciate Mulroney's government as superior, in policy terms, to anything for the previous thirty years (although Black acknowledged the prime minister's "hyperbole, platitudes, dalliance with outright dissimulation, the questionable conduct of associates, and the appearance of vanity [that] have seriously damaged his stature.") On abortion, Black said no resolution of the controversy was possible "without some reconciliation of polarized views. It is as unrealistic to think of eliminating abortions altogether or of inflicting childbirth as a punishment on unlucky or careless women as it is to represent abortion as merely another manifestation of an individual's sovereignty over her own body, endowed with no more moral or social significance than a bowel movement."[155]

Black was moulding his own public persona with his trenchant opinions, but this came with a cost. When he attacked Canadians for being less competitive, individualistic, creative and generous than Americans, he was strongly refuted by nationalists who feared he wanted Canada to become a carbon copy of the United States. The Canadian left was upset with his feisty defence of "integral conservatism," and his growing profile in the media and the corporate world.

Black developed this brand of conservatism slowly, at a time when his business practices were hotly contested — from snatching Argus to dumping Massey, from gutting the Dominion employees' pension fund to being slapped with serious charges by the SEC. His right-wing ideology seemed an affected and unnecessarily grand justification of what he had already done, rather than a clear mission and vision statement guiding him in what he was about to do.

Maude Barlow, a left-wing author and director of a non-governmental organization who co-wrote a book about Conrad Black and Barbara Amiel's right-wing views (*The Big Black Book*), said she first met Black during a visit to Canada by Prince Charles and Princess Diana in 1983. "I was just about to become Pierre Trudeau's senior adviser on women's issues," she said. "Conrad Black and I approached a bowl of strawberries, and there was one left. I offered to split the last strawberry with him, and he speared it and walked off."[156]

Barlow challenged Black in the media, and eventually in the courts. "He's a show-off," she said. "He's a public guy, calling attention to himself and, in so doing, he has become a target for what people most dislike about unregulated capitalism. He called it on himself, and he articulated a set of values that people assume is what goes on in the boardroom. He revels in his class and financial superiority and his ability to do what he wants. I think he is ideological. He is right wing. He is very bright. His ideology may be a cover for his fairly ruthless business practices. He believes there should be a class system in Canada. He is a son of privilege. He thinks that's good. He believes the captains of industry should play a key role in identifying the future direction of the state."

When Black declared war on protectionism, inflated wages, currency debasement and falling productivity — charging much of it was orchestrated by labour unions — the subtext was that others could make economic sacrifices, but he was a proprietor taking substantial risks, and if he reaped huge rewards, he deserved it. Economic salvation, he said, was to be found in harder work, lower wages, heightened productivity, increased competitiveness and, above all, free trade with the United States, which is "the only way to avert the country's excruciating economic demise."[157] He was in favour of abolishing universal social programs, believing government aid should only benefit those who really needed it. But Canadians were more centrist than Black had hoped, rejecting his neo-conservative ideal of the way he felt they should be.

He defined his oft-used "integral conservatism" as "the maximization of individual latitude and liberty, up to the point that the exercise starts to interfere with the possible exercise of similar rights by other people." He believes most people are fairly conservative. "Even figures of the left are often quite conservative in some ways. Very few people are really nihilists who want to destroy everything. Almost everybody gets comfortable with something and wants to conserve that. I am not a knee-jerk supporter of anything with a bit of seniority . . . I would say I was really rather more of a reformer than a conservative, and more of a seeker of constructive change than a reflexive upholder of the status quo. One tries to be a pragmatist after all, and do the sensible thing."

Black acknowledges that his outspoken positions have sometimes worked against him. "When I started out as a corporate figure in Canada with any stature, I thought that I was accomplishing something for business in general by helping to break down the stereotype of businessmen as inarticulate and reluctant to put any kind of interesting front on much of what they were doing — with a few exceptions — and in practice, I thought that was probably a mistake, because what it really did was bring down upon myself a great deal of obloquy as a kind of caricature of an insensitive capitalist, which I don't think is in fact representative of my real views. But that's not the point. I put myself — in public relations terms — in harm's way, where if I had to do it over again, I think I'd be a good deal more discreet than I was."

The provocative image Black projected as a columnist was reinforced by what he wrote about himself. In his July 1987 column, he felt "emboldened" to review his own corporate performance, in glowing terms, mentioning the takeover of Argus, the trading up of assets over the years and the reorganization of subsidiaries, sometimes resulting in substantial layoffs. "Those who invested with us in 1978," he concluded, "have profited handsomely. Argus common and preferred shareholders have gained 65 per cent to 120 per cent (to 1985 when the company was virtually taken private); Standard holders by 110 per cent; and Hollinger and Dominion shareholders have gained 136 per cent and 167 per cent since 1978, with bright prospects for continued appreciation. We have completed the transition from fragile control and fictitious ownership of a decrepit and ramshackle congeries of unionized retail food stores, iron ore and farm equipment assets and good but somewhat geriatric radio stations, to real and unencumbered ownership of a rich, well positioned, competently managed international newspaper company. Our past and future courses should now be unfathomably clear. Occult and myopic conjurings of 'factors' in evaluating Hollinger's performance seem, mercifully, to have subsided. The recent past has satisfactorily served its purposes but as my friends on the left used to say, 'We have seen the future, and it works.'"

Days after Black's boastful column, the *Globe* published a lengthy, critical feature by reporter John Partridge, entitled "Citizen Black." The article was an anthology of all the worst things anyone had ever said, thought, or written about Black. Whatever the motive, Partridge seemed to be replying directly to Black's columns in *Report on Business* magazine, "where he has been holding forth for the past 2½ years." Partridge made serious charges of corporate misconduct, based on hearsay and anonymous sources, offering no supporting evidence and ridiculing his subject: "Mr. Black doesn't care to discuss the matter at present. He is in London for the summer . . ." Black's London houseguest at the time, Emmett Cardinal Carter, the archbishop of Toronto, saw the article and said it was certainly libellous.

Black sued the *Globe* for $7 million, saying the article "alleged that my habitually unnamed critics considered that I 'milked' corporations and institutions, oppressed minority shareholders, pocketed other people's pensions, 'destroyed' public companies, and had been caught with my 'hand too close to the cookie jar.' The article conceded some positive aspects and concluded by acknowledging that I had unshakeable control of Hollinger, which I had at least managed with some degree of financial success."

Black felt that neither the "hard-bitten political left," nor "the grumbling detritus of the Establishment Old Guard" was responsible for the article, which was, instead, the work of "the sulphurous" Canadian spirit of envy predominant among young journalists.[158]

In a settlement reached nearly two years later, the *Globe* issued a retraction and apology, which said, in part: "In reviewing Mr. Black's business history, the author referred to prior characterizations of him and also expressed some of his own views. Mr. Black brought a libel action against *The Globe and Mail* in which he claimed the characterizations and comments in the article contained passages that were malicious and defamatory. Mr. Black says that this and some other examinations of his business activities in this newspaper and elsewhere have failed to include important aspects of his career."

With the *Globe* apology, Black dropped his lawsuits. It is interesting to note that Peter Atkinson, Hollinger's legal counsel defending Black in this case, faced fraud charges alongside Black during the criminal trial in Chicago in 2007.

In the months that followed Black's takeover of the *Telegraph*, he kept a low profile, moving ahead cautiously, fully aware that he was no longer dealing with the complacent and easily intimidated business and media crowd of English Canada. Black was facing unique challenges — class barriers, a different code of behaviour and a tradition of snobbery about the "colonies." Even the way English was spoken and written was different — the same words had a different meaning. Black's first move was to appoint Andrew Knight as chief executive of the *Telegraph*.

"My agreement with Black," Knight recalled, "was that, if he did get control, then I would be chief executive, and he would remain in Canada until we got things going. And that worked in picture-book style for the best part of four years. For example, the printers always blackmailed newspaper owners, and I would say to Black, 'you must remain in Toronto and pretend you are an ogre and not interested — that will force the printing chapels to deal seriously with management, which otherwise they never do.'

"Conrad played this hands-off role brilliantly, keeping his distance from day-to-day operations, making occasional and brief papal visits to London in an elderly Rolls-Royce, and things worked really well. It suited him partly because he had other big headaches in Canada at the time, partly because of his aversion to long-haul travel, but mainly because he agreed with the strategy and, with each success, gained confidence in it."

Two other key appointments were the new editors- in- chief of the daily and Sunday newspapers. For the daily, Black wanted Max Hastings, who had distinguished himself as a war correspondent, reporting on the final evacuation of American troops from Vietnam in 1975 and strolling into Port Stanley with a walking stick ahead of the British Army during the Falklands War in 1982. Hastings was a well-known military historian, a "wet" Tory who had managed discreetly to push his political agenda without taking himself too seriously.

Arriving in Toronto in February 1986, Hastings visited the Hollinger offices at 10 Toronto Street. "During a brief wait in his room," Hastings wrote later, "I studied the paintings, which reflected his passion for military and naval history. We were on common ground here. Conrad's heavy figure, clad in an ill-fitting double-breasted suit, steamed through the door not unlike a capital ship entering a harbour. I pointed to the picture behind his desk: '*Warspite* attacking Narvik in April 1940?' I have no idea whether he was impressed, but it seemed to get our conversation off on the right foot. I told him I made no bones about my passionate enthusiasm to take on the *Telegraph*. I was convinced I could resurrect the paper, and work well with Andrew. We talked about politics. I said I was a left-of-centre Tory."[159] Hastings noted Black's pro-American views might prove a problem.

Black's choice of editor-in-chief at the Sunday paper was a conservative British journalist and old friend of William F. Buckley and Richard Nixon, Peregrine Worsthorne. Sir Peregrine recalled his first meeting with Black in the winter of 1986: "He made me editor of the *Sunday Telegraph* in 1986. In those days, he was living in Toronto. I had never heard of him. It was snowing — thick snow. The taxi drove around his large Toronto estate, and we couldn't find our way in. I climbed a fence and trod through the snow like good King Wenceslas. Black came to the door and asked me to wait in the library, since his wife was just delivering a baby. He came later to the library and sounded me out on points of British history about which he is very knowledgeable."[160]

With a CEO and two editors-in-chief in place at the *Telegraph*, Black ruled by proxy from Toronto. He didn't feel confident enough to throw his weight around. But he was always very clear about his defence of the Anglo-American alliance and the Reagan administration. Sir Simon Jenkins, former editor of *The Times*, sees Black as a mid-twentieth-century newspaper proprietor in the mould of Beaverbrook, willing to promote an agenda of sorts.[161] However, this was not obvious during the first few years of Black's proprietorship. He was quietly studying the press barons of the 1980s, Rupert Murdoch and Robert Maxwell, for clues as to how he should (and should not) run things.

Black's search for spirituality, prompted by his discovery of Quebec's *ancien régime* traditions, the bouts of anxiety he suffered in the 1970s, his parents' decline and his marriage to Shirley, nudged him closer to Catholicism. In the mid-1980s, under Cardinal Carter's guidance, Black continued his "lengthy, cautious, and stately paced personal progress towards Rome."[162] His old friend from Quebec, Father Jonathan Robinson, taught him the Catholic catechism. He later founded, with others, the Montreal Oratory under the patronage of St. Philip Neri and approved by the Vatican. Robinson had also been chairman of the philosophy department at McGill University. In 1979, he moved the oratory to Toronto at the invitation of Cardinal Carter. Oratorian priests and brothers eventually assumed responsibility for Holy Family Church and the St. Vincent de Paul parish — both in Toronto.

After many conversations and debates with Carter and Robinson, Black "concluded that I believed in the occasional occurrence of miracles and that if a miracle can happen, logically any miracle can, even the virgin birth and the physical ascension of Christ. But I couldn't go further than to acknowledge that they and other such scientifically improbable events might have happened. The Cardinal assured me that I was still eligible, as long as I accepted the resurrection."

Carter told him that without belief in the resurrection, his whole life as a priest and cardinal and his "entire personal faith" would be nothing more than "a fraud and a trumpery."

After hearing that, Black said he could not fail to admire Carter even more "as a highly learned and talented person who had frankly gambled his entire life on an intelligent and precise act of faith."[163]

He converted from nominal Anglicanism to Catholicism in 1986 in a highly publicized ceremony in Toronto (although as a baptized Anglican, he did not have to renounce Satan); then sued an author who had questioned the conversion. (For good measure he also sued the author's printer.)

But Black embraced an idiosyncratic, wealthy man's form of Catholicism, the faith of a proprietor. At least that is what showed in public — he did not like talking about what he experienced in the private domain of the spirit. Being new to the fold didn't prevent Black from speaking out in his acerbic fashion. In 1987, he criticized Canada's Catholic bishops for the "naive, sophomoric mishmash" of their social pronouncements, and he called one bishop a "jumped-up little twerp" in a public dispute during a strike at the *Calgary Herald*, one of his newspapers. Mark Abley, former feature writer at the Montreal *Gazette* and a liberal Anglican, once said to Black: "You don't seem to believe in papal infallibility."

"It was a consolation prize invented by Cardinal Manning for Pius IX," Black replied. "What I actually had to believe in was the physical resurrection [of Christ]. There is nothing in my beliefs that would separate me from the Anglican Church."

Then Abley asked about the New Testament dictum that it's more difficult for a rich man to get to heaven than to pass a camel through the eye of a needle.

"It gives me some pause," said Black, "but on examination, a number of things emerge. The practice was that most wealthy people [at the time of Jesus] were exploitative employers, so the parable is more of a statement on exploitative practice in first century Palestine than a political doctrine. Christ himself had no particular prejudice against the rich. He dressed rather richly."[164]

When Black moved to London, he chose the parish of

Brompton Oratory, in the upscale borough of South Kensington, a short walking distance from his mansion in Cottesmore Gardens (which he bought in 1992 and would sell in 2005) and a few streets from Peter Carrington's house on Ovington Square. The oratory was built in the 1880s of Portland stone — with a portico of coupled pillars — in late Italian Renaissance style. But the spirit of the place is more counter-Reformation. Sometimes called a liturgical oasis (in a secular urban desert), the church is the home of the Oratorian Fathers, who still say Mass in Latin, and expect the faithful to receive the Holy Communion kneeling. Its nave is broader than that of St. Paul's Cathedral. It has twelve oversized statues of the Apostles that once stood in the Siena Cathedral. True to the oratorian tradition of praying for the conversion of England, the church has a chapel devoted to the English martyrs, St. Thomas More and St. John Fisher — Catholics killed on the orders of Henry VIII.

The church has a certain aristocratic grandeur, and one of its priests is Sir Charles Dilke, the deaf descendant of a nineteenth-century government minister and baronet. This became part of Conrad Black's religious world — the rich incense, the "Ora pro nobis" murmur of Latin litany and priests in cassocks hearing confession. It is one of London's architectural landmarks and continues the tradition of long-suffering English Catholicism.

The historical continuity, traditions and order of Catholicism appealed to Black on his visits to London, allowing him to develop his conservative worldview with richer spiritual and cultural layers. Peter White said Brompton Oratory "is pretty high church, and very impressive, a lovely building and a very ornate, elaborate service and liturgy. And I think it's one of the things Conrad likes about Roman Catholicism. He basically takes the historian's view that if you're going to be a Christian, you might as well be a mainstream Christian and go right back to the source, which is the Holy Mother Church, and not get involved in any of these offshoots, like the Anglicans, or any of the other Protestant religions. And of course there's a long unbroken tradition of that sort of Catholicism in England. But I also think that Conrad loves the pomp and ceremony and all the physical aspects of the liturgy, which are so theatrical and are so impressive and have done a great deal over the years, over the centuries, to keep the faithful interested."

Black took a liking to the writings of John Henry Cardinal Newman, a nineteenth-century former Anglican who converted to Catholicism. "To be deep in history," Newman wrote, "is to cease to be a Protestant." Father Jonathan Robinson maintains that "Newman's position was vindicated by the Second Vatican Council, which taught that tradition plays an indispensable role."

Black's interest in Newman intensified after he met Sir Zelman Cowen, the former governor general of Australia and the provost of Oxford's Oriel College. "My wife and I were in London one weekend [in 1990], staying with Lord Weidenfeld," said Cowen. "We were invited to dinner, and Conrad Black was present. The party was for Arthur Miller, who wrote *Death of a Salesman*. Conrad Black was walking and moving as Conrad Black does. We talked about Newman and Oxford. There were Newman papers at Oriel, and I remember saying to Black that I could arrange for him to see the New-mania, as I called them."[165]

Black increased his knowledge of Newman and later invited Cowen to serve as chairman of the Tourang Group, when it controlled Australia's Fairfax newspaper chain on behalf of Hollinger.

Some conservative Catholics join the secretive Opus Dei that, although legitimized by the Vatican and Pope John Paul II in 1982, is considered by many Church liberals as dangerous and cultlike, with fascist roots.

When the *Telegraph's* religious correspondent Clifford Longley (a former editorial writer at *The Times*) wrote a critical article about the organization in the *Telegraph*, "Black told me I was quite wrong about the Opus Dei . . . But he would not be a good candidate for the Opus Dei. He would not want to submit to anyone else's orthodoxy. He would want to create his own orthodoxy."[166]

Conrad Black had seen Barbara Amiel off and on since 1977,

and they had long appreciated each other's conservative views and found their "fairly frequent encounters convivial." Amiel took over as editor of the *Toronto Sun* in 1983, and the next year Black attended her wedding to cable tycoon David Graham. Amiel approached Black in his new role as proprietor of the *Telegraph* for a job.

Black mentioned to his editor-in-chief, Max Hastings, that his long-time Canadian friend, Barbara Amiel, recently divorced from Graham and now the girlfriend of aging publisher Lord Weidenfeld, would be interested in writing a column for the *Telegraph*. Her fiery right-wing newspaper columns about the sexiness of power and the way women married up were as stunning as her fashion-model appearance. "On the appointed day," Hastings wrote, "a vision of fine cheekbones and huge deep, penetrating eyes surmounted by a mane of black hair swept into my office, swathed in furs. I have seldom been so discomfited. Like many middle-class Englishmen, I am not at my best dealing with glamorous and formidable women. Not to put too fine a point on it, I was terrified."[167]

Hastings sent a memo to Black describing the encounter: "She said she thought I misunderstood her essentially sensitive and vulnerable nature. I said that I had perhaps been overhasty in doubting that any friend of George Weidenfeld's could be over-endowed with either characteristic. She said she feared that I was laughing at her rather than with her . . . I do not think it was a great meeting of minds." Nothing came of the meeting, although once Amiel married Black, in 1992, she became a regular columnist at the *Telegraph*.

In the meantime, she went to write columns for *The Times*, earning the nickname of "Iron Lady of Wapping" for her anti-liberal views. Wapping is the docklands suburb where *The Times* was printed, not far from her grandparents' original home.

One of the perks of Black's new position was an invitation to lunch with Prime Minister Thatcher in her official residence at Chequers, a sixteenth-century country house at the foot of the Chiltern Hills, in Buckinghamshire. Thatcher impressed him as a woman of power, "almost Elizabethan in her cunning, courage, and in the feasts and famines of her likes and dislikes." They discussed political issues of the day. On departing, Black gushed rather clumsily, "'the revolution you have wrought in this country is more important by far than the episodes in British history that usually enjoy that description. What were the decapitation of Charles the First or the deposing of James the Second compared to what you have done?' She patted me indulgently on the forearm and said, 'That's very good. Do come back, won't you?' I assured her she wouldn't have to ask twice."[168]

By the end of the twentieth century, with Britain harmonizing some of its legislation with that of Europe, the House of Lords seemed archaic. The mélange of appointed life peers, hereditary peers, bishops and Lords justice often seemed an anachronism. Lord Strathcona and Mount Royal — the bearded great-grandson and spitting image of the man who in 1885 drove the last spike of the Canadian Pacific Railway — explained that "the House of Lords was quite a well-regarded institution, but in the early twenty-first century it didn't deserve to be. It just had rather sensible people who ran it. I would hate to have to defend the principle of an inherited right to be a legislator. It really is totally indefensible in my book. Certainly, Upper Chambers in some other countries vary in the respect, which they have. For some extraordinary reason, the House of Lords worked rather well although it was not defensible, in principle. That was the difficulty. The idea of a hereditary peerage holding sway over the House of Lords struck many people as undemocratic. Now we have a very complicated system, which combines many different types of peers."[170]

"In our unwritten constitution," said Peter Carrington, who sat for many years on the board of the *Telegraph*, "the power of the House of Commons is practically unlimited. The House of Lords can delay things for a year or so, but it can't really *affect* things. And it is an unelected body, not so much hereditary as nominated by the prime minister of the day. And I don't think it can really be considered a credible House, nor will the House of Commons take any notice of it, because it's not elected. And the reason we don't have an elected Second Chamber is basically because the House of Commons doesn't want any rival which is elected. I wouldn't give it the same powers as the House of Commons has, but I would give it more powers than it has now."

On the private members' terrace at Westminster, over white wine and smoked salmon, Lord Gilmour of Craigmillar — a gaunt Scottish peer with hollow cheeks and wavy, white hair — said people "don't pay much attention to the House of Lords, and why should they? Some of the speeches are quite good. But so what? If we were an elected chamber, it might be more representative. Who are we to take strong lines, since we are not elected?" As former editor of *The Spectator* and a minister in the first Thatcher government, Gilmour's views have some weight among their Lordships. He was portrayed by the *Financial Times* of London as the quintessential aristocrat, with the Queen, the Queen Mother and Queen Mary all attending his wedding. His brother-in-law the Duke of Buccleuch (pronounced "Buckloo," with the stress on the second syllable) owns more than 270,000 acres of real estate. Ian Gilmour would like to see the House of Lords replaced by an elected Senate. There would be a ten-year term for senators and no re-election, with a third of the Senate elected every three years, on fixed dates. "They would have legitimacy, having been elected, and would not sit just because they were sons or grandsons of somebody or have been named by the prime minister."[170]

The *Telegraph* faced a serious business challenge — dealing with the print unions, which would be seriously affected by the new printing technology being installed in the Docklands. Print unions, resistant to technological change, made newspapers uneconomical by holding up the presses, deciding who did what and who got paid how much. Print delegations would attempt to prevent articles from appearing. This placed printers not simply in conflict with owners but also with journalists. According to Charles Moore, who later replaced Hastings as editor-in-chief of the *Daily Telegraph*, "Printing was an old hereditary business of old East Enders, all white. Once you changed technology, you could go from four hundred printers to twenty, and the paper was still better."[171]

While Australian media mogul Rupert Murdoch subdued

the print unions bringing out *The Times*, which he had bought from Kenneth Thomson in 1980, Black let Knight deal with the *Telegraph*'s unions. "We kept on throwing the dice. Whenever I needed Conrad's support against more cautious advisers and members of the board — for instance, in taking minutely planned but big risks with the trade unions — Conrad gave it unstintingly by telephone or fax. He was the model arm's-length owner."

Murdoch could not have acted without the full support of the Thatcher government. When his printers went on strike, they believed they could bend the will of the owner and block new technology. But he fired the strikers, who were completely unaware he had already trained an alternative production force, signed them up as members of the Electricians' Union, and installed them behind the barbed wire of a completely new printing facility in Wapping. In the House of Commons, Thatcher backed Murdoch, declaring that if "there are 10,000 rioters, there will be 10,001 policemen."[172] The ruthless way in which Murdoch transformed *The Times* improved the professional status of journalists "because they got back control of their copy."[173] It also eased the way for Black to complete the *Telegraph*'s move out of Fleet Street.

Black found Thatcher's Britain attractive. She rolled back what was, in the decade prior to her accession as prime minister, the ascent of the left. In the view of former Labour MP Tony Benn, "Mrs. Thatcher influenced the thinking of a generation."[174] Her legacy was the taming of the unions, the allowing of management to manage, the reducing of taxes and the introduction of widespread privatization, not just in state-owned companies such as airports and British Steel but also public housing — council houses that were sold to their occupants at "gift" prices. In foreign policy, she brought the "special relationship" between the United States and Britain back to what it had been at the time of Roosevelt and Churchill.

On June 21, 1988, at the G7 summit in Toronto, Margaret Thatcher had been guest of honour at a magnificent dinner at the Toronto Club, and in the presence of Canadian Governor General Jeanne Sauvé, Prime Minister Brian Mulroney and

Henry Kissinger, she commended Black on his takeover of the *Telegraph* in 1985, adding: "Of course, we're used to Canadians in Fleet Street — Lord Beaverbrook and Lord Thomson — and Conrad Black is continuing a great tradition."[175]

Black was surely flattered by such glowing words from Thatcher. And in the decade following her speech, he entered the charmed circle of the British aristocracy, which was a triumph of negotiation considering most in that elite group were firmly grounded in the past, fascinated by their lineage and disdainful of those who invented heritage for themselves. He was now on his way into a firmly closed world of power and wealth on the global scale — a world he had first seen as a young bystander, witnessing the Queen's coronation procession in 1953.

To Black's satisfaction, there had been a closer unity of view between Thatcher and Reagan than there was between Churchill and Roosevelt. When Black decided to move to London in 1989, he was lionized by high society, invited to all the glittering receptions, introduced to the popular and the powerful. His encyclopedic knowledge of history was unusual. He commanded facts more than interpretation but drew on his photographic memory to dazzle his audience. John Julius Norwich, the author of best-selling works on Venice and Byzantium, was impressed with Black's knowledge of history.[176] But Roy Hattersley said many thought Black "a powerful and slightly ridiculous figure. People have not allowed him to have influence. His obsession with gaining a peerage, his habit of writing signed letters in his own newspapers, his penchant for going to fancy dress balls, and his lavish spending — which has proved far more lavish than we thought — have all made him a figure of ridicule."

The Blacks' move to London proved a strain — first to his marriage (his Canadian wife had a hard time finding her place in London society, changing her name from the pedestrian "Shirley" to the patrician "Joanna") and then to his working relationship with Andrew Knight.

"Things began to get muddled only when Black prepared to

move to London in 1989," Knight said. "Conrad was right to come to London. He had taken the financial risk four years earlier when nobody else would, and success was now his inheritance. From earliest days, I had been encouraging him to come to London — once the *Telegraph* was out of the woods and into profit. It was totally right now that he did, for we had become royally profitable. Equally, however, it was obvious to everybody that when Conrad did finally come to London, there would not be room for the two of us in the *Telegraph*."

The newspaper group was in the midst of a major internal upheaval, which Knight was sponsoring in a drive to strengthen the Sunday paper. "We will never know whether my scheme to cure the weakness of the Sunday paper would have worked — it was probably too radical even by my standards. What is certain is that it foundered through the loss of clear authority as Conrad appeared on the horizon. He wanted to act as the effective chief executive with me burnishing the status of his team by keeping the role in name. My problem was that I sympathized with his desire to be in London, and the only way of bringing that about without major confrontation at the *Telegraph* was for me to fall on my sword."

Knight decided to leave the *Telegraph* in late 1989, and his departure marked a falling out with Black. The outgoing CEO pocketed a windfall from the sale of shares he had been promised as an incentive to come to the *Telegraph* in 1985 and then moved to the Murdoch organization, News Corp., with such speed that some people wondered whether he had not prepared his exit strategy long in advance. "I would not forget or soon pardon Andrew's shabby leave-taking, but I never forgot his contribution to my financial welfare and to the *Telegraph's* recovery," Black wrote.[177]

Knight's departure coincided with Black's final consecration as the publisher of the *Telegraph*. The quality, circulation and financial position of the newspaper were improving — one of the most impressive turnarounds in newspaper history. "In the year ending 31 March 1989," the historian of the *Telegraph*, Duff Hart-Davis wrote, "the company made a profit of £29 million, and forecast one of £40 million for the year that followed — a transformation so startling that one participant suggested that it should be written up as a case history for study in business schools."[178]

It was from this point that the paper's editorial policy shifted. Black had appointed Peregrine Worsthorne because of his knowledge of American and world politics and his friendship with Richard Nixon. But according to Worsthorne, the *Telegraph* was becoming more or less a propaganda sheet for the American administration and neo-cons in the United States.

During the late 1980s, the *Telegraph* under Hastings covered the inexorable decline of Thatcher, occasionally to the annoyance of Black, although he did not intervene as much as one might have expected. A rift was opening within British conservatism, between Thatcher's ideological conservatism and what her former cabinet minister Ian Gilmour called "empirical conservatism." In Gilmour's words, "conservatism should not be ideological, but it has become ideological over the last twenty years. In some ways Peter Carrington and I are to the left of Labour. Conservatism should adapt to the ground as you move along, build on what you've got, keep the country together, try and make the country prosperous and free, deal with things empirically rather than ideologically."

Thatcher's downfall in November 1990 placed Black in a dilemma: if the *Telegraph,* a conservative newspaper, took an overtly ideological line rather than an empirical one, then wasn't it more concerned with defence of the Thatcher revolution, now trailing off, than with the changing political landscape of the country? But Black wanted to defend Thatcher, whom he idolized. This placed him in conflict with his own editorial staff, who realized that the newspaper would survive, whereas Thatcher, politically, had not. Hastings gives an account in his book *Editor* of the discreet role behind the scenes and in print that the *Telegraph* played in finding a successor to Thatcher. Among several candidates was John Major, a self-educated man who had never been to university. Although Major won the nomination, his relationship with the *Telegraph* was strained because he suspected he was socially unacceptable to the editorial staff. And in the days after Major became prime minister, Black was annoyed that the *Telegraph* did not readily support him. Black's policy had been to staunchly defend Thatcher even when she was down and then to support her successor. One way for him to maintain political influence was to support 10 Downing Street, much like Murdoch, who always managed to back the winner.

As he looked back over the previous twenty years, Black had every right to feel satisfied. His dream of being a powerbroker on a world scale was a reality. And through the *Telegraph*, he was helping to orchestrate the transfer of power at 10 Downing Street. He was on his way to being a press lord, and it was only a matter of time before he was offered a life peerage. After feeling insecure, isolated, even rejected many times since his childhood, he had now joined a select group of powerbrokers at the top of the heap. Different standards applied to this group — different rules.

One of Black's competitors, Robert Maxwell, was in deep trouble. Maxwell had incurred staggering debts acquiring the *Daily Mirror*, as well as publishing companies and newspapers in other parts of the world. A Czech Jew, he was notorious for his friendships with Stalinist dictators in the East Bloc (who offered him lucrative printing contracts) and mysterious transactions with offshore companies. It was not clear who was backing Maxwell's outrageously leveraged buyouts of companies or who might call in the loans when Maxwell's voracious greed got the better of him. Was it the KGB? Or the Mossad? Speculation was rife. The Department of Trade and Industry had judged several years previously that Maxwell was not fit to run a public company. It was alleged that he had defrauded many clients over the years, shamelessly promoted himself in the *Mirror*, repeatedly humiliated female staff, indulged his egocentric mania and used his journalists to advance his personal business interests.[179] On November 5, 1991, Maxwell's bloated corpse was found in the sea off the coast of Tenerife, not far from his luxury yacht *Lady Ghislaine*. It turned out that he had robbed thirty thousand Mirror Group pensioners of £440 million worth of pension funds and had taken an equivalent amount from the company itself to prop up the failing share price of the *Mirror*. (The combined fraud was the equivalent, in 2007 dollars, of $2.7 billion.)

"We always knew Maxwell as a rogue," Roy Hattersley said. "He was humorously referred to as 'the bouncing Czech.' We knew he had smuggled scientific texts out of Eastern Europe as an army officer during the war. I thought he was a normal sort of crook, a corrupt businessman. But I was astonished by his death and the scale of his plundering. I was always careful with him. As deputy house leader of the opposition, I refused grants from him to operate my office. Maxwell would be a man to exercise leverage."

Black liked Maxwell. "He was a very entertaining, colourful figure," Black told me, "very amusing in his way, rather likeable — a likeable scoundrel. I rather enjoyed him, personally. He was a character, but he couldn't lie straight in bed, you know. He was a very devious man. But he was, I thought, rather likeable. Some of the stunts he pulled were a bit much. You know, selling blank books to the Nigerians at the full price of a school text, when there was nothing in them. And this whole business at the end of lifting money from the pension fund — I was sure that Bob had no intentions at all of short-changing the widows and the orphans, but there was a pool of cash, and as far as he was concerned, he was borrowing the money, but he should have known — and he must have known — that what he was doing was completely illegal."

I was astonished that Black should use this sort of language in describing Maxwell to me when all the facts about Maxwell's massive fraud were publicly known. But then Black was unbelievably indulgent toward colourful rogues.

Hastings said Black asked him to go easy on Maxwell after his death. "Don't be too hard on Bob," Black told him. "I know he was a crook, but he was a not uninteresting character. He had his moments." Hastings disagreed. "In my view, Maxwell was an unredeemed scoundrel," he said, "but I, too, was inclined to err on the side of generosity in the first hours after the man's death, before the vast scale of his defalcations was known. . . . When the scope of the man's crimes became apparent, I felt cross with myself for having succumbed to an impulse of generosity."[180]

Evidently, being a press baron had its perks even in death.

Black could help public figures in their rise, just as he could soften their fall. But with Maxwell gone and the revelations about him surfaced, the media took a closer look at Black. The *Sunday Times* wrote: "As the swashbuckling media proprietor who pops up to buy newspapers all over the globe, has a web of companies, heavy debts, a pattern of shuffling assets between his companies — and a penchant for libel litigation — Black realized comparisons between him and Maxwell are inevitable. He tackles them head-on and at length."[181]

AP Photo/Lock/Daily Telegraph

CHAPTER EIGHT

THE SUN SHALL NEVER SET

IN THE LATE 1980s, Conrad Black began assembling one of the largest newspaper empires the world had ever seen. He had in many respects outgrown the provincialism of Canada, dreading its bleak winters as much as its liberal culture. He disparaged the country's media as "irresponsible, narcissistic, self-righteously biased, unqualified to exercise the power they have, over-indulged . . . by owners afraid to offer any ethical direction."[182] But it was still a nice place for his "Canadian cottage" on Park Lane Circle.

Ever since he had devoured a biography of William Randolph Hearst during a Spanish holiday with Brian Stewart in the early 1960s, Black had been fascinated by the power of print to inform, entertain, influence and persuade. He had started out in the newspaper business, then when he took over Argus, delved into farming equipment, forestry products, grocery stores and petroleum. In the mid-1980s, he started buying up newspapers titles and chains. Control gave him the chance to gut the editorial staff of each paper, replace liberals with neo-conservatives like himself and set the agenda in the community where each paper operated. He finally had become kingmaker, backroom boy, and Machiavellian. Through his papers, he defended "integral conservatism," a gloomy, personalized blend of

Spengler, Darwin and Nietzsche that cast the newspaper tycoon as a grand strategist, monitoring the moral and intellectual development of civilization. Triumph took a lot of manipulation. But it was all about winning. As Machiavelli said, the ends always justified the means.

Black had become a global press baron in order to promote a fiercely conservative agenda of his own. He built up his personal ideology of "integral conservatism" — something like neo-conservatism but with original historical and religious spices added — as a reaction to everything he hated about Canada. But the globalization of Conrad Black marked a shift in his political views. Profiting from the international network he had laboriously built up over the years since the 1978 takeover of Argus Corp., Black now aspired to be the godfather of neo-conservatism, the person driving a right-wing revolution in the world's leading English-speaking countries.

Black often derided Canada's compassionate social attitudes, a legacy of the Louis St. Laurent government of the 1940s and 1950s, when the welfare-state mantra of the governing class was socialism, wealth confiscation and redistribution. This message, Black believed, was endlessly promoted by the media, in particular, by the public Canadian Broadcasting Corporation (CBC). As early as 1969, Black was attacking the CBC for promoting French-Canadian nationalism on its French network and anti-Americanism on its English network. "Unless the majority of French Canadians are at least cryptoseparatists, and the majority of English-speaking Canadians Americophobes, the Corporation is attempting to subvert public judgement," he said, while attacking journalists for being "reflex ultra-liberals."[183]

Veteran broadcaster Patrick Watson first met Black around 1967 and found him ebullient, funny and arrogant. In 1980, Watson was the presenter of *Ten Toronto Street*. And Watson and Black were later on the advisory council of the Canadian Centre for Arms Control and Disarmament.

"One afternoon, after a meeting," said Watson, "he asked if I was returning to Toronto, and we took the corporate jet together."

"You know what, Watson," said Black on the flight, "I always

thought you were a good interviewer, but I thought your interviews were terribly tendentious — don't you agree?"

On another occasion, Black invited Watson and veteran
broadcaster Lister Sinclair for cheap wine and cold pizza at
Hollinger's corporate office in Toronto, where Black expounded
on the state of world, the decadence of Europe, and the leadership of America.

In 1989, Watson was appointed chairman of the CBC, a position he held until 1994. "The CBC's journalistic bias is generally
conceded by people working there," Watson said. "They have a
social-democratic view, which is somewhat antiquated, about
the common good — the *res publica*. I think there is an intellectual commitment to diversity of views, but it is more of an intellectual commitment than a practical one. You don't hear from
neo-cons in a representative or proportionate way. There has
been a steady and unrepentent attitude on Israel, which has
upset a lot of people." [184]

In the face of this journalistic bias, Black saw in newspapers
the opportunity to promote his conservative social and political
agenda, not by direct control of news coverage and editorial
comment but by hiring editors who were broadly in agreement
with him. It was a strategy much like that of Rupert Murdoch,
said John O'Sullivan, a British journalist who has worked for
Murdoch in Britain and for Black in Canada and the United
States. [185] In fact, O'Sullivan proved to be a Black loyalist at the
Chicago trial — it came out in testimony that he had lived for
eighteen months in the mansion at 26 Park Lane Circle, while
working for Black. He said Black was a non-interventionist but
a man with powerful conservative ideas and an intimidating
presence.

But Black had changed since 1969 when he and his Quebec
friends David Radler and Peter White had first gained control
of the Sherbrooke *Record*. Almost twenty years later, he maintained many of the same intellectual interests — a love of
French Quebec history; an attraction to clerical Catholicism;
and a desire to forge *la bonne entente*, uniting Canada's rival
English and French populations. Now, as the proprietor of the
Daily Telegraph, he knew the advantages of having a powerful

platform from which to cajole, provoke, and occasionally harangue the public. The shoddy way he felt the *Globe and Mail* had treated him served as a reminder of the media's temptation to abuse its power.

In 1987, Black came back to an idea he had first expressed to Cardinal Léger in 1971 — purchasing *Le Droit*. Much had changed in the intervening time. Ownership of *Le Droit* had passed from the Catholic Oblate Fathers of Mary Immaculate to the Unimédia group of newspapers, controlled by Quebec businessman Jacques Francoeur. Unimédia had a large broadsheet in Quebec City, *Le Soleil*, as well as a number of smaller properties in other cities. Francoeur mentioned to Black and Peter White that he would be interested in selling the company to Hollinger for $50 million, which was more than Paul Desmarais of Power Corporation was willing to offer. In the ensuing highly politicized controversy over who should buy the chain, it was ironic that the staunchly federalist Desmarais, a Franco-Ontarian by birth and education, should be on the same side as the pro-independence Parti Québécois in opposing Hollinger. But Black and White won control of the newspaper chain by promising to offer prominent Quebeckers the right of first refusal if Hollinger later decided to sell Unimédia and by securing high-profile francophone Quebeckers as executives.

In 1976, Black had approached Pierre DesMarais II, urging him to take over leadership of the flagging Union Nationale, the old party of Maurice Duplessis. But DesMarais turned him down. The two men had sat for a time on the board of directors of Carling O'Keefe brewery. In 1987, DesMarais became the chairman and CEO of Unimédia, bringing many years of political experience and a reputation for integrity to his job. Together, White, DesMarais and Black — sought to streamline the company. The disposal of unprofitable assets netted $60 million — $10 million more than Hollinger had paid for the entire group. Journalists at *Le Droit*, accustomed to a generous labour contract under the Oblate Fathers, went on strike. But Unimédia managed to put out the paper without them, resulting in more savings. "Black made enemies with some journalists by challenging them on the record," DesMarais said. "But in the twelve years I was involved with Unimédia, he never intervened in the editorial content of the newspapers. I spoke to people on staff to make things clear, particularly where separatism was concerned."[186]

Gilbert Lavoie, editor of *Le Soleil*, also said that Hollinger allowed a good deal of editorial autonomy to newspapers in the Unimédia group.[187]

A leftover Catholic asset from the Oblate years was the Novalis division, which published theological works as well as prayer books for use during Mass. Once he had stepped down as archbishop of Toronto, Cardinal Carter was named to the board of Unimédia. Carter was not only Black's friend and mentor, but he was the ecclesiastic who had presided over the private ceremony the year before during which Black had converted to Catholicism. "I give credit to Conrad for having a cardinal on the board," DesMarais said. "I remember Cardinal Carter saying at a board meeting he was upset with one of our publications at Novalis, a book written by [liberal ecclesiastic] Bishop De Roo. But I said we should be open to books written from the Christian perspective . . . and make money publishing them."

Another publishing opportunity arose in July 1987 when *Globe and Mail* editor Norman Webster and two siblings — heirs to a major industrial fortune in Quebec — decided to sell *Saturday Night*, a money-losing Canadian literary magazine. Black, whose relations with Webster were complicated (it was Webster who fired Black from the *Globe* in 1988 for starting up a rival broadsheet in Toronto), decided to take over. Who paid whom for *Saturday Night*, and how much, remains a mystery to this day. "It's a secret," said Robert Fulford, who was editor of the magazine until Black moved in. "They made a deal, shook hands and signed a paper. My view is that Norman did not understand what was in the agreement. I am convinced he paid Conrad to take *Saturday Night* off his hands. Conrad was so much smarter and richer, and would be able to continue harassing Norman until he won out."

Fulford met with Black and quickly sensed that the editorial independence of the magazine was at stake. "Conrad outlined how he ran things at the *Telegraph*. He picks up the phone, tells one of the writers whose work he doesn't like what he should be doing. That was so far from what I imagined tolerating that I asked myself, 'Why stay? Why be in a position where I would have to lie as editor?' No, I thought, it would be better to say nothing and submit my resignation." Black quickly named John Fraser to replace Fulford. Fraser was his former classmate at Upper Canada College and the author of a laudatory article in the *Globe and Mail* about Black's 1985 takeover of the *Telegraph*. In his years at the magazine, Fraser never felt Black was his boss. "*Saturday Night* was beyond 'bossery.' I didn't see him in any hierarchical sense. I knew him only too well. I was never frightened of him."

Black had discussions with his old friend William F. Buckley, Jr. about how to develop a credible conservative voice at *Saturday Night*, but Buckley said nothing concrete came of the discussions.[188] It was hard to imagine that Black could be content for long with the small-town Sterling newspapers, the Unimédia group, *Saturday Night* and the media properties he had acquired in Britain and the United States. In 1971, he had patched together a bid with Bud McDougald for the failed *Toronto Telegram*. But the *Telegram* was instead pulled off life support and allowed to die quietly. Black had studied the successes of Roy Thomson and his son Kenneth — the father had built up a newspaper empire in small-town Ontario on the way to becoming a leading press baron in Britain; the son was responsible for transforming that empire into the world's fifteenth-largest private fortune (by the early twenty-first century). Given the scope of his newspaper ambitions in Canada, Black needed a national voice. In February 1988, he got his chance. Doug Creighton, publisher of the *Sun* group, joined Black and the *Financial Times* of London in converting the *Financial Post* from a weekly to a national daily newspaper to rival the *Globe*. At first, Black controlled 15 per cent of the shares in the *Post*. That rose in 1991 to 20 per cent. The *Post* was a conservative and thoughtful newspaper, combining original political coverage and commentary with a rich diet of business news. It was a natural fit for Black. For its part, the well-written *Financial Times* was about to become a global paper, setting down roots in foreign countries, investing massively in satellite editions of its own salmon-covered daily in the United States and Europe and acquiring the Paris business daily *Les Echos*. Black incrementally took control of the *Financial Post* as other shareholders lost interest. It would be the foundation for the new *National Post* broadsheet in 1998.

In the years that followed, Black wrote periodically for the *Financial Post*, and as a minority shareholder was allowed to rant without interference or fear of being criticized. He was now truly his own man. Some of Black's most caustic and quotable articles and speeches date from the *Financial Post* period. In 1988, he attacked the Vatican's certification of a labour union, charging "clerical and janitorial jobs are so sought after in Rome that there is always a herniating mass of applications for any vacancy in the city-state's bloated work force. The Pope should have learned from his own experience the disastrous consequences of giving the store away to the unions or of accepting unions as infallible engines of social reform."[189]

At the time, the way Black blasted the Vatican struck me as odd, since he was a recent Catholic convert. Was his faith rooted in history? Was it a private spiritual matter? Was it something that gave additional punch to his public ideology of "integral conservatism"? People are all equal before God, but I wondered whether Black approached religion from his lofty social position. I was not surprised when he later refused to discuss his faith with me. I did not understand what Black meant by Catholicism. All I could say was that it was obviously important for him.

In 1990, demonstrating the benefits of ownership, the *Financial Post* ran a 1,510-word excerpt from a speech Black had given at the British Conservative Party annual conference that year.[190] And in 1991, Black complained about Ontario's New Democratic government, and "the hobnailed fiscal jackboot of [Ontario premier] Bob Rae. . . ."

Black said that Hollinger Inc. was creating jobs, expanding payrolls and paying dividends in Britain, twenty-eight (U.S.) states, Israel and in many Canadian provinces — but not in

Ontario, because of the government's "implacable bias in favour of labour union bosses and against the shareholder."[191]

In a column the following year, Black traced Canada's demise back to the mid-1950s when "the bureaucrats, journalists, academics, left-wing clergy, labour leadership and trendies in business and the learned professions, clambered spontaneously, unquestioningly, and almost unanimously, on to [Louis St. Laurent's] new bandwagon. . . . Of course, we must always care for the disadvantaged, but 'compassion' is not a fair description of the wholesale purchase of the people's affections with the people's own money."[192]

The tone of Black's articles in the *Financial Post* was not that much different from the columns he had earlier written for the *Globe and Mail Report on Business* magazine. The difference was that Black now had the last word. His language was bombastic, even obscure, and served to create social distance from his readers and — he hoped — authority.

Brian Mulroney's Conservative government, now in its second mandate, was scandal ridden. And there was increased public hostility toward the prime minister's courageous but widely unpopular policies such as free trade with the United States, which many thought threatened Canadian sovereignty. For some Canadians, there was something suspect in the relationship Mulroney — the junior partner — had with Ronald Reagan. Former secretary of state Henry Kissinger understood this ambiguity well. "Canada is geographically sort of an extension of the U.S.," he told me, "but it wants to be more separate than reality permits it to be, so this sets up a duality of Canadian motivations."

Mulroney was too close to the centre for Black's tastes, hamstrung by Pierre Trudeau's constitutional and political legacy. Two stunning majority electoral victories by Mulroney had come at a heavy cost — absorbing into the ranks of his federalist party a large number of fiery Quebec nationalist MPs, many of whom were opportunistic would-be separatists.

The fragility of the Conservative alliance became clear after the Meech Lake Accord of June 1987, Mulroney's bold attempt to recognize "that the existence of French-speaking Canadians, centred in Quebec but also present elsewhere in Canada, and English-speaking Canadians, concentrated outside Quebec but also present in Quebec, constitutes a fundamental characteristic of Canada; and . . . that Quebec constitutes within Canada a distinct society." But Meech Lake would have amended Trudeau's 1982 Constitution constitution (the fundamental law of the land) as well as laws concerning immigration, nominations to the Supreme Court, and the holding of constitutional conferences. It therefore had to abide by the existing amending formula of the constitution, which required unanimous ratification by the federal Parliament and all legislatures of Canadian provinces and territories. Under the formula, all this would have to be accomplished by June 23, 1990, or the accord would die. Trudeau now returned to the political scene to defend his constitutional record and to denounce Mulroney's attempt to recognize Quebec as a distinct society: "Since the Meech Lake Accord is bad for Canada, and since Quebec doesn't care all that much about it, why don't we agree together that Canada will be better off if the Meech Lake monster were to drown at the bottom of the lake from which its hideous head should never have appeared in the first place," he said.[193] When Clyde Wells, the premier of Newfoundland, failed to ratify the accord by the deadline, many Quebeckers felt betrayed by this "rejection." Mulroney's nationalistic lieutenant Lucien Bouchard resigned from the Conservative government to form the Bloc Québécois, his own pro-independence party in the federal Parliament.

This was a bitter pill to swallow, Mulroney told me: "Even when, at Meech, I obtained the unanimous agreement of ten provincial premiers representing four political parties, plus the two political parties in Opposition in the House of Commons, plus my government . . . everyone in unanimous agreement . . . the amending formula was so difficult that it allowed, in three years, Mr. Wells to repudiate an agreement given by the Newfoundland legislature, and then . . . to repudiate his own agreement, and sabotage it at the last minute — guided by Mr. Trudeau and Mr. Chrétien and the rest of them."

In 1988, for $17 million, Hollinger added the *Jerusalem Post* to its growing media empire — an empire on which Black hoped the sun would never set. For him and associates David Radler and Dan Colson, the purchase represented something new — in terms of influence and readership. Moving beyond its Canadian base to acquire London's *Daily Telegraph*, Hollinger was now poised to further expand its international holdings.

Ever since biblical times, Jerusalem had exerted a strange fascination on Jews, Christians and Muslims alike. The city was blessed by all three monotheistic faiths, but their claims to ascendancy overlapped. In Jerusalem, religious transcendence had long ago fused with politics, which gave a non-negotiable, absolutist character to long-term strategic moves as well as short-term tactical ploys.

In more recent times, Jerusalem has become the focal point of the conflict between Israel and Palestine. At the Temple Mount, Jews in skull caps and prayer shawls line up at the Western Wall, to insert prayers into cracks between the ochre stones and lament the fall of the Second Temple in 70 AD. The amplified voice of the muezzin booms verses from the Quran from the minarets of the golden Dome of the Rock and Al-Aqsa Mosque, as if to smother the murmur of Jewish prayers. Christians stand back, for once, wherever refuge can be found from the blazing vertical sun, among the bougainvillea and red hibiscus.

Given Black's penchant for integral conservatism and his desire to develop a global presence for Hollinger, the *Jerusalem Post* was an attractive opportunity. As the owner of an English-language newspaper in one of the world's most explosive geopolitical regions, Black gained a powerful editorial voice with an influential readership in the diplomatic community and among English-speaking Israelis at home and abroad. As Barbara Amiel wrote in the *Jerusalem Post*, "Israel was established to spare Jews physical danger and anti-Semitism. The irony is that nowhere in the world does being a Jew carry a higher price-tag than in Israel."[194]

Historically, the *Jerusalem Post* had been close to the old Mapai Labour Party establishment, and Black saw it as "severely critical of the Likud block under Menachem Begin and Yitzhak

Shamir and . . . relentlessly hostile to every aspect of the occupation of the lands taken over by Israel following the 1967 war."[195]

Conrad Black was a Christian Zionist. He considered the four main options for peace in the Middle East: the proposal by the Labour Party's old guard (the *Post*'s original constituency), which called for a return to 1967 borders with the exception of an undivided Jerusalem; the Land for Peace option (promoted by Yitzhak Rabin and the right wing of the Labour Party), with its "more restrained notion of territorial give-backs; the more liberal Likud position of substantive discussions of a conservative definition of Israel's security needs . . . and the no-compromise, no-negotiations group led by Ariel Sharon." Black's own views fell midway between the second and third of these options.[196]

As it played out, however, the *Jerusalem Post* opted largely for the proposal of Likud, a right-wing party founded by Menachem Begin that opposed territorial concessions to the Palestinians and supported the status quo on religious matters. The *Post*'s new publisher, appointed by Hollinger, was Colonel Yehuda Levy, whose editorial interventions led to protests in the newsroom.

David Horovitz, editor of the *Jerusalem Report* since 1998, served for several years as the *Post*'s London correspondent. He said Levy, who has since died, "made clear that the editorial policy, which had basically been pro-Labour and in favour of territorial compromise with the Palestinians would now be shifted to the right, rejecting any notion of relinquishing territory in the West Bank and Gaza Strip. The moment of truth came when the publisher prevented the editor of the *Post* from publishing a fairly unremarkable editorial in the international edition, reversing the right for the newspaper to criticize the government. It was clear this was an interventionist publisher. And it was also clear that Hollinger unquestionably backed Yehuda Levy. In Israel, politics is incredibly central, a matter of life and death. The newspaper had stood for certain values that I, for one, believed were vital to the Israel I wanted to live in. And now it was going to stand for something else."

It was then that Horovitz and most of the senior editorial staff decided to quit the paper. "There was a group of about thirty of us who left," he told me, "not long after Hollinger took over." It was a troubled beginning for Hollinger. But the mass departures didn't faze Black, who felt the *Jerusalem Post*, with more than a quarter of the *Telegraph's* workforce but one-fortieth its circulation, was grossly overstaffed. "By sheer and fortunate coincidence," said Horovitz, "the *Jerusalem Report* was already in the process of being established at that time, early 1990. And several ex-*Post* staffers, myself included, came to work at the *Report*. It was somewhat ironic, to put it mildly, that the *Jerusalem Report* was itself subsequently acquired by Hollinger in 1998. The *Report* is widely perceived as being liberal and pluralistic — hardly the perceived Hollinger mindset. But with David Radler as chairman of the board, we were never subjected to any editorial pressures from Hollinger. There was no intervention."

Although the *Jerusalem Post* has never been a big money-maker, it provided Conrad Black a forum for debate on Israel's role in the Middle East and the world. And it offered Black a neo-conservative political platform. In 1990, he named a number of high-profile conservatives to the *Post's* board, including Richard Perle, the former U.S. assistant secretary of defense (well known for his links to Likud); British publisher Lord Weidenfeld; and former Israeli military intelligence chief General Shlomo Gazit. Between 1989 and 1993, the editorial staff was reduced by half, and Hollinger upgraded printing facilities to produce a more attractive and readable paper. The editorial quality of the paper was, however, not its strength.

"The current *Jerusalem Post* is a disgrace," *Jerusalem Report* editor Hirsh Goodman was quoted as saying at the time. "It's got no competition, it's the only view of Israel that every foreign correspondent, every diplomat sees, and it's bad. Its editing is bad, because the guys aren't professionals."[197]

The *Post* was Radler's baby. By pushing it to the right, Hollinger was anticipating a major shift in Israeli politics. Amidst ongoing conflicts in Lebanon and with the Palestinians, Israel's multi-party system became increasingly polarized during the 1990s.

The ability of Ariel Sharon to survive politically was a case in point. He had distinguished himself as an army officer, but his actions in the 1982 invasion of Lebanon — where more than eight hundred Palestinian and Lebanese civilians were massacred in the Sabra and Chatilla camps by a Lebanese forces militia group — were later investigated by the Kahan Commission, headed by the president of the Israeli Supreme Court. It found Sharon "responsible for ignoring the danger of bloodshed and revenge when he approved the entry of the Phalangists [Christian militia forces] into the camps as well as not taking appropriate measures to prevent bloodshed." The commission recommended that Sharon be removed as minister of defence, but he stayed with the government, holding a number of ministerial portfolios. In 1999, he won the leadership of Likud and two years later became prime minister.

Jerusalem Post editorial writer Saul Singer told me that Sharon was considered unelectable but "in a way, the people of Israel put the Kahan Commission behind them in two successive landslide elections. . . . A lot of people have made the point that Arafat elected Sharon — after the most hopeful period for peace . . . I don't think most people think of Sharon as a war criminal."

The justification for the invasion of Lebanon was that it would improve Israeli security. But the twenty-year occupation that followed resulted in thousands of civilian deaths and increased hatred and polarization on both sides.

For much of his career, Sharon was a strong supporter of Jewish settlements on the West Bank, declaring they had been promised in the Bible to the descendants of the patriarch Abraham. And he was opposed to granting concessions to bring the Palestinians to the negotiating table. "We should say to Arafat, 'You want to come to the table, come to the table — if not, stay where you are,'" Sharon told the Montreal *Gazette* editorial board (of which I was then a member) in 1994. "That would be the normal reaction of any country." His military reputation and uncompromising attitudes eventually brought electoral success, supported by Israelis desperate for security after the despair of repeated failures of the peace process. Facing increasing terrorist attacks, and tit-for-tat reprisals, Sharon later was advocating a removal of settlements and building a wall around Israel to protect its citizens.

The *Jerusalem Post* changed along with Sharon, expressing admiration for his political courage. Saul Singer said that by the late 1990s the paper was not as right wing as it had been under its first publisher, Yehuda Levy. Several momentous events occurred, blurring the historic distinction between Israel's right and left — the breakdown of the peace process, the Palestinian intifada and, perhaps most importantly, the unilateral Israeli withdrawal from southern Lebanon, which was interpreted by the radical Islamist movement Hezbollah as victory over Israel and by Palestinians as an invitation to escalate their attacks.

"The right has pretty much adopted the left's view that Palestinians cannot be absorbed," said Saul Singer. "Since they can't become citizens and can't be expelled, this means the Palestinians need a separate state. There is now a consensus on that issue, and it is a consensus I share."

David Horovitz said if the country cannot find "a safe means of relinquishing control over much of that non-Jewish population, we will lose the Israel that is primarily Jewish in demographic character and democratic. The Palestinian leadership will cease to even purport to seek a two-state solution, Israel and Palestine side-by-side, and instead advocate a single, bi-national state in which, given that the Muslim birth rate is higher than the Jewish birth rate, the Jews would come to constitute a diminishing minority. We will have lost the crucial control of our own destiny. A two-state solution is thus Israel's vital, existential interest."

Black has long held a natural sympathy for Israel and for Judaism, as his newspaper articles and 2003 biography of Franklin Delano Roosevelt attest. In terms of political networking, Black's Zionism and control of the *Jerusalem Post* and *Report* expanded his access to Jewish political, financial and intellectual circles. And his marriage to Barbara Amiel surely increased his awareness and understanding of Zionism and of the reality of anti-Semitism around the world. It was unusual that Black, a convert to Roman Catholicism, would embrace

Zionism — most Christian Zionists are Protestants, many of them Evangelicals.

Ever on a lookout for growth opportunities, Conrad Black turned to Australia. John Fairfax Holdings was a leading Australian publisher of newspapers and a media empire that went back to 1841, when John Fairfax and Charles Kemp bought the ten-year-old *Sydney Herald* from Frederick Stokes for £10,000. The paper (renamed *Sydney Morning Herald*) in 1853 became the first Australian newspaper printed with steam-powered presses. By the early twentieth century, Fairfax published a number of Australian newspapers and magazines. Television stations were added in the 1950s. In 1990, after taking the company private with a bid of $2.25 billion, Warwick Fairfax, Jr. fired the board of directors and took over as CEO and chairman. Later that year, the company went into receivership. "Operating results were improved significantly," Black later recalled, "but sky-rocketing interest rates, recessionary revenue declines, and an inability to spin out assets quickly and advantageously enough laid low the company and brought Warwick's wild escapade to its sad and widely predicted end."[198]

Black may have felt a sense of déjà vu, as he considered the prospect of getting involved in Fairfax. Just six years previously, he had seized the opportunity of Lord Hartwell's fumbling ownership and imprudent borrowing and had won control of the *Daily Telegraph* relatively cheaply. Could he now do the same with Fairfax? There were some important differences. For one thing, Warwick Fairfax's overly leveraged buyout had left the group in dire financial straits. But the company's media assets — particularly its valued broadsheets the *Sydney Morning Herald* and the *Age* — were attracting the attention of several investors. Black sought advice from fellow media mogul Rupert Murdoch, an Australian by birth and owner of *The Times*. Murdoch could not make a bid for Fairfax, since he had already purchased the rival Herald and Times Group in 1987. Murdoch warned Black that "the bottom-fishers will start . . . but it will get past that stage and it's hard to guess who will emerge until we know who the players are. Foreign ownership and cross-media will be a problem."[199]

Competition from other potential buyers was not Black's only challenge. Australia had a strong national culture thanks to its geographical isolation. And it was far from Black's bases of operation in North America and Britain. It meant long-distance flying, which Black abhorred. His former Laval classmate and long-time friend and associate Dan Colson made the red-eye trips.

In addition, protectionist laws restricting cross-ownership of Australian newspaper groups also applied to foreigners. That was a significant obstacle for Black, who preferred maximum control of his media properties. Working through the *Telegraph*, Black created a new bid vehicle, Tourang Ltd., which would hold 14.9 per cent of Fairfax. He needed partners and turned to polo-playing billionaire Kerry Packer, whom Murdoch had warned was "the most outrageous bottom-fisher of all." But Black wasn't worried because Kerry controlled other media properties. Under Australian law Packer was restricted to 14.9 per cent ownership and was not allowed to sit on the Tourang board of directors. A third player — for another 14.9 per cent of the joint bid — was a San Francisco fund manager, Hellman & Friedman.

Dan Colson had been working for ten years "almost full-time in various capacities with Conrad." Then a senior partner at the London offices of the Canadian law firm Stikeman, Elliott, Colson had been involved in negotiations over the purchase of the *Telegraph* and the *Jerusalem Post.* "Hollinger was in a very acquisitive mode," he said.

Joining a troika was something new for Black. "I made it clear that I wasn't interested in being a fig leaf and that if this consortium was to have any credibility politically," he said, "it would depend on my ability to convince a great commonwealth I had never set foot in that I was not a flag of convenience for Packer. I felt equal to that task, as it was nothing less than the truth, but I wanted it understood in advance that I expected to be treated like the senior shareholder and the principal newspaper manager in the group and not as a witless dummy in an Australian corporate salon farce."[200]

When Black visited Canberra in July 1991, he met Australia's Labour prime minister Bob Hawke and the federal treasurer, John Kerin. As Black later explained, he wanted to accommodate any reasonable political concerns the government had and wanted to know to what level his shareholding could rise. "It was at this point that Kerin uttered his remark that 'up to 35 per cent, concerns for foreign ownership are piffle.' He subsequently disputed employing the word '*piffle*,' but that is precisely what he said and I obviously took careful note of it and repeated it."[201] The comment would later be scrutinized by a committee of the Australian Senate, since it implied that the government had indicated a willingness to allow foreign ownership of a print media company beyond the limits of established law.

There was government concern that Kerry Packer was seeking secret control of Fairfax, but he denied that in testimony before a parliamentary media inquiry. "Last year I suffered a major heart attack and died. I didn't die for long, but it was long enough for me. I didn't come back to control John Fairfax. I didn't come back to break the law. And I certainly didn't intentionally come back to testify before a parliamentary inquiry."

The troika's bid was approved, but Black's status as a press baron was somewhat diminished in Australia, since he was unfamiliar with the country and had seldom visited it. Colson was Hollinger's main representative in Australia. "It was at the end of 1991 or early 1992 that I finally became 'legitimate' and joined Hollinger full-time," Colson said. "In the case of Fairfax, I spent a year in a very acrimonious and highly public takeover. I did something like sixty-eight return trips to Australia over the five and a half years that we were involved with Fairfax. Which adds up to about four and a half months of your life spent on the airplane back and forth to Australia, and that's apart from all the other travelling."

Black needed to surround himself with prominent and acceptable Australian personalities. Sir Zelman Cowen, the former governor general of Australia who had served as chairman of the British Press Council from 1983 to 1988 and who shared Black's interest in Cardinal Newman, was one of them.

"Conrad Black wrote to me saying that he was making a bid

for the Fairfax press, and he would like me to consider the chairmanship if he was successful," Cowen told me in a crackly telephone interview from Melbourne. The Tourang consortium's $1.39-billion bid was successful, and on December 23, 1991, Cowen received a phone call inviting him to a meeting to draft a company constitution. "In due course, I was the foundation chairman at Tourang. I was there for five years, the first three as chairman." With Bob Hawke's Labour government in power, Black had weathered an intensely nationalistic campaign and was confident Fairfax could deliver substantial returns with improved management and a leaner staff.

Three days after the Tourang bid was accepted, the Australian Labour Party named Paul Keating, federal treasurer from 1983 to 1991, as party leader and prime minister to succeed Bob Hawke. One of the issues he had to face was Black's involvement with Fairfax. "Black used to saunter in, a silk handkerchief in his breast pocket," Keating recalls. "Every sentence was a study of words. He sort of swallowed the dictionary. My dealings with Black were always entertaining and proper. There was a certain charm and gaiety about him, which made him easier to deal with. As for the thinly disguised sense of pomp, it was almost a put-on."[202]

Keating, the glum-faced, dark-haired son of a boilermaker of Irish Catholic descent, was a financially astute politician with considerable knowledge of the newspaper business. He had watched the Fairfax family gradually lose its grip over their newspapers, which he felt were not only arch-conservative but operated with scant editorial guidance. Even with news stories, it seemed journalists were publishing their own interpretations and opinions, with little regard for the facts. Coverage of the national government was often erratic and inaccurate. Keating yearned for an Australian "newspaper of record" like the *New York Times* or the *International Herald Tribune*. He appreciated that Black "wanted to move the *Herald* and the *Age* more toward the British broadsheet standard of accuracy. And I said to him this is a good thing, this needs to happen, there should be more presentation of news and less of views. . . ."[203]

Keating's political need for a serious "newspaper of record" was understandable — but was it his job to favour Black's creating one? This was a possible conflict of interest.

As they had done with the *Telegraph*, Black and Colson sought to increase their shareholding in Fairfax upon assuming control — not an easy goal considering Australia's apparently strict rules on foreign ownership. But because foreign investment rules and procedures applied in the earlier Fairfax decisions were confusing and ill defined, there was some hope.

Black discussed Fairfax with Keating early in 1993 — an election year. A Senate committee report later said the prime minister attempted to "improperly influence the political coverage of Fairfax newspapers by holding out to Mr. Black the prospect of increased investment in Fairfax in return for balanced coverage. . .All Mr. Keating's actions suggested he was more interested in using the unique leverage of his position to influence the political coverage of the Fairfax press in his favour in the lead-up to the [March] 1993 election."[204]

Keating told me Black had approached *him*, complaining, "He couldn't run the papers at 14.9 per cent. The newspapers were an anarchy, empowered by the collapse of the Fairfax family. Black felt he was a joke at 14.9 per cent. . . He said, 'So I will need some executive authority which I don't get with 14.9. I am looked on as an itinerant who's in it for the dollar.' He made the case for a controlling interest. . . ."

It is tantalizing to consider that a prime minister could have peddled influence — authorizing and even championing a foreign investor's increased shareholding in a national newspaper group — in exchange for "balanced" coverage. That was how the Senate committee saw it. But Keating remembers it differently. "I never asked Conrad Black for favourable coverage. At my level of political professionalism, I don't *ask* for anything. All I asked of Black was that he deliver balanced journalism. Asking Black for some sort of bias, when he couldn't deliver *any* sort of editorial line, was shooting oneself in the foot. . . . Black said, 'Give us control' and I said, 'Conrad, give us papers of record and we'll think about it. These papers are the same old spittoons. The journalists regard you as a bag of wind.' " In media interviews in Australia in 1993, Black took much the same line —

there was no *quid pro quo,* and the prime minister had not asked for favourable coverage.

Eventually, the Keating government did approve an increase of the *Telegraph*'s holding in Fairfax to 25 per cent. But Black transformed neither the *Sydney Morning Herald* nor the *Age* into a true newspaper of record. Black wrote in Hollinger's 1995 annual report that "the change in Australia's government produced by the March 2 [1996] election is difficult to interpret in its impact on foreign ownership levels in the media. . . . Ultimately for it to be successful, [the Fairfax] investment must be transformed into one of unquestionable control or liquidated.

"In Australia, as elsewhere, we are not interested in being a holding company living off dividends. We have an unrealized capital gain of over $250 million on our investment." And, after six years, in November 1996, the *Telegraph* sold its share of Tourang to a New Zealand firm — for more than double its investment.

"Black suffered from truancy," said Keating, echoing the indignant view of many Australians. "He took it as an investment, but the responsibilities of ownership meant that he had to come on quarterly visits, which he dreaded."

In his 1993 memoirs, Black wrote warmly about Australia and its people. But many of them look on him as a money-grubber who had no plans for a long-term commitment to the Fairfax newspapers and who ducked out with a bag full of money.

Black's global newspaper empire had a strong metropolitan presence in Canada, Britain, Israel and Australia. Using proceeds from asset disposals as well as strong cash flows at the *Daily Telegraph*, Chicago-based Hollinger subsidiary American Publishing acquired nearly three hundred community newspapers in the United States between 1986 and 1992 for more than $300 million. David Radler was made its chairman and CEO. American Publishing embarked on a strategy of acquiring newspapers with circulations from 4,000 to 25,000 — in suburban and industrial communities — small enough that most other buyers wouldn't be interested. Often, the papers were in monopoly markets.

The strategy echoed that of Roy Thomson early in his newspaper career. He recognized there were considerable advantages to buying up small newspapers. "Most of the people who owned and ran newspapers in Canada and America and in Britain did so because they liked the prestige and the power that newspaper ownership gave them," said Thomson. "I, on the other hand, was wholly profit-oriented."[205]

The Black and Radler formula for financial success had changed little since their days at the Sherbrooke *Record* and the Sterling Newspaper chain — count desks, slash jobs, manage cash on a group basis and boost advertising revenues regionally. With several hundred newspaper titles, American Publishing was in a position to obtain volume discounts from newsprint suppliers, which Radler was adept at negotiating. "I never wavered in my faith in Reagonomics, in the revival of the Rust Belt, and in the determination and confidence of the American industrial worker," Black wrote. "I had 'in rust we trust' translated into Latin as a device for the division. Technology had touched our end of the industry just enough to make central management of so many small units possible, but not enough to be as threatening as it was to metropolitan newspapers. It was rarely practical to wire-cable our towns. Unions were rare and reasonable. . . . We worked hard to improve the editorial product at minimal cost, even using the *Daily Telegraph* news service, and American Publishing grew steadily, by about 100,000 paid daily circulation per year, through the eighties and into the nineties."[206]

But American Publishing was Radler's responsibility — as Black's defence lawyers took pains to point out, over and over again, during the criminal trial in Chicago. Black was not really content to be the owner of the *Punxsutawney Spirit*, the *Wapakoneta Daily News,* or the *Hawaii Pennysaver*. If he balked at the idea of travelling to Australia, he had even less interest in going to gritty mill towns in the Midwest. After Andrew Knight's 1989 departure from the *Telegraph*, Black settled into the role of chairman and CEO. He was welcomed by British high society and cultivated new friendships among London's elite. He wanted more of the same in the United States.

After Robert Maxwell's death, just prior to public revelations of his billion-pound fraud, his son Kevin contacted Black to see if he was interested in acquiring additional media properties. After the meeting, Black told Barbara Amiel that he was determined his children "would not have to make such a financially embarrassed call to anyone following my death."[207]

Of particular interest to Black was the *New York Daily News*, a tabloid in chapter 11 bankruptcy protection. Its circulation had plummeted from four million after the Second World War to 800,000 at the time of Maxwell's death. A five-month strike the year before had not helped. The *News* offered enormous potential and the prestigious corporate platform Black had long coveted in the United States. If he managed to snatch it up, he would finally be joining the big leagues of U.S. newspaper publishing. Founded in 1919 as New York's picture paper, the *Daily News* rivalled Hearst newspapers. Its headquarters in the 1930s and 1940s served as the model for the *Daily Planet* building in the Superman movies, while its journalists had won many Pulitzer prizes.

The *News* appeared viable, but it needed new management, a reduction of the work force by a third and a new printing plant. Black was interested but only if the price was right. "I have no interest in coming to New York to clasp my lips around an exhaust pipe," Black warned at a meeting with the *News* board of directors.[208] In a December 1991 meeting at Lord Weidenfeld's London home, TV personality Barbara Walters offered to put Black in touch with media buyer John Veronis who subsequently worked with Black and Radler to put together a complicated Hollinger bid. Mort Zuckerman, a former Montrealer who had bought the *U.S. News & World Report* and the *Atlantic Monthly*, also announced he was interested in making a bid. Black asked Zuckerman to make a joint bid, offering his friends Henry Kissinger and Richard Perle as adjudicators. But Zuckerman was determined to go it alone. Hollinger could not complete labour negotiations by the deadline set by a judge, and its bid expired. Zuckerman signed generous deals with several unions and won the *News*. In his 1993 memoirs, Black said Zuckerman "demonstrated again that the bane of the newspaper industry has been the well-to-do amateur making non-economic deals to get into the glamour and influence business, especially in very large cities."[209]

In 1993, Hollinger's American Publishing acquired the *Chicago Sun-Times*. With a circulation of 523,000, it was the eighth-largest newspaper in the United States, with only 174,000 less fewer subscribers than the *Chicago Tribune*, which had a stronger readership in the suburbs.

Historically a liberal tabloid and supporter of the Democratic Party, the *Sun-Times* had been owned briefly by Rupert Murdoch — until the U.S. Federal Communications Commission gave him the choice of dropping a Chicago TV station he owned or the *Sun-Times*. A leveraged buyout firm took it over but couldn't turn a profit. It sold to American Publishing for $180 million. On a visit to his latest acquisition, Black looked over the *Sun-Times* building and said, "For such an architecturally well-endowed city, it really is a humdrum building, isn't it? I wouldn't say it's ugly. It's just sort of pedestrian."[210]

In Chicago, he and Radler implemented the same strategy that had worked so well for them in other markets. The number of *Sun-Times* reporters and editors represented by the Chicago Newspaper Guild fell from 255 to 185 after Hollinger took over.[211] Coverage in many areas, including Illinois state politics, was reduced as editorial budgets were slashed and printing was shifted to a modern facility at another paper owned by American Publishing. Over the next decade, several innovations were introduced. A new $100 million printing plant was opened in 1999. By moving newspaper staff out of the "humdrum building" on North Wabash Street, the Hollinger group freed up the downtown property for a proposed joint venture with Donald Trump to build the world's tallest skyscraper. And Hollinger fundamentally changed the character of the newspaper.

Over the period from 1993 to 2004, Black and Radler increased the value of the *Sun-Times* from $180 million to more than $1 billion. "Black, through Radler, has brought a fair amount of misery to the *Sun-Times* — an oppressive stinginess combined with a political turn so hard to the right that the [traditionally conservative] *Chicago Tribune* is now, astonishingly, the city's moderate voice," reported *Chicago* magazine.[212] Black ran columns by neo-conservative commentators from George F. Will to John O'Sullivan.

Black now had the U.S. power base he needed to push his political agenda. A tabloid was less prestigious than a broadsheet, but the *Sun-Times* was a significant metropolitan newspaper in the country's second-largest city. As owner, he could afford to devote less time to cultivating important opinion makers. They would come to him.

In the wake of the *Sun-Times* takeover, the board of directors of Hollinger Inc. agreed in early 1995 to reorganize the company's international newspaper operations. Under the plan, Hollinger International became a new operating subsidiary into which investments in the *Telegraph*, the *Jerusalem Post* and Fairfax were folded. Black noted in the 1995 annual report that "the reorganization positioned Hollinger International for future growth. It is expected to improve the marketability and liquidity of its stock and provide greater access to major North American capital markets."

Here, finally was a big-city title in the country he admired the most. Black gained a U.S. power base in taking over the *Sun-Times* and in folding his worldwide newspaper assets into a Chicago-based operating subsidiary. But he also now faced an operating environment that was radically different from anything he had known in Canada or Britain. The decision to raise new capital in the United States through a publicly traded company incorporated in Delaware would prove a fateful move for Black. While he was right in thinking that his new Wall Street shareholders were investing money in *his* company, he seemed to forget that once he took Hollinger International public, and raised capital through several initial public offerings, he was now answerable to those public shareholders — he was working for *them*.

Black withdrew into his own private bubble. If there was any adapting to be done, let America adapt to *him*. He maintained out-of-date business practices typical of Argus in the 1940s and 1950s, intensified his "integral conservatism" and traditionalist Catholicism to the point where they hardened into a personal ideology, and calmly opened the tap as hundreds of millions of dollars of management fees, non-compete payments, loans and other benefits began to flow toward him, his close associates, and their respective private holding companies.

As Black considered how to expand his Canadian media holdings, he was troubled that conservatism was in such disarray. He had moved from liberalism to conservatism at the end of the 1960s, and after several years enjoying the bracing air of the Thatcher Revolution and Reagonomics, he had hoped that a similar shift to the right would occur in Canada. But with Mulroney's Conservatives now disintegrating, Black felt more keenly than ever the danger for Canada of a return of Trudeau-era thinking. Newspapers were one way to prevent that from happening.

Black said Mulroney's attempt to bring separatists, such as Lucien Bouchard and Marcel Masse into the same fold with Westerners "who went all the way from sceptical to intolerant about what they regarded as excessive indulgence of Quebec" was too ambitious. "And in the end, the Conservative Party blew up. The Bloc Québécois took practically all their Quebec support, the Reform Party took almost everything west of Ontario, and they [Reform] were popular in Ontario as well. So Brian was a pretty good prime minister, and a very capable party leader — the only prime minister since St. Laurent to win two consecutive majorities. But he does carry the can for the self-destruction of the Conservative Party."

Black had approached the Southam family in 1985 with a view to becoming a minority shareholder in their national chain of metropolitan newspapers. About 20 per cent of the shares were held by two hundred relatives. The chain went back to 1877, when William Southam bought the *Hamilton Spectator*. Twenty years later, he began acquiring newspapers across the country. According to Russell Mills, former publisher of the *Ottawa Citizen*, "the autonomy of the newspapers was deep in the culture of the Southam family, going back to the time when William Southam's family ran different papers. It was a great place to work, but it was chaotic at times. The editorial autonomy was great, but some publishers refused to buy bulk newsprint as a group because that would diminish their autonomy. The inefficiencies built into the group made it vulnerable to a take-over."[213]

After several generations, it was inevitable that the network of cousins would come apart and the family would lose its power over the group. The Canadian properties, Black was aware, were awash in money. But earnings were inadequate and the product fairly lacklustre. "With the rarest exceptions," Black wrote, "Southam newspapers tended to be illustrative of the bland worthiness, inhibitedness, and derivative impersonality, of much of Canadian life. The general air was banal sanctimony, 'Proudly participating in the Canadian experience,' as one annual report boosterishly put it, beside a majestic west-coast color photoscape."[214]

Southam had an absolute monopoly in Vancouver; broadsheet monopolies in Calgary, Edmonton and Ottawa; and an English-language monopoly in Montreal — but no daily paper in Toronto. Black's initial advances were rebuffed, and Southam swapped shares with white knight (and pro-Liberal) *Toronto Star* to prevent a hostile takeover. Black complained that this hastily arranged swap did not receive proper approvals and infringed on the Securities Act. The formal connection between the companies was eventually dissolved, although once issued, the shares were not cancelled. By 1989, Hollinger had quietly accumulated 5 per cent of Southam stock but sold it off at a modest profit. Black observed Torstar's increasing dismay over spendthrift management at Southam, while waiting for the right moment to make a move. Also watching was Paul Desmarais, who through Power Corporation controlled *La Presse* in Montreal and other newspapers. His strategy was timing — selling off investments just before they went into decline; getting into investments just before anyone realized their profit potential; and holding on to mountains of cash when the conditions were not ripe.

From his operational base in London, Black continued to keep a close eye on Canadian politics. A subsequent attempt at constitutional reform, the 1992 Charlottetown Accord, also failed. I remember introducing Trudeau to the assembled *Cité Libre* crowd in the Maison Egg Roll in Montreal's working-class district of St. Henri the night he gave his famous Charlottetown speech in October 1992. I was the master of ceremonies that evening. Trudeau launched into a passionate defence of classical liberalism, saying that citizens were being asked to vote in a definitive referendum to amend the constitution on the basis of consensus documents that had not yet been finalized. I felt the speech was an exercise in narcissism — Trudeau wanted to preserve a constitutional legacy that would remind Canadians of his own struggles and actions — forever. I had seen Trudeau turn on a dime when his personal interests were at stake. I did not see him as a man of principle. He wanted the 1982 constitution to be preserved as a permanent memorial to his greatness. A few weeks later, the accord was clobbered in several provinces in a referendum. There were actually two referenda — one in Quebec and one in the rest of Canada. In both cases, the accord was defeated.

After two failed attempts to amend the constitution, and a mountain of other problems, the stage was set for the defeat of the Mulroney government. Black's assessment of Mulroney is that, although competent, "he'd been in a rather subordinate position before, and he wasn't obviously qualified for the position. . . . Unfortunately, in his absolutely sincere zeal to create a durable resolution of the French–English problem in Canada, he projected the old Maurice Duplessis–Daniel Johnson technique, which required great finesse, of getting Conservatives and nationalists within Quebec to vote together."

In late 1992, Torstar invited Hollinger to buy its 22.6 per cent block of 14.25 million shares in Southam at a premium of 15 per cent (which meant no offer needed be made to the other 77.4 per cent of the shareholders). The $259-million transaction was approved November 13, 1992.

But Paul Desmarais was still watching. On March 10, 1993, Black learned that Power Corporation was being offered a larger block of shares out of the treasury than Hollinger owned, and at a lower price. Black called on Desmarais in his Palm Beach home, explaining his plans to integrate Southam with Fairfax and the *Telegraph* and remove incumbent directors who opposed such moves. According to Black, Desmarais "pledged fidelity to an alliance he would make with us and said he had some precise proposals. We agreed to reconvene the next day. On that occasion his very convivial son André was present, and we agreed on a system of assured parity between us and a community of objectives, especially profit enhancement and editorial improvements. We would effectively become co-controlling shareholders without either of us paying a control premium."[215]

Although forced to share power with Desmarais, in Southam, Black finally had the national newspaper base in Canada he had always wanted.

The men were opposites in many ways. Black loved the spotlight: he had a punchy vocabulary and aggressive manner that exaggerated his importance and kept him in public view. Desmarais was a sophisticated, cautious billionaire who rarely gave interviews, shielded his private life from public view, and held court from the top floor of Montreal's venerable Canada Steamship Lines building, with its oil portrait of Cardinal Richelieu; private collection of Krieghoffs; enormous Chinese flag (for state visits); and a surprisingly small team of influential corporation men who wielded power on the international scene. Black had scored brilliant coups over the years, leaving a trail of controversy. Desmarais had built up a global financial empire and had succeeded in grooming his two sons, Paul, Jr. and André, to run the two roughly equal halves of his business, Power Financial and Power Corporation.

Black was interested in gaining more control of Southam. "When he came into Southam as a minority shareholder," said former *Ottawa Citizen* publisher Russell Mills, "he was asked by the *Globe and Mail* what he thought of the Southam newspapers. He replied that 'soft left envious pap flowed like sludge through the major pages.' I didn't find him to be an ideologue. What he expressed to me was that he wanted room for people like him who held conservative views. He didn't want the newspapers to be exclusively right wing. He was the best proprietor I worked for. He respected editorial autonomy like the Southam family but was a far better businessman than they were."[216]

In 1993, Black snagged a significant minority holding in Southam and finalized his memoirs, *A Life in Progress*. The 522-page book was odd. Black was not yet fifty — far too young to be writing his memoirs. He was candid and self-deprecating at times but generally solemn about his achievements and intelligenc — and given to ostentatiously lofty language and shameless name-dropping.

"He thinks exploring Conrad Black is a truly interesting endeavour," Robert Fulford told me, "and I wouldn't disagree with that. . . . He is a person with a lot of dimensions."

After the October 1993 victory of Jean Chrétien's Liberals, Black was disappointed to find Trudeau's legacy front and centre once again. Mulroney's Conservatives had split into several factions. The rump of the party had taken just 16 per cent of the popular vote, leaving it with a pathetic two seats in the House of Commons compared to fifty-four for Lucien Bouchard's Bloc Québécois and fifty-seven for the Western Canada-based Reform Party. The Liberals, with 41.3 per cent of the votes, had a clear majority with one hundred seventy-seven seats. In the secure and near-monopoly situation of being the only leader of a national party with elected representatives from every region, Chrétien's first decision was to keep the option of constitutional reform *off* the national agenda. Rough-edged, a keen judge of other people's interests, he seemed the ultimate political survivor — like a submerged crocodile ready to strike. Chrétien was proud to have been one of the artisans, as Trudeau's justice minister, of the 1981 repatriation and subsequent redrafting of the constitution. "Of course, I would have preferred that the National Assembly of Quebec had agreed to the repatriation," Chrétien told me, "but that's not the real question. I would have preferred things that way. But that couldn't have worked out, since the Quebec government of René Lévesque believed at the time that giving a constitutional charter to all Canadians would consolidate what could be called the Canadian 'personality' at the expense of Quebec's distinct character. For the separatists, that was simply unacceptable."[217]

Lined up against Chrétien was the charismatic, cunning, unpredictable charmer Lucien Bouchard. Bouchard would go on to lead the Quebec independence movement to just a fraction short of 50 per cent in the 1995 referendum. When I asked why he considered Canada, but not Quebec, divisible, he replied, "because Quebec constitutes — because of its territory, historically and by virtue of international law — a true entity, which existed before the creation of the Canadian federation." After the failure of the Meech Lake Accord, Bouchard had given up on the viability of a bi-national state. As leader of the Bloc Québécois and subsequently as premier of Quebec, he sought (not very convincingly) to redefine Quebec nationalism to include people who were not of old French-Canadian stock.

He brushed away any difficulties associated with Quebec independence while exaggerating support for it in Quebec and abroad. In 1994, he told me that the next referendum would contain "a clear question, so the answer would have an incontestable political meaning: 'Do you wish Quebec to become sovereign?'" [218] That a far more complicated and misleading question got onto the referendum ballots the following year showed that the Quebec independence movement was now in a trap: contrary to what Bouchard said, it could only hope for a referendum majority by posing an ambiguous question that in turn could only lead to an ambiguous answer.

With Chrétien's near-monopoly on the one hand and the circular arguments of Quebec's self-defeating independence movement on the other, the country stagnated politically. Black resented the return of the Liberals to power. He attacked them in print, under his own name and occasionally through his newspapers. As the biographer of Duplessis and a man of ideas committed in his own way to *la bonne entente*, Black deplored the disappearance of Mulroney's alliance of Conservatives and Quebec nationalists.

Black was infuriated by the slow-moving and repetitive nature of Canadian politics, the way debates on issues got stuck in the sand and people divided into communities, each with its own historic complaints and self-righteous stances. He wanted to use his newspapers to promote an aggressive right-wing agenda — even if it meant becoming the unofficial Leader of the Opposition himself, in Canada — a country he had come to despise.

At the same time, he continued his empire building. Turning his attentions to Southam, Black started boosting revenues, gutting staff (particularly if they were Liberals) and taking management fees. Hollinger succeeded in buying out Power Corporation's shareholding in 1996, taking Southam private. In 1997, Black declared a special dividend of $70 million on his shares in Hollinger Inc. In addition, Southam paid Ravelston $17.5 million for management services for the fifteen-month period ending December 31, 1997, and a further $1.3 million for expenses. However, Black still lacked a Toronto flagship for the chain. He told me that Southam without a Toronto broadsheet "is a rusticated Diaspora."

Now that Black had a worldwide newspaper empire, with major metropolitan titles in London, Jerusalem and Chicago, he needed a national flagship in Canada from which to promote his vision of integral conservatism. Launching the *National Post* in Toronto would address that problem.

The period from 1985 onwards marked the globalization of Black's business interests. It also signalled a significant change in his personal life.

His wife, Joanna, was not interested in the glam set — the prodigious network Black had built up of princes, billionaires, political commentators and movie actresses. She felt ill at ease with the lavish spending, the unending stream of celebrities passing through their homes, the long absences while Conrad dropped everything and ran off for another high-profile meeting with the rich and influential.

According to Black's goddaughter Lisa Riley (the daughter of his double first cousin Jeremy Riley), "Joanna is terrific. A family values person who kept it all together. She's someone who had not seen as much of the world as Conrad had, but she kept him in the reality of what was important today and tomorrow, rather than social aspirations. She is an intuitive person, and her intuitions are very right. She has done a lot of good for the family and deserves recognition for that."

But Joanna seemed unwilling to be everywhere at her husband's side as he took on the mantle of jet-setting newspaper tycoon. Their marriage may have been a catalyst to his converting to Catholicism, but he said there seemed always to be priests around, and it began to irritate him. "What proved to be a mortal blow to our marriage was my wife's almost unquenchable interest in the company of selected members of the Roman Catholic clergy," he said. "Our houses were virtually turned into seminaries, where I was not her de facto preferred male company. There was some, though little, acrimony. Almost imperceptibly, excruciatingly, the marriage died. In May 1993, she married one of the clergymen, after he had changed his occupation to environmental studies. Given my long and complicated contemplation of the Roman Church before adhering to it, this twist was richly ironic."[219]

After separating from Joanna in late 1991, Black said he felt intensely lonely, longing for female companionship as much as for love. "As I observed from my conservatory the twilight of autumn and of conjugality," he wrote, "I scanned the range of women acquaintances in a way I had not over the eleven or twelve years in which I thought I had a reasonably happy marriage. Gradually, tentatively, and then with greater fixity and deepening conviction, and finally with intense determination, my thoughts and hopes settled on Barbara Amiel."[220]

"Beautiful, brilliant, ideologically a robust kindred spirit," Black wrote of his 1991 courtship of Amiel in his dense, neo-Victorian prose, "a talented writer and galvanizing speaker, chic, humorous, preternaturally sexy, a proud though not a religious Jew, tempest-tossed in marriage, disappointed in maternity, a fugitive from Canada assuredly making her way from and towards poles not unlike my own, a cordial acquaintance for many years, she shortly became the summit of my most ardent and uncompromising desires. I was amazed, relieved and, lest it be unrequited, worried to discover that I was profoundly in love. My amazement at this turn of events was easily surpassed by Barbara's."

"Barbara is an intellectual and social equal to Conrad, rather than a nurturing intuitive mother," Lisa Riley said, "and, in that sense, very different from Conrad's first wife."

Barbara Amiel had a lot of qualities Conrad admired — she was a beautiful, articulate, sassy, in-your-face neo-conservative and Zionist, she could hold her own in the salons of Britain debating politics, just as she could play the perfect hostess at those summer garden parties. But after everything she had written over the years about the virtues of gold-digging, many people assumed she had simply married Conrad Black for his money. In a November 1993 column for the *Sunday Times*, she wrote: "My husband is very rich, but I am not. I don't regard my husband's money as my own. Having married very wealthy men before my current husband, I can guarantee that I parted from them leaving both their fortunes and my opinions intact. I have been a bitch all my life and did not need the authority of money to be one. My detractors were calling me a fascist bitch long before I had a penny. I am a North London Jew who has read a bit of history. That means I know this: In a century that has seen the collapse of the Austro-Hungarian, British and Soviet Empires, reversal of fortune is this rich bitch's reality. One might as well keep walking and have the family's Vuitton suitcases packed."

She married Black in July 1992.

The Canadian Press/Maclean's/Peter Bregg

CHAPTER NINE

HIS FINEST HOUR

WITH HINDSIGHT, it is now clear that Conrad Black's finest hour was in the late 1990s. It was the apogee of his personal prestige — the moment in time when his lifelong study of strategy and networking brought him to the crest of the wave. He had taken huge financial and political risks that were exacerbated by his confrontational style, personal vanity and a hardening of his political positions. But the payoff had also been huge. And now he had fame, fortune, and unparalleled access to the corridors of power.

Barbara Amiel was there at his side, ready to share his interests and offer her fiery opinions. She was strongly attracted to this man of the world, by turns charming and brutal, to this righteous proprietor who waged a battle of words and deeds against shareholders, labour unions and competitors, in the name of a personal ideology he had invented — "integral conservatism." Given his wide-ranging business interests, she had to work hard to maintain her own profile.

Black provided Amiel with a few opportunities to add to her CV. She was happy to be named executive vice-president of the *Chicago Sun-Times*, in 1999, at a salary of $276,000 per year. And she didn't even have to turn up at the office!

By 1999, Black had completely reinvented his business and

public image on a grand scale. In Canada, he now controlled nearly half of English-language and 18 per cent of French-language newspaper circulation. In the United States, he owned the *Chicago Sun-Times* and a large chain of community newspapers; in Britain, the prestigious *Daily Telegraph* and other publications; and in Israel, the symbolic but significant *Jerusalem Post*. Altogether, these newspapers had more than four million readers worldwide.

He had avoided the boom/bust Internet craze that brought financial devastation to thousands of companies and investors and was working in partnership with comeback king Donald Trump to redevelop the *Chicago Sun-Times* site at 401 N. Wabash Avenue, along the Chicago River, into the world's tallest building — a 150-storey skyscraper — forty storeys higher than New York's World Trade Center and Chicago's Sears Tower. He had access to world leaders including U.S. presidents and British prime ministers and was now a full-fledged transatlantic businessman, able to defend his views and take on political adversaries and business rivals from a position of strength.

On the wood-panelled wall of Hollinger International's New York boardroom, next to Black's office, was a huge watercolour depicting the cruiser USS *Houston* in 1934 — Stars and Stripes snapping in the wind and honour guard at attention on shore as she bore Franklin Delano Roosevelt through Miraflores lock in the Panama Canal. In an age of heroes, FDR had personified the transatlantic alliance, with superpower diplomacy requiring him to steam back and forth across the Atlantic aboard grey, clipper-bowed warships. Always cheerful and composed, even under severe adversity, FDR during the Second World War brushed off the risk of enemy torpedoes with a shrug of his broad shoulders. The watercolour in the Hollinger International boardroom was a metaphor for the perils of business.

Conrad Black had always wanted to be a leader of men. Unlike the great president, however, Black's instruments of "war" were newspapers. His role model might well have been Lord Beaverbrook, the Canadian newspaper magnate who made a fortune in newspapers in Britain; played an invaluable role in both World Wars and served as a Cabinet minister and

Churchill's personal envoy on wartime missions to Roosevelt and Stalin.

Black's war was different. Since the early 1990s, he had been engaged in a vicious ongoing circulation battle with archrival Rupert Murdoch, owner of the *Times*. In developing his transatlantic business, Black was heeding the words of German philosopher Oswald Spengler: "The press campaign appears as the prolongation — or the preparation — of *war by other means*." There was a distinctly military tone to Black's speeches. Combining his passionate interests in business strategy and military history, he promoted the neo-conservative values that mattered most to him — providing the United States with the means to realize its expansive geopolitical goals; strengthening the U.S. alliance with Britain and other like-minded countries; isolating Western countries such as France and Germany that did not buy into U.S. expansionism; supporting Israel; unmasking Islamist terror; restricting the role of the state in all its forms (except where defence spending was concerned); supporting free-market reforms and lower taxes and attacking political correctness and "soft-left" attitudes. One of the pillars of Black's neo-conservatism was an admiration for Richard Nixon that downplayed the forced exit from the White House and dwelled on the disgraced president's sometimes inflated reputation as a foreign policy strategist.[221]

Some of Black's journalists agreed with his neocon point of view. Others openly expressed their disagreement (earning his respect, although he occasionally attacked them in print). And a third group incessantly pandered for his approval. Black soon discovered there was a sympathetic audience for his ideology in the United States and Israel. But in Canada and Britain, where he was perceived as more belligerent than persuasive, it did not go over well and he made a lot of enemies.

Just before Easter 1997, as Prime Minister Jean Chrétien was contemplating another federal election, Black contacted journalist Ken Whyte about the idea of developing a national newspaper. The two men were concerned about the fragmentation of the federal Opposition into several impotent regional parties, virtually guaranteeing the Liberals a long-term monopoly on

power. In the aftermath of Brian Mulroney's departure from
office in 1993, the Progressive Conservative Party had split into
three incompatible fragments: the Bloc Québécois, a protest
party with the incongruous mission of promoting Quebec sovereignty from within the federal Parliament; the rump of the old
Conservatives; and, in the west, the Reform Party, later to be
repackaged as the Canadian Alliance. Leaving aside the Bloc's
10.7 per cent of the popular vote, the Conservatives and
Reformers commanded 38.2 per cent of the electorate in 1997
— just 0.3 per cent less than the Liberals. But with these feuding
entities vying for sole leadership of the right, the prospect of
uniting them as a national political alternative was remote at
best. Whyte, a blond, youthful-looking former executive editor
of *Alberta Report* and a non-practising Catholic from
Edmonton, had attracted the attention of Black and Barbara
Amiel while serving as western columnist for the *Globe and
Mail.* He quickly rose from western editor at Black's *Saturday
Night* magazine to editor at the age of thirty-three. "Barbara
encouraged Conrad to devote more time to me," said Whyte.
"They both asked me to keep an eye on the Southam papers
and write occasional memos on the strengths and weaknesses of
various papers. That became part of my role."[222]

Whyte was named founding editor of the *National Post*,
which started out with the concept of a sixteen-to twenty-page
newspaper. It would be a Canadian version of the *International
Herald Tribune*, with very little original content. The Paris-based
Herald Tribune had long consisted mostly of recycled articles
from the *New York Times* and the *Washington Post.* Similarly, the
Post was going to recycle copy from newspapers in the Southam
Group. It was at that point that Whyte became a Black loyalist
— he testified in his defence at the Chicago criminal trial in
2007.

"Black was very clear about it all," Whyte said to me. "With
the printing and distribution resources of Southam, the launch
of a broadsheet would be supported by the chain. We had
thought of building the *Ottawa Citizen* into the flagship of the
Southam chain. Forty years ago, the Montreal *Gazette* might
have been an option [as flagship], but not in the late 1990s.

"Having looked at these metro newspapers and worked at the *Globe*, I believed most Canadian papers were fundamentally boring. They had no personality, wit, or human interest. The idea of metro papers at the time was to write nice things about people in the community and have nothing hard or political. I talked a lot to Conrad and Barbara, and we agreed on that. We wanted to broaden the debate and gather a critical mass of talent together and see what happened."

Black had grown used to the colourful literary tradition at the *Telegraph*, which was in marked contrast with Canadian newspapers. But the model that most inspired Whyte was American. He liked the cheekiness of the *New York Observer* and the *New Republic*, and he studied the *New York Herald Tribune* from the 1960s and *Esquire* magazine from the 1970s. "We learned some things from British papers," said Whyte. "We had some guys from the *Telegraph* come over, but we couldn't produce a British-style paper in Canada with such a different readership and expectations. Besides, we wanted to do a different style of Ottawa coverage from the *Globe*'s, which was very insider, 'one-day scoop,' government agenda. We wanted our own agenda, and we wanted to create tension around that, hiring aggressive reporters. We investigated Ottawa as it had not been investigated."

At first, the launch of the *National Post* was widely seen as a symbol of Black's entrepreneurial flair and thoughtful conservative leadership. From the start, the *National Post* was an ambitious financial and political project. It was also an indication of Black's intention to shape events in his own image. Black's plan was to include the recently acquired *Financial Post* as a section in the new paper using its circulation list as the springboard to turn the *National Post* into the flagship of the Southam Group, shake up his old nemesis the *Globe and Mail* (which still belonged to Kenneth Thomson), and promote a right-wing agenda in Canada. It was an ambitious plan, considering that in the third quarter of 1998, the *Financial Post* had a daily circulation of 77,757 while the *Globe*'s was 309,046.[223]

The launch of the *National Post* in the fall of 1998 coincided with the release of *Render unto Caesar*, a much-reworked second edition of Black's 1976 biography of Maurice Duplessis — a book that now contained a forty-two-page editorial on everything Black disliked about Canadian politics. In the new edition, he removed the flattering appreciation of fascist historian Robert Rumilly that had prefaced the first edition.

Shortly before the launch of the *National Post*, Black took the stage at a party in Toronto. After ripping into the CBC, the federal Liberals, and the *Globe and Mail*, he presented his latest creation with the boast that "we're going to change this country."[224] It was reminiscent of the newspaper wars that raged in Toronto beginning in the late 1940s, when George McCullagh, the wealthy owner of the *Globe and Mail*, purchased the *Toronto Telegram* and announced his aim was to teach the *Toronto Star* a lesson. "I'm going to knock that shit-rag right off its pedestal," he vowed. (The *Star* survived and the *Telegram* folded in 1971). Black, still smarting from his stint at the *Globe* in the mid-1980s when he had been invited to write a column for the paper and was later libelled in a mocking feature article, was determined to put the *Globe and Mail* in its place.

The first week's press run of the *Post* was 500,000 copies per day, many of them distributed for free or at minimal cost to Southam subscribers. The *Post* would be sassier, wittier, informative, emotional, reaching out to women — all in an attempt to attract some of the *Globe*'s upscale readers. Southam executives estimated the group would spend $100 million to $130 million on the new broadsheet over five to seven years, with paid circulation settling in the 350,000 range. The projections proved unrealistic.

The first issue of the *Post* came out on October 27, 1998. Under the heading "A vigorous new voice for an exciting future" appeared Whyte's statement of principles. Canada had never had a national newspaper, he wrote, although papers published in Toronto had claimed to speak for the whole country. Canada had thrown off its old cultural timidity to become a country of resourceful free traders. "We need a newspaper that will reflect the new vitality and sophistication of the Canadian people, an articulate, vigorous voice for an exciting future." Canadians wanted a quality newspaper that was not a chore to read, so the *Post* had recruited well-known writers, from satirical novelist Mordecai Richler to veteran journalists Allen Abel and Andrew Coyne. Whyte thanked Conrad Black. "The creation of a new newspaper on this scale requires vision, courage, and a considerable commitment of resources. He supplied all of that, and by doing so has enhanced the prospects for a genuine national community in Canada."

Articles in the first issue had a marked neo-conservative slant, promoting Canada's unite-the-right movement, blasting the recent arrest in London of General Augusto Pinochet and mocking a book that questioned the ethics of former Conservative prime minister Brian Mulroney.

Neo-conservative journalist David Frum (who eventually moved from the newspaper's founding team to the White House, where he served as one of George W. Bush's speechwriters) said "the launch of the *National Post* in 1998 upended the old conformist cartel [of stodgy Canadian papers]. Nothing like it had ever been seen before in Canada — or just about anywhere else. Yes it was conservative and unashamedly so. But it was also far and away the best-looking paper in Canada — the best written, and the most amusing. It gleefully defied the old dogmas — and broke stories nobody else dared touch, from Prime Minister Chrétien's financial scandals to the Jenin massacre hoax. . . . It was a happy, eccentric place. Editorial conferences were held around a ping-pong table. Journalists who had been working one beat for years found themselves suddenly reassigned to something radically different — and doing the best work of their careers."[225] Frum later co-wrote a book on the state of the world with Richard Perle, the controversial neo-conservative, Hollinger insider and defence consultant.

The *Post* gave Black a national political soapbox. During the 1960s, when he was still a student at Ottawa's Carleton University, he got to know his way around Parliament Hill — the imposing Gothic revival building, dominated by the copper-roofed Peace Tower, the House of Commons and Senate chambers in the Centre Block and the maze of administrative offices in the East and West Blocks. Now the Hill became the unlikely setting for a power struggle pitting Jean Chrétien against

Conrad Black. Chrétien's Liberals handily won the June 1997 election, forming a second majority government and continuing to dominate Parliament as they had for nearly three-quarters of the century. The Liberals felt invincible and able to rule as they pleased. The splintered Opposition seemed no match for Chrétien, who rose in Parliament each day to fend off and even scoff at their questions.

Across the sea, Black, comfortably settled in his mansion in Cottesmore Gardens, decided to establish himself as an effective voice of opposition. He would wage war on Chrétien and the Liberals. And with the 1998 launch of the *National Post*, he finally had the weapon he needed. He would make it personal.

Chrétien often entertained guests on the magnificent back lawn of the official prime minister's residence overlooking the Ottawa River at 24 Sussex Drive — a Gothic stone mansion, discreetly hidden by trees, and standing across the road from the even more spectacular Rideau Hall, home to Canada's Governor General. At these gatherings, waiters in livery might serve champagne to an assortment of businessmen and their chic female companions in Chanel suits while strategists, speechwriters, pollsters and public relations and advertising executives — the butterflies of the opinion-shaping industry — fluttered around federal ministers and the presidents of Crown corporations in the hope of landing contracts. Party bagmen stood along the hedge, drinking and watching in silence. I remember running into a Quebec printer at one of these parties — Jacques Corriveau, a debonnair, white-haired opera lover who always dressed in black and who complained to anyone who would listen that the Liberal Party owed him a fortune for fronting party printing costs back in the 1993 election. He eventually obtained $9 million of government contracts in what became known as the Sponsorship Scandal.

Then along would come Chrétien — escorted by a few Mounties wearing earpieces and dark suits — passing through the crowd, shaking hands, offering Cuban cigars (he once said Fidel Castro was his supplier), and posing for snapshots with the party faithful. All eyes would turn to him, the CEO of the federal government, which accounted for 17 per cent of Canada's GDP, or Can.$195.6 billion.

Ken Whyte recalled that the *National Post* was about six months old when reporter Andrew McIntosh came in "with a little story about the prime minister buying into a golf course and losing some money. We all got more interested over time. It attracted the attention of the Prime Minister's Office, who called us and made a mountain out of a molehill. Chrétien himself called Conrad directly, and we ended up publishing a statement by Chrétien himself. But the story continued. Chrétien got angrier and angrier, but Conrad wanted us to be cautious, which was frustrating for Andrew McIntosh, our investigative reporter. We demonstrated that the prime minister of Canada had personally intervened in the affairs of a Crown corporation [the Business Development Bank], so that it loaned money against its rules to a sometime business associate of the prime minister."

With no viable or even visible opposition in Parliament, Black's *National Post* attacked Chrétien personally, excoriating him for his involvement in "Shawinigate," as the money-losing investment in a golf course in his Quebec riding of Shawinigan came to be known, and for just about every other impropriety or failing it could uncover. The newspaper also condemned the government as incompetent and corrupt for mishandling millions of dollars channelled to Liberal-friendly advertising firms in Quebec. After several years of obfuscation and stalling by the government, a public inquiry into the scandal began in February 2004.

Black's assessment of Chrétien was "not very positive. Look, to be fair to him he appears to have consistently had the support of the majority of Canadians, so I have to allow for that, and indeed that was one of my motives in leaving the country. I didn't really wish to be a citizen of a country that thought he was a good leader. Because I don't think he is."

Black said Chrétien was a sincere federalist and fighter with some positive qualities. And although he panicked during the 1995 referendum, he fought for what he believed in. But as prime minister he actually didn't do much. He also benefited from the Opposition's disarray that ensured the Liberals' solid grip on power. "He is the only person in the history of Canada elected to the position of prime minister — who has been thrust out of office as prime minister by his own party," said Black.

While Black led the public charge on the Liberals, his long-time friend and Hollinger associate Peter White served as a major fundraiser for the Canadian Alliance. A former principal secretary to Brian Mulroney, White faced the daunting task of raising millions of dollars for a party rooted in Prairie reformism and not generally considered a viable alternative to the Liberals. Developing a new Opposition party was a worthy goal, but their transparent methods — Black's bold political advocacy through the *Post* and White's fundraising centred in Hollinger's corporate suite — were questionable.

"I don't believe Conrad's principal aim in acquiring newspapers in Canada was to improve the standards and quality of Canadian journalism," said Kenneth Thomson, who still controlled the *Globe and Mail* during the first three years of the *National Post*. "He clearly wished to operate his newspapers profitably, but he also had a political agenda. It was this agenda that led to the launch of the *National Post,* which had a very conservative bias under his ownership. When the support of the *National Post* failed to re-energize the Conservative Party in Canada, the *Post* did to some extent, by default, become the official Opposition to the Liberal government in Ottawa. I don't believe these developments have in any way changed the role of the *Globe and Mail* as Canada's national newspaper of record."[226]

Meanwhile, Black's Canadian newspaper flagship was in serious trouble. He had hoped to build up a readership for the *Post* with a highly discounted subscription price by delivering the paper along with other Southam papers and by giving away for free almost three times as many copies as the *Globe* did. The *Post* relied heavily on an appealing design, discounted subscriptions and cut-price advertising rates. Even with the bottom falling out of the national advertising market, the subscription price was about 45 per cent lower than the *Globe*'s. Many copies were given away or distributed for less than six cents, and losses were mounting. The *Post*'s circulation lagged well behind that of the *Globe*, which moved to the political centre, where most Canadians seemed comfortable. The *Post* damaged its own credibility by attacking the Liberals at every turn while providing the most craven, effusive, uncritical coverage of the right-wing Canadian Alliance. The low point came on July 10, 2000, when an eight-page supplement, entitled "Day's Victory," praised Stockwell Day, the newly appointed leader of the Canadian Alliance, as an "agent of change on a mission." The supplement presented Day as a politician of the future. The "courageous, irrepressible grassroots politician" and "contemporary traditionalist not afraid to speak his mind" was shown in a T-shirt and shorts, tottering on in-line skates and flashing a dim smile. His "coronation marks a new era in Canadian politics," proclaimed the *Post*.

Most embarrassing in the supplement was the prose of Black's former biographer and *Post* columnist, Peter C. Newman, describing Day as "light on both feet, cheeky, bushytailed and looks as if he might overdose on testosterone at any nanosecond ... Canada's political landscape changed forever when the neo-conservative cause in Canada, which had been an impulse without clout, finally breached itself into the political mainstream." Newman seemed to be either at people's feet or at their throat.

The packaging of Day as sexy protagonist didn't impress anyone. His leadership ambitions died quickly. In the November 2000 election, the Canadian Alliance was held to 17.6 per cent of the popular vote, while Chrétien's Liberals boosted their share of the popular vote to 45.8 per cent, moving from 155 to 172 seats in the House of Commons.

No wonder that Izzy Asper, the founder of CanWest Global, compared Black's *National Post* to *Izvestia* or *Pravda*.

Instead of costing $100 million to $130 million over five to seven years, as originally predicted, the *National Post* lost $200 million in the first eighteen months alone. Black announced the *Post* would turn a profit in the fourth quarter of 2000 and would break even in 2001, but Hollinger was highly leveraged and could not sustain the losses. Net earnings at Hollinger Inc. had gone from $51.9 million at year-end 1998 to a paltry

$2.6 million at year-end 1999. Having raised money on capital markets, Black could not absorb such disappointing results indefinitely.

The *Post* was becoming a financial drain on the Southam Group. Stephen Jarislowsky had been concerned for some time about the rich payments Conrad Black was receiving. "I was chairman of the compensation committee of the Southam board," he recalls, "and I remember asking Conrad to provide a justification for the fees he was getting. He replied that he would get back to me in due course, but of course he never did. In 1999, I resigned from the board, and we sold the stock we held under management in Southam. I also contacted the Ontario Securities Commission about the situation, but they never did anything about it."

But the *Post* also posed problems from the editorial point of view. "There is nothing wrong in principle with a newspaper that nails its political colours to the mast," said Philip Crawley, publisher of the *Globe and Mail*. "But it isn't always good for business, and the *National Post* has proved that in spades. I have no quarrel with the ethics of what Conrad Black tried to achieve in providing a rallying point for right-wing conservatism. It's what the *Daily Telegraph* in London has done for years. Where it went wrong for Black was that he was arrogant enough to believe that his power and influence, through the *Post* and his Southam papers, could persuade the Canadian public to think differently about its political choices. He set out his stall in the *Post* to unite the Right, and yet the Right became even more fragmented and unelectable.

"My argument is that Black allowed his political beliefs to override his business sense. The policies which the *Post* relentlessly promoted, through its news reports, its columnists and its editorial opinions, failed to impress the majority of his target audience. He had made it clear that he believed the *Post* could win over readers from the *Globe* and the *Toronto Star*, both of which were labelled in his remarks as representing the 'wet' liberalism which was causing Canada to fall from grace. But a national newspaper that spent most of its time criticizing Canada — its politicians, its foreign policy, its business competency — was a tough proposition to swallow for many people. I accuse Black of bad business caused by 'folie de grandeur.' He made the mistake of putting politics before dollars and cents."[227]

But Black was not through with the *Post* just yet. In April 2000, Hollinger announced it was offering its stable of Canadian community newspapers for sale in order to raise up to a billion dollars. According to Hollinger executive Peter Atkinson, "We also said that we would be willing to talk about affiliations with regard to the large metro newspapers like Montreal, Vancouver and Calgary. But at that time we did not contemplate that anybody would come forward and express interest in the whole group."[228]

Izzy Asper at CanWest Global initiated discussions with Black. Asper eventually offered to buy the entire Southam chain of fourteen major daily newspapers, eighteen other dailies, half of the *National Post,* and the Internet portal canada.com. The closing price — $3.5 billion (later reduced to $3.2 billion) — was an offer Black could not refuse.

"The purchase price will be payable as to approximately $700 million (Can.) in shares of CanWest," ran Hollinger's laconic press release on July 31, 2000, "and as to the balance, 75 per cent in cash and 25 per cent in subordinated debentures of a senior company in the CanWest group. Hollinger will nominate two directors to the CanWest board, commensurate with its opening equity interest of 15 per cent. Conrad Black, Hollinger's Chairman and CEO, will be the Chairman of the National Post. . . . The sale is expected to be completed by September. . . . This transaction is consistent with Hollinger's stated objective for its Canadian restructuring initiative launched earlier this year." A non-compete fee amounting to Can.$82 million including interest was part of this transaction. Asper said CanWest offered the non-compete to Hollinger, which subsequently decided who would receive the fee. Ultimately, Black and the private holding company he controlled, Ravelston Corporation, took 73 per cent of the fee, while Hollinger executives David Radler, Jack Boultbee and Peter Atkinson shared the remainder. This provided the basis for one of the criminal charges in the 2007 trial.

The sale of Southam sent shock waves through the Canadian media community. Christie Blatchford, a columnist at the *Post*, remembered a couple of parties before the sale "where Conrad got up and, in his wonderful articulate way, shat on the naysayers. The sense that you took from whatever he would say publicly about our newspaper was that he was in for the long haul." When the sale was announced, "I felt significantly betrayed and sort of . . . pissed off with him. I felt it wasn't the writers. Editorially, none of us had ever let him down. We gave him the product that I think he wanted. . .When Conrad came out, they put it to him that way, they said, 'Some of your reporters are feeling betrayed.' And his answer was something like this: 'Well, if that's how they feel, let them put their $200 million in it then.' And when I heard that, I thought, 'You prick! We DID give the equivalent.' "

Another *National Post* columnist, Robert Fulford, offered a more charitable view. "Erratic behavior, or the appearance of it, will open any powerful figure to severe criticism, because a certain consistency is a quality we need and desire in our leaders. This is one reason why it was easy to pounce on Conrad Black. . . . To change willingly, in the speed of a press release, from the best and most important publisher in Canada to the owner of one half of one newspaper — certainly this will look to just about anyone like erratic behavior, no matter how reasonable it seems to Mr. Black and his shareholders."[229]

The combination of CanWest Global's television assets and the newly acquired Southam, the leading newspaper chain in the country, posed a serious threat to the *Globe and Mail*. The largest transaction in the history of Canadian newspaper publishing had made CanWest the country's number-one media company, and a leader thanks to its strategy of convergence. Given this precedent, Kenneth Thomson's Toronto-based private holding company, Woodbridge, began discussions with BCE, the Montreal-based telephone utility, which led to the $4-billion merger in mid-September 2000 of their media assets, including the *Globe and Mail*, into a new multi-media company. Thomson had been selling off his father's newspapers for years as part of a strategic and extremely lucrative shift to electronic publishing.

On November 10, 2000, Hollinger announced the sale (reportedly for $150 million) of its Unimédia chain of French-language newspapers to Gesca Ltd., a subsidiary of Power Corporation, which was controlled by Black's wily old rival Paul Desmarais. The sale virtually completed Black's departure from the Canadian media scene (only his 50 per cent interest in the *National Post* and a few smaller publications remained). Black may have wanted to change the country with the *National Post*, leading Canadians to a bright neo-conservative future, but Canadians did not want to follow. The *Post* had some editorial and reporting strengths, but the line between editorial support and obvious propaganda had become seriously blurred. The paper lost credibility by totally committing to a losing politician — Stockwell Day — and a losing cause — the Canadian Alliance. Whatever Ken Whyte and his journalists wanted to make of the *Post*, the newspaper seemed to be Hollinger's instrument of all-out war, alongside Peter White's fundraising efforts on behalf of the Canadian Alliance.

Black initially offered to sell off the Southam and community newspaper assets of proven value in order to hold on to the *Post*, which provided him with a prestigious if money-losing platform. In hindsight, he was fortunate to pull off a deal selling the entire chain to CanWest. The huge price tag ought to have resolved financial problems at Hollinger Inc. and its U.S.-based subsidiary, Hollinger International. But Black had sold off the assets that provided continuous cash flow, preferring to focus on prestigious core assets such as the *Telegraph*, the *Sun-Times*, and the *Jerusalem Post*. These core assets suffered sharp declines in operating profit due to the disastrous advertising market in 2001, the intifada in Palestine, and, ultimately, September 11. Besides, as Izzy Asper pointed out, the *National Post* forced dramatic improvements at the *Globe*.

Black, his closest associates, and his holding company, Ravelston Corp., collected management fees of $32 million (U.S.) in 1998, $38 million in 1999, $37.3 million in 2000, $30.7 million in 2001, and $25.6 million in 2002 — while Hollinger International saw revenues drop 45 per cent after the sale of Southam, resulting in a $36 million loss in 2001.

On December 4, Black held a surprise birthday party for
Barbara at the exclusive Manhattan restaurant La Grenouille.
This $63,000 party — one-third charged to Conrad Black per-
sonally and two-thirds to Hollinger International — became
the focus of a criminal charge in Chicago. On the one hand,
the party was all about his love for his wife. On the other hand,
the guest list included many movers and shakers in Manhattan
and the party could have helped him maintain his tycoon profile there. While Metropolitan Opera mezzo-soprano Jossie
Pérez sang selections from Bizet's *Carmen* and Saint-Saëns's
Samson and Delilah, guests went through $16,875 of dinner,
beluga caviar and ceviche de homard au concombre, $912 of
cocktails, and $13,935 of Dom Perignon champagne, as well as
some select vintages of Chassagne Montrachet Prosper
Maufoux, Clos Vouegot Vougeot Prosper Maufoux and
Sancerre Jean Claude Chatelain. Tips for the cooks and waiters
came to $7,930. The guest list included blue-chip names such
as "Happy" Rockefeller and Kate Ford II; top model Melania
Knauss and her billionaire fiancé, Donald Trump (Twenty-six
years younger than Trump, Knauss had posed nude in the
January 2000 issue of *GQ* magazine in his personal Boeing 727,
next to an attaché case brimming over with fabulous jewels —
this image of the jet-set starlet seemed the perfect evocation of
America's myth of sex, money and power. They got engaged
four months later); fashion designer Oscar de la Renta and his
wife, Annette; the billionaire mayor of New York, Michael
Bloomberg; *New York Daily News* owner Mort Zuckerman;
Ghislaine, daughter of the late press tycoon and Robert
Maxwell; TV celebrities Barbara Walters and Peter Jennings; and
the usual gang of neo-cons and Hollinger executives and board
members. Arthur M. Schlesinger, Jr., the Pulitzer Prize–winning historian and biographer of Franklin D. Roosevelt, told
me he also attended. Given the guest list, it was hard to picture
how singing "Happy Birthday" to Barbara would result in new
business opportunities.

In his 1993 memoirs, Conrad Black had written admiringly of
how one of Montreal's Scots — Lord Strathcona — had spent

long years in Labrador with the Hudson's Bay Company before getting his due: a post as Canadian High Commissioner in London and a peerage. He did not mention that Strathcona had made hundreds of millions of dollars by manipulating railway stocks. When Black established his presence in London in the late 1980s, he was well aware that rescuing a declining pro-Conservative newspaper from oblivion and making it a media leader in Britain and internationally could fulfill his long-time dream — a life peerage.

Provoked by Black's bluster and advocacy, Canadian prime minister Jean Chrétien found what he thought was his opponent's weakness — vanity. Sensing that Black craved the prestige of a peerage, the prime minister did his best to block the honour. With the peerage finally within his grasp, Black was forced into a vigorous defensive position, which reinforced his reputation for more than a touch of snobbery. It was payback time for Chrétien. The focus of the conflict between Black and Chrétien now moved from Ottawa to the Mother of Parliaments — Westminster.

Black's love of provocative language caused strong reactions, and he was not universally liked in Britain. There was considerable controversy when he engaged in the intense debate over how deeply Britain should integrate into Europe, writing in the *Telegraph*: "My position continues to be that the UK is nearer in all respects except geography to North America than to Europe, must remain close to both and should not in the clearly foreseeable future subscribe to the euro."

He testified before the U.S. Trade Commission in Washington, defending his view that Britain should join the North American Free Trade Agreement rather than Europe. There were other controversies. After *Spectator* columnist Taki Theodora-Copulos denounced Israeli forces "shooting at kids" and "assaulting rock-throwing youth with armor piercing missiles," Black implied Taki (his own employee) was little better than a Nazi: "In both its venomous character and its unfathomable absurdity, [his] farrago of lies is almost worthy of Goebbels or the authors of the *Protocols of the Elders of Zion*. The Jews, according to Taki, have suborned the U.S. government, direct that country's military like a docile attack dog, and glory in the murder of innocent or mischievous children. He presents the universal Jewish ethos as brutish, vulgar, grasping and cunningly wicked."[230] Black accused Ian Gilmour (a former editor of the *Spectator* and a minister in the first Thatcher cabinet who has long worked for Palestinian causes) of being "an almost pathological Americanophobic myth-maker. And in his febrile hostility to Israel, he does himself the injustice of seeming little better than a common or garden Jew-baiter masquerading as a champion of the Palestinian 'underdog.'"[231]

Black sometimes attacked the British Foreign Office, the BBC, the *Independent*, the *Guardian*, the *Evening Standard,* and other leftist or trendy media organizations. In a 2003 profile of Black, the *Independent* counterattacked: "Black is urbane and intelligent. Like that other Canadian press giant, Lord Beaverbrook, he is also an impressive historian — he has just finished writing a biography of Franklin D. Roosevelt, and is said to be able to name every single galleon in the Spanish Armada. As broad as a rugby prop and sometimes as menacing, he can deploy a doleful tone in conversation that throws his interlocutors off balance. But don't let that fool you. He loves debate, but enters it for only one reason — to prove he is right. This is not a man who changes his mind readily.

"Black's friends are the sort who think small talk is for small people and who, if they aren't calling the shots any more, feel they ought to be: Henry Kissinger, Margaret Thatcher, Richard Perle, Lord Carrington . . . Black is a leading member — is there any other type? — of the Bilderberg group, the high-powered think-tank that meets in near-secret and is much beloved of conspiracy theorists as a result." The profile concluded that "with Henry Kissinger and Richard Perle at his side, Black has steered the *Daily Telegraph*'s editor, Charles Moore, further and further to the Euro-sceptic Zionist right; nowadays it appears to be talking to a neo-conservative clique of true believers."[232]

Black's increasingly strident neo-conservatism was of concern even to close colleagues at the *Telegraph* because it seemed to imply that Britain's interests should be subservient to those of the United States. "As far as Conrad is concerned," said

Peregrine Worsthorne, editor of the *Sunday Telegraph* from 1986 to 1989, "the neo-cons are his lot. They believe that if America is strong enough and determined enough, and not held down by lily-livered guilt-stricken intellectual Liberals, and if people are frightened enough of you, America will prevail. I remember Nixon saying to me that the secret of his foreign policy was that the rest of the world should be frightened of America, and that was the best guarantee of world order. That might have worked with the Soviet Union. But this neo-con belief in willpower, a very Nietzschean view, doesn't work in the Middle East. Nixon absolutely told me his view." Worsthorne's conservative credentials are impeccable: "I was one of the few British journalists who supported the United States during the Vietnam War."

Ian Gilmour said, "The neo-cons are pretty much of a disaster — they just talk to each other and despise everybody else. Are there any in Britain? There are at the *Telegraph*."

Brian MacArthur, associate editor of *The Times*, said, "On issues like America and Israel, the *Telegraph* reflects Conrad Black's views. There are those who think he has atlanticized the paper. There is a constituency for this view in Britain."

There is some irony in the fact that the Republican George W. Bush, whom the *Chicago Sun-Times* endorsed during the 2000 presidential election, found such a ready partner in Tony Blair, a former British Labour prime minister and devout Anglican, who articulated his bipolar view of the world in the starkest us-and-them terms. The *Telegraph* did not support Blair in the June 2001 election: that support would come later, once Blair became a bold promoter of the Atlantic alliance and Bush's junior partner.

One of the reasons the neo-conservative Black got on so well with the Labour prime minister is that Blair faithfully maintained the transatlantic "special relationship" between the United States and Britain.

By 1999, Conrad Black had lived eleven years in the United Kingdom, although he remained a citizen of Canada. In recognition of his role at the *Telegraph*, the leader of the British Conservative Party, William Hague, informed Black in February 1999 that he planned to nominate him for appointment by the Queen as a life peer. Black said he did nothing to get the peerage: "I did not lift one finger to have it happen, but once I was up for this position, as has been every proprietor of the *Telegraph* since the newspaper was founded, I felt I was entitled to it. I'm an internationalist, and I felt that was completely compatible with being a Canadian citizen. And legally that was the case."

However, his long-time friend and business associate Peter White laughs at the claim: "Of course, he did *everything* he possibly could to get the title."

At first sight, there was something unusual about this nomination, since a Canadian was being invited to sit in the Upper House of Parliament of a foreign country without being a citizen of that country. The nomination was accepted and sent on to the British Government. First came the protocol, the niceties between governments. Three months later, on May 24, the British Government contacted the Government of Canada, asking for confirmation that there was no legal impediment to the honour. The Honours Committee of the Canadian Government reviewed the case, and Black was informed there was no statute to prevent him from accepting the peerage, although it was customary that the two governments involved consult each another in such cases. Five days later, on May 29, Prime Minister Blair told Black that he could accept the title as long as he became a British citizen and did not use the title in Canada. The Canadian Government provided written confirmation of Blair's position on June 9. The way was open to British citizenship, which Black applied for and obtained on June 11. Evidently on the fast track, Blair informed him the nomination had been passed on to the Queen and he would be made a peer on June 18, 1999. The fast track turned to mud when Prime Minister Chrétien decided to step in. The day before the peerage was to become official, Blair told the unsuspecting Black that the Canadian prime minister had blocked the appointment on the grounds that it contravened the little-known Nickle Resolution. Instituted by the Canadian House of Commons in 1919 just after the First World War, it requested that King George V not confer any titles on his Canadian subjects.[233]

By invoking the Nickle Resolution, Chrétien blindsided Black, who immediately took the matter before the courts, suing the prime minister for "abuse of power, misfeasance in public office and negligence." In addition, he sued the Government of Canada, represented by the Attorney General of Canada, for negligent representation, seeking declaratory relief and damages of $25,000. Although the Upper Chamber in Ottawa had never adopted the Nickle Resolution, it had become a custom of sorts.

Despite the questionable image of Britain's House of Lords, Black wanted in, and he was furious that Jean Chrétien would deny him membership by blocking his peerage. There is no doubt in Black's mind it was personal. Explaining his actions to Black over the telephone, Chrétien reminded him that media coverage of the Liberal government in the *National Post* had been consistently negative. In his legal challenge in the Superior Court of Ontario, Black charged that the prime minister was conducting a personal vendetta.

The legal dispute was rich in irony, given that Black had wanted to use the *National Post* to "change the country." First, there was the title of the court case — *Black versus Canada (Prime Minister) 2000*. Then, there was the matter of Black seeking a British title for himself, although he would just as soon see Canada without a Queen. Chrétien did his best to block Black's "foreign" title but has done more than any other Canadian, with the exception of Pierre Elliott Trudeau, to cast the Canadian constitution in stone and ensure that the British sovereign remains the Canadian head of state forever.[234] The dispute reopened a long-festering wound — Canada's ambivalent relationship with Britain, underscored by more than a century of Liberal actions that simultaneously strengthened and reduced Canadian sovereignty. Finally, there was the precedent (which not even Black seemed to remember) of Canadian cardinals becoming princes of the Church and serving in the Vatican "Senate," where they were eligible at least for ministerial roles serving under the Pope, an absolute monarch. If it was acceptable in Rome, then why not in London?

In May 2000, Ontario Superior Court Chief Justice Patrick

LeSage ruled that Chrétien had every right to "give advice and express opinions on honors and foreign affairs" and was under no obligation to explain his reasons. Furthermore this "prerogative" power was not reviewable by a court of law. Black quickly appealed the decision. Justice John Laskin of the Ontario Court of Appeal reaffirmed the lower court's decision in May 2001, stating: "The refusal to grant an honour is far removed from the refusal to grant a passport or a pardon, where important individual interests are at stake. Unlike the refusal of a peerage, the refusal of a passport or a pardon has real adverse consequences for the person affected. Here, no important individual interests are at stake. Mr. Black's rights were not affected, however broadly 'rights' are construed. No Canadian citizen has a right to an honour." Black's appeal and a government cross-appeal were dismissed with costs. The Canadian taxpayers' share of the legal tab to defend the prime minister and file the cross-appeal was $168,000.[235]

"Chrétien had things his way, and he had the satisfaction of seeing me cease to be a Canadian citizen," Black said. "But whether the prime minister of Canada is contented or discontented is not a matter that concerns me particularly. I would have preferred, of course, to retain my Canadian citizenship, but he effectively required me to choose. What does disappoint me a bit is that first of all, I had to make that choice, and secondly that, for the most part, my motive has been assumed to be exclusively to take up the peerage. But that was only part of it."

Black said he was also making a statement about Canada. "I really felt that there was practically no hope for Canada as I wished it to evolve, that I perfectly, serenely, submitted to the majority view in that country, and as a sovereign people, it will make its own decisions. It was, in fact, a recognition on my part that the vision I had for Canada has, I think, effectively no possibility of success. . . . I think that rather got lost in the whole business of my becoming a peer . . . there were the two elements to my decision to renounce my citizenship. There is no point to my continued Canadian citizenship at all. And it was a gesture, and it just became a passport of convenience that in fact, I don't use much."

Dan Colson, Black's right-hand man in London, disagrees. "His decision to give up his Canadian citizenship was one of the saddest events in his life. Because he has always considered himself to be a patriotic Canadian."

Black's introduction into the House of Lords demanded a heavy personal price — one not paid by other life peers. This was his apotheosis, his social consecration. But it was also the culmination of a long, acrimonious and, at times, surrealistic struggle, pitting him against the prime minister of Canada. Like many struggles in his life, it was played out in full public view.

Conrad Black often took pride in his strategic prowess. Yet his downfall can be traced back to two catastrophic errors of strategy. His first strategic blunder was the decision, in the mid-1990s, to go public in the United States by folding worldwide newspaper assets into a U.S.-based public company, Hollinger International. This first blunder was now followed by a second one — to give up his Canadian citizenship. In the end, Black's snobbery overcame his prudence. By giving up his Canadian citizenship to claim a vain title in Britain, he was exposing himself to a huge liability. If he was ever convicted of a crime in the United States, he couldn not apply for a transfer to a softer, gentler Canadian prison. Instead, he would be sent to a federal medium-security penitentiary in the United States, where he would likely share a cell with a convicted drug dealer, as 57 per cent of all inmates in federal penitentiaries have been convicted of drug offences.

Now that he had sold control of the Southam Group to Izzy Asper, Black could not use his Canadian newspapers to hammer Jean Chrétien. Asper and Black were both prepared to interfere directly in editorial policy, but Asper was a long-time Liberal (he had once been leader of the Liberal Party in Manitoba). In a letter of January 5, 2001, Black wrote to Asper: "I am aware that considerable pressure has been exerted by David Asper [Izzy's son] on behalf of Chrétien. This is not reconcilable with our agreement and I am sending an unexceptionably worded memo to the most senior editorial people at the *National Post* saying that should they receive any request from representatives of affiliated companies for material alteration of the editorial content of the newspaper, the inquiring parties should be referred to [Hollinger executive] Peter Atkinson or myself. The fact is that given the malicious, cowardly, ignorant, dishonest and illegal assault of Chrétien upon me, I have shown great forbearance in encouraging as tolerant a tone in our coverage of him as I have."

On March 13, 2001, Asper criticized Black for attacking a cautious article by David Asper about Chrétien's business affairs: "Neither you nor I would profit from a public battle, which would give great pleasure to those who wish neither of us well, but regrettably, you have chosen to publicly throw a gauntlet, administer a public slap in the face which has both embarrassed, humiliated and held up to ridicule and dishonour both my family and my company."

In reply the next day, Black wrote: "I have told you, David and [Izzy's other son] Leonard many times that there is a way to alter the general tone of a serious newspaper and I have offered advice, without being asked, on how to do that. I believe it is, in fact, contrary to the spirit of our arrangement and to CanWest's corporate interests for you people to tinker so recklessly by these interferences with the credibility and therefore the value of these franchises which my associates and I so swiftly built up. I must add that going back to the days of my civil relationship with Chrétien, I beseeched him to resolve these matters [Black's desire to maintain his Canadian citizenship while gaining entry to the British House of Lords] by the time honoured method of a few honest answers. Instead he has consistently lied to Parliament and the public. . . ."

A final breach between Asper and Black was inevitable. On August 23, 2001, Black announced the sale to CanWest of his remaining 50 per cent interest in the *National Post* (which had already lost $22.7 million in the first quarter that year).

Black received official confirmation of his life peerage on the day of the September 11, 2001, terror attacks in New York and Washington. The *Independent* pounced on the unfortunate coincidence. Noting that Black had been known in his early years at the helm of the *Daily Telegraph* as a non-interventionist, the *Independent* said, "The non-interventionary Black is [now] impossible to recognize. When his peerage was announced . . .

the *Telegraph* managed to find space for nearly 500 words on the event. Most other newspapers did not have room for such fulsome reports, given that a few hours after Downing Street revealed Black's good fortune, hijacked aeroplanes had flown into the twin towers of the World Trade Center and the Pentagon."[236]

Black's newspaper interests were seriously affected by the terror attacks. Plans for the 150-storey skyscraper in Chicago were scaled down to a more manageable 90 storeys. But the real estate market recovered only slowly, and the plans were put on hold.

But that was not all. Although October 31, 2001, was set for Black's becoming a peer of the realm, the sunny, successful outer Conrad Black was dogged by a darker, tortured inner personality. While he was tasting victory in London, the beginnings of defeat were looming in New York. Just two weeks *before* his introduction, Tweedy, Browne Company (which owned about 18 per cent of Hollinger International's class A common stock) started to challenge the practice of paying management fees to Ravelston, the Canadian-based holding company controlled by Black. The campaign waged by Chris Browne and his financial analyst Laura Jereski ultimately led to Black's ouster from the company.

Along the ashen Thames, wending its way eastward through the middle of London, a stocky man of wealth with a forceful personality and something restless and proud in his bearing donned parliamentary robes — an ermine-lined, gold-embroidered scarlet cape.

His eyes were cold, his jaw square and his large hands hung heavily from his costume. An historian and a romantic at heart, he felt a powerful sense of the moment. Conrad Black was entering the House of Lords — one of the most ancient parliamentary institutions in the world, and one that has long symbolized Britain's archaic class structure, hereditary privilege and heavily concentrated land ownership, while serving as a part-time occupation for the idle rich. Black was about to be introduced as a life peer, Baron Black of Crossharbour — the name of a tube station near Black's east London offices and, perhaps more appropriately, the name of the neighbourhood where Black and his close associate Daniel Colson, deputy chairman of the Telegraph Group, made a lot of money in real estate in the 1980s.

According to Ian Gilmour (Lord Gilmour of Craigmillar), "If you buy a London newspaper, you buy a peerage at one remove. But you would be more or less out of your mind if you bought a newspaper in order to get a peerage." Other prominent social positions in Britain are a sure guarantee to a seat in the Lords — as the historian John Julius Norwich mused: "Even the secretary of the boilermaker's union is going to end up in the Lords." Norwich's own grandfather was a medical man knighted for treating King Edward VII for gonorrhoea — or was it piles? The title of Viscount came courtesy of Norwich's father, who had been a British ambassador.

Black's parliamentary introduction was a personal apotheosis. It took his quest for social and financial standing to the ultimate level — the culmination of his thirty-two-year career as a brilliant, ruthless, larger-than-life press baron who controlled Hollinger, one of the world's leading media empires. It meant that he had gone one better than the old snobs of Argus, such as E. P. Taylor and Bud McDougald. Why did a peerage matter so much to Black? It may be that he saw membership in the House of Lords as the ultimate personal link binding him to historical figures he admired. He knew that Sir Winston Churchill had given many of his most stirring speeches during the Second World War from the dispatch box of the House of Lords (after the House of Commons had been damaged by Nazi dive-bombers). He knew that British aristocrats had been figureheads of political power in Canada right up to the Second World War. He surely thought back to that 1953 coronation cruise. Now, millions of Britons could be expected to cheer *him* along, or at least to show him deference.

Black's seat in the Lords instantly turned him into a legislator in Britain. But there was something bittersweet about the pageantry — a certain irony in the timing of his title in that it coincided with a groundswell of shareholder allegations.

The British know how to organize colourful rituals, and Black's introduction in the House of Lords was somewhere between brilliant heraldic pageant and tongue-in-cheek high theatre. There was an air of self-deprecating nostalgia for Britain's bygone glory years. Despite the dignified pace, and the wigs and bowing, there was something vaguely comic about it — a subtle, mischievous joke that would come to you a day later.

According to a time-honoured ritual, the Gentleman Usher of the Black Rod, with his Rod of Office over his right shoulder, led each new peer into the Lords with the peer's two supporting peers and the Garter King of Arms, wearing his tabard of the Royal Arms and carrying a sceptre in his right hand.

Black Rod, bowing profusely, and the bewigged Reading Clerk, bearing the Letters Patent from the Queen, first escorted a Scottish lady, who would become Baroness Michie of Gallanbach. She elected to take her oath of office in English and in Gaelic, the ancestral language of the Scots.

Then amid the relaxed hubbub of the dukes, earls, barons, Lords justice and bishops, Conrad Black readied for his entry. Flanked by Lady Thatcher and Lord Carrington, he proceeded to the centre of the House of Lords. All three bowed deferentially to the Lord Chancellor, who sat in court dress, gown, full-bottomed wig and tricorne hat on the woolsack. The Lord Bishop of Bath and Wells read prayers. Then the Reading Clerk, who lifted a scroll to eye level, began reading:

> Elizabeth the Second, by the Grace of God of the United Kingdom and Northern Ireland and of our other realms and territories Queen, Head of the Commonwealth, Defender of the Faith, to all Lords Spiritual and Temporal and all other subjects whatsoever, to whom these presents may come, Greeting! Know Ye that of our special grace, certain knowledge and mere motion, in pursuance of the Life Peerage Act 1958 and of our other powers in that behalf us enabling, do by these presents advance, create and prefer our right trusty and well-beloved Conrad Moffat Black, member of Our Privy Council for

Canada, Officer of the Order of Canada, to the state, degree, style, dignity, title and honour of Baron Black of Crossharbour, in our London borough of Tower Hamlets, and for Us, Our heirs and successors, to appoint, give, and grant unto him, the said name, state, degree, style, dignity and honour, of Baron Black of Crossharbour, to have and to hold unto him, for his life.

"Historically," Black said of the occasion, "I was standing at the dispatch box, where a good many famous people have stood, including in the latter part of his time as prime minister, Disraeli . . . and the Marquess of Salisbury . . . the Duke of Wellington, when he was prime minister, and others. Just because I stood where they were doesn't mean I take onto myself the grandeur of those men. It was just an interesting position to be in. And I was particularly gratified that Margaret Thatcher and Peter Carrington were my presenters, and that Dr. and Mrs. Kissinger were in the gallery on my behalf. I couldn't help thinking how pleased my mother would be. She was a very Commonwealth-oriented person, and she was from that era, when the summit of what a Canadian could achieve would be some recognition in the Commonwealth as a whole, and in a sense, that would have fit that criteria."

In 2001, Conrad's new baronial title created more authority and social distance for him; it justified his life struggles, appealed to his snobbery, washed away his sorrows, and redeemed his some-times tattered reputation as a feisty Machiavellian.

His title also made Barbara a baroness. She, too, had finally arrived.

Discretion is the greater part of valour, but both husband and wife flaunted their glamorous celebrity lifestyle, despite the. first open confrontations with enraged Hollinger International public shareholders.

Even though she was now a baroness, Amiel's taste for the upper crust of British society rang of self-parody. "I have an extravagance that knows no bounds," she told *Vogue* in 2002, "I don't want to be mutton trying to be lamb. And I'm always wor-ried about cleavage. It's good in your 30s and okay in your 40s, but after that it's not on. I keep saying 'higher', but I seem to keep spilling out of things." The *Vogue* article featured a photograph of Lady Black in her living room, wearing a Carolina Herrera blouse with sable cuffs and plaid pants; Tony Duquette ring; and Manolo Blahnik shoes; as she reclined on a sofa below the watchful gaze of a mega-sized portrait of her husband by Andy Warhol. And there were the jewels. "Until I was about 45 years old, diamonds and other gemstones were simply not in my life," Amiel told *FQ* magazine in 2003. "I had never seen any and I certainly didn't miss them. Then I married again ... and vaulted into circles where, for some people, jewellery is a defining attribute, rather like your intelligence or the number of residences you have. I got [from Conrad Black] a fantastic natural-pearl and diamond brooch that has stayed in my safety deposit box for about six years, unworn because it is so large that I simply can't carry it off."

Such attention-seeking quotes gave the impression Amiel liked to boast about her lifestyle, to show off her trophies and glory in a social status she only fantasized about in her early years. The public shareholders took notice. But one of Amiel's friends, the *National Post*'s Elizabeth Nickson, defended Amiel in a column, saying that the hateful things being written about her were 90 per cent politically motivated and "the rest is just plain envy."[239] Nickson was European bureau chief of *Life Magazine* in London, where she met Amiel, then a columnist for *The Times.*

"I admit that in London, I found Barbara's ideas shocking," she wrote. "I liked her despite her thinking. It is a brutally hard thing to make it in London as a colonial, especially in society. Thousands of cultivated well-born Ivy league-educated American and Canadian beauties attempt the summit every year and turn tail within weeks. Barbara was a middle-aged, freelance columnist who grew up in Hamilton, Ontario, with no money of her own, who was also Jewish. Odds on her making it, let alone virtually re-creating London society? Almost zero. Of all the women, the Canadian cultural establishment routinely throws up for us peons to worship, not one of them has a scrap of the bravery of Barbara Black."

Ken Whyte, founding editor of the *National Post*, said, "Barbara is amazing. At times, she has been the most charming woman I ever met; at other times she can be quite aloof. She is incredibly committed to the craft of journalism. Conrad became a lot more entertaining after he married Barbara. She loosened him up. They argued incessantly about issues but also about each other, reducing each other to stereotypes — national, religious, racial. But he would play the doting husband, while she would tease him after parties, when he had been surrounded by so many women. Their politics on many things were similar, but they found a lot of uncommon ground."

"The marriage has been extremely successful," said Larry Zolf. "Lord and Lady Black are among the world's leading couples. . . . When Black met Barbara Amiel it was like the sky opened up for both of them. Now Black had added true love to his repertoire. It was a real meeting of minds and bodies. The beautiful Amiel was as conservative as Black, as Ayn Randish, as Zionist, as rugged an individualist. And even better, she was a convert to Black's conservatism before she ever knew him."

Nickson said Amiel risks herself over and over again, and though her "ferocity of purpose might make her frightening, it does not make her evil."

Despite all the fame and fortune, Barbara's skeptical this-world-is-an-illusion attitude never left her. In her own mind, she was still a wandering Jew, with her toothbrush handy. Ken Whyte remembered spending time with her in Toronto during the glory years. "Yes, I'm living well now," she told him as they drove in her limousine, "but before I met Conrad I was living in a one-bedroom flat in London, and I may be back in a one-bedroom flat one day."

In November 2001, three weeks after Black became Lord Black, New York papers were abuzz with news that Black and a syndicate of investors were planning to launch a new daily paper in Manhattan in early 2002. Dan Colson said the *Sun* would be "very up market" and "certainly neo-conservative in its ideological views." The *Sun* would prove a modest success, providing columns from the *Telegraph* and *Jerusalem Post*. This was certainly an act of faith in a city reeling from the shock of the September 11 terror attacks.

Returning to Canada in November 2001, Black delivered a speech to the Fraser Institute, a right-wing think-tank. His words were repeated in the *National Post* under the heading, "I dreamt of Canada" and summarized his most important experiences in the land of his birth: "From the age of eight . . . when I first saw New York and London, in both of which cities I am a homeowner now, I dreamt of a Canada where the most talented and ambitious people would not feel irresistibly drawn to those and other great foreign cities. . . . Almost all practising Canadians, including me when I was one, felt the urge to help lift the country that final rung we were told in school we were pre-destined to climb, to the summit of national achievement. In pursuit of this objective, I moved to Quebec in 1966 and took as a holy crusade the pursuit and propagation of a spirit of bonne entente between the French- and English-speaking Canadians . . . I retreated to Toronto in 1974 and began the noisy championship of, in Quebec parlance, a distinct society vis a vis the United States . . . I believed Canada could evolve to a more confident, spontaneous, individualistic, enterprising and unenvious society than it had been by its own methods, not imitative ones.

"With only 11 per cent of the U.S. population and a less temperate climate, Canada had a less complicated sociology. I thought most Canadians perceived that Canada does have the potential to be one of the world's ten most important countries and a fairly distinct and much admired political laboratory. I believed it myself for a long time, and advocated it strenuously, as a commentator, a business spokesman, and ultimately as a publisher, arguably the country's leading newspaper publisher."

Black had renounced his Canadian citizenship, pulled up roots in his native land. He now publicly conceded in the speech that his dream of reinvigorating conservatism in Canada had failed. His agenda for the country, not as an elected politician but as a newspaper proprietor, had been rejected. And this agenda included his calls for "an end of pre-emptive concessions to Quebec. . .lower taxes, fewer regulations and a steady move toward a government less socialistic than the United States but still generous to the disadvantaged . . . reinforcement of the Canadian currency to restore value to Canadians and impose discipline on Canadian industry and labor . . . a restoration of private medicine and tax treatment for private education to help emancipate Canadian children from the teachers' unions . . . [an end to] continued truckling to Castro and pandering to the Third World and . . . restoration of Canada's ability to play a NATO security role."

The Fraser Institute speech was a strange, narcissistic rant. He was brilliant, omniscient, immune, but the average Canadian did not appreciate him. In launching the *National Post*, he had promised, "We're going to change this country." But Canada had refused to live up to his dreams. If Canada could not be altered, then it was only worth discarding. Call it the Grandiosity Gap.

But Black's long-time friend and business associate Peter White sees Black's 2001 departure from Canada in a different light. "If you would say Conrad was to judge his own success on his intellectual leadership [in Canada], he would have to judge it a failure, as he has. He basically said, 'Look, I tried to do my best for this God-forsaken country — essentially, they were too lumpen to listen and to pay attention, and I'm leaving.'"

Why did Black take the court cases, the renunciation of his Canadian citizenship and the acrimony leading up to his British peerage as a deeply personal humiliation? Why use such moralistic language, blaming Canada for rejecting him and forcing him to start a new life on the greener shores of Britain? Why should Canadians treat him like Beaverbrook, a transatlantic warrior, a living bridge both political and economic between Canada and Britain? He even claimed during his speech that there was a brain drain of Canada's best and brightest to Britain, although to most Canadians, no such brain drain had ever been observed.

The fact was, he simply slammed the door on Canada in 2001, the way he had abruptly left Quebec in 1974, full of acrimony, insults and accusations. Despite all the invective, the fact was that Black's business interests had changed. After his disgrace in 2003 and the mounting financial and legal troubles starting in 2004, it was highly ironic that the only place where he had any dignity left was his $20-million "cottage" back in Toronto.

Black still had Canadian roots and deserves recognition for that.

Joanna and Black's children were now coming of age. Jonathan Black, a strapping young man with red hair, a Marlon Brando face and full lips, had taken up modelling in 1996. In 1999, he told a reporter that being the son of Conrad Black had not opened doors for him in the fashion world: "To be honest with you, apart from here [in Canada] and London a bit, in New York and other places, my father is not really a household name. In the business, especially in New York, Milan, Paris, they're oblivious to what my father does . . ." As for the modelling, "My mum [Joanna] is really into it. My dad likes it too. Sometimes, he sees me in London, because he was there. He sees some stuff that I've done, because I've done some work over there, and he's really proud of me." Alana Black moved to Montreal to study at Concordia University. And son James entered Upper Canada College — which meant that Conrad his father had put his 1959 expulsion from the same school behind him.

In late 2001, Black was preoccupied by the deteriorating health of his brother, Monte, who had a form of liver cancer. They had shared so much over the years, and it was hard to see the vigorous, personable Monte go down to a fatal disease. In early January 2002, Monte lay dying in Toronto's Sunnybrook Hospital. By a quirk of fate he was two rooms away from his former wife, Mariellen Campbell. They died of cancer within a day of each other. "My brother was a delightful man who faced a terrible ordeal with great dignity and good humour and will be greatly missed," Conrad Black said.

By the beginning of 2002, Black had achieved many of his personal goals. He headed an international press empire that was publicly traded on the New York Stock Exchange. He was a member of the House of Lords. He felt he could afford to devote considerable time and resources to researching and writing a biography of Franklin Delano Roosevelt (launched in November 2003). He made it clear that he had left Canada largely because of its soft-left social democracy. He promoted neo-conservatism through his newspapers in Britain, the United States and Israel. The *International Herald Tribune* opined that Black's ambition was to become "the godfather of neo-conservatism" and that he was recruiting and handsomely rewarding the likes of Kissinger and Perle to his boards of directors, "even if they seem to have taken their fiduciary duties somewhat lightly." And in his London newspapers, Black was promoting a group of writers "whose devotion to American power was all the stronger because they belong to that curious category, self-hating Canadians. Black himself, his wife Barbara Amiel, David Frum and Mark Steyn all loathe their native country, evidently under the impression that Canada is on the brink of Bolshevism because it has a national health service."[238]

In mid-2002, former prime minister Brian Mulroney told me he crossed the Atlantic in the hopes of luring Black back to Canada. This was just a few weeks after Black's maiden speech in the House of Lords. "I told Conrad in London, that, given the [political] divisions we had lived with, I thought he would be quite uniquely qualified to seek the leadership of the Progressive Conservative Party and bring the [PC and Canadian Alliance] parties together on an honourable basis. He was known as a Conservative, was very articulate, bilingual and successful, and would have brought an entirely different dimension to the leadership of the party. Now, you just *know* that the Liberals would have salivated at the idea of having a Colonel Blimp whom they could massacre across the floor of the House of Commons. But that's the way the Liberals are — they underestimate everybody. . . . And they would have underestimated Conrad Black at their peril."

Mulroney's offer showed an utter lack of judgment. How could someone who had given up his Canadian citizenship in order to become a British baron return to Canada and lead the Progressive Conservatives to victory? Could he be a member of the national legislatures of two countries simultaneously? Would Black really have a chance of becoming Canadian prime minister in 2002? Would he have had to reapply for citizenship first? How could Canadians be expected to vote for a national leader who had renounced his Canadian citizenship and slammed the door on the country, in a blaze of blistering acrimony and wounded pride?

The Canadian Press/AP/Nam Y. Huh

CHAPTER TEN

COMPLETELY OUTMANEUVERED

KISSINGER DESCRIBED IN *A World Restored* Prince Metternich's great spiderweb of political networks — and Black's web stretched from London to New York, Palm Beach and Toronto. In these cities, he owned residences worth close to $100 million. As he well knew, international jet-setters are drawn to those willing and able to dazzle guests with splendidly decorated mansions, abundant trophies (whether artwork or wives), and extravagant entertainment. Networking in this environment costs a fortune and requires a high-maintenance lifestyle.

Attended by presidents, prime ministers, princes, millionaire industrialists, movie actresses, top models, rock stars and well-known intellectuals, Black's glittering dinner parties served as potent symbols of his prestige and wealth.

But Black wasn't inviting guests merely to bathe in their reflected glory. He cultivated the company of people who had information, perspectives and contacts worth trading.

For example, in 1985, Black got advance warning from Kissinger that a big change in oil prices was likely, important information to Black, who at the time was in the oil business through his control of Norcen Energy Resources. "I had met with Henry Kissinger when passing through New York in December," Black wrote, "and he had told me that in recent contacts with Saudi leaders, including the king, he had been advised that the world oil price would decline from the mid-twenties to under ten dollars a barrel. It seemed clear enough that supply was outstripping demand and that a decline in the world oil price, perhaps a fairly sharp one, was inevitable. I had thought Norcen could endure that without too much effect on its performance. . . . A decline on the scale Kissinger was fore-casting was less easily assimilable . . . It became necessary to contemplate parting with Norcen."

Black periodically defended Kissinger in his newspapers, as did Barbara Amiel. For example, Black denounced a Kissinger biography by Christopher Hitchens, which drew attention to Kissinger's role in the indiscriminate bombing of Cambodia (leading to hundreds of thousands of civilian deaths) and the 1973 *coup d'état* in Chile that overthrew the Allende govern-ment, among other controversies. "This is not really a book at all," Black wrote. "It is a malicious polemic from a notorious pamphleteer."[239]

And after getting to know Andrew Knight through the Bilderberg conferences, Black learned from him of the financial problems at Lord Hartwell's *Daily Telegraph* — a timely discovery that provided Black with his greatest negotiating coup and assured Knight of a brilliant run as CEO of the *Telegraph* as well as considerable financial rewards.

Among Black's other important Bilderberg contacts were former U.S. national security adviser Zbigniew Brzezinski; Peter Carrington; former U.S. assistant secretary of defence Richard Perle; and conservative columnist George F. Will.

Black's networks were drawn together by a community of interests, whether financial, political or intellectual. In the 1990s, Black named Kissinger to Hollinger International's advisory board along with other Bilderberg contacts, Brzezinski, Will, former British prime minister Margaret Thatcher and the Cath-olic conservative intellectual William F. Buckley, Jr.

"For showing up once a year with Lord Black to debate the world's problems, each was typically paid about $25,000 annu-ally (until the board was disbanded in 2001)," the *New York Times* reported. "Mr. Brzezinski's personal records show that he collected almost $170,000 for attending eight such meetings in the 1990s, according to an aide. Mr Buckley estimated that he had earned perhaps $200,000 or more. Mr. Will could not recall how many meetings he attended; an aide later confirmed that the per diem for each meeting was $25,000."[240] Buckley and Will sometimes defended Conrad Black in their columns, without disclosing the fact they were on Hollinger's payroll.[241]

It seemed Black was paying a fortune of company money just to make friends. He was also using his business to support a powerful network of neo-conservative allies intent on imposing themselves on the world.

Hollinger International board member Richard Perle served as chairman of the Pentagon's Defence Policy Board until he had to step down in March 2003 because of an apparent conflict of interest. A hard-core neo-conservative and advocate of a more aggressive U.S. foreign and defence policy, Perle is co-manager of Trireme Partners, which invests in electronic security and encryption technology for defence purposes. Kissinger served as an adviser to Trireme. And Hollinger's board authorized a $2.5-million investment in Trireme.

According to journalist and author Seymour Hersh, Perle attempted to recruit Saudi arms trader Adnan Khashoggi to convince ten wealthy Saudis to invest $10 million each in Trireme, which in turn would invest in companies dealing in technology, goods and services of value to homeland security and defence. Trireme wrote to Khashoggi that the fear of terrorism "would increase demand for such products in Europe and in countries like Saudi Arabia and Singapore." The Saudi millionaires were aware that Perle had been a strong advocate for war on Iraq and was very upset with the complacent Saudi response to terrorism. Between 1996 and 2002, Perle received $300,000 in annual salary and $2 million in bonuses as chairman of Hollinger subsidiary Hollinger Digital, a company that invested $14 million in Cambridge Display Technology — a UK-based company specializing in advanced virtual technologies. Perle also had shares in Cambridge. But as Hollinger International's 8-K amended filing of May 7, 2004, later made clear, the bigger controversy was that Hollinger Digital allegedly paid $15.5 million in incentive bonuses to Black and several associates from 1997 to 2003, while recording losses of $65 million on investments of $190 million.

Perle stated his view of the world in a book co-authored with fellow neo-conservative (and *National Post* columnist) David Frum. *An End to Evil: How to Win the War on Terror* puts forward their beliefs on why the United States should not submit to the authority of the United Nations and should disregard the sovereignty of any potentially threatening country; why Washington was right to prosecute the war on Iraq; how both Saudi Arabia and France have betrayed the United States; and how Israel's war against terror is fundamentally the same as America's. The book, which treats the greater part of the world with contempt, is particularly noteworthy given Perle's wide-ranging business ventures, many of them in the defence and security fields.

In the aftermath of the September 11 attacks, Black supported the pre-emptive war in Iraq, saying that the United States "is a tremendously powerful country prepared to take the initiative . . . and isn't asking us to make any huge sacrifice. Let us rejoice in the fact that there is such a country prepared to use its power for such a good end . . . The president of the U.S., Bush, was absolutely right when he spoke to the UN [on the issue of Iraq, in fall 2002] and said, 'We are acting based on the upholding of international law, and to make sure that the UN is taken seriously, and is not ineffectual the way the League of Nations was.'"

Black mobilized the resources of his newspaper empire to support the Coalition rationale for the March 2003 invasion of Iraq: namely, that Saddam Hussein possessed weapons of mass destruction (based on a British intelligence report); had developed operational links with al Qaeda; headed a totalitarian dictatorship based on gross human rights violations; and was a menace to the region.

For example, in a February 2003 speech before Britain's right-wing think-tank the Centre for Policy Studies, Black said, "Western intelligence estimates that Iraq has hundreds of tons of sarin, mustard and vx nerve agent, 30,000 projectiles for the delivery of these chemical and biological weapons, a mobile biological weapon development program, and an extensive nuclear weapon delivery program. These are all prohibited by treaty and a long succession of supporting United Nations resolutions, and all is hidden from the present contingent of 108 overworked UN inspectors. No other regime in the world possesses the combination of Saddam Hussein's notorious sponsorship of terrorism, his record of invading neighbouring countries, his fervent pursuit of mass destruction weapons and the capacity to fire them on other countries, as well as his barbarous mistreatment of his own citizens, as he has murdered tens of thousands of them. Saddam Hussein is also the leader of the militant Islamists. His is a secular government, and he does not tolerate religious, or any other dissent. But he is the undoubted standard-bearer of all the Arab world's militant Muslims, who yearn for a violent defeat of the West, as Bin Laden's endorsement of him this week indicates. He is the custodian of the hopes of all Moslems who rejoiced, as Saddam himself publicly did, at the massacre on September 11, 2001. We must certainly avoid a clash of civilizations, and one of the ways to do so is to demonstrate that Saddam's form of barbarism is a political model it is dangerous to emulate."

In this grossly exaggerated speech, Black seemed to be thumping his chest and calling for all-out war on Iraq. Being a global press baron, his position counted for some people. It could be argued that it contributed in a modest way to the panic leading to the U.S.-led invasion of Iraq. In fact, Black supported Bush and Tony Blair in both the justification and launch of the war. And it was no secret that Hollinger International board member Richard Perle was also a strong advocate for war.

The *Telegraph* was a leading source of information about the war in Iraq. Sir John Keegan, defence editor at the *Telegraph*, told me in mid-2003, "We have put huge resources into covering the war. We had dozens of correspondents covering the war — in the Middle East, Washington, etc. We cover wars as comprehensively as anyone. It is very expensive running war coverage."

The newspaper supported the Coalition rationale. "Like every government building in Baghdad," the *Telegraph* reported in April 2003, "the foreign ministry has been pillaged to destruction. It also suffered an American cruise missile strike in the second week of the war. Almost every room has been stripped bare and bands of looters still roam its corridors. Documents are strewn across the floor of every storey. Here, blowing in the wind are the crucial documents of a regime that was once among the most secretive in the world."

Shortly afterwards, reporter Inigo Gilmore wrote that "Iraqi intelligence documents discovered in Baghdad by *The Telegraph* have provided the first evidence of a direct link between Osama bin Laden's al Qaeda terrorist network and Saddam Hussein's regime." (In fact, there was widespread speculation that these "intelligence documents" were planted.)

In December 2003, the *Sunday Telegraph* published a story quoting Lt. Col. al-Dabbagh, an Iraqi officer who had commanded a front-line unit, to the effect that he was the source of top-secret information passed to British intelligence on Saddam's weapons of mass destruction. (He also said the reports that Saddam Hussein did indeed possess weapons of mass destruction were accurate.)

These news stories, speculative though they might have been, tended to justify the war in Iraq. Barbara Amiel's columns in the *Telegraph* supported the same position. "Saddam already has modest stockpiles of biological and chemical weapons," she wrote, "and needs only fissionable material for a nuclear device. Saddam has made it clear that he intends in his madness to be the leader of the Arab world. This requires him to be the leader of the Islamist movement whose goal, clearly stated and hideously demonstrated, in New York City last September 11, is the eradication of the West and its values."

Actually, Saddam had few or no weapons of mass destruction; was not on the point of acquiring nuclear weapons; and was not well-liked by the Islamist terror groups Amiel claimed he was about to lead in an insane quest for domination of the Islamic world. The fanatical ideology of *Islamism* should not be confused with *Islam* itself, which according to the Quran consists in complete devotion to God.

"I think the Iraq War was a great success, and was well conducted," *Telegraph's* defence editor John Keegan said in mid-June 2003. "Clearly it has had a messy aftermath, but wars do have messy aftermaths. The coalition had a perfectly straightforward approach, but Saddam didn't: he probably destroyed his weapons of mass destruction but was too proud to admit he destroyed them. He could not publicly admit that, since the weapons were a symbol of his prestige and power and deterred the Iranians from attacking him."

In Keegan's view, Islamist terrorism is a new development that will last as long as there are terrorists. "Al Qaeda are longing to get their hands on nuclear weapons and are longing to use them," he said. "They would only be too happy to use one."

In April 2003, shortly after the outbreak of war in Iraq, I went to New York for a long interview with Conrad Black. He kept me waiting a few hours that day, which was only to be expected. He always kept people waiting. I felt a combination of dread and boredom, wandering along the corridors of Hollinger International's executive suite. In the boardroom, I read Daisy Suckley's correspondence with Franklin Roosevelt. She died at the age of ninety-nine, and her heirs offered the revealing letters for sale. Black got a tip from the auction house Sotheby's, of which he was a director, and quickly bought them at reduced price. I also flipped through copies of Hollinger newspapers, noting the death notice of Sir Jean Paul Getty, whose stunning steam-powered yacht *Talitha G*, a miniature version of the passenger liner *Normandie*, Black had boarded several times on holidays.

Black had always shown tolerance for colourful rogues, from Maurice Duplessis and Robert Maxwell to Richard Nixon, while expressing unbounded admiration for heroic historic figures from Napoleon to Sir Winston Churchill and Franklin Delano Roosevelt. Black had enthusiastically embraced unfettered free enterprise, "integral conservatism," and the Catholic faith while worrying, along with Oswald Spengler, about the decline of the West. His tactics and manipulation of power could be stunningly inappropriate. Through his invective and bullying style, he created a great deal of antipathy. As long as his companies did well, he had the world at his feet. But when he began to falter, as in early 2003, and his tactics were revealed, many people turned against him.

Considering the backdrop of grandeur and wealth — the mansions, the private jets, the Ivor Roberts-Jones bronze statue of Sir Winston Churchill, the gold-framed FDR letters — I wondered whether he was a colourful rogue himself. Was that the leitmotif — of all the challenges and responses of his life? Was there something artful, cunning and duplicitous in his way of handling business? Did he promote a view of "the winner takes the spoils" with a knowing, self-deprecating wink? I wondered whether the speeches and editorials and books were a diversion — a brilliant blaze of verbiage to attract the audience's attention away from some of the other things that were going on.

Finally, Conrad Black turned up, apologizing for the delay. In the comfort of his New York office, with the sirens of fire engines drifting up from busy Fifth Avenue, Black expressed strong views about the values he would like to transmit to his children. There was a hint of sadness in his voice.

I wasn't sure whom I was talking to — the sunny, outgoing Black, or the gloomier, destructive Black, stealing like the moon across the surface of the sun and eclipsing its golden light.

"Try to separate questions of principle from questions of tactic, and be clever in tactics, but be inflexible on principle," he told me. "It's easy to say that, but in practice, we all face this all the time. It's hard. And we all get it wrong sometimes, but . . . recognize it as the problem that it is, constantly recurring through life, and do your absolute best to deal with it. The tendency that we all have is often to try to ignore things like that, and try to pretend that they aren't crises of judgment. But such crises do frequently occur, and all you can do is consider them carefully, act decisively, and do what you think is best. So, like all advice, it tends to be sort of clichéd, but that would be it, I think. Just recognize when questions of principle are in play, and try to uphold the principle . . . but not go so far that you become one of these priggish, self-righteous people who translates every act, no matter how mundane, and has some great moral crisis. We all know people like that too, and it's very tiresome."

Black said one must learn from experience, "otherwise life becomes very complicated indeed. My grandfather used to say, 'For some people experience is a slow teacher' — I hope I am not one of them." Black said he "succeeded less than fully many times, but again, that is the nature of our lot in life. I don't want to be absurdly platitudinous here, but not even Alexander the Great or somebody like that was always completely successful. I think rarely have I failed completely at anything serious, but I am not talking about a chess game with my son or something. Some things . . . if I had to do over, could have been done better — sure."

Conrad Black had a detached, bird's-eye view of winning and losing. He sounded as if he was dismissing shareholder complaints the way someone would swat flies.

Two weeks after my meeting with Black, Hollinger International held its 2003 annual shareholder meeting.

Toronto filmmaker Debbie Melnyk hid a portable video camera in her purse and made her way into the Metropolitan Club in New York in the hopes of catching some of the exchanges at the meeting. The raw footage she shot in the white marble Renaissance revival club on Fifth Avenue was eventually subpoenaed by the SEC, in time for the Chicago criminal trial. In her documentary, *Citizen Black*, a shareholder rises to complain: "You mentioned that you're going to scale back your use of the corporate jet. Could you tell me what type of corporate jets, the nature of the fleet and the number of hours flown for business versus private use?"

"None for private use," Black replied, with a blistering glare. "It has been made to appear that my associates and I are overpaid, we are self-indulgent and we're rather forgivingly adjudicated by our independent directors. . . . Our compensation method has been in place for many years. . . . There were, as has been amply demonstrated, a number of related-party transactions. The chairman of the audit committee, Governor Thompson, has said that every one of these transactions was demonstrably in the company's interest and was the best arrangement available."

According to Chris Browne, managing director of Tweedy, Browne, one of Hollinger International's institutional shareholders, "It would appear that the management fees were excessive. From the way Black had constructed the balance sheet at the holding company level — and it was only subsequently disclosed that the management service fee at Ravelston was pledged to cover the interest on debt — it was clear that the fees could not go below that level. And that had absolutely nothing to do with the executive services we were receiving as shareholders of Hollinger International. At the 2003 annual meeting, I asked Black about the non-compete payments, and he said they were common in the industry. I said, if they were common in the industry, could he cite some examples. And he did not." According to Browne, more than $300 million of questionable payments are at stake.

Melnyk provided evidence in her film that one independent director at least — Henry Kissinger — got additional perks, such as abundant use of the executive jet. So did William F. Buckley, Jr., another of Conrad's pals, who was not even a company director.

In early 2003, Black had considered taking Hollinger International private, although the price then seemed too high. Since the major focus of corporate governance is the balance of interests of majority and minority shareholders, it generally has less relevance to private companies than to public ones. By buying out minority shareholders and going private, Black might have avoided the showdown with institutional shareholders that led to his removal as chairman of Hollinger International and subsequently of the *Telegraph*. But the cost of privatization would have been too great, according to Chris Browne.

On June 17, 2003, as a direct result of a shareholder revolt, the Hollinger International board of directors struck a new special committee of the board, advised by Richard Breeden. He had already made a name for himself as chairman of the Securities and Exchange Commission. He had also served as the court-appointed corporate monitor of WorldCom Inc., uncovering the largest corporate fraud behind the largest bankruptcy in U.S. history. The special committee began an investigation into alleged improprieties at the company, some of which involved Black.

In June 2003, while shooting her documentary about Conrad Black, Debbie Melnyk set up a camera across the street from the Blacks' £13.1-million mansion at 14 Cottesmore Gardens, to immortalize the summer party held by them that year. A staff of liveried butlers, under-butlers, cooks and maids scurried around the 12,390-square-foot mansion with its seven bedrooms, four bathrooms and five reception areas, setting a table for twelve in a magnificent sunken dining room. In 1998, *Tatler* magazine voted Conrad Black and Barbara Amiel to its list of couples you would most want to invite to a party, just behind Mick Jagger and Jerry Hall. Together they formed part of London's upper-crust social circuit. Conrad regularly featured on the *Sunday Times'* Rich List, as well as the *Evening Standard's* "Top 50 residents of Kensington and Chelsea," alongside actor Rowan Atkinson, singer/songwriter Robbie Williams, and international banker Sir Evelyn de Rothschild

Leading members of the "glam set" turned up, from Prince Andrew to Anne Robinson, the "Queen of Mean" host of the quiz show *The Weakest Link*, *Spectator* editor Boris Johnson, British Home Secretary David Blunkett, accompanied as always by his seeing-eye dog, and the leggy Australian model, actress and *Playboy* cover girl Elle Macpherson.

TV stars and striking top models such as Macpherson were likely produced as bait to ensure that older, more ponderous and surely more boring movers and shakers of high finance and international politics also showed up. Macpherson was a Catholic — just like Black. But she was more than a trophy guest with light brown hair and a voluptuous 36-25-35 figure. Macpherson was a former law student who had become seriously wealthy through sales of her designer lingerie and nude photo shoots for various magazines. Her net worth was probably greater than Black's.

In September 2003, Black's niece and goddaughter Lisa Riley, a Canadian banker working in London, told me: "Conrad and Barbara have a summer party every year, and it is *the* party everyone talks about, and wants to be invited to."

But the June 2003 summer party was to be their last extravaganza in London. Four months later, Black was forced out of the executive suite of Hollinger International, and his fairweather friends stopped returning phone calls. The Blacks' social standing took a nose-dive.

In 2000 and 2001, Black's energies had been focused on becoming a baron. In 2002 and early 2003, he was absorbed in a 600,000-word manuscript biography of FDR. *Franklin Delano Roosevelt: Champion of Freedom* required a huge investment of time, energy and emotion on Black's part, but its launch was overshadowed by the news that he had been forced to relinquish his position as executive chairman of Hollinger International.

"Since I don't write for a living, I start a book when [I get] that old feeling," Black said. "I know there's a book inside me, somewhere. Well, when it roused itself up to the point of propelling me to my machine to start typing, that was when I started the book. That was really the same with my previous books. Once I started, I just stayed out and apart. For two weeks on holiday in the Pacific, I contributed something to that text every night." He wrote the original 600,000-word draft in fifty-three weeks.

I inferred that this must have been the 2001 trip when he used Hollinger International's executive jet for a South Pacific holiday with his wife — a trip that later figured prominently in the criminal charges in Chicago. I pictured him in Bora Bora, hammering away at a laptop computer.

Black sent a draft of the manuscript to Public Affairs publisher Peter Osnos.[242] The New York publisher is an admirer of legendary investigative journalist I. F. Stone, *Washington Post* icon Ben Bradlee and Robert L. Bernstein, former chief executive of Random House and the founder of Human Rights Watch. Osnos felt Black's manuscript was significant, but that "you couldn't just publish this book by putting covers on it. There was a substantial draft by the time it got to us, but it was edited with tender loving care by Bill Whitworth," the former editor of the *Atlantic Monthly* and associate editor of the *New Yorker*.

Naturally, I wondered whether Conrad Black had actually written this back-breaking tome himself.

According to his diary, Whitworth worked on the FDR biography for thirteen months, starting September 9, 2002. "I know for a fact that nobody wrote the book for him," said Whitworth. "I worked with him on tiny details and got corrections in his handwriting. My journalistic background is one of researchers and fact-checkers — but we didn't have that. He is his own fact-checker. It is amazing that someone running newspapers and companies could write such a long book. He would sometimes break for dinner, then call me back [in Arkansas] at three in the morning London time, to go over new changes. . . . An editor is doing a number of things. I was supposed to cut the book some. We didn't cut quite as much as Conrad and I both hoped to cut. Some of these matters he had been working on for so long, he couldn't bear to cut. I was line editing — going through it line by line — we did this three times for the whole book. I alerted him if I thought a paragraph or passage was not clear . . . I would say we had a very smooth and easy relationship. I admit I was concerned about that at the beginning, since I knew he owned a lot of newspapers and might tend to order editors around rather than taking advice from them. He was very patient and responsive. Conrad is a talented and lively writer, shrewd and entertaining in his descriptions of personalities and politicians. He is sympathetic to men of power and action who accomplish things. You can tell in the book that he is deeply interested in people with power and in how they wield power."[243]

This doesn't wash with Chris Browne. "The average CEO probably works about seventy hours a week running the company. If you spend seventy hours a week running Hollinger, I don't think you can write a 1,280-page book."

Osnos said Black "is a paradox. I don't know what happened on the financial side. I have no idea. But in his interactions with us, he was very courteous to our staff, handled himself well, and met all deadlines. He is very eloquent — very lucid." He describes Black's "grandiosity" as "a form of energy . . . And his appetite for research reflects that."

In the 1970s, Black wrote his biography of Duplessis partly in the hope of addressing a political problem — how to divert the raw energy of Quebec nationalism from a revolutionary separatist movement to conservative nationalism. His FDR book addressed a different set of problems. Now Black was integrating his life experiences as a mature business tycoon and student of power; distilling his knowledge of history and politics; affirming his admiration for the United States while crafting a complex portrait of FDR. It meant building a bridge between the liberalism of his youth and the neo-conservatism of his middle age. (There was an implicit contradiction between his own conservative beliefs and the fact that Roosevelt was a liberal of the 1930s waging political war on the largely Republican financial sector with the goal of regulating the economy in order to lift up the poor and dispossessed.)

Overcoming a strong pre-war isolationist mindset, Roosevelt was able to build the nation's defences and emerge — with Sir Winston Churchill — as one of the decisive Allied leaders of the Second World War. To Black, FDR was a heroic figure and architect of a New World Order. It probably helped Roosevelt's early political career — first as assistant secretary of the navy and later as governor of New York — that his distant cousin was the distinguished former U.S. president, Theodore Roosevelt.

Black describes Roosevelt as having great style: "his powerful, handsome, animated appearance — cigarette holder at a rakish upward angle; flamboyant gestures; hearty and contagious laugh; skill at repartee; and evident love of his work and his job, made him an irresistible personality. Even some of his sartorial flourishes, the fold in his hat, his naval cape, a walking stick, were widely emulated. His idea of how to be president was to be himself." FDR's tenacity and courage kept him in public life even after he contracted polio, which required him to use a wheelchair. He went on to win four successive terms as president of the United States and a place as one of the great political figures of the twentieth century.

Arthur M. Schlesinger, Jr., who wrote the three-volume *Age of Roosevelt* in the late 1950s and early 1960s, said, "Above all else, the victory over polio confirmed the Rooseveltian inheritance of optimism. A cheerful strength radiated from him, which roused in others not pity but exhilaration and a sense of their own possibilities. He could communicate confidence by the intonation of his voice, the tilt of his head, the flourish of his cigarette holder."[244]

Black said Roosevelt "not only triumphed over a terrible infirmity, he had to disguise it, which is a good deal more challenging. In those days, it was assumed that a handicap of that type would be a real electoral problem. So with the co-operation of the press, he disguised the full implications of it. For example, I have at home an extract of a letter in which he claimed in 1932 that he had a brace on one leg. Now, once in his life, he did walk with the help of a person on each side, with a brace on only one leg. But in fact, he had braces on both legs. He was constantly trying to minimize the impact of this. To achieve what he achieved in his condition makes it an even greater achievement. He set out to change the world, and he did change the world, and . . . he is one of the few who have actually changed it for the better. Napoleon set out to change the world, and he did change the world, but he didn't actually change it for the better. And Lenin and Hitler set out to change the world, and they did, but certainly not for the better."

Black's view, said Osnos, "is that Roosevelt saved the world from tyranny. One of the more elevating definitions of conservatism is to defend democracy from tyranny. The bad kind of conservatism is the flip side of Stalinism. Conrad is essentially a proponent of freedom."

In September 2003, Henry Kissinger told me Black is an intense student of history: ". . . extremely penetrating intellectually and a very warm friend personally. He wrote what I think is a significant book. I read, I think, all the sections [of the unpublished manuscript] that dealt with Roosevelt's foreign policy, and one or two of the sections on domestic politics. I think it's a seminal book. It's one of the most comprehensive and thoughtful, if slightly 'Euro' version, books on Roosevelt."

Kissinger said he and Black share a respect for Roosevelt's long-term vision and basic policy "even if the vision was semi-instinctive. But he was a man who had a very clear sense of direction. And Roosevelt's insight into the nature of international politics in the mid-1930s in America was comparable to Churchill's in England, although Roosevelt operated in a much more difficult environment because the Congress had just passed three neutrality acts in 1936 and 1937, and Roosevelt was heading the country towards support of the Western countries in the looming crisis with Germany . . . I have never seen such a systematic account of how Roosevelt went from the Quarantine Speech in Chicago to the entry into World War II. And how consistently he dealt with the attempt to show an engagement in the outcome of the crisis, even before there was a war. I've read a lot of books about Roosevelt. I have never seen the mechanics of how Roosevelt operated described in such details and in such felicitous language."

"The point I'm trying to make," Black said, "is that Roosevelt was the most important figure of the twentieth century . . . because he did bring the Americans to the world. He was, with Churchill, the co-saviour of Western civilization, and he was the leading architect of the post-war institutions prior to the Cold War institutions, and he did create this durable imbalance of power in the world in America's favour."

In singling out FDR and Churchill, Black remained true to the messianic view of political leadership that he had demonstrated in *Duplessis*. He also affirmed the importance of unique individuals in moulding events and indeed whole epochs of history. According to Black, FDR not only saved Western civilization and made the world "safe for democracy at last," he also anchored the United States in the world and mastered the American political system.

The tension between American liberalism and conservatism was accentuated during the 1960s when FDR's progressive legacy was wounded by the assassination of John F. Kennedy, the failed promise of Lyndon Johnson's Great Society, racial unrest and the quagmire of the Vietnam War. Along with the general drop in support for the Democratic Party during the late 1960s and early 1970s, Black's own commitment to liberalism weakened. He was stung by the Vietnamese defeat of the United States and through the 1970s and 1980s, warmed to Republican leaders —

in particular, Ronald Reagan, who vowed to "make America great again."

William F. Buckley, Jr. said that although "liberal consensus is that FDR went in the correct direction . . . he was a founder of the modern version of the welfare state. He was an interventionist, a very discreet *dirigiste* who sometimes did things that were at variance with what he said. Conservatives are negative about Roosevelt. They acknowledge him as an important wartime leader, but their resentment of his enhancement of state power is still very strong."[245]

There was an obvious contradiction in Black's work. How could Black, a one-time liberal who had become a fiery "integral conservative," admire FDR, a patrician who built up the state in order to declare war on financial speculators and other capitalist profiteers in America in the 1930s?

To answer the question, I sought out John Kenneth Galbraith, the progressive economist, at his house on Francis Street, next to the Harvard Divinity School in Cambridge, Massachusetts. He was the last person living I could think of, who had known Roosevelt personally. (He died April 29, 2006.) Born in Iona Station, Ontario in 1908 of Scottish descent, Galbraith was a living legend — a giant physically and intellectually, who had served in the administrations of Franklin D. Roosevelt, Harry S Truman, John F. Kennedy and Lyndon B. Johnson. Galbraith was an eyewitness of some of the most important events of the twentieth century. After practically running America's war economy from 1941 to 1945, he interviewed several Nazi war criminals awaiting the Nuremberg tribunal, including Hermann Goering, Adolf Hitler's second in command, who took a potassium cyanide pill rather than hang. Galbraith's house was full of wooden statues of elephants and photographs showing him with Indian prime minister Jawaharlal Nehru, from the time when he had served as American ambassador on the subcontinent. His aged wife brought in a clattering tea-tray. They had been married close to seventy years. I sat down with "Ken." Aged ninety-five, he had a full head of hair and lively, penetrating eyes, a strong square face, a beaklike nose and an immense frame folded into a chair with a blanket over his knees.

Galbraith told me right off the bat that he was not a fan of
Conrad Black. He felt Black was too right wing, had a fantas-
tical vision of Roosevelt that was not accurate, and was exactly
the kind of manipulative businessman Roosevelt had targetted
when he set up the SEC.

According to Galbraith, his generation regarded Roosevelt as
"the only clear-cut hope of relieving the hardships of the
Depression. And the New Deal was the fulfilment of that hope.
There was an intensely adversarial community in the
Republican Party and the financial community. Most of the
affluent in the U.S. divided their time between some identification with the New Deal and a much larger group that spent a
lot of time fighting it since they felt it threatened their financial
interests."[246]

For Galbraith, one of Roosevelt's greatest achievements was
to regulate the financial sector, through the 1933 creation of the
Securities and Exchange Commission. "The SEC's creation," said
Galbraith "was a response to the corporate scandals that were
revealed in and after the great crash of 1929. The Depression and
the crash of the stock market revealed a substantial area of corporate scandal. We had a galaxy of primeval Enrons, and it was
to that that the SEC was directed." Galbraith found it highly
ironic that Black should admire FDR, since it was Roosevelt who
had set up the SEC — the very commission that investigated
Black in 1982 and again during the Hollinger scandal of
2003–04.

Schlesinger, who was Galbraith's best friend and next-door
neighbour during their Harvard years, said the New Deal
"accomplished a fantastic series of reforms, any one of which
would have staggered the nation a few years earlier. It established the principle of maximum hours and minimum wages on
a national basis. It abolished child labor. It dealt a fatal blow to
sweatshops. It made collective bargaining a national policy and
thereby transformed the position of organized labor. It gave new
status to the consumer. It stamped out a noxious collection of
unfair trade practices."[247]

Galbraith thought it was also ironic that Black's book is peppered with references to Roosevelt's masterful manipulation.

"Even as a child and a schoolboy," Black wrote, "Franklin Roosevelt was frequently duplicitous. As a political leader he was almost compulsively devious. While he found some of the exigencies of political life distasteful, gentleman as he was, he resorted to them naturally and was proud of his manipulative virtuosity and skill as a dissembler." The great tour de force of the 1932 presidential election campaign "was in fact largely an unsettling melange of socialism, atavism, humbug and snobbery." During his first presidential press conference, in March 1933, Roosevelt "completely charmed the 125 journalists, was a master of the duplicitous answer and of the partial, evasive, or half-true answer, and always knew how to give most of the journalists something useful. He exuded a comprehension of the requirements of their job and manipulated them with such surpassing finesse that few of them realized the extent to which they were being used, or were flattered to play the role. . . . At the end of the press briefing the reporters broke into spontaneous applause."

Galbraith maintained that FDR was *not* as Machiavellian as portrayed in Black's book. "FDR was required, on occasion, to change his mind," said Galbraith. "He didn't consider himself a manipulator, although he considered himself required, on occasion, to accommodate circumstances."

Schlesinger conceded to me that beneath FDR's perennial optimism "there remained the other man — tougher than the public man, harder, more ambitious, more calculating, more petty, more puckish, more selfish, more malicious, more profound, more complex, more interesting. Only intimate friends saw Roosevelt in these aspects, and then in enigmatic and sometimes terrifying glimpses." Schlesinger concluded ". . . at bottom, Franklin Roosevelt was a man without illusions — clearheaded and compassionate, who had been close enough to death to understand the frailty of human striving, but who remained loyal enough to life to do his best in the sight of God." Of course, said Schlesinger, "Roosevelt was Machiavellian and manipulative. In a democracy, as a leader, you have to be. Persuasion in a democracy is a popular term, where manipulation is a negative term."[248]

Like Schlesinger and Galbraith, Black accepts the progressive legacy of Roosevelt, although he believes the New Deal was not an unqualified success. He said FDR involved the government "in many areas where its presence had been limited or non-existent — industrial recovery, reflation, large-scale workfare programs, Social Security, reform of financial institutions, rural electrification, flood and drought control, stabilization of farm production and prices, conservation, refinancing of home mortgages and farm loans, reform of working conditions, public sector development and distribution of hydroelectric power, generous treatment of veterans as well as the repeal of Prohibition."

Anyone visiting Black's Palm Beach palazzo or the New York executive offices of Hollinger International could attest that Black was fulfilling a long-standing dream by writing the Roosevelt biography. He knew the corridors of power himself. He controlled widely read newspapers in major world cities (The *Chicago Sun-Times,* which he owned, had been a staunch supporter of Roosevelt.) He had been a regular guest at the White House and had cultivated the company of a number of presidents, particularly Nixon, Reagan and George Bush Sr.

He wanted to become a transatlantic warrior in his own right. Black identified with FDR in a romantic and personal way. He wanted to create links between his hero and himself and, more than that, he wanted to possess them. Perhaps he projected FDR's glory onto himself, and his own manipulation onto FDR. In Palm Beach he proudly displayed the presidential Stars and Stripes that had flown over FDR's White House during the Second World War, while in the Manhattan executive suite there were all those gold-framed letters from FDR to Daisy Suckley.

In November 2003, just when Conrad Black was due to embark on an author's tour for Public Affairs Press, the financial scandal at Hollinger International erupted. It was unfortunate timing for what should have been a triumph for Black.

"It is completely bizarre that on the very day his book came out and was praised as a magnificent achievement by many knowledgeable people, his business should get trapped in the maelstrom of so many issues," said Peter Osnos.

From November 2003 to well into 2004, the deepening crisis at Hollinger International received saturation coverage in the world's financial and mainstream media. A strategic selling-off process, run by New York investment bank Lazard LLC on behalf of Hollinger International, got underway in mid-November 2003 and was to be completed by mid-2004, with the company being sold as a single entity or in up to seven groups of assets. The special committee's growing appetite for independent action convinced Black its real purpose was to curtail or break his grip on the newspaper empire, largely at the instigation of minority shareholders seeking short-term profits. Claiming he had received incomplete and inaccurate information, he refused to repay the non-compete fees despite coming to an agreement only weeks before that he would. He also moved unilaterally to amend Hollinger International's bylaws to strip the special committee of any control over the sale of Hollinger International's assets. And on January 17, he accepted an offer from the billionaire Barclay brothers of Britain for control of Hollinger Inc., disregarding Hollinger International's auction. Black and his close associate Peter White, now chief operating officer of Hollinger Inc., invoked an exception clause in the agreement with Hollinger International, claiming the sale to the Barclays was necessary to prevent the holding company from defaulting on a debt payment in March.

After three years of acrimony between him and Hollinger's minority shareholders, it was a watershed moment for Black when he appeared in Delaware's Court of Chancery in the New Castle County Courts building February 20, 2004.

Since so many American corporations are registered in Delaware (well known as a corporate haven), Chancery has become the foremost court for solving corporate legal disputes in the world's most litigious country. As a court of equity rather than a court of law, it can issue temporary injunctions and declaratory judgments. Under direct and cross-examination Black testified about the strategic process at Hollinger International, his negotiations with the Barclay brothers to sell the Canadian holding company Hollinger Inc., and his attempt unilaterally to amend Hollinger International's bylaws. Black was portrayed in court as an insensitive majority shareholder, allegedly willing to run roughshod over minority shareholders. Martin Flumenbaum, a lawyer representing Hollinger International's independent directors, wanted confirmation that Black had written an e-mail in August 2002 calling unhappy shareholders "a bunch of self-righteous hypocrites and ingrates." Black said some shareholders fit that description. "The stock is up 140 per cent since then, Mr. Flumenbaum," he added.

"Does that give you the right to steal other people's money?" retorted Flumenbaum.

"Objection!" shouted one of Black's attorneys.

"The answer is no," said Black calmly.

Responding to questions from Vice Chancellor Leo Strine, Black said he found it "very disappointing to read testimony in deposition by directors comparing my offer to the antics of the Nazi government of Germany prior to the occupation of Bohemia in 1938." Strine delivered a blistering decision on February 26, striking down the amended bylaws Black had imposed on U.S.-based Hollinger International and approving a poison-pill defence to protect independent shareholders. He also slapped a temporary injunction on the Barclay brothers' offer for Hollinger Inc.

Strine disputed Black's claim that Hollinger Inc. needed to be sold to meet liquidity problems. "As former Chancellor Allen has said, the most interesting corporate law cases involve the color gray," wrote Strine in his decision. "Regrettably this case is not one of that variety." He said Black had "repeatedly behaved in a manner inconsistent with the duty of loyalty he owed his company." According to Strine, Black violated his newly undertaken obligations under the restructuring agreement of November 2003 "by diverting to himself a valuable opportunity presented to [Hollinger] International . . . by using confidential company information for his own purposes without permission, and made threats, as he would put it, of 'multifaceted dimensions' towards [Hollinger] International's directors . . . I conclude that Black breached his fiduciary and contractual duties persistently and seriously."

Strine scrutinized Black's fiduciary responsibility to Chicago-based Hollinger International as its CEO and lead shareholder but didn't mention Black's identical responsibilities for Toronto-based Hollinger Inc., where he was also CEO and major shareholder. In the conflict between these two responsibilities lay the key to the whole drama, but Strine did not allude to it.

Strine scolded Black for entering into an agreement — as a tactical ploy — with no intention of respecting it. Black "recognized that he was vulnerable to a serious investigation not only from the Special Committee but from the Securities and Exchange Commission," said Strine. "He wanted to head off actions by the independent directors that would tend to elicit immediate SEC scrutiny and to take the steam out of the Special Committee process by focusing the independent directors on a strategic process involving [Hollinger] International. Put simply, Black feared SEC scrutiny, and even a possible criminal investigation."

Strine rejected any suggestion that Black should not be bound to his agreement based on arguments that he acted under duress. "Black is a sophisticated man, who knows how to bring a lawyer into a room when he needs one, especially when a highly skilled advocate is waiting in the other room at the ready. Nor is Black a meek man, easily intimidated by others. The contrary is true . . ." Strine found that Black had deliberately misled his fellow directors to achieve a tactical benefit over the Hollinger International strategic process.

Strine also mentioned the relationship Black had with his independent directors at Hollinger International. "First, he communicated the confidential advice provided to the International board to both the Barclays and to Triarc [another potential bidder] — without permission from the International board. Second, he called director Kissinger and threatened to remove the [Hollinger] International board if it adopted a rights plan [a so-called poison pill]. Negotiations then ensued between Black and his legal advisers . . . on the one hand, and the [Hollinger] International board, through its advisers, on the other. During this process, Black threatened to sue the directors on the Special

Committee and audit committee, mentioning that he knew where directors Seitz and Savage had personal assets that he could seize."

As to Black's claims that he withheld repayment of non-compete fees because he had found evidence they had been properly authorized, Strine ruled, "Those assertions were erroneous as Black continued to possess no evidence of proper approval . . ."

Finally, in assessing Black's credibility, Strine accused him of "pulling a Benedict Arnold," found him to be an "evasive and unreliable" witness and said "his explanations of key events and of his own motivations do not have the ring of truth. . . . It became impossible for me to credit his word." Strine said Peter White, Black's old friend and business associate, was "so faithful to Black personally that it was difficult for him to be dispassionate." He described White's claim that Hollinger Inc. might have to file for bankruptcy as a "nihilistic tactic" that "seems to a neutral mind absurd, when advanced by the director of a corporation with three times more assets than liabilities." (Hollinger's refinancing in April 2004 proved Strine was right.) And Strine dismissed Black's allegation that board minutes provided evidence of the directors' approval of non-compete payments made to Black and others. According to Strine, they did nothing of the sort. And if they were intended to have that effect, they "might have been called constructive fraud. The inference from the record one inescapably inclines towards is that the consents were drafted to give the least possible notice of their non-compete references, were not actually placed before the board, and were ratified by a board that never saw them. . . . The consents do not even approve specific non-competition contracts. If ever there was a time when this sort of approval process would be deemed 'proper,' that time is long distant. At worst, the [Hollinger] International board was purposely duped and there was fraud on the board. At best, they were entirely uninformed. In either instance, the [Hollinger] International independent directors did not properly approve the non-compete payments under Delaware law."

Peter White was disgusted by the experience of going to court in Delaware. "I thought we would get a fair hearing. I was completely disabused of that notion. Everything was cooked in advance. I learned that the U.S. court system is incredibly influenced by the media. They all work together on things and that has continued . . . I can't imagine a Canadian or British judge writing anything as incendiary as Strine — but he's a little tinpot dictator."

The Delaware decision was humiliating for Black. And it made headlines around the world.

"The resulting 133-page document deserves a place in the annals of character assassination," a *Financial Times* columnist wrote of the ruling.[249]

The *Chicago Sun-Times*, controlled by Black, said the decision was an outright defeat and he "still faces a raft of other problems. In addition to Hollinger International's $200 million lawsuit, shareholders have filed suits charging him and his top aides with looting the company while the directors did nothing to stop them."[250]

Britain's BBC News reported, "The 59-year-old peer is suddenly having to endure a crash course in humility . . . Hollinger International would no doubt claim Lord Black is the author of his own downfall, thanks to an age old vice — greed. . . . Although Lord Black was the third biggest newspaper magnate in the world, his holdings are not in quite the same league as Mr. Murdoch's News Corp, which spans satellite broadcasting, film, book publishing and newspapers. [Black's] downfall will cause much gloating in his native Canada where his appetite for newspaper acquisition, outspoken conservative views and abrasive tongue had made him a *bete noire* for liberals."[251]

"The decision," said the *Globe and Mail*, "paints a picture of a duplicitous man who made promises and almost as quickly cast them aside to pursue his own schemes with the Barclays. It will be painful for the vain Lord Black to see himself characterized so harshly by the judge. Not quite as painful, one suspects, as the realization that, for once in his life, he was completely outmaneuvered. . . ."[252]

The *International Herald Tribune* speculated, "It is conceivable that if no settlement is reached with Hollinger International, the result could be that Black would realize no money from the sale of the press empire he built. He still could seek to negotiate a deal, but his bargaining position is much weaker than it was before Strine issued his decision."[253]

The most devastating coverage, however, may have been in the *Telegraph* — the crown jewel of Black's empire — which devoted several articles to the judgment in its February 28 issue. It included a large portrait of Black with Barbara Amiel sitting at his side on the day of his introduction to the House of Lords. The headline said: "Feistily direct but evasive and unreliable: U.S. judge's damning verdict on Lord Black." In the same issue, *Telegraph* columnist Tom Utley brooded about the indignity of Britain's leading broadsheet being sold at auction to the highest bidder.

In response to the Strine judgement, a press release was issued from Toronto stating that "Hollinger Inc. and Lord Black respectfully disagree with Vice Chancellor's view of the facts and equities in his decision. They nonetheless recognize that the decision points the way to a realization of full value for shareholders of both Hollinger Inc. and Hollinger International Inc. through the active pursuit of the strategic process being conducted for International by Lazard LLC. Both Hollinger Inc. and Lord Black look forward to the prompt and effective pursuit of Lazard's work, and to the presentation to International and Hollinger of a course producing value superior to that presented by the Barclays' tender offer for Hollinger and proposed bid for International."

"It has been very trying," Black wrote me a week after Strine's decision. "However, the strong performance of the stock price indicates the value that we have built into the company, so the financial outcome should be reasonably benign. Most of the legal skirmishing is nonsense, but the venomous atmosphere created by the corporate governance lobby and the systematic defamation of me by my enemies could make some of the litigation dangerous."

Once Vice Chancellor Leo Strine handed down his blistering decision, it was clear that Black had tried and failed to navigate his way through the Delaware Chancery Court hearings. Two and a half months later — on May 7, 2004 — Hollinger International filed an amended complaint that was the result of the special committee's investigation. The amended complaint sought $1.25 billion in damages, including $484.5 million in allegedly improper payments to Black, several associates, and their investment vehicles, $390.6 million in damages and $103.9 million in prejudgment interest. The damages include allegations of $217.8 million of excessive management fees; $90 million of non-compete/unauthorized payments; $1.4 million paid to personal staff; $23.7 million to pay for two corporate jets; $1.9 million for corporate apartments; and $353,000 for automobiles.

The special committee, advised by Richard Breeden, had turned up a lot of evidence while building its case. Any allegations would have to be proven in a court of law. But Black was facing an extremely powerful adversary. The payments were being hyped by Hollinger International in order to justify a trial under terms of the Racketeer Influenced and Corrupt Organizations (RICO) Act. This act had originally been designed to give authorities sweeping powers to go after the Mob, but in recent years it has increasingly been used and abused in cases of corporate malfeasance. It was hard for Black and White to defend their position publicly, since they would only gain access to Hollinger International records if and when the case went to trial.

In June 2004, Hollinger International announced the sale of the *Telegraph* to the Barclay brothers — the same reclusive Scottish business tycoons with whom Black had tried to make a deal in January 2004. The price of sale — £665 million, or $1.21 billion — showed that Black was right in thinking he had built a lot of value into the company. But the sale took place over his objections: Black contested the proposed sale in Delaware Chancery Court on the grounds that Hollinger Inc. as the largest single shareholder in Hollinger International had the right to vote on the sale of all or substantially all company assets.

On July 1, Black was still hopeful. He wrote me that "dramatic things could well happen this month. As a result I am extremely preoccupied. . . .You are chasing a moving target and would not want to close this story just as the last chapter was beginning." Five days later, Black wrote again, saying, "I am preparing for the case in Delaware that will determine the future ownership of the *Daily Telegraph* and cannot do anything before that case is resolved. . . . I agree that this entire matte will probably go on longer than a month, but there will be some important news this month, and perhaps not all of it will come from Delaware."

On July 16, 2004, Black and Hollinger Inc. paid $30 million to Hollinger International as ordered by the Delaware Chancery Court. (Both Black and Hollinger Inc. indicated they would appeal the order.)

Vice Chancellor Leo Strine heard presentations from Hollinger Inc. and Hollinger International on July 23 regarding the right of shareholders to vote on the proposed sale of the *Telegraph* to the Barclay brothers. On July 29, Strine ruled that no vote was necessary, removing Black's last chance of blocking the sale and holding on to control of the *Telegraph*. The Delaware Supreme Court rejected Black's appeal of the Strine decision. Along with other members of the corporate review committee of the Hollinger International board, Henry Kissinger and Richard Perle voted in favour of the sale of the *Telegraph*, over the vehement objections of their former friend, Conrad Black. Hollinger International was believed ready to place Black's share of the proceeds in escrow or some other structure pending the resolution of lawsuits and other claims.

By late 2004, the corporate war between the Hollinger International special committee and Conrad Black was raging. And it was far from clear who would gain victory in the end. The special committee started out with a strategy of "sneak attack" that it hoped would quickly lead to Black's annihilation. The committee mounted a vigorous press campaign, hyped allegations in various suits against Black and several of his associates, and scored a few early gains such as the sale of the *Telegraph*. But that strategy could not be sustained. The press campaign waned in intensity. The media grew jaded. The special committee published a litany of allegations in one report after another. But over time, each report commanded less media attention than the previous one. The strategy of annihilation gave way to a strategy of attrition, seeking to wear Black down, drain his resources and weaken his position to the point where he could be destroyed.

On August 30, the special committee filed what should have been a devastating complaint in U.S. District Court in Illinois, repeating many of the allegations that had been made in May, but taking them further. The authors of the report — Gordon Paris, Graham Savage and Richard Breeden — tried to show a flair for colourful language, referring to their 513-page document several times as the "Hollinger Chronicles," as if they were writing the screenplay for a soap opera. They used every rhetorical device they could think of. The complaint compared Black to a bank robber looting a company he treated as his private piggy bank; implied he felt guilty about reaping the privileges of his proprietor status; chastized him for spending too much time writing about FDR and sitting in the House of Lords; mocked David Radler for fast-tracking excessive payments in the time it took to eat a tuna sandwich and slammed Black's leadership team for "ethical corruption" that was so pervasive, systematic and self-serving, it justified a trial under RICO. The special committee still sought $1.25 billion from Black, several associates and various companies, which included treble damages under provisions of RICO.

Some allegations documented in the complaint were troubling — particularly those concerning related-party transactions; other allegations seemed speculative. Any allegation would have to be proven in a court of law, where the standard of evidence was nothing like the standard of evidence in the world's financial newspapers. Most allegations were technical and contextual. And since few people had access to the full details, it was hard to form a judgment. Many journalists and authors were only too happy to repeat the allegations without critical analysis. After all, when the special committee called itself "independent," people naturally assumed its reports were a rigorous and objective presentation of facts. No one seemed to have noticed that the special committee was selecting and constructing evidence in the most damaging way possible, while vigorously pursuing an agenda of its own. The special committee condemned Black for manipulative handling of corporate directors — but the special committee itself exerted more power over the board than Black ever did. It could, on the one hand, prosecute directors while, on the other hand, offering them the prospect of mediation and a peaceful settlement.

Under the circumstances, it was natural that directors should go on record saying they were not properly informed by Black, not aware of the true nature of transactions and payments, not happy with the end result. That was their only possible defence. The special committee presented its findings as objective. But it was in a position to bend the will of the people it summoned to interviews. And it cost a fortune. With the meter running, Richard Breeden needed to produce spectacular results in order to justify the level of his own fees, which were also spectacular.

The special committee's credibility was damaged on October 7 when Judge Blanche Manning of U.S. District Court in Illinois dismissed all counts in Hollinger International's suit against Black and various associates. She did not rule on the merits of the case, but she said the case as filed did not fit the definition of racketeering and therefore did not belong in a federal court. Black took the dismissal of the RICO case as a personal vindication.

During the course of October and November 2004, a flurry of activity showed that Black was trying to take the offensive. On October 27, Hollinger International conceded that he had a right to his share of proceeds from the sale of the *Telegraph*. In exchange, Black accepted (for the time being) an extension of an injunction blocking him from resuming his position as chairman and CEO. Two days later, Black made a bid to privatize Toronto-based Hollinger Inc. which, if successful, meant that he would no longer be subject to the evolving morality of corporate governance. He would be the main shareholder of a private corporation, which could no longer be held to account by minority shareholders and would no longer need to publish financial results.

But the same day, Hollinger International counterattacked, filing a new amended complaint in U.S. District Court in Illinois that dropped references to RICO and added new allegations, particularly concerning Richard Perle. The company was now seeking $425.2 million in damages plus prejudgment interest of $116.7 million, for a total of $541.9 million. The tone of the complaint was now more subdued, the colour commentary and sarcastic references having largely been removed.

Three days later, Black resigned as chairman and CEO of Hollinger Inc. in order to make it easier for independent directors of Hollinger Inc. to scrutinize his bid to take the company private. It was clear that he had developed a strategy of his own — but what was the strategy? To answer that question, one would have to return to Black's early years when he re-enacted the battle of Austerlitz with Hal Jackman's toy soldiers and devoured books on the battles of Midway and Leningrad. Many people facing the intense media campaign attacking Black would have turned and run. But in Black's mind, the new isolation he experienced gave him a chance to reflect. The debacle of 2004 could be — *no, had to be* — transformed into an opportunity. The many liabilities he faced — whether legal, financial or political — could be made into assets that would help him to win ultimate victory. There was nothing accidental or improvised in the steps he took. On the contrary, it was all part of a coherent, well-ordered plan, and one that he interpreted by analogy.

"With the RICO victory," Black noted, "the refinancing of Hollinger Inc., the defeat of the effort to avoid distributing us our share of the *Telegraph* proceeds and of their effort to stop our Hollinger Inc. privatization from going forward, and then the launch of the privatization, they [Black's adversaries, particularly the special committee] are being rolled back. I doubt if my enemies now possess the ability to conduct a war of attrition. They will be '*attritted*,' to put it in 'Pentagonese.' So I would say it is like the Pacific or Russian campaigns of World War II, where there was fierce action and heavy casualties, but a decisive result and not attrition on a scale that enervated the victorious powers."

Just what was a strategy of attrition? In 1521, Machiavelli warned in *The Art of War* of the dangers of a strategy of annihilation, writing that "it is better to subdue an enemy by famine than by sword, for in battle, *fortuna* has often a much greater share than *virtu*." Destiny plays a greater role in warfare than valour or purposeful awareness. In Machiavelli's day, decisive battles were rare. During the Renaissance, there were advantages in the wasting, desolate strategy of attrition — organized famine, continual sniping and repositioning.

Hollinger International and Black were armed with the modern-day equivalent of the sword. They were ready to bloody one another and bring famine. More litigation would cost more money, which, in turn, would reduce the relative benefits for either side of ultimate victory in court. If the special committee's work cost $56.1 million between June 2003 and September 2004, then each quarter would see legal and other costs added to the company's ledger sheet. At the same time, Black's legal bills would climb higher and higher. Victory would go to the side with the last dollar.

Amid the desolation, Black had done some soul-searching. With hindsight, he conceded he would have done things differently in his capacity as chairman and CEO of Hollinger International. He would have reduced his own vulnerability to the attacks of institutional investors and enforced tighter corporate controls so that decisions conscientiously taken were completely documented and "unimpeachable." With those changes, he would not have amended his views. He would not have suggested, for example, that board members themselves respond sooner and more tactfully to the questions or concerns of minority shareholders. "In Canada, Britain and the United States," Black told me, "the *zeitgeist* is hostile, and there is great hostility to executives who can be portrayed as self-indulgent, and a tendency to regard anyone in my position as a crook. The public relations debacle will gradually subside as the financial and legal facts improve, as they are now doing, and it becomes clear that assimilating me to law-breakers, and Hollinger to bankrupt companies like Enron, is seen to be unjust, as the personal attacks on Barbara and me are seen to be excessive, and as the faddish invincibility of the corporate governance zealots abates. My enemies have done a good professional job of poisoning the wells. But in the end, it will backfire."

Did Black think that the special committee's position, and the threat of personal liability against the directors, had influenced the actions of the directors individually? "Some of the directors have been intimidated by Breeden," Black said. "This is the abusive way the corporate governance system often works in the U.S."

Clearly the special committee was concerned about actions (transactions, payments, expenses) that it considered immoral, I continued. It portrayed these actions as illegal. Is there a difference between the two, between morality and legality?

"None that I am aware of were objectively immoral or illegal," Black said. "There is certainly a difference between the two, but the special committee has tried to create a climate of moral outrage in order to influence courts and regulators against us. They seem to have had some success, but once in front of a serious tryer of fact, the vendetta becomes much harder to sustain in the absence of evidence, as the RICO dismissal demonstrated."

Should there be any distinction between the two? "Yes," Black responded. "The law doesn't determine morals."

The question as to whether board members knowingly approved various actions is a technical and contextual one. It involves establishing whether they were adequately informed prior to taking decisions, whether they understood their fiduciary responsibilities, and so on.

What were Black's views of the skills and training needed for an effective Board?

"Intelligent, experienced, conscientious people are required," he said. "I think it helps if they have some stake in the business, or identify with those who do, as it tends to make them more entrepreneurial and braver. Intelligence, integrity and commercial aptitude are the qualities most needed. It is becoming academic as almost no one of these qualities will continue to serve as a director in the terrorized atmosphere that has been created."

Did the special committee, I asked him, have a political agenda — objectives quite beyond the work it had done related to Hollinger International?

"Breeden wants to make himself Mr. Corporate Governance — the efficient destroyer of prominent executives with any vulnerability at all. The committee is completely dominated by him. I doubt that they have any motives of their own, other than Paris's avarice, as he clings to his post, receiving $60,000 a week for pretending to be an executive."

How did Barbara react, since allegations have also been made about her?

"Bravely and stoically, and with the same determination I have to prevail over our enemies."

What did he think would be the ultimate outcome of the various complaints concerning him?

"They will be exposed as almost completely without merit, exacerbated by the frenzied and dishonest way they have been pursued and publicized. All those responsible will be legally punished. It will be a lengthy but ultimately satisfying process."

Black said he now felt a sense of detachment about things that used to matter. After renouncing his Canadian citizenship in 2001, he had not re-applied for Canadian citizenship, nor did he have any intention of doing so. He maintained a palatial residence in Toronto, and his main investment vehicles — Hollinger and Ravelston — were still based in Toronto. But, he said, he had no particular interest in Canada.

"I dissent from the Canadian national raison d'être of being to the left of the United States, and I think that in the end it will be a failure, alleviated and disguised only by the great wealth of Canada and the possible ambition of the waves of relatively unassimilable immigration to try a different course in public policy. My impression is the Chinese and Indian Canadians are much more capitalistic than the natives. With that said, I really don't follow Canadian public affairs closely, and feel that it is inappropriate for me to comment publicly on it. I said when I renounced my citizenship that I would explain why I did so and then say nothing more. In democracies, those that strongly dissent are free to leave and explain why they left, but should not inflict their opinions unduly on populations from which they have seceded . . . Canada is, federally, almost a one-party state, as it has been since the First World War. I don't think it's a good system, but it doesn't affect me any more."

As for Britain, Black put his Cottesmore Gardens home up for sale and said he no longer reads the Daily *Telegraph*. After winning the price war against Rupert Murdoch's *The Times* and pulling out of newspapers in Britain, Black now felt a sense of relief. There was some irony in the fact that *The Times* had now gone down-market, changing format from a quality broadsheet to a tabloid.

"Murdoch is a tabloid man, in newspapers and television. He is so cynical: he has no feel for product quality or integrity. That ultimately is why we [at the *Telegraph*] won the price war. He thought price-cutting was a fast track to market leadership. It wasn't; it was a hideously expensive failure he was able to hide in the figures of News Corp. and its Australian accounting practices. This is his latest lunge at a quick victory. I don't read the *Times* or the *Telegraph*. I have no further interest in how their competition unfolds. It was nerve-wracking, and I am relieved no longer to be bothered with it and with Murdoch's relentless and fanatical competition though, obviously, I would have preferred to have exited the London newspaper business in a more dignified way."

Black said that in late 2004, he had lost his faith in newspapers except in "small-centre monopolies at the right price and special growth situations. I have no faith in newspapers as a growth industry and have not for some years, which is why I began disassembling our company, a process that has been very successful financially."

And then there was his position in the corporate world. As a press baron running the world's third-largest newspaper empire, he was a titan, used to dominating shareholders' meetings with his trademark force of character, bluster and occasional exasperation. Now he saw things differently. "I don't want ever again to have any role in a public company. It will become impossible to recruit serious directors, to operate a business with any executive decisiveness, and the stock market will lose ground to exchanges of debt instruments having some equity characteristics, regulated but not vulnerable to the antics of rapacious institutional investors. I am glad to be one of the relatively early departures from a battlefield that will become steadily more contested and inhospitable. Our company will be an operating company; holding companies are nonsense. And we will invest where we think returns are good. That will include some newspapers."

Rob Kirkpatrick, managing director of Cardinal Value Equity Partners (a leading minority investor in Hollinger International), whose complaint was unsealed in Delaware Chancery Court in January 2004, warned there was a good prospect of a long, drawn-out war of attrition between Hollinger International and Conrad Black, in which the only victors will be lawyers on both sides. "It might be good to have a settlement," he said. "That all depends on what the details are. I would be astonished, personally, if Conrad Black did anything other than slugging it out."

Hollinger International and Black had gathered their forces, settled into their respective positions and occasionally fired suits and countersuits at one another. If a ruling were to come down favouring one side, then the other side could find grounds for an appeal. The slugging-it-out approach applied to both sides in the conflict — slugging it out and investing in a strategy of famine.

"For Cardinal," Kirkpatrick said, "we simply want to maximize the share price of Hollinger International. And we will take actions that we believe will accomplish that. From a more altruistic point of view, the best outcome might be to litigate and set a new, higher standard for the actions of directors of publicly traded U.S. corporations."

It was reported that some of the attorneys working on behalf of Cardinal and Tweedy, Browne were working on a contingency basis. That meant they would get a cut of the damages that could eventually be won from Conrad Black, several of his associates and various companies under their control. Corporate lawyers working on contingency are something like medical malpractice lawyers — it is to their advantage to inflate damages as much as possible as a way of increasing their own lawyers' fees.

On November 15, the SEC filed a seventy-six-page suit for civil fraud in Illinois against Conrad Black, David Radler and their holding company, Toronto-based Hollinger Inc. The suit blasted them for allegedly developing "a fraudulent and deceptive scheme" to divert more than $85 million in non-compete fees to themselves and close associates between 1999 and 2003; accused them of "misstatements and omission of material fact" to Hollinger International's board and audit committee, as well as in regulatory filings; and slammed them for "cheating and defrauding" public shareholders "through a series of deceptive schemes and misstatements." These schemes, it was alleged, included non-compete payments, related-party transactions through which Black, Radler and their associates diverted Hollinger International assets to themselves, and the $2.5-million investment in Trireme Partners, Richard Perle's venture capital fund. Anyone operating a business is supposed to abide by the law. But in its suit, the SEC noted that Black had additional obligations. Between August 2002 and August 2003, Black had "signed and certified Hollinger International's annual and quarterly reports filed with the SEC pursuant to the Sarbanes-Oxley Act of 2002"; and in 1982, he had signed a court-ordered consent decree promising to comply with securities regulations in the future.

A conviction for civil fraud could result in financial penalties but not a prison term. The SEC's agenda was three-fold: to ban Black and Radler from any future role running a public company; to recover an unspecified amount of money that it alleged had been fraudulently diverted; and to raise a rigorous new standard for disclosure in regulatory filings and public shareholder meetings — a standard applying to cases such as Hollinger's, where a dominant private shareholder wields effective control over a company. The SEC suit made headlines around the world. But analysts noted that the case could take several years to be resolved and that the new allegations had yet to be proven in a court of law.

Surprisingly, the SEC was silent about two burning controversies that had riled Tweedy, Browne starting in October 2001: the more than $200 million in management fees paid over a seven-year period to Conrad Black and several associates and the responsibility of Hollinger International board members for questioning, criticizing, approving and/or ignoring decisions taken during their tenure. The SEC's silence was curious. For whatever reason, it had clearly chosen to disregard several important shareholder allegations.

The ongoing crisis at Hollinger International since early 2003 had left many important questions unanswered. What was Conrad Black's responsibility for the various controversial payments? What was the Hollinger International board's responsibility for these same payments? What if the Hollinger International board had knowingly approved the payments? Tweedy, Browne and other shareholder activists set in motion a process that ultimately dislodged Black as chairman and CEO, deprived him of the right to vote on the fate of Hollinger International, and resulted in the sell-off of the company's prize assets. Should there be any limit to the ability of shareholders to manipulate legal proceedings against the executives of a corporation? Were the timing and circumstances of the *Telegraph* sale appropriate? Would a higher price have been obtained (that is, greater value for shareholders) if the sale of the *Telegraph* had been delayed? Would the shareholders have been better off if there had been no sale at all? Given Conrad Black's use of principle strictly for tactical, short-term reasons, did he damage his own credibility?

"Conrad lost a level of sensitivity I would have expected him to have in these matters of governance and personal lifestyle," said Senator Michael Meighen, who has known Black since the 1960s. "It is a question of scale and proportion. He went over the top. When that happens, you lose touch with some elements of reality. Some of the amounts paid to top executives in the corporate world are just obscene — the options, management fees — they are out of proportion with what is appropriate and generous remuneration for a good job well done."

I met Conrad Black for an hour in July 2005, in the lobby bar of the Intercontinental Hotel on Bloor Street near Avenue Road in Toronto. He was fifteen minutes late. When he arrived, I was surprised how humble he was, how easy he was to talk to compared to other times. The waitress was cute and very perky.

She glowed with recognition at having this celebrity called Conrad Black in her bar. We kept her busy. He drank three large glasses of Chardonnay, I drank three large glasses of Shiraz. Black's chauffeur, John Hillier, paced nervously outside, beside a very long, double-parked, navy-blue Cadillac. This stern-looking man had helped Black remove twelve bankers' boxes from 10 Toronto Street on May 20, 2005 — all of which was captured on security video cameras, and would serve as the basis for the obstruction of justice charge in Chicago.

While downing our first glass of wine and munching on some stomach-turning pretzels, I asked how his family was doing. "My daughter, Alana, has just sent me an e-mail from Honduras," he said, "where she is on a scuba-diving holiday. She was surprised to see security guards around the scuba-diving resort, armed with machine guns. This is actually a common occurrence in Latin America, and not something exceptional."

"Well, Conrad . . . How do you feel about everything?"

"Richard Breeden has campaigned as hard as possible to get the U.S. government to charge my associates and me. But if, after eighteen months, the DTI [Department of Trade and Industry] still hasn't come up with so much as a letter, that means they have nothing substantive to go on. I have nothing but disgust for Breeden, with the vicious media campaign waged in the press, with the idea that the corporate governance lobby can take a company away from someone on the presumption of guilt without documented proof of wrong-doing."

"But it isn't just a corporate governance lobby at work here. Hasn't the Sarbanes-Oxley Act made the obligations for CEOs of public companies much more clear?"

(I remembered how he had once told me Sarbanes-Oxley was "an insane law" with "all sorts of absurd conditions that are in part locking the barn door after the horses have fled and in part penalizations of the habitually law-abiding.")

"There is no real need for Sarbanes-Oxley, since it rehashes already existing legislation," Black told me now.

"Given all the things that have happened, I wonder whether you found it intoxicating to run a newspaper empire — did it go to your head at some point — all these journalists and wordsmiths writing for you, all the readers hearing your voice through the newspaper?"

"Yes, I did find it intoxicating to be a press baron, owning the *Daily Telegraph* and other newspapers."

"Conrad, I have always seen you as motivated fundamentally by curiosity — you wanted to be an eyewitness to historical events, to use your position as press baron to get a ringside seat and know political leaders well and at least to maintain access, in order to hear their views in private."

"I had a moderate amount of access. Senior people in London or Washington would take my call. But it is not as if I ever had a lot of influence on policy — I had a moderate amount of influence, nothing more."

This comment surprised me. We drained our first glass. I had always listened to him boasting of visits with British prime ministers and American presidents. Having unique access to power was part of his public persona.

He leaned forward. "George, how do you feel about your book?" It was a funny question. He was trying to size up whether I could be of any use to him.

"It was hard to write — you are, after all, a public figure much in view, you have sued a lot of people, and the story is constantly changing. A lot of people want to hear the negatives about you, the malicious gossip or anonymous denunciations, the things you have done wrong, without hearing the other side. My publisher has since gone bankrupt. . . . I have begun teaching in the university world to get away from all the manipulation. In fact, all the manipulation around this story has grossed me out."

At this comment, he winced — he must have realized I was referring to his own manipulation as much as everyone else's.

"Conrad, I don't know what I would have done in your position: you have to be someone who can focus on the positive aspect of things, in order to survive."

"My position isn't that bad," he replied. "Once the various lawsuits fizzle out, I intend to go after people for libel. Ravelston is currently in receivership because of its cashflow position but is not at all bankrupt. I have just been named to the board of Blackpool Energy, and the stock price doubled on the news of my appointment."[254]

"Your experiences must have showed you who your real friends are."

"Well, Ted Rogers, Paul Desmarais, Ken Thomson, the Westons and others have been very good to me throughout it all — whereas the Eatons, the Bassetts, and others have been very bad to me. Which I consider awful, given how much I have had done for them, including paying them rich fees."

When he said this, I couldn't help feeling he was wrong about Ken Thomson, who had told me privately how Conrad Black had been greedy, and how badly things would turn out for him in the end. And the Desmarais family may have continued publicly inviting Black to the occasional social gathering but had privately taken the decision to dissociate themselves from him business-wise after sharing majority ownership of Southam with him, for a few years. Black's attitude was as if he had received celebrity endorsements and could produce these on demand. He had banked on fairweather friends, people he had paid to keep him company, and Establishment figures who publicly showed him courtesy while privately sharpening their knives.

"That's fine where rich people are concerned," I said, "but you must have friends who are not wealthy — who are just interested in ideas." (I was thinking of Brian Stewart and Larry Zolf.)

"These friendships are doing well. My American and British friends have stuck by me, although the British media have assumed that Breeden's charges of 'looting' would lead directly to criminal charges. In some people's minds, I must have committed embezzlement, whereas that is completely untrue. I have found some media commentary reasonable, although a lot of media commentary, particularly in the *Globe and Mail* and in Murdoch's papers, has been consistently spiteful and horrible. Peter White is doing well, and has an article appearing tomorrow in the *Financial Post* about the fact the new Hollinger Inc. directors are paying themselves $1 million annually each, to serve as directors — they are now the highest-paid directors in the world!"

We then went on to discuss his Roosevelt book. He was interested to know my impression of John Kenneth Galbraith, Arthur Schlesinger, Peter Osnos and Bill Whitworth.

He said he was leaving with Barbara for a holiday in England and Provence.

I asked whether he was still Catholic, and in an answer that made me laugh, he said, "Of course I am still Catholic, although some people only become Catholic for a time — like Hemingway, I believe."

Finally, it was time to go. He asked whether he was paying — or I was. I picked up the tab for $79.

John Hillier looked anxiously to right and left, then opened the door of the Cadillac for Black. The limo seemed more like a boat than a car. After they left, the waitress came up to me. "You know who that is?" she asked. "Do you?" I asked. "Sure, that's Conrad Black, he's on the front page of all the papers! So . . . *you* know him?" I shrugged my shoulders.

Five weeks after my meeting with Black, U.S. federal prosecutor Patrick Fitzgerald announced criminal fraud charges against David Radler, Mark Kipnis and Ravelston Corp. Radler copped a plea, offering his full co-operation with the Department of Justice. On November 17, 2005, Fitzgerald laid criminal charges against Conrad Black, Jack Boultbee and Peter Atkinson. Black pleaded not guilty on December 16 and was released on a $20-million bond.

The Canadian Press/Dave Chidley

CHAPTER ELEVEN

CONVICTION

KEN THOMSON AND CONRAD BLACK were Canada's two
remaining global press barons with seats in the British House of
Lords. Thomson told me things would end up badly for Black.
And he was right.

Events toward the end of Black's criminal trial in 2007
underlined the huge difference between the two men and the
legacies they left behind.

Thomson had struck me as an astute man, modest and kind
— almost an accidental billionaire. Black, on the other hand,
was a self-destructive genius, full of savage, self-righteous bluster
— a man who rose to fame and fortune but continued rising
beyond his normal trajectory until his guidance system failed
and he came crashing downwards.

In early May 2007, Ken Thomson's legacy, the tremendous
company he and his father had built up for his family and other
shareholders, made a $17.5-billion bid for the century-old Reuters
news and financial data company. Once it got through various
anti-trust investigations, the newly merged company — to be
called "Thomson-Reuters" — would be a global information
leader, rivalling the New York-based Bloomberg data company.

There was something down-home about Ken, the gentle
giant from North Bay, Ontario, who had turned his father's

ownership of *The Times*, the *Scotsman* and North Sea oil into one of the world's largest fortunes. The last time I visited him in his Toronto office, we got down to some straight talking about Canadian art and the state of the world's press. I was careful never to appear to be asking him for anything. Ken was having fun chatting, but his executive secretary was concerned I was taking up too much of his limited energy. It was time to go. I reached out for his hand, which struck me as surprisingly warm for such an old person. But Ken wouldn't let go — he may have felt this was the last time we were going to meet. Then, clutching me by the hand in a fatherly sort of way, he led me down the corridor, introducing me to different senior officers of his company. "George is an honest man," he said, presenting me to a somewhat startled John A. Tory, president of Thomson Investments Ltd., and Richard Harrington, president and CEO of the Thomson Corporation. Their offices seemed cramped compared to offices at Hollinger International, even though the Thomson group of companies was far larger and more successful than Black's companies had ever been.

Then there was Conrad Black's legacy. A few days after the Thomson-Reuters announcement, with his criminal trial continuing in Chicago, Conrad Black gave a sit-down interview to Olive Burkeman of the *Guardian*.[255] The pretext for the interview was to discuss Black's weighty new biography, published March 2007, of disgraced U.S. president Richard M. Nixon, *The Invincible Quest*. "The former media mogul Conrad Black has a broad face," she and Andrew Clark wrote, "as impervious as an Easter Island monolith and nearly as motionless; he expresses himself by tiny adjustments in the narrowness of his eyes, which are narrow to begin with. In court in Chicago, where he is facing up to 101 years in prison for fraud, he assumes a detached, sceptical air, as if the trial were mildly amusing, and happening to someone else. Occasionally, when a former friend enters the witness box to testify against him, he flashes an icy glare. Then there's his third expression — a feline look of pleasure, eyes almost closed — which is rarely seen these days, but which will return, presumably, should he be acquitted of all charges."

The interview got underway about the way the American

people had misunderstood Nixon's greatness. Another of Black's "fallen giant" stories, evidently. Then he made an appalling outburst. The government's case against him was "bullshit . . . a joke . . . an outrage . . . and a complete fraud." He noted the promise in the Fifth Amendment "of no seizure of property without proper compensation. It's an outrage. Due process is guaranteed. It's not happening." He then lost his cool completely. "I'm sending everyone a message. I'm saying, *This is war.*" The notion that he and Barbara lived an extravagant lifestyle was "complete and total rubbish." Besides, it was no wonder the prosecution were "suffering mood fluctuations" since they were headed for "a complete wipeout." He said he wouldn't go so far as to say "'The game is won, I'm on an inexorable march to victory . . .' This [criminal case] still has its scary moments. But I see the trend. My strategy is working."

Actually, Black's strategy was *not* working. He wrote me that "the Nixon book will come out about May 22 in Canada and the UK, and at Labour Day in the U.S. No launch is planned at the moment, but it will undoubtedly be widely commented on. . . . We are flourishing in Chicago, and the general press perception that the government is not making its case, and doesn't really have a case, is catching on heart-warmingly."

Once again, the brilliant, sunny Black was being eclipsed by a darker Black, who was undoing all that the other side of him had just achieved with the Nixon biography.

In 1994, over a glass of wine in Montreal, a Canadian bank president told me that success in business involved "doing what you want with other people's money." Times had changed since that statement, however. If anything, the prosecutors in Black's trial wanted to establish that the company's money wasn't other people's money — it belonged to the shareholders and was only entrusted to the company they had invested in — in fact, success was now supposed to involve respecting the fact the company was dealing with other people's money.

Within a few days, the jury heard testimony from Paul Healy, Hollinger International's former investor relations officer (who turned state's evidence in exchange for immunity from prosecution). Healy said the May 2002 shareholders meeting was "the most contentious" he had ever seen. In an e-mail shortly before the meeting, Black wrote to Healy that shareholder concerns were "an epidemic of shareholder idiocy. . . . Much as I would like to blow their asses off, I don't want a sour atmosphere at the shareholder's meeting." Although Black was directly challenged by shareholder complaints about millions of dollars in non-compete payments made directly to Black and other executives, Healy was stunned that Black did not even mention the complaints at a directors' meeting later the same day. When Healy wanted to inform audit committee chairman James Thompson about the complaints, Black blasted him. "He said I had overstepped my bounds," Healy told the jury. "This is my company, he said, I'm the controlling shareholder and I decide what the Governor needs to know and when."

Shortly after this shareholder's meeting, Black and Healy met potential investors who asked pointed questions about management fees and company perks such as the use of company jets. "Black said, 'I can have a 747 if I wanted,'" Healy told the court. The investors decided to take a pass.[256]

A few days later, Black's former executive secretary, Joan Maida, whom I had met at 10 Toronto Street, was subject to cross-examination. Assistant U.S. Attorney Jeffrey Cramer openly ridiculed the story she gave about helping Black to remove twelve boxes of documents from the building, on May 20, 2005. An Ontario judge had issued a court order, forbidding the removal of any documents. The SEC had sent a request for documents, which amounts to a court order, on May 19, 2005. Maida, Black and chauffeur John Hillier had been caught in the act on a security video tape.

"Do you remember anyone talking to you about a Canadian court order?" Cramer asked.

"No," Maida said.

"You don't know whether he [Black] knew about the document-retention policy?" Cramer asked.

"No, I do not," she answered. She claimed repeatedly she could not remember what Black said when he was caught on camera moving the boxes to his waiting Cadillac.

Cramer showed Maida a photo of Black pointing up to a security camera in a hall. "Maybe he's pointing to me," she offered.

"Do you remember him pointing?" asked Cramer.

"No," she said.

Cramer projected a blow-up of Black's stubby, outstretched finger onto the big screen so the jury could take in this high-impact image, but Maida's answers were evasive, contradictory, and simply not believable. She admitted she had mailed out T-shirts bearing the words: "Conrad will win."

"You're hoping Conrad will be acquitted in this case, you're hoping Conrad will win?" Cramer said.

"Yes," she replied.[257]

Early one morning I went to courtroom 1241 to make sure I got a seat. No lawyers were present. I took my accustomed seat in the back left corner, next to the wall. Judge Amy St. Eve took her seat at the bench, organizing her papers, and chatting with Joe Rickhoff, the court reporter who sat at a desk in front of her.

A few sullen spectators had slipped into the courtroom to watch. A big, burly man with cornrow hair and an orange jumpsuit dragged his chained feet before Judge St. Eve for his arraignment, as armed marshals looked on. His drug trafficking charges were read out, and he nodded his head when asked if he understood the penalties he could face — life in prison and a $4 million fine. I wondered whether this was the kind of man Black would share a cell with in federal prison, if he got convicted.

While listening to the case, I had come to see lawyers as something akin to cancer surgeons. They were paid whatever the outcome, and they had to be detached from the work they did. The outcome in a trial could not be predicted either, especially when a jury of twelve citizens chosen virtually at random had the last word.

The case had begun to take its toll on all of us journalists. Some remained loyal to Conrad Black, confidently predicting his acquittal. They held in reserve a neo-conservative counterargument, that the government had shown itself to be fundamentally corrupt during this trial. Other journalists wondered whether Black would seek asylum in Belize or even take a cyanide pill, rather than face a guilty verdict and imprisonment. We all speculated about the verdict.

I had a hard time imagining how, if found guilty, Black would survive imprisonment, or how, if acquitted of criminal charges, he would survive more than a billion dollars' worth of civil suits awaiting him once the verdict dropped. Neither prosecution nor defence had been particularly convincing. From day to day, I did not know which side to believe. Black steamed down the hallway at the break, nodding the way people do at a church service, and occasionally making a quip, while the loyalists bobbed along adoringly in his wake. He was not supposed to give interviews. He must have found the pressure of his own silence in court unbearable. On June 12, he declined the last chance offered to him to take the stand in his own defence.

I wearily continued to maintain the presumption of innocence. "Objectivity" now struck me as a philosophical ideal rather than something a journalist could actually attain. Instead, I felt I should be fair — I could make impartial, balanced and hopefully honest judgments, but they would depend on my understanding of the case. This case — all the evidence, legal arguments and objections back and forth — had nothing to do with philosophical ideals and everything to do with power relationships.

One day the jury was absent, and no other journalists had turned up to listen. The morning session would be devoted to a jury instruction conference.

Within a few minutes, I realized the conference — involving judge, prosecution, and defence in Black's case — was all-important. Judge St. Eve discussed a crucial point with the prosecution and defence teams. Would she be giving the so-called Ostrich Instruction to the jury? This instruction would mean that the jury would be asked to consider whether the accused simply hid their heads in the sand, did not ask and did not tell about an ongoing fraud from which they benefited. Did they engage in deliberate avoidance? In other words, the jury would be asked to interpret the evidence and testimony from a broad rather than a narrow perspective.

Black's defence had been that he did not know there was anything wrong about the payments. But an Ostrich Instruction would send a clear signal to the jury to consider whether he received payments of a million dollars a month while *deliberately* staying out of the loop where the mechanics and legality of the payments were concerned.

The defence team were palpably nervous. One defence lawyer muttered to the judge that convictions were a possibility. The defence wanted to ensure that the Ostrich Instruction did not amount to directing the verdict, lining things up in such a way that the jury was bound to come to a guilty verdict.

"I have two questions for the government," said St. Eve. "You have presented a brief in support of the Ostrich submission. You give some examples of evidence that came in that a defendant shielded other defendants from knowing — in other words, that this defendant, instead of shielding himself, shielded others. . . . You allege that in regard to the CanWest and Community [CNHI] non-compete payments, Black's response was to draw a line and refuse any inquiry into the payments. But was that concealment?"

"Even giving Black the benefit of the doubt," replied Sussman, "he was saying, 'I don't want to know anything more about these payments.' We [the government] are arguing an Ostrich Instruction about Black and the payments. In the case of the Paxton and Forum payments [two contested non-compete payments that lay at the heart of the criminal charges in Chicago], he receives his cheque for these payments, he certainly knows that there was never a non-compete agreement . . . He put his head under the sand."

St. Eve said she would take the matter under advisement and respond the next day. In a written ruling on Thursday, she said the government had provided sufficient evidence to warrant "an inference of deliberate avoidance." In making the ruling, she had doubtless studied the trial of former Enron executives Kenneth Lay and Jeffrey Skilling, as well as WorldCom CEO Bernard Ebbers — all three were convicted on a similar basis.

Assistant prosecutor Julie Ruder, a tall, personable brunette with a razor-sharp mind, gave the closing arguments for the government. She portrayed Black and the other co-defendants as fraud artists who had systematically stolen money from Hollinger International shareholders.

"It was stealing, plain and simple," she told the jury. The defendants took a "slice of their company's profits" creating "a phony paper trail to make their actions appear legitimate. . . . Did they try to cover their steps? That's *exactly* what they have done," she said. "It is your job to expose the cover story for the lie it is."

Ruder handled the mass of evidence more clearly than the lead prosecutor Eric Sussman had. "We are not here because somebody made a mistake," she said. "We are here because five men systematically stole over $60 million from the shareholders of Hollinger International. . . . In one case, Conrad Black was paying himself not to compete with himself. That's ridiculous!"

In taking various non-compete fees, she said, the defendants had cheated shareholders. Non-compete payments were tax-free in Canada, and Black needed the funds to support his lavish lifestyle.

"Ladies and gentlemen, the goose was Hollinger and the golden egg was the money he was stealing from shareholders. And it *wasn't* his money," Ruder concluded.

When Ed Genson began his closing arguments in Black's defence, I remembered how he had identified with Arthur Bannister in *The Lady from Shanghai*. For most of his life, he had contended with physical infirmity. It was part of his personality. And it was part of his pleading in court to shift on his uncertain legs, held up by his braces. The jury listened, impassively, attentively, in silence, rarely taking notes, as Genson declaimed against the prosecution's charges. "Racketeering is relatively simple. It is by far the most serious charge in this case. They're [the prosecution] saying there's a racketeering scheme. They're saying these four [Black, Boultbee, Atkinson and Kipnis] are in a scheme, an enterprise. . . . There was no scheme and no enterprise. People don't talk to each other and nobody tells anyone else what to do. . . . The last substantive charge and probably the one that gets me more worked up than anything else is [Black's] obstruction of justice charge."

Genson paused to take a deep breath. "Black took some documents [from his former Toronto office], and he returned them. What you're going to say is there were personal effects — photographs of his houses in London, his personal chequing account, his brother's estate. He took personal papers. The government has to prove two things — first of all that Conrad concealed or attempted to conceal evidence, and second that he tampered with it. There has not been one accusation in this case that he tampered with anything. The fact of the matter is he was not served with a First Request for Production of Documents [by the SEC], and he didn't know about it."

Genson mocked the prosecution, but in addressing the jury directly, he also played with his voice, making it sound intimate, as if he were speaking to a long-lost friend instead of twelve jurors who would soon have the power to decide on Black's fate.

"Did you ever lose something and can't find it although it isn't worth much, and then you get mad and start looking for it? That's what the prosecution is doing. I guess I'm the only compulsive person here. . . ."

He looked exhausted and mopped his brow. "I had a nervous breakdown last night at four-thirty, when I produced a twenty-page summary. You're not going to remember what I am going to say. Instead, I'm going to give you references to specific documents and I'm going to ask you to read them. . . . I'm not going to be tricky. And you know when you get into your room, and realize you are in charge, you are going to forget half of everything the lawyers said, then you'll look at the documents yourself. . . . There will be a [prosecution] rebuttal, and I expect it will be a very robust rebuttal. Conrad Black is a good man. Conrad Black did a lot of good things for Hollinger. You've been very patient. I'm just about at the end. Conrad isn't American. But he has a kind of dream of hard work. He did not steal or intend to steal. He was a very successful, hard-working businessman. My wish is that you listen to the evidence. It has been very hard for Conrad and his family. The government in this case has overreacted, has manipulated the facts."

The following week, while the other defence attorneys in the case were presenting their final arguments, I had a last meeting with Conrad Black. In the bar of the Ritz-Carlton Hotel, he turned up in a beige suit, egg-blue Oxford-cloth shirt, and gold tie. He had the bitter, exhausted eyes of a warrior. He ordered a glass of Chardonnay.

"Today is the fiftieth anniversary of Maurice Duplessis's fifth electoral triumph of June 20, 1957. . . . So we agree that this is off the record — until after the verdict?"

I felt daunted. Judge St. Eve had repeatedly asked him not to speak to the press during the trial. Black's mid-May outburst in the *Guardian* showed he felt no remorse, and imagined he could single-handedly wage war on the government of the world's only superpower.

"Shall we say this is off the record?" I said. "Certainly — until after the verdict."

"I found it interesting in court today, because the prosecution has forced the defence teams together, although there is no real community of interest. Gus Newman and Patrick Tuite [the defence attorneys of Boultbee and Atkinson, respectively] took stands that actually strengthened our position. The government's case is so weak that it will be smashed over the next two days. And when I am acquitted, things will move up to a new level. You have informally canvassed people. What do they say?"

"I haven't been seeking out 'experts,'" I said. "They are armchair authorities and may not really know what they are talking about. Besides, some media interview experts who are former prosecutors, and they have a particular mental framework."

"What are the people you know saying?" asked Black, leaning forward in his seat.

"Of the journalists in the courtroom, some made up their minds a long time ago, some are not too sure, and some are supporting you. The only one who has been predicting a clean sweep for you from the very beginning is Steve Skurka."

"But he's a lawyer," said Black.

"Yes. . . . The people I know haven't really been following the case closely. They say the prosecution has tried to throw many charges against you, hoping some will stick. I feel some of the charges are, on the face of it, speculative, whereas four or five others are more damaging. But the damaging charges also seem to concern mistakes, errors in judgment, rather than fraudulent actions with criminal intent. I am not sure they justify your incarceration, since that is what the prosecution is seeking. It is very hard to know how the jury will react."

"It takes a unanimous verdict," said Black. "I can guarantee you that. The jury seem to be attentive, to be doing a good job."

"They have blank faces and listen carefully. But it's hard to know what they are thinking. So much money is at stake. I figure the direct costs of this trial — including the company investigations, the insurance, the legal fees — is about $500 million."

"It's much more than that! More like $1.5 billion, including losses in the share price."

"But that could be recovered eventually."

"No. . . . But the direct costs must be something like what you say, George — around half a billion dollars. Of course, when I am acquitted, we are going to ramp things up and I will recover my position. In fact, my acquittal will completely change the way corporate governance is dealt with. I am lucky to be in such good shape. When my brother, Monte, was the age I am now, he was suffering from a fatal illness, and by this age [sixty-two] my mother had already succumbed to a fatal illness."

"I wanted to say I regret all these things that have happened," I said. "It must have been a terrible experience. We will have to wait and see the outcome. I admire the way your children have supported you."

At these words, his expression changed. I could almost hear him snarling like a tiger behind the bars of his cage. He must have felt I was predicting his conviction. I got the impression he was waiting to hear some words from me, like "good luck," but I looked at him, in silence. Much to my surprise, he paid for drinks.

Black's biography of Richard M. Nixon had come out in late May. The book justified a lot of what Tricky Dick had done, admitting his faults but seeking to redeem an unappreciated and wholly unlikeable politician, even though Nixon had sabotaged himself. Reading the book, I couldn't help drawing parallels between Black and Nixon, both of whom, at least according Black, had been victimized by "smear jobs" and had achieved great international stature only to be brought down by a baying crowd of liberals. Shortly before the book's publication, Black had explained to me what he meant by "Machiavellian," since he had used the word in reference to Franklin Roosevelt. "I meant that Roosevelt was extremely secretive, devious, inscrutable and conniving, but working always toward the implementation of a plan that no one could divine. His ends were admirable, and his means were not unconstrained by ethical factors, but he was as I described." This, in a nutshell, seemed to be what Black himself had aspired to since the 1960s.

Then again, he had written several biographies — first of Duplessis, then of Roosevelt, now of Nixon — in addition to his own autobiography. He had studied the character of greatness. Did he feel empathy for the people he had written about, or for his employees? "I have felt about the people I have written about (apart from myself) as George C. Scott said he felt about General George S. Patton: 'He was a splendid anachronism and I rather enjoyed the old gentleman,' in the case of Duplessis and up to a point Nixon. Roosevelt was such an overpowering and successful figure, it was hard not to admire him even when he was not especially likeable. As for employees, the employer feels some responsibility for them as a group. Empathy is a matter determined on a case-by-case basis."

Black had studied historical greatness, had dogged it and analyzed and recorded it. He had built up a collection of memorabilia associated with greatness, from presidential flags and bishop's thrones to Napoleon's shaving bottles and his heroes' letters in golden frames. In his own inimitable way, he had fused himself with the people he admired, adding a dose of intellectual self-justification — Nietzsche for his belief in superhumans specially fitted to rise above normal moral standards and dominate their epoch, Spengler for his belief that world historical personalities can reverse the course of civilization and save the West from decline, and Darwin for seeming to validate whoever prevailed as if they alone were fittest to survive, by crushing others.

Conrad Black wanted others to believe in his historical greatness, but the mantle had slipped off, and in Chicago, disgrace was looming — on a grand scale.

It would be hard to portray Black as a stag brought down by wolves, as an idealistic man laid low by the envious or to compare him to Shakespearean heroes. The only character I could think of comparing him to was Shakespeare's hunch-backed, plotting Richard III, the very personification of the Machiavellian villain of the Renaissance, who betrayed everyone and then was betrayed himself. At the end of the play, Richard's enemies are closing in on him, and all he can do is cry despairingly, "A horse! a horse! my kingdom for a horse!" In Chicago, Conrad Black had simply run out of options. He had nowhere left to go.

Listing Hollinger International shares on the New York Stock Exchange was a huge strategic error for a master strategist such as Black. U.S. investment and securities regulators have a history of strict and aggressive enforcement compared to their Canadian counterparts. Giving up his Canadian citizenship was also a colossal strategic mistake.

The mark Black left on journalism will long be debated, as will his record as a business tycoon. His bold start-up of the *National Post* and his takeovers of Argus Corporation, the *Daily Telegraph,* and the Southam Group were remarkable and will be weighed against his business practices and his fall from power. And it was under Black's leadership that the *Telegraph* ultimately won the price war against Rupert Murdoch's *The Times* by concentrating on the quality of *Telegraph* reportage. Given the enormous financial resources of News Corp., Black's achievement was considerable. He built up a tremendous amount of value at the *Telegraph*, which he acquired in 1985 for some $60 million and which was sold in July 2004 for $1.21 billion. He did the same with the *Chicago Sun-Times*, which he bought for $180 million in 1993 and which Vice Chancellor Strine valued at more than $1 billion in July 2004.

But he had left an enormous amount of wreckage behind. Besides, unlike Ken Thomson, Paul Desmarais, Sr. and other media magnates, Black had not managed to groom the next generation, ensuring the orderly transmission of control of his press empire. But then his children are much younger. In the end, just as he failed to revive conservative nationalism in Quebec during the 1970s, or to launch a new conservatism in Canada, Black's defence of U.S.-style neo-conservatism lost him support in Britain and his Hollinger troubles landed him in criminal court in the United States.

In the last days of the trial, the Boultbee, Atkinson and Kipnis defence teams hammered the jury with swirling facts and arguments, spreading as much doubt as possible about the charges facing their clients. The government was trying to confuse the jury, they said; the government wanted the jury to come to a verdict based on incomplete information; the government had manipulated the facts; the prosecution witnesses had simply lied about what they knew; the three audit committee members who had testified for the prosecution (Governor Thompson, Ambassador Burt and Marie-Josée Kravis) had knowingly signed one approval of payments after another; the government had threatened them with lawsuits, fines and possible disbarment from serving on corporate boards in the future; the government had pressured prosecution witnesses into perjuring themselves; the government had relied on its star witness, David Radler, who had told a new version of his story each time he spoke, lying repeatedly; in exchange for his testimony Radler had derived benefits from the government, such as a reduced sentence and a transfer to a Canadian horse farm to serve it; the government case was built on lies and deception; the burden of proof was there to protect the citizens from the awesome power of the government; this was a criminal case — not a game; just because the government called something false, that didn't magically make it false; the jury had seen the power of the government but that power ended at the jury room door. The jury would receive fifteen boxes of exhibits, and have to make up its own mind . . .

With all the emotional pressure in courtroom 1241, one of the jurors had a sudden malaise. The judge called a five-minute recess. We all stood while jury and judge filed out. Then the tension dropped as we wondered what we were all doing on our feet. Everyone began talking animatedly to the next person — prosecution and defence lawyers, multi-millionaire defendants and their families, journalists, spectators and bailiffs. I wondered where the champagne and oysters had got to.

The time came for Eric Sussman to present the governmental rebuttal of the defence's closing arguments. Under the American system, during the rebuttal the government can introduce new evidence if it wants to — evidence to which the defence cannot respond. Sussman asked Judge St. Eve for an hour and a half to two hours — which mushroomed into a full day.

"It's been almost four months," said Sussman, pacing back and forth in front of the jury. "We have had over forty witnesses and thousands of documents. In the case of each of the defendants, there is a defining moment, a moment of truth. For Mr. Black, that moment was when he paid himself not to compete with himself." Sussman then went through the moments of truth for the other defendants. "For all of them, for each of these defendants, the moment comes together when they lied to the audit committee and to the shareholders. Why were these men getting paid for non-competes, when the buyers [of Hollinger International newspapers] had not asked for them? Why were these men entitled to take this money and lie about it? And when they are defending this case we didn't charge — that the non-competes are valid — they have disregarded portions of the prosecution testimony that did not suit them, and have casually accused government witnesses of perjury. There is an old lawyer's adage. When you have the facts on your side, you argue the facts. When you have the law on your side, you argue the law. And when you don't have either, you argue that everyone else is perjuring himself."

Sussman forged ahead. With cries of "Look! Come on! Okay! You know! Who cares?" he appeared to be appealing to the working-class jurors. The chief federal prosecutor, Patrick Fitzgerald, sat glowering in the front row, unsmiling, with crystal eyes and hunched shoulders, like a shark or meat-eating boxer.

"Get a conviction, dammit," his whole body language seemed to shout at Sussman.

"We essentially have two themes from the lawyers of Conrad Black," Sussman continued. "One is that our star witness, David Radler, is a liar. Two is that Conrad Black is being persecuted and is the victim of class prejudice. The defence wants this case to be about David Radler. . . . Whose case is David Radler? He was on the witness stand for two days, he was cross-examined for about a week. They [the defence] rely on David Radler. David Radler provided the colour commentary, the insider view of what had happened. Of course David Radler was part of our case. But you don't need to believe a single word David Radler told you, and still convict each and every one of the defendants."

The spectators gasped. This seemed a strange argument for Sussman to make, since the prosecution's case depended more than anything else on Radler's testimony.

"David Radler is a criminal," Sussman continued. "David Radler is a fraudster. He lied to the special committee and to the SEC. He lied to us. . . . Who picked David Radler as our star witness? Conrad Black picked him, when he started doing business with him thirty years ago. Do you think David Radler turned into a criminal overnight? Birds of a feather nest together. You know what? Conrad Black and David Radler nested together for over thirty years. . . . Presumably, David Radler would lie to you if it were in his interest to do so. His plea is structured so that the incentive is on him to tell the truth. If David Radler's only job was to lie to you, to stay on the script as the defence has suggested, don't you think he could have done a better job than that?

"We were told that David Radler ran Western Canada and Conrad Black ran Eastern Canada. Well, ladies and gentlemen, while we have all been here in court, a tremendous event has occurred. David Radler has taken over *all* of Canada, and Conrad Black is a small island! The fact is — Conrad Black was involved in *every* transaction, he signed them and he presented them to the board. He knew, and he knew the details. He knew everything that was going on in his company. . . . Just because the security guard was asleep does not excuse these men of committing crimes. If you don't like what the audit committee did, it doesn't mean what they [the defendants] did is okay. We're not here because the audit committee skimmed the files. We are here because five men skimmed the company. . . . Conrad Black knew exactly that the non-competes were a vehicle for extracting money from Hollinger International."

Then there was the matter of perks. "We *don't* care how Conrad Black spends his money," said Sussman. "We *do* care about how Conrad Black spends shareholders' money. It's not surprising that the defence has not made that distinction, because Conrad Black certainly did not make that distinction. . . . One of the reasons the perks are relevant is because they give you a window onto his attitude of fiduciary responsibility. They are part of a consistent scheme to harm the shareholders, for his personal benefit."

Continuing on the subject of perks, Sussman then said the mistake was not that Black took the company plane to Bora Bora — the mistake was that the company accountant found this expense. It wasn't up to Black to decide whether shareholders should pay for his wife's birthday — that was the job of the audit committee. Wasn't it surprising that Black remembered every detail of his wife's birthday expenses — but knew nothing about million-dollar payments he received?

Then there was the matter of the obstruction of justice charge, based in large part on the security camera video from May 2005, showing Conrad Black, John Hillier and executive assistant Joan Maida removing boxes of documents from 10 Toronto Street into a back alley, then loading them into a black Cadillac. Sussman mocked the idea that Black could have turned up at 10 Toronto Street with his chauffeur and personal assistant to remove boxes of documents the day after the SEC had copied him on a document request. "Why do you think this guy lugged boxes out of 10 Toronto Street — to create a home office? You know why. He knew there were things in there that he did not want the SEC, the grand jury or yourselves to see. You heard he brought them back. He was ordered to bring them back. We don't know what he took — we only know what he returned."

"Ladies and gentlemen," Sussman said as he came to the core of the government's argument. "This case is not a disclosure case. It is not about false disclosures to the SEC. The fraud is the 'why' of why they [the defendants] were being paid these non-compete payments — they lied to the shareholders about why they were getting the non-compete payments. In twenty-five hours of closing arguments, not one of them [the defence attorneys] answered Ms. Ruder's question — why these five men [Black, Radler, Boultbee, Atkinson and Kipnis] got non-compete payments that were not requested by the buyers. . . . Why does anyone commit a crime? People commit crimes for millions of reasons — money, power, friendships, passion, anger. There are millions of reasons. You are not asked to consider that. You are asked to evaluate the facts and the law and decide whether a crime is committed. . . . We have proved that David Radler was not Santa Claus, handing out millions of dollars to these men, then lying to them about it."

Sussman then presented two enormous glossy black poster boards to the jury — one marked "honesty" in white, the other "loyalty."

"When you evaluate the transactions in this case, and remember these two words, you will see they are not what the shareholders got."

In closing, with biting sarcasm in his voice, Sussman flashed a memo on the big screen, so the jury could read Conrad Black's words of May 25, 2002, to Paul Healy, who had got immunity in exchange for agreeing to testify for the prosecution. The e-mail referred to the shareholder outrage at the Hollinger International shareholders meeting a few weeks before. "Two years from now," Black had written, "no one will remember any of this."

The following day, Conrad Black, his wife, Barbara, her former husband, George Jonas, and Black's three children filed into court one last time, to hear Judge St. Eve give her instructions to the jury. Black nodded stiffly at Ed Genson and Ed Greenspan, then sat down. Barbara Amiel had a vacant, otherworldly expression on her face, as if she were on some powerful sedative. She seemed to be almost leaning in exhaustion on the shoulder of Jonas, who sat next to her.

"Members of the jury," Judge St. Eve began, "you have seen and heard all the evidence and the arguments of the attorneys. Now I will instruct you on the law.

You have two duties as a jury. Your first duty is to decide the facts from the evidence in the case. This is your job and yours alone. Your second duty is to apply the law that I give you to the facts. You must follow these instructions, even if you disagree with them. Each of the instructions is important, and you must follow all of them.

Perform these duties fairly and impartially. Do not allow sympathy, prejudice, fear, or public opinion to influence you. You should not be influenced by any person's race, colour, religion, national ancestry, sex, or economic status.

Nothing I say now, and nothing I said or did during the trial, is meant to indicate any opinion on my part about what the facts are or about what your verdict should be.

The evidence consists of the testimony of the witnesses, the exhibits admitted in evidence and stipulations.

A stipulation is an agreement between the government and one or more of the defendants that certain facts are true or that a person would have given certain testimony.

You are to decide whether the testimony of each of the witnesses is truthful and accurate, in part, in whole, or not at all, as well as what weight, if any, you give to the testimony of each witness.

In evaluating the testimony of any witness, you may consider, among other things: the witness's age; the witness's intelligence; the ability and opportunity the witness had to see, hear, or know the things that the witness testified about; the witness's memory — any interest, bias, or prejudice the witness may have; the manner of the witness while testifying; and the reasonableness of the witness's testimony in light of all the evidence in the case.

You should use common sense in weighing the evidence and consider the evidence in light of your own observations in life.

In our lives, we often look at one fact and conclude from it that another fact exists. In law we call this 'inference.' A jury is allowed to make reasonable inferences. Any inferences you make must be reasonable and must be based on the evidence in the case.

Some of you have heard the phrases 'circumstantial evidence' and 'direct evidence.' Direct evidence is direct proof of a fact or an event, such as the testimony of an eyewitness. Circumstantial evidence is the proof of facts from which you may infer or conclude that other facts exist. The law makes no distinction between the weight to be given either direct or circumstantial evidence. You should decide how much weight to give to any evidence. All the evidence in the case, including the circumstantial evidence, should be considered by you in reaching your verdict.

Certain things are not evidence. I will list them for you: First, testimony that I struck from the record, or that I told you to disregard, is not evidence and must not be considered. Second, anything that you may have seen or heard outside the courtroom is not evidence and must be entirely disregarded. This includes any press, radio, or television reports you may have seen or heard. Such reports are not evidence and your verdict must not be influenced in any way by such publicity. Third, questions and objections by the lawyers are not evidence. Attorneys have a duty to object when they believe a question is improper. You should not be influenced by any objection or by my ruling on it. Fourth, the lawyers' statements to you are not evidence. The purpose of these statements is to discuss the issues and the evidence. If the evidence as you remember it differs from what the lawyers said, your memory is what counts.

It is proper for an attorney to interview any witness in preparation for trial.

You may find the testimony of one witness or a few witnesses more persuasive than the testimony of a larger number. You need not accept the testimony of the larger number of witnesses.

The information in this case (the 'information') is the formal method of accusing the defendants of an offence and placing them on trial. It is not evidence against the defendants and does not create any inference of guilt.

Defendant Conrad Black is charged with the offences of mail and wire fraud in Counts One and Five through Twelve. He is charged with the offence of concealing documents from an official proceeding in Count Thirteen and the offence of racketeering in Count Fourteen. Defendant Black is also charged with the offence of aiding or assisting the preparation of a false corporate income tax return in Counts Fifteen and Sixteen. Defendant Black has pleaded not guilty to the charges.

Defendant John Boultbee is charged with the offences of mail and wire fraud in Counts One and Five through Twelve. He is also charged with the offence of aiding or assisting the preparation of a false corporate income tax return in Counts Fifteen and Sixteen. Defendant Boultbee has pleaded not guilty to the charges.

Defendant Peter Atkinson is charged with the offences of mail and wire fraud in Counts One and Five through Nine. He is also charged with the offence of aiding or assisting the preparation of a false corporate income tax return in Count Sixteen. Defendant Atkinson has pleaded not guilty to the charges.

Defendant Mark Kipnis is charged with the offences of mail and wire fraud in Counts One through Nine. He is also charged with the offence of aiding or assisting the preparation of a false corporate income tax return in Counts Fifteen and Sixteen. Defendant Kipnis has pleaded not guilty to the charges.

The defendants are presumed to be innocent of each of the charges. This presumption continues during every stage of the trial and your deliberations on the verdict. It is not overcome unless from all the evidence in the case you are convinced beyond a reasonable doubt that the defendant is guilty as charged. The government has the burden of proving the guilt of a defendant beyond a reasonable doubt.

This burden of proof stays with the government throughout the case. The defendants are never required to prove their innocence or to produce any evidence at all.

A defendant has an absolute right not to testify. The fact that a defendant did not testify should not be considered by you in any way in arriving at your verdict.

Judge St. Eve then provided some qualifying information about two prosecution witnesses.

You have heard testimony from Paul Healy, who received immunity; that is, a promise from the government that any testimony or other information he provided would not be used against him in a criminal case. His receipt of immunity is not to be considered as evidence against the defendants. You have also heard testimony from David Radler, who has pleaded guilty to an offence. Radler received benefits from the government, including a promise of a reduced sentence in return for his cooperation. His guilty plea is not to be considered as evidence against the defendants.

You may give the testimony of Healy and Radler such weight as you feel it deserves, keeping in mind that it must be considered with caution and great care.

Judge St. Eve went on to review the charges against the four defendants with great care. Then she came to the Ostrich Instruction.

When the word 'knowingly' or the phrase 'the defendant knew' is used in these instructions, it means that the defendant realized what he was doing and was aware of the nature of his conduct, and did not act through ignorance, mistake or accident. Knowledge may be proved by the defendant's conduct, and by all the facts and circumstances surrounding the case. You may infer knowledge from a combination of suspicion and deliberate indifference to the truth. If you find that a defendant had a strong suspicion that criminal conduct was occurring, yet intentionally shut his eyes for fear of what he would learn, you may conclude that he acted knowingly, as I have used that word. You may not conclude that a defendant had knowledge if he was merely negligent in not discovering the truth.

I do not anticipate that you will need to communicate with

me. If you do need to communicate with me, the only proper way is in writing. The writing must be signed by the foreperson, or, if he or she is unwilling to do so, by some other juror. The writing should be given to the court security officer, who will give it to me. I will respond either in writing or by having you return to the courtroom so that I can respond orally. If you do communicate with me, you should not indicate in your note what your numerical division is, if any.

You should make a determined effort to answer any question by referring to the jury instructions before you submit a question to me. If you do submit a question, I must show it to the lawyers for each side and consult with them before responding. I will either answer your question, or explain why I cannot answer your question.

The verdict must represent the considered judgment of each juror. Your verdict, whether it be guilty or not guilty, must be unanimous.

You should make every reasonable effort to reach a verdict. In doing so, you should consult with one another, express your own views, and listen to the opinions of your fellow jurors. Discuss your differences with an open mind. Do not hesitate to re-examine your own views and change your opinion if you come to believe it is wrong. But you should not surrender your honest beliefs about the weight or effect of evidence solely because of the opinions of your fellow jurors or for the purpose of returning a unanimous verdict.

The twelve of you should give fair and equal consideration to all the evidence and deliberate with the goal of reaching an agreement which is consistent with the individual judgment of each juror.

You are impartial judges of the facts. Your sole interest is to determine whether the government has proved its case beyond a reasonable doubt.

With that, Judge St. Eve concluded her instructions and dismissed us. It had only taken fifty-five minutes.

In the lobby of the Dirksen building, TV cameramen and press photographers lined up in the pit, waiting for Conrad

Black to steam past. But when he and Barbara appeared, with George Jonas trailing just behind them, it seemed the three had developed curvature of the spine. Led by James and Jonathan and followed by Alana, the three looked weathered and broken. They stepped around the shouting journalists and labyrinth of TV cameras and boom mikes out onto South Dearborn Street, climbed into a white Chevy stretch van and sped off.

After eleven days, the verdict finally came back. Conrad Black was found guilty on three counts of fraud and one count of obstruction of justice. This would translate into a significant forfeiture of assets and a stiff U.S. prison term in medium security. The testimony relating to the three counts of fraud involved some of the lesser transactions, and had barely been reported in the press at the time. In one fraudulent transaction, Black, Radler and several others paid themselves non-competes when they sold American Publishing, a string of small-town newspapers. Black himself pocketed $2.6 million in this deal. But by the time the non-compete agreement was drafted, American Publishing only had one last weekly paper in California. A company controlled by Black and Radler picked it up for just one dollar. Was Black paying himself not to compete with himself? Talk about a larger-than-life personality!

The security video of Black removing boxes of documents had made a huge impression on the jury. After the verdict came down, jurors told the press they had not believed David Radler's testimony, they had found Black's Toronto defence lawyer Ed Greenspan essentially disagreeable, and they had resented suggestions they did not understand the issues in the case. They had taken their work seriously. The easiest charge of all, for the jury, was Black's obstruction of justice. "Oh, guilty!" juror Monica Prince told the *Toronto Star.* "They had him on tape taking those files out and they told him not to take those files out. And he took them, like: 'I'm Conrad Black, I'll take what I want,'" she said, chuckling.[258] According to Prince, the jurors would have liked to find Black guilty on all counts. (Peter Atkinson, Jack Boultbee and Mark Kipnis were also convicted on three fraud charges but face a lighter sentence.)

This had been a huge story, with many psychological dimensions, and over the years covering it I had often reached for analogies in the world of cinema, trying to explain — at least to myself — what was at stake. After meeting Conrad Black in Toronto in July 2005, I mailed him a DVD copy of the Alfred Hitchcock courtroom drama *I Confess*, in which a killer confesses to his crime and tries to get off, while the priest who hears the confession is falsely accused of murder and is just barely acquitted towards the end. I knew the film would appeal to Black, because it had been shot in 1953 in Quebec City. Maurice Duplessis had authorized Hitchcock to film scenes in the Legislative Assembly as it was then called, while other scenes were shot in the Catholic cathedral.

But another film kept coming back to me: *Citizen Kane*. Conrad Black had been the first to compare himself to William Randolph Hearst. This was in the early 1960s while he was on holidays with his friend Brian Stewart. In the years since then, he had occasionally suggested in writing or in conversation that he was like Citizen Kane, although he would sometimes object in mock surprise that anyone would make such a comparison. He fed others so they would feed him back.

Over the years, I asked a number of people for parts of the puzzle that is Conrad Black. I felt like the reporter in *Citizen Kane* who is trying to figure out the meaning of the word *Rosebud*. It was the last word that rolled off Kane's lips, as he lay dying. Find out what it meant, and you could explain the secret of his existence. *Rosebud*, for Kane, was a symbol of his lost innocence, of the good times in his childhood before the wrenching power struggles, outrageous success and equally outrageous failure of his later years. In the final scene, we see a sled pitched into the flames, its painted name *Rosebud* bubbling and curling, then vanishing.

"I have watched Black's rise and fall up close," I wrote in the *Christian Science Monitor* in March 2007, "trying, like some journalist-witness in *Citizen Kane*, to make sense of a larger-than-life press baron who has, on a personal level, seemingly sabotaged himself through greed, provocative behavior, and exhibitionism."

Naturally Black quickly retorted that I had completely lost the "vision" — the grand vision, I suppose — of his acquittal on all charges and his rise back to glory from what I counted as his fall. And if he wasn't acquitted, then he would win on appeal.

The one experience in Conrad Black's life that has a "Rosebud" quality was the coronation cruise in 1953. Everything was safe back then, his parents were well, the family was all together, and they steamed across the Atlantic on the world's most glamorous passenger ship to witness the near rebirth of Britain, the crowning of the young queen, while millions lined the streets. That Conrad Black continued identifying with this formative experience of childhood is illustrated by the way he filled several rooms of the enormous house at 26 Park Lane Circle with the most extraordinary custom-made models of the great passenger and battle ships of the first half of the twentieth century. No matter what he was doing — entertaining royalty, princes, rock stars, top models, billionaires, intellectuals or his own family; hammering out a caustic neo-conservative article for publication; proof-reading a biography of Roosevelt or Nixon; or developing some new Machiavellian strategy — he could cast a glance at his ship models and get some of that "Rosebud" sense of security that everything was still safe, innocent, serene, in its rightful place. He wouldn't be able to look at these ship models, however, once he got to prison.

Chicago Sun-Times court reporter Mary Wisniewski told me over lunch during the trial that Black and the other co-defendants seemed "to be running Hollinger International like a pirate ship." That comment put a completely new spin on the ship metaphor!

The TV crews faded into the background, and in my mind's eye, I pictured $500 million going up in smoke. Or was it $1.5 billion, as Conrad Black had said? I imagined an immense pile of bank notes raked together, with dark grey smoke coiling outwards, snake-like, from the mass of paper, coiling and slowly, relentlessly, inescapably building into a brilliant sheet of orange flames. Then, as I stood imagining, the bank notes morphed into pages of newsprint. This was the definitive end of the world's third-largest newspaper empire.

What was Conrad Black's claim to historical greatness? Of all Canada's greatest robber barons, he was the one who got caught.

1. Peter C. Newman, *The Establishment Man*, p. 78.
2. Author's interview.
3. Author's interview.
4. *Fortune*, October 13, 2003.
5. Author's interview.
6. Author's interview.
7. Author's interview.
8. Unless otherwise noted, all quotes from Conrad Black in the text are from interviews and correspondence with the author.
9. *Fortune*, October 13, 2003.
10. *Washington Post*, December 4, 2003.
11. *Wall Street Journal, Globe and Mail, Financial Times*, November 18, 2003.
12. Black was referring to the increase in the value of his shares *after* he resigned as company CEO.
13. Author's interview.
14. *Globe and Mail*, October 18, 2003.
15. According to a filing made by the Sun-Times Media Group (the former Hollinger International), by July 2007, legal fees paid on behalf of Black and various co-defendants passed the $60-million mark.
16. Black also laid out this point in an e-mail to the author.

17. The breakdown of these penalties is: $7 million in 2003; $21.18 million Radler agreed to pay to settle a civil suit filed by Hollinger International, since renamed Sun-Times Media Group; $23.3 million from North American Newspapers Ltd., owned by Radler; $11.78 million from Horizon Publishing Co., and $7.15 million from Bradford Publishing Co. *Chicago Sun-Times*, March 19, 2007.

18. This fine is part of the previously cited figure of $71 million that Radler and his companies agreed to pay back.

19. *The Australian*, October 21, 2000.

20. With his brother Lord Northcliffe, First Viscount Rothermere, 1868–1940, he built a successful newspaper empire that included the London *Daily Mail*. During the First World War, he served as first secretary of state for air in the British government; in 1934, the pro-fascist *Daily Mail* proclaimed "Hurrah for the Blackshirts," throwing its support behind British extreme right leader Sir Oswald Mosley.

21. Maurice Hecht interview with George Black, 1973, E. P. Taylor Archives.

22. *Saturday Night*, March 26, 1955.

23. Author's interview. David Culver served as chairman of Alcan Inc., one of the world's leading aluminum manufacturers.

24. Conrad Black, *A Life in Progress*, p. 2.

25. *Daily Telegraph*, January 14, 2002.

26. Author's interview.

27. Author's interview.

28. Author's interview.

29. Barbara Amiel, *Confessions*, 1st edition, p. 15.

30. *Ibid.*, pp. 23 and 59.

31. William Dendy, *Lost Toronto*, p. 188.

32. Author's interview.

33. John Fraser, *Telling Tales*, pp. 75-76.

34. Author's interview.

35. Black, *A Life in Progress*, pp. 11-13.

36. Newman, *The Establishment Man*, p. 31.

37. Author's interview.

38. Author's interview.

39. Robert Lacey, *Little Man: Meyer Lansky and the Gangster Life*, p. 409.

40. *Daily Telegraph,* January 30, 1997.

41. Amiel, *Confessions,* 1st edition, pp. 53-54.

42. *Ibid.,* p. 130.

43. Author's interview.

44. Amiel, *Confessions,* 1st edition, p. 144.

45. Author's interview.

46. Author's interview.

47. David Halberstam, *The Powers That Be,* p. 409.

48. Black, *A Life in Progress,* p. 31.

49. Black, *A Life in Progress,* p. 34.

50. Author's interview.

51. *Ibid.,* p. 34.

52. Author's interview.

53. Author's interview.

54. Black, *A Life in Progress,* p. 44.

55. "Hero Worship," *CBC News Viewpoint,* October 24, 2003.

56. Author's interview.

57. Montreal *Gazette,* August 24, 1978.

58. Nick Auf der Maur, *Nick: A Montreal Life,* p. 107.

59. *A Life in Progress,* p. 74.

60. Author's interview.

61. Black, *A Life in Progress,* pp. 52-53, and author's interview.

62. *Diagnostic and Statistical Manual of Mental Disorders,* 4th edition, pp. 393-395.

63. Black, *A Life in Progress,* p. 54.

64. Graham Greene, *The Quiet American,* p. 24.

65. Sherbrooke *Record,* Friday, October 2, 1970. "(*Record* Publisher Conrad M. Black is visiting South Vietnam, as part of a fact-finding tour of the Far East. His hour-and-a-half-long interview with South Vietnamese President Nguyen van Thieu is one of the most wide-ranging of recent times.)"

66. Kissinger, *Diplomacy,* pp. 655-656.

67. Black, *A Life in Progress,* p. 56.

68. Author's interview.

69. Black, *A Life in Progress,* p. 94.

70. Author's interview.

71. Max and Monique Nemni, *Trudeau, fils du Québec, père du Canada,* volume 1, especially chapters 8-9. Montreal: Editions de

l'Homme, 2006. The Nemnis based their account on their privileged access to Trudeau's personal archives, after his death.

72. The correspondence between Robert Rumilly and Jacques de Bernonville, and between Rumilly and Conrad Black, can be consulted at the Archives nationales du Québec in Montreal.

73. Author's interview and Black, *A Life in Progress*, p. 12.

74. Author's interview.

75. Author's interview.

76. Conrad Black, *Render Unto Caesar*, p. 500.

77. Author's interview.

78. Conrad Black, *Duplessis*, p. 173.

79. *Duplessis*, pp. 660 and 661.

80. Black, *A Life in Progress*, p. 72.

81. Author's interview.

82. Black, *A Life in Progress*, p. 143.

83. Peter C. Newman, "Titans: How the Canadian Establishment Seized Power," Empire Club speech, November 10, 1998.

84. CBC TV documentary, *Ten Toronto Street*.

85. Black, *A Life in Progress*, pp 149-151.

86. Newman, *The Establishment Man*, p. 96.

87. Black, *A Life in Progress*, p. 154.

88. Author's interview.

89. Newman, *The Establishment Man*, p. 78.

90. Black, *A Life in Progress*, pp. 168-171.

91. *Ibid.*, p. 106.

92. Spengler, *Decline of the West*, vol. II, p. 461.

93. *Ibid.*, vol. II, p. 474.

94. Newman, *The Establishment Man*, p. 175.

95. Author's interview.

96. CBC-TV, *Ten Toronto Street*.

97. Black, *A Life in Progress*, p. 213.

98. *Toronto Star*, June 17, 1978.

99. *Globe and Mail*, July 17, 1978.

100. Newman, *The Establishment Man*, p. 109.

101. Black, *A Life in Progress*, p. 288.

102. *Globe and Mail*, June 7, 1979.

103. Newman, *The Establishment Man*, pp. 259-260.

104. Black, *A Life in Progress*, p. 251.

105. *Vanity Fair*, February 2004.

106. *Ibid.*

107. *New York Times Magazine*, August 15, 1999.

108. Cook, *Massey at the Brink*, p. 240.

109. *Ibid.*, p. 259.

110. Black, *A Life in Progress*, pp. 250-251.

111. *Ibid.*, p. 140.

112. Henry Kissinger, *A World Restored*, pp. 329 and 322.

113. *Ibid.*, p. 286.

114. Author's interview.

115. *Maclean's*, February 21, 1983.

116. According to Brigadier General S.F. Andrunyk's introduction to Barbara Amiel's speech before the Empire Club of Canada, Toronto, February 4, 1982.

117. Fraser, *Telling Tales*, pp. 64-65.

118. Author's interview.

119. *Chatelaine*, September 1985.

120. *The Times*, November 23, 2003.

121. Author's interview.

122. Amiel, *Confessions*, 2nd edition, pp. 251-252.

123. *Chatelaine*, 1980.

124. Ann Finlayson, *Whose Money Is It Anyway?* p. 105.

125. Black, *A Life in Progress*, p. 327.

126. Newman, *The Establishment Man*, p. 14.

127. Author's interview.

128. *Architectural Digest*, April 1988.

129. A.J.P. Taylor, *Beaverbrook*.

130. Roy Thomson, *After I Was Sixty*, p. 171.

131. Author's interview.

132. Peter Hennessy, *The Prime Minister*, pp. 102-143.

133. Author's interview.

134. Duff Hart-Davis, *The House the Berrys Built*, p. 155.

135. *Ibid.*, p. 285.

136. Black, *A Life in Progress*, p. 336.

137. Black was in good company. Rothschilds and Hambros also managed investments for the Vatican bank, among many other blue-chip clients.

138. Hart-Davis, *The House the Berrys Built*, p. 301.

139. Black, *A Life in Progress*, p. 338.

140. *Globe and Mail*, June 14, 1985.

141. *Report on Business Magazine*, June 1986.

142. Letter of September 2003.

143. *The Spectator*, November 23, 1985.

144. *Ibid.*, December 14, 1985.

145. *Matthew* 5:14.

146. Margot Kidder, in Nancy Southam (ed.), *Pierre*, pp. 255 and 257.

147. Author's interview.

148. Author's interview.

149. Black, *A Life in Progress*, p. 36.

150. Newman, *The Establishment Man*, p. 69.

151. Author's interview.

152. Author's interview.

153. Northop Frye, *Anatomy of Criticism*, p. 236.

154. *Report on Business Magazine*, March 1986.

155. The quotes in this paragraph are from columns by Black published in *Report on Business Magazine* between November 1985 and August 1987.

156. Author's interview.

157. *Report on Business Magazine*, January 1988.

158. Black, *A Life in Progress*, pp. 387 and 388.

159. Max Hastings, *Editor*, p. 22.

160. Author's interview.

161. Author's interview.

162. Black, *A Life in Progress*, p. 288.

163. Black, *A Life in Progress*, p. 103.

164. This exchange is based on Mark Abley's unpublished notes from the interview.

165. Author's interview.

166. Author's interview.

167. Hastings, *Editor*, pp. 236-237.

168. Black, *A Life in Progress*, p. 367.

169. Author's interview.

170. Author's interview.

171. Author's interview.

172. Black, *A Life in Progress*, p. 363.

173. According to Brian MacArthur.

174. Hennessy, *The Prime Minister*, p. 398.

175. Richard Siklos, *Shades of Black*, p. 184.

176. Author's interview.

177. Black, *A Life in Progress*, p. 410.

178. Hart-Davis, *The House the Berrys Built*, p. 329.

179. Such practices are documented by John Pilger in *Heroes* and by many others.

180. Hastings, *Editor*, p. 249.

181. *Sunday Times*, July 5, 1992.

182. *Financial Post*, July 18, 1989.

183. Black, Radler and White, "A Brief to the Special Senate Committee on the Mass Media from the Sherbrooke *Record*, the voice of the Eastern Townships," November 7, 1969, p. 20.

184. Author's interview.

185. Author's interview. John O'Sullivan worked for Rupert Murdoch as associate editor of *The Times*, for Conrad Black as effective editorial-page editor of the *National Post*, and more recently as editor of the *National Interest*, a conservative publication, subsidized by Hollinger, specializing in foreign affairs, and based at the Nixon Center in Washington.

186. Author's interview.

187. Author's interview.

188. Author's interview.

189. *Financial Post*, November 30, 1988.

190. *Ibid.*, October 26, 1990.

191. *Ibid.*, June 15, 1991.

192. *Ibid.*, May 2, 1992.

193. Pierre Elliott Trudeau, *La Presse*, March 10, 1989, quoted in Trudeau, *Against the Current*, 1996, translated by George Tombs, p. 241.

194. *Jerusalem Post*, February 23, 2001.

195. Black, *A Life in Progress*, p. 391.

196. Black, *A Life in Progress*, pp. 391-392.

197. Siklos, *Shades of Black*, p. 209.

198. Black, *A Life in Progress*, p. 433.

199. *Ibid.*, pp. 436-437.

200. Author's interview.

201. Black, *A Life in Progress*, p. 441.

202. Author's interview.

203. *Lateline*, November 29, 1993, quoted in *Percentage Players: Report of the Senate Select Committee on Certain Aspects of Foreign Ownership Decisions in Relation to the Print Media*, p. 112.

204. *Ibid.*

205. Roy Thomson, *After I Was Sixty*, p. 6.

206. Black, *A Life in Progress*, pp. 376 and 378.

207. *Ibid.*, p. 476.

208. *Vanity Fair*, November 1992.

209. Black, *A Life in Progress*, pp. 486-487.

210. *Chicago Tribune*, September 18, 1994.

211. *Chicago*, November 20, 2003

212. *Ibid.*

213. Author's interview.

214. Black, *A Life in Progress*, p. 332.

215. *Ibid.*, p. 501.

216. Author's interview.

217. *Politique Internationale*, no. 63, Spring 1994, p. 324.

218. *Politique Internationale*, no. 63, Spring 1994, p. 337.

219. Black, *A Life in Progress*, p. 461.

220. *Ibid.*, p. 463.

221. Nixon had been named an "unindicted co-conspirator" by the grand jury investigating Watergate; resigned rather than face impeachment; received a pre-emptive pardon from his successor, Gerald Ford; and was alleged in 2003 by Jeb Magruder, an official in the Nixon administration, to have personally ordered the Watergate break-in by phone.

222. Author's interview.

223. Newspaper Association of America, *Presstime*, September 1998.

224. *Globe and Mail*, November 18, 2003.

225. *National Review*, May 5, 2003.

226. Author's interview.

227. Author's interview.

228. Allan Levine, *From Winnipeg to the World*, p. 165.

229. *National Post*, August 10, 2000.

230. *The Spectator*, March 3, 2001.

231. *Ibid.*, March 17, 2001.

232. *The Independent*, May 24, 2003.

233. "We, Your Majesty's most dutiful and loyal subjects, the House of Commons of Canada in Parliament assembled, humbly approach Your Majesty, praying that Your Majesty may be graciously pleased: (a) To refrain hereafter from conferring any title of honour or titular distinction upon any of your subjects domiciled or ordinarily resident in Canada, save such appellations as are of a professional or vocational character or which appertain to an office. (b) To provide that appropriate action be taken by legislation or otherwise to ensure the extinction of an hereditary title of honour or titular distinction, and of a dignity or title as a peer of the realm, on the death of a person domiciled or ordinarily resident in Canada at present in enjoyment of an hereditary title of honour, or titular distinction, or dignity or title as a peer of the realm, and that thereafter no such title of honour, titular distinction, or dignity or title as a peer of the realm, shall be accepted, enjoyed or used by any person or be recognized. All of which we humbly pray Your Majesty to take into your favourable and gracious consideration." The Nickle Resolution is available in many resources — online, in constitutional books, and elsewhere.

234. In crafting the patriation of the Canadian constitution in 1982, Chrétien and Trudeau made it practically impossible for Canadians to abolish the constitutional place of the British sovereign: according to Article 41 of the Constitution Act of 1982, "An amendment to the Constitution of Canada in relation to the following matters may be made by proclamation issued by the Governor General under the Great Seal of Canada only where authorized by resolutions of the Senate and House of Commons and of the legislative assembly of each province: the office of the Queen, the Governor General and the Lieutenant Governor of each province . . ." In other words, the unanimous consent of two Houses of Parliament and ten provincial assemblies is required — which will never be obtained.

235. *Globe and Mail*, October 31, 2001.

236. *Independent*, May 24, 2003.

237. *National Post,* March 20, 2004

238. *International Herald Tribune*, March 15, 2004.

239. *Ottawa Citizen,* June 3, 2001.

240. *New York Times*, December 22, 2003.

241. *Ibid.*, December 23, 2003.

242. Author's interview.

243. Author's interview.

244. Arthur Schlesinger, *The Age of Roosevelt,* v. I, pp. 408-409.

245. Author's interview.

246. Author's interview.

247. Schlesinger, *The Age of Roosevelt,* v. II, p. 174.

248. Author's interview.

249. *Financial Times,* February 28-29, 2004.

250. *Chicago Sun-Times,* February 27, 2004.

251. *BBC News,* February 27, 2004.

252. *Globe and Mail,* February 27, 2004.

253. *International Herald Tribune,* February 28, 2004.

254. According to an affidavit filed by Peter White with the Superior Court of Ontario on April 19, 2005, "the principal asset of Ravelston Corporation Ltd. is its direct and indirect interest in Hollinger. As of April 15, 2005 the market value of such interest was approximately $164 million although, because of . . . cease trade orders, the Applicants (Ravelston Corporation and Ravelston Management Inc.) are not able to dispose of their interest in such shares. Other assets of Ravelston Corporation include cash and cash equivalents (which as of April 15, 2005 was approximately $218,000), other fixed assets with a book value of approximately $750,000 and accounts receivable, including amounts due from related companies. . . . Given the extremely limited immediately available resources, the Applicants (Ravelston Corporation and Ravelston Management Inc.) intend to conserve cash within the next 30 days, and all spending will be within the control of RSM Richter Inc." According to RSM Richter's *First Report to Court* on May 14, 2005, an unaudited balance sheet review as at January 2, 2005, showed Ravelston Management's assets at $84.3 million and Ravelston Corporation's assets at $216.8 million. Ravelston Management is a wholly owned subsidiary of Ravelston Corporation. As a result of a Management and Insider Cease Trading Order issued by the Ontario Securities Commission on June 1, 2004, RSM Richter notes, "Ravelston Corporation and its Receiver are precluded from selling shares of Hollinger until full compliance by Hollinger with filing requirements or a lifting of

the Management and Insider Cease Trading Order by the OSC, on terms acceptable to it."

255. *Guardian*, May 19, 2007.

256. *Chicago Sun-Times*, May 23, 2007.

257. Associated Press, May 31, 2007.

258. *Toronto Star*, July 15, 2007.

259. *Guardian*, May 19, 2007.

260. *Chicago Sun-Times*, May 23, 2007.

261. Associated Press, May 31, 2007.

262. *Toronto Star*, July 15, 2007.

Books

Amiel, Barbara. *Confessions.* Toronto: MacMillan, 1980.

Auf des Maur, Nick. *Nick: A Montreal Life.* Montreal: Véhicule Press, 1998.

Barlow, Maude and James Winter. *The Big Black Book: The Essential Views of Conrad and Barbara Amiel Black.* Toronto: Stoddart, 1997.

Bell, Ken. *A Man and His Mission: Cardinal Léger in Africa.* Scarborough: Prentice-Hall, 1976.

Black, Conrad. *The Career of Maurice L. Duplessis as Viewed through his Correspondence.* Montreal: McGill University, unpublished M.A. thesis, 1973.

——. *Duplessis.* Toronto: McClelland & Stewart, 1976. (& French translation: *Maurice Duplessis.* 2 vols. Translated by Monique Benoit. Montreal: Éditions de l'Homme, 1977.)

——. *Franklin Delano Roosevelt: Champion of Freedom.* New York: Public Affairs, 2003.

——. *The Invincible Quest: The Life of Richard Milhous Nixon.* Toronto: McClelland & Stewart, 2007.

——. *A Life in Progress.* Toronto: Key Porter, 1993. (& French translation: *Conrad Black par Conrad Black.* Translated by Jean-Pierre Fournier. Montreal: Québec-Amérique, 1993.)

———. *Render unto Caesar.* Toronto: Key Porter, 1998. (& French translation: *Maurice Duplessis.* Translated by Jacques Vaillancourt. Montreal: Éditions de l'Homme, 1998.)

Bouchard, Lucien. *A visage découvert.* Montreal: Boréal, 1992.

Buckley, William F. *Up from Liberalism.* New York, Hillman, 1961.

Bull, George. *Inside the Vatican.* New York: St. Martin's, 1982.

Cameron, Stevie. *On the Take: Crime, Corruption and Greed in the Mulroney Years.* Toronto: Seal, 1995.

Carrington, Peter. *Reflecting on Things Past.* New York: HarperCollins, 1988.

Chesterton, G.K. *Orthodoxy.* London: Unicorn, 1939.

Chrétien, Jean. *Straight from the Heart.* Toronto: Key Porter, 1985.

Conrad, Joseph. *Works.* New York: Doubleday, 1925.

Cook, Peter. *Massey at the Brink.* Toronto: HarperCollins, 1981.

Debrett's Baronetage and Peerage. London: Debrett's. Various editions.

Diagnostic and Statistical Manual of Mental Disorders (DSM-IV). Fourth edition. Washington: American Psychiatric Association, 1994.

Dendy, William, *Lost Toronto.* Toronto: Oxford University Press, 1978.

Finlayson, Ann. *Whose Money Is It Anyway? The Showdown on Pensions.* Markham: Viking, 1988.

Fisk, Robert. *Pity the Nation.* Oxford: Oxford University Press, 1990.

Fraser, John. *Telling Tales.* Toronto: Totem, 1987.

Frum, David and Richard Perle. *An End to Evil: How to Win the War on Terror.* New York: Random House, 2003.

Frye, Northrop. *Anatomy of Criticism.* Princeton: Princeton University Press, 1957.

Fulford, Robert. *Best Seat in the House.* Toronto: HarperCollins, 1988.

Galbraith, John Kenneth. *The Anatomy of Power.* Boston: Houghton Mifflin, 1983.

———. *The Great Crash 1929.* Boston: Houghton Mifflin, 1961.

———. *Name Dropping: From FDR On.* Boston: Houghton Mifflin, 1999.

de Gaulle, Charles. *Mémoires.* Paris: Livre de Poche, 1966. 3 vols.

Godin, Pierre. *La révolution tranquille: la poudrière linguistique*. Montréal: Boréal, 1990.

Goldenberg, Susan. *The Thomson Empire*. New York: Bantam, 1985.

Grafftey, Heward. *Portraits from a Life*. Montreal: Véhicule, 1996.

Haines, Joe. *Maxwell*. London: MacDonald, 1986

Halberstam, David. *The Powers that Be*. New York: Alfred A. Knopf, 1983.

Hart-Davis, Duff. *The House the Berrys Built: Inside the Telegraph 1928-1986*. Toronto: Stoddart, 1990.

Hastings, Max. *Editor: An Inside Story of Newspapers*. London: Macmillan, 2002.

———. *Going to the Wars*. London: Pan, 2000.

Hennessy, Peter. *The Prime Minister: The Office and its Holders since 1945*. London: Penguin, 2000.

Higgins, Michael W. and Douglas R. Letson. *My Father's Business: A Biography of His Eminence G. Emmett Cardinal Carter*. Toronto: Macmillan, 1990.

House of Lords: A Thousand Years of British Tradition. London: Smith's Peerage, 1994.

Hitchens, Christopher. *The Trial of Henry Kissinger*. New York: Verso, 2002.

Johnson, Lyndon. *The Vantage Point*. New York: Henry Holt, 1971.

Karel, David. *La collection Duplessis*. Quebec: Musée du Québec, 1991.

Kissinger, Henry A. *Crisis: The Anatomy of Two Major Foreign Policy Crises*. New York: Simon & Schuster, 2003.

———. *Diplomacy*. New York: Simon & Schuster, 1994.

———. *A World Restored: Metternich, Castlereagh and the Problems of Peace, 1812-1822*. London: Phoenix, 2000.

Knightley, Philip. *The First Casualty*. San Diego: Harcourt, 1975.

Lacey, Robert L. *Little Man: Meyer Lansky and the Gangster Life*. Boston: Little, Brown, 1991.

Lachance, Micheline. *Le prince de l'Église & Le dernier voyage*. Montreal: Éditions de l'Homme, 1982 & 2000.

Lavertu, Yves. *The Bernonville Affair: A French War Criminal in Quebec*.

Translated by George Tombs. Montreal: Robert Davies, 1995.

Lévesque, René. *Attendez que je me rappelle.* Montreal: Québec Amérique, 1986.

Levine, Allan. *From Winnipeg to the World: The CanWest Global Story.* Winnipeg: CanWest Global, 2002.

McCall, Christina and Stephen Clarkson. *Trudeau and Our Times.* 2 vols. Toronto: McClelland & Stewart, 1990.

Machiavelli, Niccolo. *The Art of War.* Translated by Ellis Farneworth. Cambridge, MA: Da Capo, 2001.

Malraux, André. *Les chênes qu'on abat.* Paris: Gallimard, 1974.

Maurras, Charles. *Enquête sur la monarchie.* Paris: Nouvelle librairie nationale, 1925.

Morris, Edmund. *Dutch: a Memoir of Ronald Reagan.* New York, Random House, 1999.

Nemni, Max and Monique. *Trudeau, fils du Québec, père du Canada,* volume 1. Montreal: Editions de l'Homme, 2006.

Newman, John Henry Cardinal. *Apologia pro vita sua.* London: Longmans, Green, 1947.

Newman, Peter C. *The Establishment Man.* Toronto: McClelland & Stewart, 1982.

——. *Renegade in Power.* Toronto: McClelland & Stewart, 1964.

Nietzsche, Friedrich. *The Will to Power.* Translated by Walter Kaufmann. New York: Vintage, 1967.

Nixon, Richard M. *Memoirs.* 2 vols. New York: Warner, 1979.

Nolte, Ernst. *Three Faces of Fascism.* New York: Mentor, 1965.

Norwich, John Julius. *Shakespeare's Kings: The Great Plays and the History of England in the Middle Eages, 1337–1485.* New York: Scribner, 1900.

Pearson, Lester B. *Mike.* 2 vols. Toronto: University of Toronto Press, 1972-3.

Robinson, Jonathan. *On the Lord's Appearing: an An Essay on Prayer and Tradition.* Edinburgh: Clark, 1997.

Rumilly, Robert. *Duplessis.* 2 vols. Montreal: Fides, 1973.

——. *Quel monde.* Montreal: privately published, 1965.

Sawatsky, John. *Mulroney: The Politics of Ambition.* Toronto: McClelland & Stewart, 1992.

Schlesinger, Arthur M. *The Age of Roosevelt.* 3 vols. Boston: Houghton Mifflin, 1957–60.

Sheridan, E.F. (ed.) *Do Justice: The Social Teaching of the Canadian Catholic Bishops.* Montreal: Mediaspaul, 1987.

Siklos, Richard. *Shades of Black: Conrad Black and the World's Fastest Growing Press Empire.* Toronto: Reed, 1995.

Spengler, Oswald. *The Decline of the West.* Translated by Charles Francis Atkinson. New York: Alfred A. Knopf, 1939.

Taylor, A.J.P. *Beaverbrook.* London: Hamish Hamilton, 1972.

Thatcher, Margaret. *Statecraft.* London: HarperCollins, 2002.

Thomson, Roy. *After I Was Sixty.* London: Nelson, 1975.

Trudeau, Pierre Elliott. *Against the Current.* Edited by Gérard Pelletier. Translated by George Tombs. Toronto: McClelland & Stewart, 1996.

———. *A Mess that Deserves a Big No.* Translated by George Tombs. Montreal: Robert Davies, 1992.

Watts, Gregory. *Catholic Lives: Contemporary Spiritual Journeys.* Leominster: Gracewing, 2001.

Westley, Margaret W. *Remembrance of Grandeur: The Anglo-Protestant Elite of Montreal, 1900-1950.* Montreal: Libre Expression, 1990.

Willson, Beckles. *The Life of Lord Strathcona and Mount Royal.* Boston: Houghton Mifflin, 1915. 2 vols.

Worsthorne, Peregrine. *Tricks of Memory.* London: Weidenfeld & Nicolson, 1993.

PRINT MEDIA

Les Affaires
Age
Annex Gleaner
Architectural Digest
Australian
Australian Business Monthly
Australian Financial Review

L'avenir de Brome-Missisquoi
Chatelaine
Chicago
Chicago Sun-Times
Chicago Tribune
Cité Libre
Compass
Daily Mail
Daily News
Daily News (Halifax)
Daily Telegraph
Le Devoir
Le Droit
Eastern Townships Advertiser (Knowlton Advertiser)
Economist
FQ Magazine
Financial Post
Financial Times (London)
Forbes
Fortune
Gazette (Montreal)
The Globe and Mail
Globe and Mail Report on Business
Guardian
GQ (British edition)
Hamilton Spectator
Independent
International Herald Tribune
Jerusalem Post
Jerusalem Report
Le Jour
Los Angeles Times
Maclean's Magazine
Le Monde
Montreal Star
National Post
National Review
New York Post

New York Sun
New York Times
New York Times Magazine
New Yorker
Observer
Ottawa Citizen
Playboy
Politique Internationale
La Presse
Presstime
Record (Sherbrooke)
Saturday Night
Selwyn House School Examiner
Le Soleil
The Spectator
Standard (Saint Catharines)
Sunday Telegraph
Sunday Times
Sydney Morning Herald
Tatler
Time
The Times (London)
Toronto Life
Toronto Star
Toronto Sun
Town and Country
Vanity Fair
Vogue
Vox
Wall Street Journal
Washington Post
World Press Review

ELECTRONIC MEDIA

ABC Radio, TV and Web site, BBC Radio, TV and Web site, CBC Radio, TV and Web site, CNN TV and Web site, Radio-Canada TV and Web site

GOVERNMENT DOCUMENTS

Archives nationales du Quebec, Montreal
Debates of the Assemblée Nationale du Quebec
Debates of the Canadian House of Commons
Debates of the Canadian Senate
Debates of the British House of Commons
Debates of the British House of Lords
Kahan Commission report
Percentage Players: Report of the [Australian] Senate Select Committee on Certain Aspects of Foreign Ownership Decisions in Relation to the Print Media.
United States International Trade Commission, documents
Various corporate annual reports
Various court documents and unpublished archives, cited in the footnotes